Gods in the Desert

Gods in the Desert

Religions of the Ancient Near East

Glenn S. Holland

ROWMAN & LITTLEFIELD PUBLISHERS, INC.
Lanham • Boulder • New York • Toronto • Plymouth, UK

ROWMAN & LITTLEFIELD PUBLISHERS, INC.

Published in the United States of America
by Rowman & Littlefield Publishers, Inc.
A wholly owned subsidiary of The Rowman & Littlefield Publishing Group, Inc.
4501 Forbes Boulevard, Suite 200, Lanham, Maryland 20706
www.rowmanlittlefield.com

Estover Road
Plymouth PL6 7PY
United Kingdom

British Library Cataloguing in Publication Information Available

Library of Congress Cataloging-in-Publication Data:

Holland, Glenn Stanfield, 1952–
  Gods in the desert : religions of the ancient Near East / Glenn S. Holland.
    p. cm.
  Includes bibliographical references and index.
  ISBN 978-0-7425-6226-4 (cloth : alk. paper) — ISBN 978-0-7425-9979-6 (electronic)
  1. Middle East—Religion. 2. Mythology, Middle Eastern. I. Title.
  BL1060.H635 2009
  200.939'4—dc22   2009009444

The Scripture quotations used herein are taken from the New Revised Standard Version
Bible, copyright © 1989 by the Division of Christian Education of the National Council
of Churches of Christ in the U.S.A., and are used by permission. All rights reserved.

Printed in the United States of America

⊗™ The paper used in this publication meets the minimum requirements of
American National Standard for Information Sciences—Permanence of Paper
for Printed Library Materials, ANSI/NISO Z39.48-1992.

Contents

	List of Illustrations	vii
	List of Maps	ix
	Time Line	xv
	Preface	xix
	Introduction: Religion and Its Characteristic Expression	xxiii
Section 1	**Egypt**	
Chapter 1	Egypt: Historical Survey	3
Chapter 2	Egypt: The Gods and the World They Made	15
Chapter 3	Egypt: The King and Royal Power	37
Chapter 4	Egypt: The World of the Dead	57
Chapter 5	Egypt: The Human World	77
Section 2	**Mesopotamia**	
Chapter 6	Mesopotamia: Historical Survey	99
Chapter 7	Mesopotamia: The Gods and the World They Made	111

Chapter 8   Mesopotamia: The World of Kings and Heroes   131

Chapter 9   Mesopotamia: The World of the Dead   149

Chapter 10   Mesopotamia: The Human World   167

Section 3   **Syria–Palestine**

Chapter 11   Syria–Palestine: Historical Survey   191

Chapter 12   Syria–Palestine: The Gods and the World They Made   199

Chapter 13   Syria–Palestine: Kings and Prophets   219

Chapter 14   Syria–Palestine: Suffering and Death   239

Chapter 15   Syria–Palestine: The Human World   257

               Conclusion: Change and Continuity in the
               Hellenistic Age   277

               Bibliography for Further Reading   285

               Glossary   289

               Index   297

Illustrations

The Great Pyramid at Giza   6
Mask of Tutankhamun   22
Head of Hathor   24
Akhenaten and his family receiving blessings at the hands of Aten   29
Partially reconstructed mortuary temple of Hatshepsut   41
Tutankhamun between the goddess Sekhmet and Ptah, flanked
     by Horus as a crowned falcon and Wadjit, goddess of Lower Egypt   51
The weighing of the heart in the Judgment Hall of Osiris.   72
Procession of the sun bark of Ra   81
Figure of a scribe   88
Sargon II and the Tree of Life   107
Akkadian seal from Mesopotamia   116
Clay mask of Huwawa or Humbaba   143
Partial reconstruction of the Great Ziggurat at Ur   170
Reconstruction of the Ishtar Gate of the city of Babylon   176
Cuneiform tablet containing part of the Flood narrative from
     the *Epic of Gilgamesh*   185
Bronze Canaanite figure of Baal   205
View of modern Jerusalem   259

List of Maps

Ancient Egypt xi
Ancient Mesopotamia xii
Syria–Palestine in the Ninth Century BCE xiii

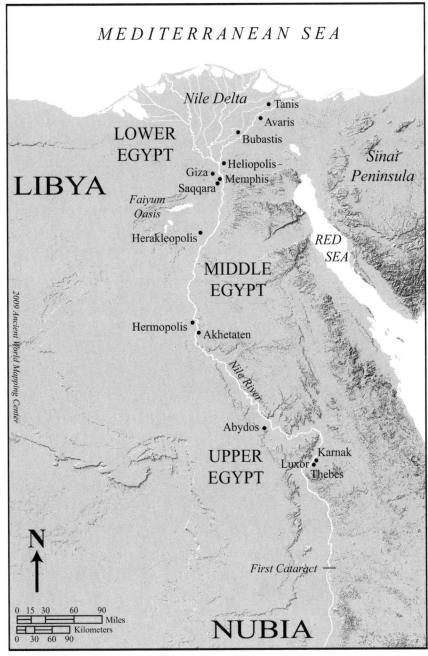

MEDITERRANEAN SEA

Nile Delta

• Tanis

• Avaris

LOWER EGYPT

• Bubastis

Sinai Peninsula

Giza •
Saqqara •

• Heliopolis
• Memphis

LIBYA

Faiyum Oasis

Herakleopolis •

RED SEA

MIDDLE EGYPT

Hermopolis •
• Akhetaten

Nile River

Abydos •

UPPER EGYPT

Karnak
Luxor •
• Thebes

N

First Cataract —

0 15 30   60   90
|—|—|—————|—————| Miles
|—|—|—————|—————| Kilometers
0   30   60   90

NUBIA

2009 Ancient World Mapping Center

Map created in 2009 by the Ancient World Mapping Center at the University of North Carolina at Chapel Hill (www.unc.edu/awmc)

Ancient Mesopotamia

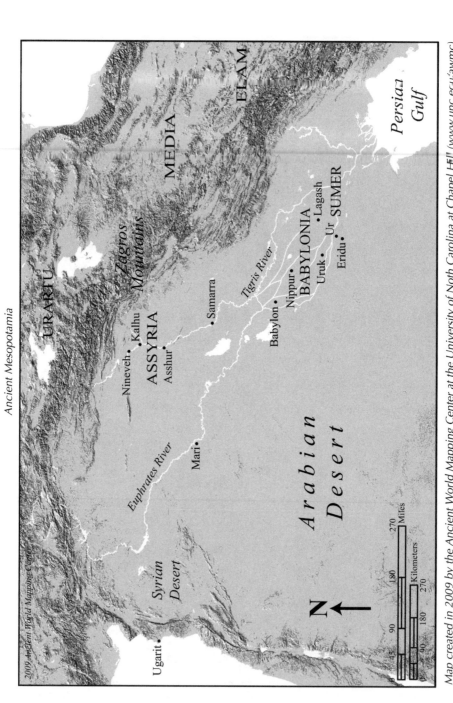

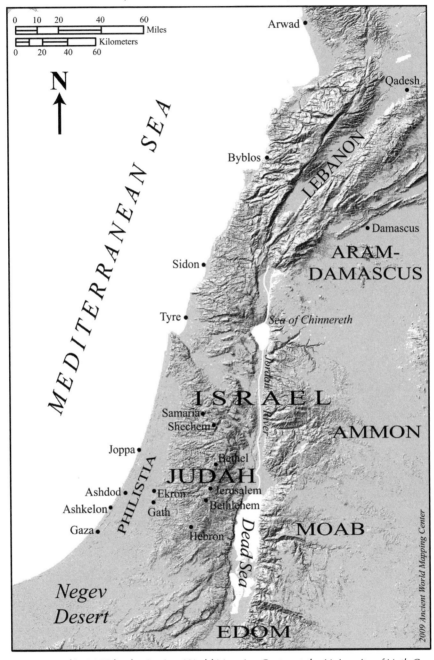

Syria–Palestine in the Ninth Century BCE

Map created in 2009 by the Ancient World Mapping Center at the University of Noth Carolina at Chapel Hill (www.unc.edu/awmc)

Time Line

c. 8300c.–4000 B.C.E.	Neolithic era (New Stone Age)
c. 5000 B.C.E.	Mesopotamia: Ubaidian culture dominant throughout the territory
c. 3500 B.C.E.	Mesopotamia: Sumerians enter southern Mesopotamia
c. 3300 B.C.E.	Mesopotamia: Development of cuneiform writing in Sumeria
c. 3000–2686 B.C.E.	Egypt: Archaic era—Dynasty 1 and 2
c. 2900 B.C.E.	Mesopotamia: Amorites settle to the north of Sumer
2686–2125 B.C.E.	Egypt: Old Kingdom—Dynasty 3–8
2667–2648 B.C.E.	Egypt: Djoser; career of Imhotep, later deified as the god of medicine
2589–2566 B.C.E.	Egypt: Khufu (Cheops)
2334–2279 B.C.E.	Mesopotamia: Sargon the Great of Akkad

c. 2200–1200 B.C.E.	Middle and Late Bronze Ages
2160–2055 B.C.E.	Egypt: First Intermediate Period—Dynasty 9–11
c. 2111 B.C.E.	Mesopotamia: Ur–Nammu establishes Third Dynasty of Ur
2055–1650 B.C.E.	Egypt: Middle Kingdom—Dynasty 11–14
1985–1956 B.C.E.	Egypt: Amenemhat I
1956–1911 B.C.E.	Egypt: Senusret I
1792–1750 B.C.E.	Mesopotamia: Hammurabi, first great king of Babylon
1650–1550 B.C.E.	Egypt: Second Intermediate Period—Dynasty 15–17
1650–1550 B.C.E.	Egypt: Hyksos—Dynasty 15
1595–1157 B.C.E.	Mesopotamia: Kassites rule Mesopotamia
1550–1069 B.C.E.	Egypt: New Kingdom—Dynasty 18–20
c. 1365 B.C.E.	Mesopotamia: Assur–uballit I (1365–1330 BCE) frees Assyria from Hurrian domination and reestablishes it as an independent kingdom
1352–1336 B.C.E.	Egypt: Amenhotep IV / Ankhenaten
1279–1213 B.C.E.	Egypt: Ramesses II
1235 B.C.E.	Mesopotamia: Tukulti–Ninurta (1244–1208 B.C.E.) of Assyria conquers Babylon
c. 1200–800 B.C.E.	Dark Age in the eastern Mediterranean; incursions of the Sea Peoples into the Near East
1115–1077 B.C.E.	Mesopotamia: Tiglath–Pilester I, king of Assyria

1069–64 B.C.E.	Egypt: Third Intermediate Period—Dynasty 21–25
c. 1020–1000 B.C.E.	Syria–Palestine: Saul, king of Israel
c. 1000–961 B.C.E.	Syria–Palestine: David, king of Judah and Israel
c. 961–922 B.C.E.	Syria–Palestine: Solomon, king of Judah and Israel
922–587 B.C.E.	Syria–Palestine: Separate kingdoms of Israel and Judah
883–859 B.C.E.	Mesopotamia: Assurnasirpal II, king of Assyria
882–871 B.C.E.	Syria–Palestine: Omri, king of Israel
c. 871–851 B.C.E.	Syria–Palestine: Ahab, king of Israel
858–823 B.C.E.	Mesopotamia: Shalmaneser III, king of Assyria
c. 851–850 B.C.E.	Syria–Palestine: Ahaziah, king of Israel
842–814 B.C.E.	Syria–Palestine: Jehu, king of Israel
786–758 B.C.E.	Syria–Palestine: Uzziah, king of Judah
785–749 B.C.E.	Syria–Palestine: Jeroboam II, king of Israel
758–742 B.C.E.	Syria–Palestine: Jotham, king of Judah
744–727 B.C.E.	Mesopotamia: Tiglath-Pileser III, king of Assyria
742–726 B.C.E.	Syria–Palestine: Ahaz, king of Judah
740–732 B.C.E.	Syria–Palestine: Rezin, king of Aram–Damascus
735–731 B.C.E.	Syria–Palestine: Pekah, king of Israel
726–697 B.C.E.	Syria–Palestine: Hezekiah, king of Judah

721–705 B.C.E.	Mesopotamia: Sargon II, king of Assyria
697–642 B.C.E.	Syria–Palestine: Manasseh, king of Judah
669–627 B.C.E.	Mesopotamia: Assurbanipal, king of Assyria
664–332 B.C.E.	Egypt: Late Period—Dynasty 26–30, Persian rule
604–562 B.C.E.	Mesopotamia: Nebuchadnezzar II, king of Babylon
556–539 B.C.E.	Mesopotamia: Nabonidus (Nabu–na'id), king of Babylon
559–530 B.C.E.	Persia: Cyrus II ("the Great"), king of Persia
486–465 B.C.E.	Persia: Xerxes, king of Persia
336–323 B.C.E.	Greece: Alexander III ("the Great"), king of Macedon
333–63 B.C.E.	Hellenistic Era
332 B.C.E.	Persia: Alexander conquers Persian possessions in the Near East
305–285 B.C.E.	Egypt: Ptolemy I Soter, first Hellenistic king of Egypt
175–163 B.C.E.	Syria–Palestine: Antiochus IV Epiphanes, king of Syria, 175–163 B.C.E.
167–142 B.C.E.	Syria–Palestine: Maccabean revolt in Judah
165 B.C.E.	Syria–Palestine: Restoration of Temple sacrifice in Jersualem
142–63 B.C.E.	Syria–Palestine: Jewish autonomy under Hasmonean rule

Preface

This book is a product of a course that I began teaching shortly after my arrival at Allegheny College in Meadville, Pennsylvania, in the fall of 1985. I wanted to provide my students with a better understanding of the religious cultures of the ancient Mediterranean world than was available in survey courses devoted to the faith of ancient Israel or the origins of the Jesus movement and early Christianity. As originally conceived, the course covered prehistoric religious culture, the religions of Egypt, Mesopotamia, and Syria–Palestine as well as the religions of Greece and Rome and the early imperial world, including the first few centuries of the Christian movement.

In 2003 I was approached by The Teaching Company to produce a series of recorded lectures based on my course about ancient religious cultures. The lectures were released under the title "Religion in the Ancient Mediterranean World" in 2005. This book owes much to my research in preparation for those lectures, although it differs from them in many ways in regard to both approach and content.

The intention of this book is the same as the intention of the course I first taught at Allegheny. I want to provide not only an overview of three different religious cultures—Egypt, Mesopotamia, and Syria–Palestine—but also through the use of primary sources to give the reader some idea of how the adherents of these different religious cultures thought about the gods, the human situation, creation, and the relationship between humanity and the gods, and—just as important—how they expressed those thoughts in words and actions.

The approach is broadly comparative. I have divided the main portion of the book into three sections, one devoted to each religious culture, and further divided each section into five chapters. The first chapter provides an historical survey of Egypt, Mesopotamia, or Syria–Palestine, beginning in prehistory and culminating with Alexander's conquest of the Near East in the fourth century BCE. These chapters are by necessity schematic, providing what scholars call "top down" overviews of kings, dynasties, battles, and conquests to give the reader some sense of the general historical contexts in which these different religious cultures flourished. The second chapter in each section introduces the gods of the religious culture and its dominant ideas about creation. The third chapter deals with the place of the king and other dominant cultural figures in relationship to the gods on the one hand and the people on the other. The fourth chapter addresses beliefs about the situation of the dead and discusses the gods of the Underworld in relation to the gods of the earth and heaven, and beliefs about human life and death. Finally, the fifth chapter in each section examines public and private expressions of religious belief: temple rituals, household religion, and particularly in the surviving literature. The conclusion discusses Alexander's conquest of the Near East, and brings the story of the religious cultures of Egypt, Mesopotamia, and Syria–Palestine up to the first century BCE, on the eve of the Roman conquest of the Near East.

I am indebted to many people who have helped to make this book possible. My students at Allegheny College over more than twenty years have inspired me through their interest and their searching questions to color and fill in more and more details of my portrayal of ancient religions on what seems to be an increasingly large canvas. My departmental colleagues over the years, most notably Carl Olson and Eric Boynton, have encouraged my work and provided models of scholarly depth and rigor that I hope I have been able to emulate here. I have also benefited immeasurably from the comments of the scholars who have reviewed my work and offered their insights.

I am particularly grateful to those associated with The Teaching Company, past and present, whose support and encouragement during the development of my lecture series was invaluable for the creation of this book. I would like to particularly thank Virginia Marbella, Maggie Lyons, Brien Lohrmann, and the others who have made my association with The Teaching Company such a pleasure. I am also indebted to Brian Romer, who first approached me about writing this book, and Sarah Stanton of Rowman & Littlefield, who has helped me bring it to completion.

The time I have spent in the creation of this book may be fairly characterized as a time of transition in my life, and transitions are by their nature never without their difficulties. As always, I have depended during this time on the love and support of my wife Sandy and my sons Nathaniel and Gregory. They have in their different ways repeatedly validated the view so often expressed in the ancient Near East that the greatest joys in life are those found in the company of one's spouse and children. This book is dedicated to them.

Glenn S. Holland
January 2009

Introduction: Religion and Its Characteristic Expression

What Is Religion?

Before we begin our discussion of religion in the ancient Near East, we really have to ask a fundamental question: What is religion?

Most of us, reasonably enough, usually begin to develop a definition of a complex human phenomenon by making a list of what seem to be its essential elements. We consider different examples—in this case, different religious communities—and try to isolate what they have in common. Then we choose those common elements that seem to be essential to the phenomenon—in this case, religion—and put aside other elements our examples might share with other ideas and activities that clearly have nothing to do with "religion." So we start out with a general idea of what religion might be, and refine and develop that idea as we determine what seem to be its essential elements.

But there are still several different approaches we might take to figuring out what religion is. For instance, we might want to think about religion in terms of what all the activity associated with it seems to be aimed at, what people are trying to do through the activities we identify as "religious." One possible answer is that they are establishing and maintaining a relationship with a god or gods by worshipping them and doing what the god or gods command. So we might say that religion is activities aimed at pleasing a god or gods.

But not all examples of what clearly qualifies as religion have anything to do with a god or gods. Some forms of religion are primarily concerned not with gods but with spirits of some sort, and some religions, like Buddhism, have no gods of any sort. Even the general idea of "worship" is a problem. On the one hand we have to define what sort of human actions might qualify as "worship," and on the other, some clearly "religious" people don't perform any actions that conform to those we usually associate with worship. As for the more general idea of pleasing a god or gods, that may be done through specifically "religious" activities or by the way we live our daily lives. But not everything we do each day can be considered "religious" in intention.

So we really have two problems to solve. First, how do we best describe the focus of attention for people who participate in a particular religious community, what they might conceive of as gods or spirits or powers or a world or concerns beyond our own? Second, how do we describe the consequences of sharing that focus of attention with other people, in terms of how a community responds to the focus of its attention through words, actions, and a distinctive way of life?

For help in answering the first question, we may turn to the German theologian Rudolf Otto (1869–1937), who devoted his 1923 book *The Idea of the Holy* to the essential nature of the focus of attention in religious communities. Otto approached this problem from a theological perspective influenced by comparative religious studies that tried to do the very thing we are trying to do now, discover what all religious communities have in common. But Otto was also influenced by the tradition of German mysticism with its emphasis on interior religious experience over exterior religious actions and behavior.

Otto identified the focus of attention in religious communities as the "Holy" and defined it with the Latin phrase *mysterium tremendum et fascinans*, "the overwhelming and awe-inspiring mystery." This meant the Holy was something people experienced as entirely "Other," that is, completely unlike anything else in human experience in both order and magnitude. For Otto religion was primarily the experience of the Holy, human encounter with the overwhelming mystery that could not be understood through rational analysis.

Otto's idea of religion has the advantage of shifting the focus from spiritual beings or the supernatural to a more general idea of the Holy as something human beings experience as both awesome and compelling. Clearly Otto thought of religion as something that was primarily interior, involving feeling and belief; he was much less concerned with the consequences of religious experience, the *expression* of religious belief in words and actions.

The French sociologist Émile Durkheim (1858–1917), an older contemporary of Otto's, also wrote about the essential nature of religion. Durkheim wished to develop a basic definition of religion based on the simplest forms of religious beliefs and behavior—what we can call "religious culture"—that would also apply to its most sophisticated forms. In his book, *The Elementary*

Forms of the Religious Life, first published in 1912, Durkheim provides this definition: "A religion is a unified system of beliefs and practices relative to sacred things, that is to say, things set apart and forbidden—beliefs and practices which unite into one single moral community called a church all those who adhere to them" (Durkheim, 47).

This comprehensive definition has both advantages and disadvantages. Among the advantages is its inclusion of the practical consequences of religious belief: a community of people who share religious beliefs and practices as well as a distinctive way of life based on those beliefs, a religious culture. This is why Durkheim calls the community created by a religion a *moral* community, because it is characterized by specific forms of behavior. He also makes it clear that the beliefs and practices typical of a given religious culture are unified and systematic—in other words, they are mutually dependent and mutually supportive, each related to the others in some way that makes coherent sense to members of the religious community.

The disadvantages of Durkheim's definition are perhaps more numerous. Durkheim defines a religious community as a "church," a distinctively Christian term. But the term also implies the idea of a "gathering" or congregation, as well as a distinction between the social community and the religious community that often does not in fact exist. In the religious cultures of the ancient Near East, for example, the social community and the religious community were the same, and did not usually include any aspects we might recognize as congregational. Durkheim's definition also places sacredness exclusively in "things," an ambiguous term that seems to imply sacred objects rather than sacred space, sacred beings, or even a more general concept of "the sacred" such as we find in Otto. Finally, by defining "sacred things" as "things set apart and forbidden," Durkheim limits the sacred to the taboo—what is forbidden—an unnecessarily restrictive idea, since in some religious communities the sacred is embraced.

But Durkheim's definition of religion is a useful one, and it is relatively easy to modify it to make it more useful. Here is a modified definition of a religion based on Durkheim's formulation: "A religion is a unified system of beliefs and practices relative to the sacred, beliefs and practices that unite into one single moral community all those who adhere to them." This definition requires a further definition of the sacred as "that which permeates, influences, and relates to material reality and yet is recognized as part of another reality not subject to the limitations of the material." This definition lacks the grace and power of Otto's definition of the Holy, but is intended to indicate more clearly how the sacred is believed to interact with the everyday reality of the religious community.

We will want to keep this modified version of Durkheim's definition of religion in mind throughout what follows. The definition will serve to reinforce several concepts basic to understanding religion: the idea of the sacred or holy, the essential interdependence of religious beliefs and practices, and the necessity of a religious community that follows particular patterns of behavior based on its beliefs.

Ways of Thinking about the Sacred

As the distinctive religious cultures of the ancient Near East began to emerge during the Neolithic era (8300–4000 BCE), particular ways of thinking about the sacred arose. First, there was the predominant tendency to think about the sacred in terms of the divine, that is, in terms of deities who are self-conscious controllers of numinous—supernatural or spiritual—power. We in the West are so used to thinking of the sacred in this way that we need to be reminded that there are other possibilities. For example, some people think of the sacred as immanent in creation, that is, as something that exists in and through all things. But this idea of the sacred does not include the idea that the sacred consciously controls or directs its own power. Instead, it falls to human beings to act in ways that will help the sacred to bring well-being to the cosmos.

Even when the sacred is thought of in terms of particular localized manifestations instead of immanent in creation, it need not be present only in beings such as gods. The sacred can also be present in places, places whose sacred nature requires that human beings behave in a particular way when they are there, or in things whose sacred nature requires that human beings treat and use them only in certain ways. Even when the sacred is thought of in terms of beings that exert an influence over human affairs, those beings may not be thought of as making conscious choices about how to treat human beings. Their actions may be thought of as more or less automatic stereotyped responses to human actions; this is how spirits, ghosts, ancestors, demons, and so on are often believed to behave, and all their interactions with human beings produce similar results.

Although the idea of the sacred in places and things is found in ancient Near Eastern religious culture—along with belief in spirits, demons, and ghosts—in general, the sacred was thought of primarily in terms of deity. This meant preeminently a collection of gods and goddesses. These gods and goddesses were identified with different aspects of creation or its divine government. Many had a specific realm of divine concern, while others were essentially personifications of divine principles or qualities.

Second, there was the tendency in the ancient Near East to think about the sacred as something different and separate from creation and its creatures. One contrast here is with monism (from the Greek *monos*, "one and only one"), the belief that everything that exists is based in and an expression of a single reality. This single reality may be thought of as cosmic mind or consciousness, or as material reality. Whatever its essential nature, in monism this single reality is believed to be manifested in myriad forms in the world, including natural forces and both animate and inanimate objects. A similar concept of the divine is cosmic duality, the idea that all that exists is an expression of one or the other of two equal, opposed, and contrasting realities that interact eternally in opposition to one another in the flow of cosmic life. But religious cultures of the ancient Near East, and Western cultures historically, have almost uniformly thought of creation as something other than a manifestation of a single or a dual divine reality. Creation may be brought into being by a god or gods, and other gods may be a result of the creative work, but the gods and the created order inhabited by them and by human beings are generally regarded as separate but interrelated realities.

Third, following on this idea, the ancient Near East shared the idea that the sacred is transcendent over the human world and yet involved in the human world by choice rather than as a matter of necessity. In other words, the gods and goddesses chose to concern themselves with human beings and what human beings do. In contrast to this idea is pantheism, a form of monism that posits that all creatures are merely extensions and expressions of the divine. This means the relationship between the divine and the human is really the relationship of the divine to itself in the human and so a necessary relationship, not a matter of choice. But in the ancient Near East and the Mediterranean world in general, transcendent deity was believed to have chosen for a variety of reasons to create and then remain in relationship with human beings.

Thinking about the sacred in particular ways unites the religious cultures of the ancient Near East and the Mediterranean world and affects the way their people understood the cosmos. They thought of the sacred in terms of self-conscious controllers of power, gods and goddesses. They believed these controllers of sacred power were superior to and separate from creation and its creatures. But at they same time, they believed the gods and goddesses chose to live in relationship to creation and its creatures. Beliefs about the nature of that relationship, however, varied from one religious culture to another.

Ways of Talking about the Sacred

These common beliefs about the sacred in the ancient Near East are the result of human beings attempting to understand and talk about the sacred and various ideas associated with it. But the very nature of the sacred prevents us from having a direct way to talk about it. Human language is based on the reality we experience in everyday life. We today usually contrast our mundane reality with what we think of or experience as part of religious belief and practice. But this has not been the case with all people throughout history. For people in the ancient world, and many people even today, the sacred permeates the mundane world and is a part—an unseen part—of everyday reality. But even for those people there is no direct way to talk about the sacred, because by its very nature it resists our attempts to make sense of it through language.

The only way human beings can talk about things and matters related to the sacred is through metaphor, using language originally meant to describe things and matters having to do with everyday reality. That means we have to use everyday language to talk about the sacred, but we use it symbolically, expressing what we know or think about it in terms of analogous experiences and ideas in everyday life. For example, when Christians talk about God as "father," they do not mean that God provided the spermatic matter involved in their conception, which is the most literal sense of the word. Even in everyday conversation we use the word "father" to denote a man who fills the role in a person's life usually filled by that person's biological father. But when Christians use "father" to talk about their god, they are using the word and the idea behind it as a metaphor or analogy. God is, in certain very specific respects, comparable to a human father. But more particularly, God is like a human father in the Jewish context of first-century Palestine, the context in which Jesus used the term in reference to God and taught his followers to do likewise.

The use of symbolic language when we talk about the sacred is a necessary result of our experience of the sacred being filtered through human consciousness. Human consciousness is structured and developed by our experience of the world. But our experience of the world is in turn dependent on the historical and cultural setting in which we live our lives. So we find each culture's ideas about the sacred realm bear a strong resemblance to its own historical models of power, wisdom, relationship, and value. Whatever is prized most highly in a given culture will be attributed to the sacred realm and its inhabitants. However society is structured in a given culture will be reflected in the social order attributed to the gods, and whatever virtues set one person apart from another will be the basis of the distinctions among the gods. In this way, not only language, but human cultural norms, are used symbolically to describe the sacred, the gods, and the realm they inhabit.

The language of religious symbolism does not only arise from cultural consensus. It might also arise from individual consciousness or be "given," that is, determined by the nature of the religious experience itself. For example, if a particular religious experience involves a vision of light, then "light" is a given symbol of the experience. But even in cases where the symbolism is given like this, there is an undeniable cultural component, and arguably the cultural context determines what is "given" by the experience. In any event, we might reasonably expect to find similarities in related cultures in the sort of language and imagery used to describe religious ideas and experience.

For example, as noted above, we find that the divine realm is most often believed to be organized on the model of human social or political organization. We find that people in the ancient Near East thought of the gods as arranged in a political hierarchy, with a chief god presiding over a body or council of subordinate gods, each of them with his or her own range of concerns. The chief god, male or female, is accorded royal honors similar to those given to kings and queens among the people that worship the chief god. But like human kings and queens who have to contend with the competing interests of their subjects, the chief god is limited in his or her ability to act by the competing interests of other gods. We also find the chief god exerting his or her power both by force and by persuasion, as well as by the force of his or her personal authority. The chief god will sometimes have to defend that personal authority in conflict with other gods, gaining victory through cunning or strength of arms or both. As we will see, royalty and its associated benefits and problems take on many forms in the divine realm and work out in different ways in ancient Near Eastern religions.

The relationship between the gods who inhabit the divine world and the human beings in the earthly realm can be understood in a number of different ways. If a given group of people thinks of the gods as a divine governing council, for example, the question is the nature of their attitude toward the human beings under their control. Human beings might be independent actors who owe allegiance and tribute to the gods, on the model of political vassals who owe fealty—loyalty and material support—to their overlords. Or human beings might essentially be slaves created by the gods to work for them. Like slaves, human beings then must submit to the will of their divine masters and put up with whatever treatment they might receive from the gods without complaint. Or it might be that human beings are related to the gods as essentially the same sort of beings. In that case, human beings might be considered as something like younger siblings who have to grow and mature to eventually become like their elders, the gods.

A religious culture's ideas about how human beings stand in relationship to the gods will have inevitable consequences for that culture's ideas about the human predicament. What prevents a harmonious relationship between human beings and creation on the one hand and the gods on the other? The answer will depend on the sort of relationship posited between humanity and the divine world, as do the possible solutions.

If the gods are set apart from humanity by their superior status, human ills may arise from human pride and presumption that leads some men and women to consider themselves equal to the gods and provoke divine jealousy. If the gods are set apart from humanity by their superior moral nature, human ills may arise from human moral failings that inflict harm on other human beings and alienate them from the morally pure gods. If the gods are set apart from humanity by their superior wisdom and understanding, human ills may arise from ignorance, and the solution may be contemplation, the accumulation of knowledge, or the exercise of wisdom. Although humanity may be alienated from the gods as a result of some human deficiency in comparison to the inhabitants of the divine realm, the nature of their deficiency will determine not only its resolution, but also how the resolution comes about, and how much of humanity may reasonably expect to escape the human predicament.

We may see, then, that there are many ways of thinking and talking about the divine world and the human world that lives in relationship to it. The peoples of the ancient Near East made certain choices in expressing their experience of the divine, and those choices have shaped their distinctive religious cultures in ways both large and small. The choices were not arbitrary; they were determined in part by the situation of the people who first used them, and in part by the subsequent growth and evolution of the religious culture that employed them. In all events, we find the divine realities believed to govern human existence are inevitably conceived of in human terms, as human beings strive to give expression to their experience of the divine in ways that make sense to them.

SECTION ONE

EGYPT

CHAPTER ONE

Egypt: Historical Survey

The Beginnings of Egyptian Civilization

Egyptian civilization began as a series of agricultural settlements along the Nile River. The Nile flows northward from the union of two of its tributaries, the White Nile and the Blue Nile, near modern Khartoum, ultimately forming a broad fertile delta before joining the Mediterranean Sea. The Egyptian part of the Nile Valley stretches from the First Cataract (the northernmost cataract) of the river at the border of ancient Nubia toward the north. Along this stretch of the Nile the valley is higher than it is farther north, so the land there was known as Upper Egypt. Farther north the valley leading to the broad river delta bordering the Mediterranean Sea was known as Lower Egypt. The distinction between Upper and Lower Egypt was basic to the historical situation of ancient Egypt, and was maintained in the designation "the Two Lands" even when Egypt was a single kingdom.

The fifth millennium BCE saw the first use of the plow and draft animals. Neolithic farmers learned how to irrigate and drain their land, making the best use of the available water, and substantially improving their yield of crops. The Egyptian climate is arid, but the Nile floods its banks annually in late summer. When the flood recedes, it leaves behind highly fertile soil that can support a wide variety of crops. The "Black Land" (*Kemet*) of the Nile valley stands in marked contrast to the "Red Land" (*Deshret*) of the surrounding desert.

By the late fourth millennium BCE small territories along the course of the Nile had begun to coalesce into larger political units under military leaders.

These regional domains may have been the basis for the later administrative districts (*nomes* in the Greek) of the Egyptian kingdom.

Egypt's culture appears to have been highly developed even when it first began to emerge into the light of early history soon after the establishment of the two kingdoms of north and south. Egypt's distinctive artistic style was already evident in surviving funerary monuments from this period. The earliest form of writing—hieroglyphic—is pictographic and was used primarily for inscriptions such as those found in tombs and temples. Later, a cursive form—hieratic—was used for record-keeping, religious texts, literature, and so on, written on such materials as papyrus, leather, and linen. The business of government was overseen by the king and a cadre of administrators, including architects, overseers, and scribes. The earliest kings known to have ruled over substantial portions of Upper and Lower Egypt were the kings called "Scorpion" (c. 3050 BCE) and Narmer, both of whom fought and overcame enemies in the western Nile Delta.

The Archaic Period

According to Egyptian tradition, the kingdoms of Upper and Lower Egypt were first united by Menes, a legendary king of Upper Egypt, around 3000 BCE. Menes may be identified with Aha who founded the First Dynasty. He moved his capital from Upper Egypt to establish a new royal capital in Memphis, about two hundred miles south of the Mediterranean coast. The distinction between Upper and Lower Egypt as separate lands was maintained long after the two regions were united. The royal title *nisu-bity*, usually translated "King of Upper and Lower Egypt" appears in the early third millennium. The king sometimes wore a double crown combining the white crown of Upper Egypt (the *hedjet*, shaped like a fat bowling pin) with the upswept red crown of Lower Egypt (the *deshret*). The king had two palaces and two burial places, although one was often only a cenotaph, a memorial stone or a structure commemorating the dead king. Aha, for example, built a tomb for himself in Lower Egypt near Saqqara and another in Abydos, a traditional cultic center in Upper Egypt.

The different major eras of Egyptian history are determined by alternating periods of unification and fragmentation, and further divided by the beginnings and ends of royal dynasties. Egyptian dynastic history begins with Aha. His reign marks the beginning of both Dynasty 1 and the Archaic Period around 3000 BCE. Notable kings before Aha—such as "Scorpion" and Narmer—are now relegated to Dynasty 0, although they probably represented several different ruling families.

The kings of Dynasty 1 and 2 mounted military actions to secure and expand the nation's borders against the Nubians to the south and the Libyans to the west of the Delta. At least one king, Den (c. 2880 BCE), even ventured north into Syria–Palestine. But this era also saw the creation of a royal bureaucracy that levied taxes and conscripted laborers for large-scale building projects, thereby consolidating royal control over an extensive kingdom. During this era kings most often presented themselves as incarnations of the god Horus, chief god of Lower Egypt. Each king would take a Horus name as his throne name and in its written form a falcon, the iconic animal representing Horus, would appear above it. But even in the early period kings might introduce religious innovations. The name of a king of Dynasty 2, Peribsen (c. 2715–2700 BCE), appears not with a falcon surmounting it, but instead with the iconic animal representing Seth, the chief god of Upper Egypt and Horus's primary divine rival. The throne name of the last king of Dynasty 2, Khasekhemwy (c. 2690–2670 BCE), appears surmounted by the iconic animals of both Horus and Seth. He reaffirmed his sovereignty over the entire nation, and symbolically reconciled the opposing forces of Horus and Seth in his own person as divine king.

The Old Kingdom

The Old Kingdom (Dynasties 3–6) is set apart from the Archaic Period by an artistic and architectural innovation: the use of stone to produce life-sized statuary and monumental buildings. Djoser (2667–2648 BCE), a king famous throughout Egyptian history for his wisdom and piety, is usually credited with initiating this new practice, since a step pyramid was built over his underground tomb at Saqqara. This first pyramid was apparently designed to replicate the primeval mound of earth on which the creator god stood while doing the work of creation. The pyramids may have also developed from the mound of earth or pile of mud bricks placed over an underground tomb. Sneferu (2613–2589 BCE), founder of Dynasty 4, completed three large true pyramids—each now with the familiar smooth limestone surface—and presided over a number of other changes in the construction and orientation of the pyramid complex as well. These changes probably reflected new ideas about the king's fate in the afterlife.

During Dynasty 4 trade flourished between Egypt and Byblos and other ports in Lebanon, and the forests of Lebanon became a major source for the wood used in Egyptian construction. Military campaigns secured the borders of the western delta against the Libyans and the borders to the south against the Nubians. Increased security and royal revenues prepared the way for the

The Great Pyramid at Giza, built by Khufu (2571–2548 BCE). © 2008 Jupiterimages Corporation

building projects of Khufu (2589–2566 BCE). Khufu (often known as Cheops) built the Great Pyramid at Giza, the only one of the seven wonders of the ancient world to survive to the present day. The pyramid was surrounded by an extensive funerary complex of tombs and temples, attesting to the centrality of the divine king in both life and death. It was also apparently during this period that the methods used to mummify bodies were first introduced and developed.

Khufu's successor Djedefra (2566–2558 BCE) was the first king to incorporate the divine name Ra into his throne name and to use the royal title "Son of Ra." Djedefra's successor Khafra (2558–2532 BCE) was the model for the human head of the Great Sphinx of Giza. His successor Menkaura (2532–2503 BCE) built the last of the pyramids at Giza. His pyramid was built on a smaller scale, in large part using granite in place of limestone.

The reign of Menkaura saw the beginning of a long period of decline in royal authority that also produced a number of religious innovations. The dominance of Ra as sun god during Dynasty 5 (c. 2494–2345 BCE) led to the building of sun temples of elaborate design dedicated to the god. Also during Dynasty 5 Egypt initiated sea trade with Punt on the Somali coast; this area would become an important source of incense for Egypt. Along with the reverence for Ra that had marked the first part of Dynasty 5, later kings of the dynasty also gave increasing attention to Osiris as god of the Underworld. The last king of Dynasty 5, Unas (2375–2345 BCE), had the walls within his pyramid at Saqqara engraved with texts intended to aid and ensure the deceased king's entry into the Kingdom of the Dead. These spells together form the "Pyramid Texts," one basis for the later *Book of Going Forth by Day*, more commonly known as the *Egyptian Book of the Dead*.

By the reign of Pepy I (2321–2287 BCE) during Dynasty 6, royal authority had been eroded by the power of provincial leaders. One of his successors, Pepy II (2278–2184 BCE), may have been the longest-reigning king of Egypt; the ancient historian Menetho put his reign at ninety-four years. But the king's personal weakness, exacerbated by jockeying for power among his ministers, undermined royal authority to the point that the king could no longer ensure economic and social well-being. Several short-lived kings and one queen regnant (Nitiqret, 2184–2181 BCE) followed Pepy II and with the last of them Dynasty 6 and the Old Kingdom ended in a fragmentation of power and Egyptian society.

The First Intermediate Period (c. 2181–2055 BCE) included Dynasties 7–11, but most kings of these dynasties ruled only a portion of Egypt and had to contend with competing rulers who also claimed the throne. Both Dynasty 7 and 8 were very short-lived and their kings held little power. Real power during this time seems to have reverted largely to nomarchs, regional rulers, some of whom claimed royal power in Herakleopolis or Thebes as the kings of Dynasties 9 and 10. These kings struggled for power against other royal claimants and regional leaders while working to resolve the internal problems of their own domains.

The Middle Kingdom

The Thebans ultimately pushed their power northward and prevailed with the final conquest of Herakleopolis and the delta around 2041 BCE under the Theban king Mentuhotep II (2055–2004 BCE) of Dynasty 11, although the details of the conquest are difficult to reconstruct. The Middle Kingdom (2055–1650 BCE) begins with the reunification of Upper and Lower Egypt under a single king. It was a period of artistic achievement in graphic art and architecture as well as literature. Mentuhotep secured the borders of his realm, revived commerce and trade, and appointed an overseer of Lower Egypt while he ruled from Thebes. Mentuhotep also undertook a massive building program, again using wood from the forests of Lebanon supplied through revived sea trade with Byblos. Mentuhotep III (2004–1992 BCE) revived sea trade with Punt and continued his father's building program. His brief reign saw further innovations in both art and architecture, and particularly fine examples survive.

The founder of Dynasty 12, Amenemhat I (1985–1956 BCE), moved the royal capital from Thebes to a site south of Memphis, although Thebes remained an important cultic center devoted to the god Amun. Under Amenemhat Egypt extended its power southward into Nubia. The king built a series of forts to defend the frontier and ensure access to Nubia's stone quarries. Amenemhat also built forts along the eastern Delta to limit access to Egypt from the Sinai Peninsula and to lay claim to Sinai's mineral riches. Amenemhat apparently made his son Senusret his coregent during his reign, setting a precedent followed by most later kings of Dynasty 12.

When he became king in his own right after Amenemhat's death in an attempted palace coup, Senusret I (1956–1911 BCE) further extended Egyptian control over Nubia, ensuring Egypt's security and initiating fifty years of relative peace. Senusret presided over the development of a particular style of art, the "royal style," that soon came to dominate Egyptian art. He also built temples for a multitude of gods. Many of these temples were built in Abydos, a ritual center associated particularly with the rites of Osiris, the god who ruled over the Underworld. Selective peace agreements between Egypt and regional states of Syria–Palestine provided renewed opportunities for trade and commerce. The Middle Kingdom also saw the importation of slaves from western Asia into Egypt to serve as laborers for building projects.

Senusret II (1877–1870 BCE) developed the Faiyum, an oasis in the western desert, by building an irrigation system that allowed its water to be used for agriculture. He also built religious monuments in the same region. Senusret III (1870–1831 BCE) consolidated royal power, initiating a realignment of political and social power in the Two Lands. He mounted a series of brutal wars against Nubia and maintained the Egyptian presence there with a heavy hand. Senusret also extended Egyptian power into Syria–Palestine, gaining control over trade routes as far north as the city of Shechem in Canaan. The many surviving statues of Senusret appear to be reliable portraits of the king and so may be identified by their distinctive appearance.

Senusret's conquests were secured and extended by his son Amenemhat III (c. 1831–1786 BCE), who consolidated his territorial gains with substantial new building, including shrines, temples, and tombs. His long and prosperous reign marks the climax of the artistic achievements of the Middle Kingdom. By contrast, the reign of Amenemhat IV (1786–1777 BCE) was brief and relatively undistinguished. He was succeeded by his sister Sobekneferu (1777–1773 BCE), the first woman to rule Egypt as pharaoh. She took female and some male titles, and one damaged statue depicts the queen wearing a combination of female and male garments. Her rule lasted only a few years, and Dynasty 12 came to an end with her death.

The kings of Dynasty 13 (c. 1773–1723 BCE) reigned for only a few years each, although at least initially the royal administration continued to function as it always had. Despite occasional indications of a resurgence of royal power under a few kings, there was a general decline in the throne's wealth and influence. After the reign of the last king of Dynasty 13, royal power passed to competing regional dynasties as the Two Lands were racked by division.

The Second Intermediate Period (c. 1650–1550 BCE) saw Egypt lose territory in both the north and the south. In part because the contending armies could no longer control the northeastern borders, groups of Semitic peoples entered the Egyptian Delta from Syria–Palestine and moved toward the south. Several of these Semitic groups established independent rule within Egypt, forming their own dynasties. Most notable among the Semitic peoples were the Hyksos, who founded Dynasty 15 and claimed authority over Upper and Lower Egypt and parts of Syria–Palestine, ruling from their capital Avaris in the eastern Nile Delta. To the south, native Dynasty 16 (c. 1650–1580 BCE) and Dynasty 17 (c. 1580–1550 BCE) ruled in Thebes. The kings of Dynasty 17 went to war against the Hyksos, mounting several military campaigns to drive them out of Egypt. When the Hyksos were finally expelled, the Two Lands were again united under a single powerful king, Ahmose, founder of Dynasty 18. His reign marks the beginning of the New Kingdom (c. 1550–1069 BCE), when Egypt would reach the height of its power.

The New Kingdom

After defeating the Hyksos, Ahmose (1550–1525 BCE) was able to consolidate his kingdom and expand its borders, bringing Egypt peace and security. Ahmose secured the delta and regained Egypt's earlier territories in the Sinai Peninsula while also reestablishing dominion over Lower Nubia with a chain of fortified outposts. He undertook a series of major building projects. Perhaps more important, he revived and reorganized the apparatus of the royal administration in Thebes. Ahmose's military and political accomplishments made it possible for his son Amenhotep I (1525–1504 BCE) to both continue his father's successes and initiate a cultural renaissance, notably in a series of royal memorials at Karnak. Amenhotep and his mother Ahmose-Nefertari were later worshipped as gods at Thebes. The military ventures of his successor, Thutmose I (1504–1492 BCE) further expanded Egyptian power farther south in Nubia. Thutmose asserted nominal control over Syria–Palestine as far northeast as Mesopotamia.

Thutmose III (1479–1425 BCE) came to the throne as a child under the regency of his stepmother Hatshepsut, who essentially ruled in his place for twenty years. She claimed all the powers of the pharaoh and was represented in art with the accoutrements of male royal power. She undertook prodigious building projects, including major additions to the temple at Karnak. Despite these assertions of personal authority, Hatshepsut was largely disengaged from foreign affairs and depended heavily on the expertise of her royal functionaries to govern the nation.

At Hatshepsut's death around 1458 BCE, Thutmose III assumed sole authority and quickly acted to reassert Egyptian power against the nation's enemies. He gained supremacy over Syria and expanded Egyptian power to its greatest extent in Nubia, as far south as the Fourth Cataract. In both instances, Thutmose controlled his new possessions through effective royal administration and Egyptian garrisons in a series of strategically placed fortresses. Thutmose's successors Amenhotep II (1427–1400 BCE) and Thutmose IV (1400–1390 BCE) followed the example of both his building programs and his military ventures.

Amenhotep III (1390–1352 BCE) did not campaign extensively. He instead devoted himself to court life and architecture, building a mortuary temple that included the so-called Colossi of Memnon, a pair of 65-foot-high stone portrait statues of the pharaoh on the west bank at Thebes. He also appears to have shared the concern with religious matters that marked the reign of his son, Amenhotep IV, better known by his later name, Akhenaten.

Amenhotep IV (1352–1336 BCE) was a devotee of Aten, god of the sun disk, and exalted Aten over the other gods of Egypt, displacing Amun as the dominant national god. Amenhotep ("Amun is gracious") changed his throne name to Akhenaten, "pleasing to Aten." He established a new royal capital between Memphis and Thebes and named it Akhetaten, "Horizon of Aten." Akhenaten also introduced a new artistic style that combined realistic elements with a highly developed iconic symbolism. During the reign of his successor Tutankhaten (1336–1327 BCE), Memphis once again became the royal capital and Amun regained supremacy. The young king's throne name was changed to Tutankhamun. The reigns of Akhenaten and his successors, called the Amarna period after the modern name of his capital, were purged from history by the kings of Dynasty 19.

Dynasty 19, founded by Rameses I (1295–1294 BCE) was stabilized by his son Sety I (1294–1279 BCE), who regained territory Egypt had lost in Syria and Nubia. Sety also restored temples and inscriptions, reinstating the name of Amun where it had been obliterated under Akhenaten. His son Rameses II (1279–1213 BCE) mounted a campaign in Syria to reclaim the territory of Amurru from Hittite control. When the Hittite king Muwatalli later attempted to secure Amurru against the Egyptians, Rameses returned north and engaged the Hittites in a battle at Qadesh. Despite the fact that the Egyptians suffered heavy losses and left the Hittites in control of Qadesh, the battle was subsequently presented in Egypt as a great victory. Rameses reigned sixty-six years, presiding over a long era of peace. He built a new royal capital, Piramesse ("House of Rameses") in the eastern Delta and continued to assert Egyptian authority in Syria through both military power and diplomatic alliances.

Beginning around 1200 BCE, the groups the Egyptians called the "Sea Peoples"—notably including the Philistines—became dominant in Syria–Palestine in the wake of the collapse of the Hittite kingdom, Mycenaean Greece, and other eastern Mediterranean kingdoms. Merneptah (1213–1203 BCE) campaigned against Sea Peoples who had settled along the eastern North African coast and joined forces with the Libyans, who had harassed Egypt's western borders for generations. Merneptah conquered rebellious cities in Palestine, while also carrying out punitive campaigns in Nubia. He commemorated his victories with a stele that includes the first reference to "Israel" in Egyptian sources.

Merneptah's death set off a struggle for power between his son Sety II (1200–1194 BCE) and a rival king, Amenmessu (1203–1200 BCE), who ruled for a few years in Upper Egypt. After Sety's death his principal queen Tausret ruled as regent with her stepson Saptah (1194–1188 BCE), and alone for two years (1188–1186 BCE) after Saptah's death. A royal official, a Syrian named Bay, wielded great power during both Saptah's and Tausret's reigns. He may have tried to rule as king himself after Tausret's death; if so, he was overcome by Sethnakht.

Sethnakht (1186–1184 BCE) ruled briefly and established a new dynasty (Dynasty 20), but his successors were all named Rameses, perhaps in homage to the great king of Dynasty 19. Rameses III (1184–1153 BCE) beat back separate invasions by the Libyans from the west and the Sea Peoples from the east. Rameses also had to contend with political and social unrest within Egypt. He may have been assassinated, but there was certainly a palace conspiracy to murder him. Persistent economic uncertainty and political unrest continued during the reigns of the several short-lived kings who followed him. The last king of Dynasty 20, Rameses XI (1099–1069 BCE), found his power increasingly usurped by his military leaders. During the last decade of his reign his authority may well have extended only to Lower Egypt.

The Third Intermediate Period (c. 1069–664 BCE) began with Egypt in isolation from the rest of the Near East. During Dynasty 21, military commanders who were also high priests of Amun held power in Thebes while the pharaohs ruled from Tanis, near Piramesse in the eastern Delta. In these uncertain times the king depended on military support from Libyan tribes. Siamun (978–959 BCE) campaigned in Syria–Palestine and captured Gezer from the Philistines, but later gave the city to King Solomon of Israel as a dowry for a princess, possibly Siamun's daughter.

A Libyan, Sheshonq I (c. 945–924 BCE), assumed power after the last Tanite king. He and his successors in Dynasty 22 are called "Bubastids" after their capital Bubastis, southwest of Piramesse and Tanis. The Libyan Bubastids were acculturated to Egyptian ways and Sheshonq was careful to maintain Egyptian traditions, overcoming the initial unease among his subjects that greeted his reign in Upper Egypt. Sheshonq's brief campaign into Syria–Palestine resulted in enough wealth for him and his son Osorkon I (924–889 BCE) to initiate extensive building projects at home. The Bubastids also placed members of the royal family in major high priesthoods.

The Bubastid dynasty apparently split after the reign of Takelot II (850–825 BCE). This led to the founding of Dynasty 23 and further disintegration of royal authority. Upper Egypt was ruled by petty kings while Libyan tribes maintained control of much of the Delta. The Libyan chieftain Tefnakht of Sais

(727–720 BCE) founded Dynasty 24. Acculturated Nubians took power in the south, establishing Dynasty 25 and reviving traditional Egyptian titles, texts, and rituals. Kings of Dynasty 25 even built pyramids in Nubia. After conflict arose between the Libyans in the north and Nubians in the south, Kushites from Upper Nubia gained control over much of Egypt, and maintained it primarily through military power. They revitalized the economy by drawing on Nubian stores of gold and initiating monumental building projects.

The Assyrians, who had brought all of Mesopotamia and Syria–Palestine under their control, turned their attention to Egypt in the first part of the seventh century BCE. The Assyrian king Esarhaddon (681–669 BCE) responded to Egyptian offensives in defense of Hezekiah of Judah in Palestine and moved down into Egypt in 671 BCE, where he made allies of the petty kings of the Delta against the Kushites. The vassal kings later revolted when Esarhaddon's successor Assur-bannipal (668–627 BCE) was occupied with other concerns. Assur-bannipal looked to recruit trustworthy allies in Egypt. One of these, Psamtek I (664–610 BCE) of the Saite Dynasty 26, reunified the Delta over a period of many years. He finally established sovereignty over Upper Egypt through careful diplomatic interaction with the Nubian dynasty to the south.

The Late Period

The Late Period of Egyptian history is characterized by the rise of a series of world empires that saw Egypt as a primary territory for conquest. The growing power of Babylon threatened Assyria and its allies in the Near East. Both Psamtek and his son Nekau remained loyal to Assyria. Nekau II (610–595 BCE) gained control over Judah and much of Syria–Palestine in the course of a campaign against the Babylonians in 609 BCE. But Nekau later lost all his conquests in the territory to the advancing power of the Babylonian king Nebuchadnezzer in 597 BCE. His son Psamtek II (595–589 BCE) campaigned against the Nubians, forcing them farther south and away from Egyptian territory. Apries (589–570 BCE) colluded with princes in Syria–Palestine in a rebellion against the Babylonians, and provided refuge to their people when they fled Babylonian retaliation once the rebellion was crushed.

The Persians under Cyrus destroyed the power of Babylon and systematically gathered up the remnants of its empire. Cyrus's son Cambyses (530–522 BCE) defeated the Egyptian king Psamtek III (526–525) in May 525 BCE and soon gained control of the entire nation. Darius I (522–486 BCE), a remarkably enlightened monarch, codified Egyptian law and governed largely through the existing Egyptian royal administration.

In the late fifth century BCE, after a prolonged period of peace, a Libyan, Amyrtaios of Sais, led a successful revolt against the Persians. He subsequently ruled for less than five years (404–399 BCE) as the only king of Dynasty 28. The kings of Dynasty 29 maintained their independence against the Persians, but the last, Nepherites II (c. 380), was forced to submit to a usurper after ruling less than a year. The triumphant Nectanebo I (380–362 BCE) founded Dynasty 30, the last native dynasty of Egypt. The kings of Dynasty 30 continued to resist the power of Persia, but the Persians regained control of Egypt under Artaxerxes III in 343 BCE. The last king of Dynasty 30, Nectanebo II (360–343 BCE), fled the Persians and escaped south into Nubia.

But the Persian Empire was itself faltering. In 332 BCE, Egypt was conquered by the armies of the Macedonian king Alexander the Great. Soon the nation came under the control of Alexander's general Ptolemy and his successors. The Ptolemies adopted the powers, titles, and symbols of the pharaohs and modeled their rule on the glories and traditions of Egypt's past.

CHAPTER TWO

Egypt: The Gods and the World They Made

The General Character of Ancient Egyptian Religion

Egypt provides the best example in the ancient Mediterranean world of a religion and a religious view of political leadership that developed and flourished in relative isolation from outside cultural influences. Although the history of ancient Egypt covers over four thousand years, the relative stability of daily life in the Nile Valley and the general conservatism of Egyptian culture ensured that religious beliefs and practices would change very little over the centuries. In fact those religious beliefs and practices became hallmarks of Egyptian national identity as well as primary indicators of political legitimacy.

But even within this tradition of religious conservatism there remained the possibility of diversity and change. Throughout Egyptian history there were local variations of the dominant religious culture. Developments and innovations in Egyptian religion arose primarily from political turmoil, since each change of dynasty introduced the possibility of religious change as well. Whenever a new king or dynasty established a new capital, for example, that would entail changes in major cultic centers, including construction of a new necropolis or cemetery complex for the king, his family, and his ministers. A new dynasty might also initiate or expand the worship of a favored god with new temples or new rituals. Such changes did not necessarily affect the religious practices and affections of the average Egyptian, but they would certainly change the face of official religion and be reflected in the public religious life (and sometimes the names) of the nation's political leaders.

Through such innovations, the overall nature and characteristic emphases of Egyptian religious culture would slowly evolve.

Over time ideas about the gods in general as well as beliefs about specific gods changed to address shifting needs and concerns among their worshippers. Sometimes divergent traditions about the gods stood side by side; at other times there was an attempt to harmonize them by creating new stories or substantially changing old ones. Sometimes one god became identified with another, leading to elements of their mythology and their worship being combined to produce something new. At other times a god's popularity might lead to a more active role in the divine realm and new titles to recognize the god's enhanced power.

As major as such changes might seem, however, they were moderated by the essential conservatism of Egyptian culture. Once the political unity of Egypt was achieved at the beginning of the Archaic Period, the models for the ideals of its cultural life were already in place. The art and architecture subsidized by the royal treasuries from the Archaic Period are notable not only because they presented these ideals in concrete forms, but also because they were designed to outlast the centuries. Similar ideals and intentions informed the work of artists employed by local officials or individuals. Egyptians, from kings to peasants, most often performed their religious duties and invoked their gods surrounded by centuries-old monuments, temples, and art that showed them what their gods looked like and how best to serve and please them. Certain religious ideas, images, and metaphors became dominant and provided the defining concepts for ancient Egyptian religious culture throughout its long history. As a result, even religious innovations tended to be expressed in very traditional terms. So for the most part we can talk about the full range of ancient Egyptian religion as a more or less homogeneous religious culture throughout its history. We should remain mindful that this is a simplification of the actual situation, and we will note significant changes and developments in religious belief or practice over Egypt's history.

The predominant characteristic of ancient Egyptian religious culture, both for its own people and in the eyes of others both past and present, was its aura of serenity and the eternal. This impression of Egyptian culture is fostered by major monuments dating back to the Old Kingdom. The Great Pyramid of Khufu and the Sphinx impress the modern viewer with the solidity and impassivity that has allowed them to survive for thousands of years. All eras of Egyptian art and architecture impress us in much the same way. The elaborately decorated and furnished tombs, the calm expressions and stylized poses of the figures in statuary and tomb paintings, all seem to convey a calm detachment from the tribulations of life and an engagement instead with what endures.

But this impression of serenity and eternity is a deliberate artistic creation of the overseers and craftsmen who created the monuments, inscriptions, murals, and statuary that reflected and shaped the spirit of Egyptian religious culture. Those artists and artisans who served the king produced works that would reflect the king's enforcement of cosmic harmony on the unruly forces of disorder. Since the king represented the principle of order (*maat*), royal monuments as well as the king's self-presentation deliberately reflected the salutary effects of a life lived under the authority of the gods' elect, the serenity that arises from cosmic harmony.

But the reality of daily life in ancient Egypt for the vast majority of the population was very different. The dark powers associated with disorder and catastrophe threatened to break into their lives at any time. Apart from political disasters in the form of war, invasion, coup, or usurpation, there were various sorts of natural disasters, any of which might trigger famine or plague. At the more personal level, the vast majority of the Egyptian population was subjected on a regular basis to the losses imposed by accident, disease, or death.

So there was a dichotomy in how the world was perceived in ancient Egypt, two different stories about the cosmos, the gods, the king, and his people. On the one hand, life in this world under the king's sway was a mirror of the eternal life of the divine realm: peaceful, joyful, and unchanging. On the other, this world was seen as a place where the forces of disorder were kept suppressed but still threatened to overwhelm the divine order at any time. The peace and order imposed by the king required a constant exertion of both strength and will and could be achieved only through the divine power at his command.

The dichotomy between order and disorder is typical of the contrasts that appear to have been a fundamental part of the ancient Egyptian way of understanding the created world: order and disorder, fertile valley and arid desert, light and darkness, life and death. The Egyptians understood these dichotomies not so much as conflicts between contending aspects of creation but as complementary parts of a whole, the expression of the temporal in the eternal and the eternal in the temporal. These were the inevitable tensions in the world the gods had made.

The Nature and Depiction of the Egyptian Gods

The gods of Egypt were depicted in specific forms with distinctive attributes, each reflecting beliefs about the nature of the divine in general as well as the nature of the specific god. The earliest forms of ancient Egyptian religion, as far as we are able to reconstruct them, represent a belief in the ubiquity of divine power suffused throughout creation. Divine power was present in animals and in human beings in varying degrees as well as in the gods.

Initially the gods were represented in animal forms. The later classic depictions of many of the gods retain aspects of their earlier animal forms, most often combining an animal head with a human body. Sometimes a god would continue to be depicted in an animal form, or as a human being with some specific indication of the god's divine identity. For example, the goddess Hathor is commonly depicted in the form of a cow, but she also appears as a woman with a cow's ears or crowned with a sun disk and *uraeus*—the sacred cobra representing supreme power—between a cow's long curving horns. Such variations in a god's appearance suggested different aspects of the god's power. As a result, the gods could be depicted in a number of forms, using a variety of symbols, because of the variety of the gods' manifestations and inexpressible divine power. Representation of the gods in concrete forms in pictures or sculpture to some extent domesticated them and made them comprehensible to their worshippers. Individualized depictions of the gods made the divine world accessible to the human imagination, and the Egyptian gods share the sort of fluidity that is characteristic of human personalities, encompassing different traits.

Traditional symbols of power and artistic traditions made the gods' divine nature evident in any depiction of them. As we have seen, the gods might be portrayed with animal heads or other animal features. Typically they were shown with their hands raised in an attitude of blessing or welcome, an indication of a god's benevolence. One hand might grasp the *ankh*, the symbol of eternal life. Some gods were depicted crowned with the solar disk as a sign of their divinity, or with the *uraeus* as a sign of their power. Many gods can be identified by the sort of crown or headdress they wear. Some gods were shown in stereotyped ways. Both Osiris and Ptah were commonly shown with their bodies mummified, wrapped in cloth strips. Seth was depicted as a composite beast, a "Seth-animal." Horus in the form of a falcon or a falcon-headed man might wear the double crown of Egypt, holding the royal crook and flail as symbols of his sovereign power over both the gods and humanity.

From Dynasty 1, divine power was conceptualized and expressed in anthropomorphic terms, so the gods were believed essentially to be human beings with divine abilities. The gods spoke and acted like human beings; they loved, made war, grew old, made plans and carried them out, expressed regret, and practiced trickery. Both the gods and humanity were part of the created order, although the creator god, whether Atum, Ra, or Ptah, was thought of either as uncreated or self-created. Both gods and human beings had a beginning in time and would have an end in time, although the lives of the gods were reckoned in millions of years. Like human beings, the gods might form family units, although there was no uniform system of relationship among them.

The gods differed from humanity not only by virtue of their divine power and length of life, but also their location. The gods lived far away from human beings and their earthly habitations. While human beings lived in the Two Lands or among the foreign nations, the gods lived in the sky, or in the Underworld. The gods might also live on the earth, but if they did, they lived far away from human beings, at the very edges of the world. Despite their spatial separation from their human subjects, the gods were believed to be present among their devotees at their temples where they were worshipped in the rituals of the state religion. They were present in their cult statues in their temples or during festivals when the statues were publically displayed. And they were also believed to be present to their worshippers and ready to respond to invocations, prayers, petitions, and magic spells when people called upon them.

The gods of Egypt simultaneously existed in two sorts of time, one the cyclical eternity of change and renewal associated with Ra, the other the eternity of the changeless associated with Osiris. The first, *neheh*, was the continuation of the cosmos in temporal terms, the perpetual passage of heavenly and earthly events that accumulated as history. It was in the realm of *neheh* that the gods experienced change. *Neheh* was associated with Ra in his daily passage from east to west, each day coming and passing like all others in the eternal cycle. It is in the realm of *neheh* that the gods interacted with human beings. The second sort of time, *djet*, was the transcendent reality of the changeless, associated with Osiris, king of the realm of the dead. *Djet* was the eternal foundation for the functioning of *neheh*, and after the cessation of *neheh*, *djet*—and its ruler Osiris—would continue. *Djet* was the eternal basis of divine action and initiative that enabled the creation of the cosmos and the possibility of its continuation.

The Egyptian Pantheon

There is no single obvious way to categorize the vast array of gods in ancient Egypt. Attempts at systematization are to a large extent a convenience to the modern person and do not reflect the way the Egyptians themselves thought about the divine world. We might classify the gods according to their place in a hierarchy of power, but the degrees of divine power are not clear and not of major importance. We might classify the gods by the nature of their primary associations, but primary associations may be less important than the amount of attention given a god in official or popular worship, or the role a particular god or goddess plays in the mythology. We should also keep in mind that many gods transcended their primary associations or attributes to become involved in a wide range of human activities and concerns.

The Ennead are the nine gods who in some accounts are the first products of divine creation. But their priority in the order of creation did not constitute a hierarchy. The gods who were involved most closely with human society and destiny were in fact last in the initial line of creation. These were the children of the god Geb and his consort Nut: Osiris, Isis, Seth, and Nephthys. Even these gods are not the immediate rulers over humanity. The chief god was either one of the sun gods, in some cases a god believed to be the initiator of creation, such as Amun or Atum, or the god who was one of the later divine products of the creative work, Horus, the son and successor of Osiris.

Horus was chief god of Lower Egypt. Later Horus became the patron of the king of Upper and Lower Egypt. The name Horus means "the Distant One," referring to his role as a sky god whose two eyes were the sun and the moon. The name Horus appears in many compound forms, notably "Horus Uniter of the Two Lands," a title associated preeminently with his role as patron of the king. Horus was represented as a falcon or as a falcon-headed human being, often with a crown or a sun disk on his head. His spread wings formed the canopy of the sky. In the story of Osiris, Horus inherits the heavenly throne and kingly rule over the gods after Osiris has been murdered by Seth, although only after a lengthy conflict with the usurper. In this respect Horus represents the legitimate succession of the king as well as the king's divine authority to rule. Horus has one of the longest histories among the Egyptian gods. He was already a god during Dynasty 0, before the Archaic Period, and was still being worshipped during the Greek and Roman periods over three thousand years later.

Gods associated with natural phenomena and those who represented different cosmic elements are important primarily in Egyptian creation stories but were also believed to contribute to the continuing welfare of the cosmos. Among the elemental gods are Shu ("Emptiness"), the god associated with the space between earth and heaven, and Tefnut, goddess of moisture. Shu and Tefnut are the first divine couple, the parents of Geb, the god whose recumbent body forms the earth, and Nut, the sky goddess whose body is stretched out over him, with Shu between them. To these elemental gods may be added the two gods associated with the moon, among other divine roles. Thoth, the divine scribe, was recognized as god of the moon in Hermopolis. Khonsu was recognized as god of the moon in Thebes, where he was one of the divine triad along with his father Amun and Amun's consort Mut, who shared royal rule with Amun as queen and divine mother.

Other gods might include aspects of the elements of creation or natural phenomena among their other attributes. This was notably the case with the various chief sun gods, who represented the sun in its different aspects, but it was also true of the goddess Hathor. Hathor was primarily a goddess of joy and erotic love. But in one myth Hathor, in her form as a cow, carries her father, the sun god Ra, into the sky when he decides to leave the earth. Ra climbs on Hathor's back and her body ascends into the sky as her legs, feet planted firmly on earth, grow longer and longer. When the ascent is finished, the underside of Hathor's body forms the firmament of heaven, decorated by stars. From that time forward the goddess gives birth to Ra from her womb in the east each morning and swallows him in the west each evening.

National deities appear to have developed from local or regional gods, either through the spread of their worship from one place to another or through their association with one of the royal dynasties. Regional gods often took on additional significance when they became identified with one another (for example Amun and Ra) or associated with other gods in divine families (for example the divine couple Osiris and Isis with their son Horus), or set in opposition (for example Horus and Seth). Other regional gods apparently were recognized from very early on as local manifestations of more universal gods, as was the case with Amun, whose primary local association was with Karnak. A god sacred to all Egypt might have a special association with a particular locality, as the divine craftsman Khnum did with the cataracts in Upper Egypt. Most gods had a particular city as the center of their worship.

Two regional goddesses in particular were significant, since their association with the king was an expression of his sovereignty over all Egypt. The goddess Nekhbet, represented as a vulture, was a protective deity over Upper Egypt. The goddess Wadjit, represented as a cobra, presided over Lower Egypt. The heads of the two goddesses appear on the double crown of the king, indicating his sovereign power over the Two Lands.

One group of gods significant for all Egyptians was the group of funerary deities, the gods who oversaw the preparation of the dead for burial and their entrance into the afterlife. The earliest gods of the dead and the Underworld were depicted with the heads of jackals, including Wepwawet ("Opener of the Way"), Khentyamentiu, and, most notably, Anubis. The jackal is a desert scavenger whose primary food is carrion, and the heads of these gods were

Mask of Tutankhamun (1333–1323 BCE), showing crown with uraeus. © 2008 Jupiterimages Corporation

black, the color of fertility and the Underworld. Anubis was both the judge and the ruler of the dead during the Old Kingdom.

Anubis was succeeded as god of the Underworld by Osiris, who is placed in that role when his name first appears during Dynasty 5. In Egyptian mythology Osiris became ruler of the afterlife after his own death at the hands of his brother Seth. Osiris presided over the realm of the dead with his consort Isis and their sister Nephthys, the wife of Seth. Osiris, like Anubis before him, was also the judge of the souls of the dead. The process of judgment involved a multitude of gods who represented the traditional nomes of Egypt, and might also include the four sons of Horus. We will discuss the gods of the Egyptian Underworld and the fate of the dead in greater detail in a later chapter.

There were also Egyptian gods associated with different occupations. Usually the god or goddess did in the divine realm the work associated with the occupation and served as a patron to those who did similar work on earth. We see Ptah, for example, not only serving as an artisan and craftsman among the gods, but serving as the divine patron of artisans and craftsmen as well. Thoth, scribe of the gods, was also patron of the scribes in the royal bureaucracy who served the king in the same way Thoth served the gods. A host of gods served as patrons of doctors. One of them, Imhotep, was a deified form of an historical official from the reign of Djoser (2667–2648 BCE) during the Old Kingdom. Other more universal gods might also be invoked by those who were ill or in need in particular situations. The goddess Isis, among her many other roles, was a source of magical spells to cure various sorts of illnesses. Some minor gods seem to have been invoked primarily as protectors, such as the grotesque dwarf god Bes, whose primary function was to frighten away evil spirits. As is usually the case with polytheistic religious cultures, the Egyptian pantheon included a host of major and minor gods, some narrowly specialized and others with a broad array of divine powers.

The Accumulation of Divine Attributes: Two Examples

Some gods and goddesses accumulated a large number of attributes, associations, and stories over the centuries. One example was Hathor, a popular goddess who filled a number of sometimes tenuously related roles. Hathor's origins seem to lie in prehistoric worship of a cow goddess that represented nature and the power of fertility. These are attributes Hathor retains throughout her history. She is usually represented as a cow with the solar disk between her long horns, as a goddess with horns and the solar disk or with a human face and cow's ears. Her name *Hwt Hr* means "House of Horus." She was identified with various abodes of Horus, including the sky, and understood to be his protector

Head of Hathor, shown in human form with cow's ears, from the mortuary temple of Hatshepsut. © 2008 Jupiterimages Corporation

and nurturer. She may have been a manifestation of Isis in early Egyptian religious culture and in that respect the mother of Horus. Hathor is also closely associated with the sun god Ra, and is often said to be Ra's daughter.

Hathor was goddess of joy and erotic love, associated with all its pleasurable aspects. She was patroness of singers, dancers, and artists, all of whose arts were conducive to romance. Hathor also protected women in childbirth; one of her titles was "Lady of the Vulva." Her associations with erotic love and joy are closely connected. In an episode from the "Contendings of Horus and Seth," Ra becomes exasperated after long days spent judging between the rival claims of Horus and Seth to the throne and retires to his tent. Hathor seeks Ra out, lifts up her skirt, and exposes herself to him. This act makes Ra break out in laughter and lifts his mood enough that he returns to his work.

Perhaps because of her associations with fertility and the cosmic cycles of the agricultural year, Hathor is also goddess of fate. In this capacity it is sometimes she, not Anubis, who first receives the dead into the Underworld in accounts of the afterlife. In this same connection, Hathor is also sometimes a prophetess, with foreknowledge of what the future holds.

Hathor's role as goddess of fate is connected with another role that at first seems in conflict with her primary attributes as a goddess of love and joy: she is also the warrior goddess of divine vengeance. It is Hathor who inflicts punishment on those who offend the gods or overstep the limits of divine prerogatives. In this role she is most often identified with Sekhmet ("the Powerful One"), the fearsome lioness-headed goddess associated with war and violence.

In another story involving Ra, "The Destruction of Mankind," the sun god has grown old and human beings are plotting to overthrow his authority. Ra discovers their treachery and orders Hathor to take vengeance on them. Unfortunately, Hathor in her aspect as Sekhmet takes to her work too readily, and by the time she stops to rest at the end of the day she has destroyed half of the people on earth. Ra realizes the goddess's thirst for blood threatens to wipe out humanity entirely. To save humanity, during the night Ra procures a vast quantity of barley beer and mixes it with red ocher, pouring it out over the face of the earth. When the goddess awakens the next morning, she mistakes the tinted barley beer for human blood and drinks her fill of it. Soon she is too intoxicated to continue her work and humanity is saved. This story may also explain why Hathor is honored as the goddess of drunkenness.

Hathor was one of the most popular gods throughout Egyptian history with worshippers from all levels of society, and her rituals and festivals reflect her primary characteristics. Her worship rituals included music and dance to the sound of her sacred instrument, the sistrum, a type of musical rattle. Everyone danced in honor of Hathor, even the king. On New Year's Day Hathor's cult statue was taken to the roof of her temple to be touched with the sun's rays, symbolically uniting her with her father Ra. Later during the same month Hathor was happily honored by a Festival of Drunkenness.

Hathor's many associations and representations are typical of the major goddesses of ancient Mediterranean religious cultures, but in this respect she is surpassed by Isis. As we have seen, Isis is the sister and consort of Osiris, but she gained greater importance over time and was ultimately worshipped as Queen of Heaven. Isis is a model of the love of a devoted wife, widow, and mother, reflecting the roles relevant to virtually all Egyptian women at different stages in their lives. Isis loved Osiris from their conception, and the two embraced while still in Tefnut's womb. After Osiris's death Isis devoted herself to finding the scattered pieces of his body and using her magic and erotic love to return Osiris to life sufficiently to conceive Horus as his heir. Isis's tears of mourning for Osiris cause the flooding of the Nile, insuring the fertility of Egypt and the continuation of the agricultural cycle. In her marriage to Osiris, Isis is essentially identified with the land of Egypt and Osiris with its bountiful harvests of grain. It is Osiris's death and revival that guarantees food and continued life for all of Egypt.

Isis is also a protector of the king, the earthly manifestation of her beloved son Horus. As a result, Isis is sometimes identified with Hathor. Isis too is often depicted crowned with a cow's long horns and the solar disk. Like Hathor, Isis was worshipped with the sistrum in worship rituals with music and dance. Isis is also a goddess of love. But unlike Hathor, Isis is associated exclusively with the domesticated erotic love of the wife and mother, and always in relation to Osiris and Horus. But she is also a trickster figure, a goddess whose cleverness takes the form of cunning, as she develops schemes to gain what she wants from others.

We will discuss Isis at greater length later in terms of the major role she plays in the myth of kingship as wife and sister of Osiris and in the *Contendings of Horus and Seth* as the mother and protector of Horus. But even this summary indicates the diversity of her roles and the hold she seems to have had on the Egyptian religious imagination.

Egyptian Solar Deities

The duplication and overlapping of functions among deities is particularly evident among the various Egyptian solar gods. Because the sun was a primary reality of life in Egypt, and understood as the source of life and fertility, sun gods were most often also identified as chief gods. Several different Egyptian gods were identified with the sun, and sometimes the same god was also credited with initiating the work of creation. Sun gods in particular seem to have risen and fallen in importance as a result of historical factors, not least among these the influence of the priests of their cult and the favor of different pharaohs. But among the sun gods, Ra remained paramount, although he was often identified with other sun gods.

Although we might think of a variety of sun gods as inconsistent, or an indication of successive conceptions of the same god, the Egyptians apparently had no trouble in conceiving of these gods as simultaneously representing the divine reality of the sun in all its different aspects, each important in its turn and in its own way. Different aspects of the sun were identified with different solar gods, some of whom, like Ra, were also important for aspects of their divinity not directly related to the sun.

The god Kheprer was identified with the sun at its rising. Kheprer was represented by the scarab or sacred dung beetle, or sometimes as a human being with a scarab for a head. The female scarabaeus beetle rolls a ball of dung backwards; in a theological modification of this act, Kheprer was believed to roll the ball of the sun before him across the sky. Atum, important primarily as the creator god in the Heliopolis cosmogony, was identified with the sun at its setting, and so was sometimes depicted as an old man, as Ra also might be.

Ra was the dominant solar deity, especially during the early dynasties of the Old Kingdom. Ra's name appears in compound forms with those of other sun gods, indicating the other gods denote different aspects of Ra as the sun and sun god. In the earliest Egyptian image of the sun's journey, Ra traveled across the sky each day in his royal barge accompanied by other gods and entered the Underworld each night to travel under the earth so he might return to his rising place in the east. Both the daily voyage and the nightly return underground were fraught with peril. Sometimes the sun's passage across the sky was thought of as a parallel to the passage of a human life, with Hathor or Nut the sky goddess giving birth to Ra each morning. As a result, in some cases the dawning sun is portrayed as an infant, while in some stories about Ra he is portrayed as an old man who dribbles at the mouth as he dozes.

Ra is not only a particular aspect of the sun but also its divine essence. Ra is the incomprehensible cosmic reality and the true source of light the Egyptians believed existed behind the merely physical aspect of the sun. The divine creative power associated with the sun as well as its elemental role at the source of life led to Ra's identification as a creator god. Ra, like Ptah, was associated with the Ta-tenen, the mound of creation on which the creator god stood to do the work of creation in the midst of Nun, the sea of undifferentiated matter. Ra was also manifested as Atum, the god who initiated the creative process.

From Dynasty 4 the king of Egypt was called "the son of Ra" as a sign of the special relationship between the king and the sun. Later, during the New Kingdom, the queen served as priestess of the sun, and Ra was believed to father her children through the agency of the king. One of Ra's names, Ra-Horakhty, "Ra, Horus of the Horizon," indicates Ra's special relationship with the king through the dynamic union of Ra with Horus, the god of kingship. Such composite names do not imply the gods are identical, nor are they names for new gods. These sorts of names are better thought of as titles expressing a god's divine nature. In the case of Ra-Horakhty, the name indicates the essential unity of the sun's different divine powers.

Amun, a primeval deity, was originally one of the Ogdoad, the four pairs of gods and goddesses responsible for creation in some traditions. Amun later gained supremacy and became the object of widespread and often nearly exclusive worship. Amun was very early on a god of Thebes together with Montu, the Egyptian god of war. As Thebes became more politically prominent at the end of the First Intermediate Period Amun became more prominent among the gods. Before 2000 BCE he was already given the name Amun-Ra, a name representing the two aspects of the god. The name Amun, meaning "hiddenness," indicated the unknowable essence of the god whose power and authority lay beyond human understanding. The name Ra indicated the revealed aspect of the god, shining over the Two Lands in the brilliant radiance of the sun. After Dynasty 18 was established under Ahmose following the expulsion of the Hyksos at the beginning of the New Kingdom, worship of Amun-Ra became an expression of Egyptian national identity and power. Two new major shrines were built for the god, one at Luxor and one at Karnak. During the New Kingdom, Amun-Ra was designated "king of the gods" and the other gods were often presented as personified facets of his divine being. At times the worship of Amun-Ra appears to have come close to monotheism—exclusive worship of a single god as the only god who truly exists—in practice if not in theory.

It was in part the power of the priests of Amun that led to the attempt to replace devotion to Amun with the worship of Aten, the solar disk. Devotion to Aten began during Dynasty 18 early in the New Kingdom, reaching its height during the reign of Amenhotep IV (1352–1336 BCE), who later took the name Akhenaten. As we've seen, Akhenaten's reign signaled a break with tradition in many ways—particularly in Egyptian art and the establishment of a new royal capital—but in no way more so than in his promotion of the worship of Aten.

Contrary to earlier practice in Egypt, Aten was not identified with any of the other sun gods, and the worship due to the highest god was given to him alone. The worship of Amun in particular was suppressed and his name removed from temples and monuments. Whether worship of Aten was meant to be truly monotheistic is an open question. It is clear that Akhenaten intended Aten to be worshipped in place of Amun. His religious innovations were not only an attack against the priests of Amun but a powerful reassertion of the pharaoh's primacy as the mediator between the divine world and the human world.

Aten was not represented in anthropomorphic form but as the sun disk, its light descending as rays ending in human hands held in a gesture of blessing and welcome. But whatever divine benefits bestowed in such depictions

Akhenaten (1353–1336 BCE) and his family receiving blessings at the hands of Aten.
© 2008 Jupiterimages Corporation

fall exclusively on Akhenaten, his wife Nefertiti, and their children. The elevation of Aten (and so also of his beloved, Akhenaten) stands in clear contrast to the rich polytheistic tradition and mythology that is otherwise typical of Egyptian religion. That tradition probably continued at some official level even during Akhenaten's reign, and it is almost certain that popular Egyptian religious practice and piety continued as it always had. Soon after Akhenaten's death Amun was again the preeminent god and the worship of the other gods had been restored. Akhenaten's capital Akhetaten was abandoned, and the monuments to Akhenaten and to Aten were defaced. The worship of Aten did not long survive the death of his most dedicated devotee.

The fortunes of the gods rose and fell not only with the fortunes of their royal or priestly followers, but also with the waxing or waning of the daily importance of the realm of human concern over which they presided. Thoth, for example, experienced a growth in importance parallel to the growth of the scribal bureaucracy. The gods of the Underworld became more important to a wider range of worshippers when entrance into the realm of the blessed dead was no longer believed to be restricted to the king and his family, but at least theoretically possible for all those who served and pleased the gods. The gods who concerned themselves with protecting worshippers from harm or healing their injuries and illnesses were invoked by people in all levels of Egyptian society. But even though the gods themselves might change and develop over time, even though certain gods might gain more worshippers while other gods lost them, the religious concepts associated with the gods, their powers, and their world remained essentially the same. Whatever their specific powers or roles, they were the benefactors responsible for all blessings and the well-being of the cosmos in all its variety through the imposition of *maat*, divine order.

The Nature of Creation Stories

Many of the fundamental Egyptian ideas about the cosmos, the gods, and humanity are expressed in the Egyptian stories of creation. Creation stories are a form of cosmogony, accounts of the origins of the universe or cosmos. Cosmogonies can represent different forms of discourse, explaining things in distinctive sets of terms. For example, some cosmogonies are scientific, explaining how things began based on a series of what we identify as "natural" causes, without any reference to further causality. Similarly, some cosmogonies are "mythic," explaining how things began based on what we would call "supernatural" causes, motivated by the conscious will of some divine agent.

Creation stories are mythic accounts of the origins of all things, since the word "creation" itself implies some sort of conscious intelligence at work to bring the universe into being. Creation stories generally understand this creative intelligence as a god or gods. Creation stories are set in a distinct "beginning" time, when things were different than they are now. In fact one of the primary functions of creation stories is to explain how things came to be the way they are now, the origins of the conditions under which human beings must now live. In polytheistic religious systems, creation stories are usually about the origins of the gods as well. The earliest gods are identified with elements of the cosmos, so the creation of the element is also the birth of the god. Later other gods come into being, most often as a result of sexual intercourse between the earlier elemental gods and goddesses.

We should note that the order of the gods' creation doesn't necessarily reflect the importance of the gods involved. In many religious cultures the earliest elemental gods are of little importance, and the gods who appear later, often the gods of the political realm, are dominant. This is because, for the most part, the initiative for creation in these stories arises more or less spontaneously out of undifferentiated primordial matter, without conscious intention or direction. But in some cases the creator god is a conscious agent who stands over against the undifferentiated primordial matter that prevails before creation begins. In most Egyptian creation stories the creator god is "self-generated," eternally present.

There are four means of creation in classical mythic cosmogonies, although there is usually more than one means of creation in any given story. There is (1) *creation by making*, when a god brings order to undifferentiated primordial matter and so makes the elements of the cosmos. The primordial matter before creation is often depicted as water or a sea, the fathomless depths of waters that people in the ancient Near East believed surrounded the created realm of earth and heavens. The god brings structure and order to primal matter through exertion of divine will and power. There is (2) *creation through conflict* between the creator god and some personified principle opposed to creation, most often some sort of sea monster the god must subdue and kill. The creator god then uses the body of his defeated opponent as primal matter to create the divinely ordered cosmos. The combat is essentially a prelude to creation by making. There is (3) *creation through sexual generation*, when a god and goddess engage in sexual intercourse and the goddess subsequently gives birth to the elemental gods. This idea of creation seems to be an inevitable result of conceiving of the divine world in terms of multiple gods and goddesses in something like human form. The final method is (4) *creation by word*, based on the idea of the spoken word as a means of identifying, and thereby controlling, the essence of all that exists. Stories of creation by word require only a creator god who gives voice to ideas in his mind, bringing them into existence by breathing "spirit" into them. Since "breath," "wind," and "spirit" may be conveyed by the same word in many ancient Mediterranean languages, when the god breathes out a word, divine spirit fills what is spoken, making it substantial reality.

These four means of creation appear to be common to all ancient Mediterranean religious cultures and reflect different attitudes toward the gods' creative work. Creation by sexual generation does not necessarily require any overt intention to create on the gods' part. By contrast, stories about creation by making, creation through conflict, and creation by word all reveal a conscious intention to create on the part of the creator god. They only disagree about the means and the substance of creation.

Egyptian Stories of Creation

Egyptian creation mythology is distinctive in portraying creation as the deliberate work of a god (or gods) with the intention to create, rather than a spontaneous action of matter. There are several cosmogonies that credit a "self-created" or "self-generated" god with initiating creation with the specific desire to create. The three godly powers necessary for the work of creation are *Hu*, divine utterance, *Heka*, magic or divine energy, and *Sia*, divine knowledge. The god's employment of all three in concert allows the cosmos to come into being and to continue in existence. The different Egyptian creation stories appear to represent variations on several basic ideas and what is essentially a single narrative plot line.

Several different methods of creation are involved in the Heliopolis creation story, probably the best known of the early Egyptian creation stories. Heliopolis ("sun city") is the Greek name for the Egyptian Iwnw (the biblical On), located in the southern delta near modern Cairo. Heliopolis was the primary cultic site for the worship of the sun god Atum as creator from the time of the Old Kingdom; Ra was also worshipped as creator there.

According to the Heliopolis creation story, Nun, the dark waters of the limitless depths, already existed before creation as a principle of inert nonexistence ("nothingness"). In the midst of Nun, Atum stood on the Benben, a primeval hillock shaped like a square-based pyramid. The Benben is identified with Ta-tenen, "the land which has become distinguishable." Atum himself is described in the story as "self-generated," meaning his existence is dependent on nothing other than itself. Atum, whose name means "the All" or "the complete one" is the creative force who contains within himself the life-essence of every other deity. Atum in some way releases the divine life-essence within himself, although how this is accomplished varies in the different sources. In the Pyramid Texts from the Old Kingdom, the process is described by a play on words, where it is said Atum "sputtered out Shu ['Emptiness'] and spat out Tefnut ['Moisture']." In the theology of Memphis, Atum released the divine life-essence through masturbation, when he employs his semen to bring order to the undifferentiated mass of Nun. This version of creation forms a complement to the story of Ptah, who spat out creation through speech, as we will see below.

The two elemental gods created in this way are Shu and Tefnut, who together are seen as the necessary elements for all further creation, the first sexually differentiated gods and the first divine couple. Tefnut represented the moist air of the heavens and the atmosphere of the Underworld, and Shu was the god of life manifested in the breath of life. Tefnut is depicted as a woman with the head of a lioness, crowned with the solar disk and *uraeus*, the sacred cobra that symbolizes supreme power. Tefnut becomes the first mother when brother and sister have sexual intercourse, and she gives birth to two children, Geb, the god of the earth, and Nut, the goddess of the sky. Her children form another couple who have sexual intercourse in turn. After Nut gives birth to two gods and two goddesses, Shu lifts Nut off Geb at Atum's command and holds her aloft as the space between the sky and the earth. As a result, Geb weeps tears that create the oceans, and Nut is often portrayed stretching over the reclining body of Geb and held up by Shu, her arched body supported by her feet and hands.

The children of Geb and Nut—Osiris, Isis, Seth, and Nephthys—are the gods of the political order. They form a link between primeval creation and the world of human beings. That world and the divine world will both at some point pass away. Then creation will cease to be, the gods will die and all things will return to undifferentiated matter. Osiris and Atum alone will survive in Nun, the primeval sea, retaining within them the potential for a new creation.

We find another presentation of the divine work of creation in "spell" 1130 from the Coffin Texts. The speaker is "Him whose-names are hidden," the "All-Lord," who may be either Ra or Atum. The god recounts his "four good deeds" in creation: He created the four winds to provide the breath of life, he made "the great inundation" of the uncontrollable sea, he made one person like another, and he set the hearts of human beings on the west, the dwelling place of the gods, so that they might honor them. Here again the creator contains within himself the essence of both gods and human beings: "I created the gods from my sweat, and the people from the tears of my eye"

(Lichtheim, 1:131–132). This last reference is based on a play on the Egyptian words for "tears" (*rmyt*) and "people" (*rmt*) and is notable for including the origins of human beings in the work of divine creation.

The creation story of Hermopolis (*Hmnw*), the city of Thoth in Middle Egypt, comes from Dynasty 12 during the Middle Kingdom. In the Hermopolis story, the agents of creation are the Ogdoad, a group of eight primeval gods divided into four pairs of gods and goddesses. The Ogdoad appear to have existed initially within the primordial sea, and sometimes are presented as four frogs (gods) and four snakes (goddesses). The four divine couples were essentially male and female aspects of principles that are in part embodied in chaos. The couple Amun and Amaunet, for example, represent the principle of hiddenness or concealed power. Huh and Hauhet represent formlessness, the force of the flood. Kuk and Kauket represent darkness. Nun and Naunet represent the limitless depths of waters, the sea within the unfathomable abyss. The gods and goddesses are here more important as couples than they are as separate male and female gods, since the emphasis in the story is on their capacity for sexual generation.

From these four couples comes an egg containing the god who is responsible for the creation of all other gods, elements, human beings, and creatures. Originally this god was probably Thoth, the patron god of Hermopolis, but in surviving versions he is Atum. Atum here becomes a part of the process of creation rather than its instigator, although he does initiate the further acts of creation. In some versions of the story, it is Thoth who stands on the Benben mound and initially creates the Ogdoad, again incorporating elements found in the Heliopolis myth of Atum, but making Thoth the self-generated initiator of the creative process.

An interesting variation on Egyptian creation stories comes from Thebes in Upper Egypt, capital of Dynasty 12, focusing on the god Khnum. Khnum is portrayed as a ram or a ram-headed man, and is a divine craftsman, a builder of ferryboats and ladders. In the Theban story, Khnum is responsible not for the creation of the cosmos, but specifically for the creation of human beings, a topic most other Egyptian stories ignore. Khnum creates human beings on a potter's wheel, creating not only their outer form but also the intricate internal systems that make human life possible, and provides for their health and well-being. As a god of the cataract Khnum was also believed to control the flooding of the Nile, another benefit for humanity. This creation story represents an unusual interest in human beings and their welfare, but it is significantly an account not of the origins of all things, but only of a divine craftsman's fabrication of human beings as part of a larger creation. In some stories from Thebes Khnum is also responsible for the individual creation of the king under the direction of Amun.

Amun became the dominant god of Egypt during the five hundred years of the New Kingdom, and among his other attributes he was designated the transcendent creator. As with Atum in the Helopolis creation story, Amun ("Hiddenness" or "the one who conceals himself,)" was believed to be the divine essence present in all the gods, making all the gods essentially projections or manifestations of Amun. Amun is "self-generated" as Atum is also said to be, and he is active in creation as the initiator of the first act, as the impulse of creative energy prompting the Ogdoad into action. This story again indicates the conservative nature of Egyptian religion. Amun can be incorporated into creation only by finding him a place in an existing creation narrative.

Finally we have an example of creation by word in the Memphis creation story involving the god Ptah, who "speaks" all things into being. Ptah was worshipped from the Archaic Period, but his distinctive character as the patron of artisans, craftsmen, and builders only became evident later. Ptah was the chief god of Memphis in Lower Egypt, and came to a prominence second only to Amun and Ra during Dynasty 4, when Memphis became the royal capital. Ptah was usually depicted as a mummified human figure holding a composite scepter that combined the symbols of life, stability, and omnipotence. In the Memphis creation story, Ptah creates by speaking a word, giving breath and spirit to a divine thought. He "breathes" or "spits out" what he has conceived in his mind by *Sia*, divine knowledge, into actual being through *Hu*, divine utterance, activated by *Heka*, divine energy. Ptah's act of creation was an act of both the heart, the seat of the intellect and understanding, and the tongue, the organ of speech and communication that gives spirit and independent life to thought. Ptah's mouth, lips, and teeth are identified in one version of the myth with the Ennead, the nine chief gods who also appear in Heliopolis cosmogony: Atum, Shu, Tefnut, Geb, Nut, Osiris, Isis, Seth, and Nephthys.

In the Memphis creation story, Ptah creates Atum and the other gods by speaking their names, that is, by giving "spirit" to each god's divine essence as contained in his or her secret name. Ptah is responsible for the creation of each god and goddess and each god's or goddess's *ka*, the "soul" that is their creative intellectual capacity. To the extent the gods and other beings exhibit creative intelligence, their *ka*, Ptah resides within them. This process of speaking and "breathing" the other gods places Ptah at the very beginning of the creative process. As a result he is sometimes identified with Ta-tenen, the mound of creation where Atum stood to begin his creative work. Again we may see how each chief creator god becomes an agent of creation only when a place may be found for him in the dominant creation narrative.

Despite the different versions of the Egyptian creation story, the dominant outline of the master creation narrative that appears to lie behind most of them is fairly clear. Before creation, there is only a primordial sea, the dark waters of the abyss. Out of the depths of the waters arises a hill of earth, and from this pyramid-shaped hill the process of creation is initiated by an act of a god or a group of gods. The process of creation moves from the creation of elemental gods Shu and Tefnut to their sexual generation of Geb and Nut, and the further generation of the gods of the political realm, Osiris, Isis, Seth, and Nephthys. These four divine couples, together with a creator god such as Atum or Amun, form the Ennead, the nine principal gods of Egypt, although in some cases, the ninth god is Horus, son of Osiris and Isis.

The creation of the cosmos is separated by three generations from the gods who have the most immediate sovereignty over human beings, although in later versions the creator god is also the chief god who continues to govern the entire cosmos. Within this drama of creation human beings play little or no part. They appear to be of interest only as a small subset of creation, and then primarily because of the intricacies of their workings, the result of careful work by the divine craftsman Khnum. But even as only a small part of the divine creation, human beings, like all other things that dwell on the earth or in the heavens, still enjoy the benefits the gods have bestowed on creation. Like the Two Lands under the benevolent rule of the king, creation flourishes under the rule of the ageless gods, whose imposition of *maat* ensures the well-being of the cosmos and all its creatures.

CHAPTER THREE

Egypt: The King and Royal Power

The King and His Relationship to the Gods

As our surveys of the Egyptian pantheon and the different myths of creation indicate, the divine realm in Egyptian religious culture is sufficient to itself, quite apart from human beings. Although human beings are subject to the gods and benefit from the divine order imposed on creation, the gods are not necessarily directly interested or involved in the lives of human beings. Although there are parallels between the divine and human worlds, human beings do not appear to be privileged over other creatures in the divine economy.

The chief beneficiary of divine blessings is the king, and he is himself understood to be in some sense a divine figure who serves as an intermediary in passing the blessings conferred by the gods to the rest of humanity. The king is at the head of the human hierarchy, standing in relation to other human beings much as the chief god—whether Amun-Ra, Horus, or some other—stands in relation to the other gods. The king is the source of his subjects' essential being and guarantor of their welfare not as individuals, but as a people. Although they live and function as individuals through the gift of the gods, it is in and through the king that they come into being as the people of Egypt, the beneficiaries of the gods' blessings.

The reality of Egyptian kingship was somewhat more complicated. The basis of the king's royal authority was ultimately military power, and it was military power that made Egypt. It was the strength of the king's armies, and his effectiveness as their commanding general, that held Upper and Lower

Egypt together and defended them against both internal and external enemies. As we have seen, there were many forces threatening the unity of the
kingdom, not least the ambitions and intrigues of some of the king's own un-
derlings and vassals. The eras of Egyptian history are defined by the successive unification and fragmentation of the kingdom. Military forays into Nubia and Syria–Palestine were for defense as well as for conquest. The kings of
Egypt built forts and installed garrisons at strategic points in or near those
territories to maintain Egyptian control of its borders. The king's first responsibility was to hold his kingdom together and ensure its security. The dif-
ficulty of the task led the Egyptians to ascribe divine power to the man who
was capable of accomplishing it.

In addition to their military responsibilities, kings of the Old Kingdom established and oversaw an extensive royal administration to help them govern their domain. There were often two chief ministers to supervise the economic activity of the kingdom. Administration required hundreds of scribes
to serve the royal bureaucracy. Some maintained records of tax revenues,
capital outlays, and other business of the royal treasury. Others were concerned with keeping track of the legions of workers needed to serve the royal
household, ensuring that the royals were clothed, housed, and fed. The
palace complex was the center of royal administration. It is significant that
the most familiar title for the king of Egypt, "pharaoh"—a title used no earlier than the Middle Kingdom and perhaps not before the New Kingdom—
is derived from "great house," making his association with the palace complex a primary means of identifying the king.

Others assisted, in ways large and small, the king's control of the nation's
government. Local nobility ruled their territories under the authority of the
king and his ministers, and had their own local administrations. Temples and
their priests were at least nominally under the king's control, and formed
their own part of the royal administration. Virtually all of the elite of Egyptian society served the king either directly or indirectly. Under the power of
the elite, the vast majority of Egyptians were subsistence farmers and craftsmen who served the king in their own way, but otherwise lived lives similar
to those of their Neolithic ancestors.

The king was a primary focus of religious concern from at least the time of
the first unification of Upper and Lower Egypt. This is hardly surprising,
since the power to unite the disparate parts of the nation militarily and politically was, in the Egyptian mind, clearly a divine power. Since the beginning of political leadership, leaders have claimed a special relationship with
the patron gods of the state, both to legitimate their own power and to cast
their enemies as the enemies of the gods as well. The king becomes the gods'

champion, fighting on their behalf against earthly opponents to their rule. He is their viceroy, acting in their stead on earth to rule over the people. But in Egypt we find more absolute sorts of claims being made for the king. He not only is endowed with divine power to rule, but is a god himself.

The kings of the First and Second Dynasty (3000–2670 BCE) during the Archaic Period were already identified as incarnations of Horus, the god who represented the forces of life and order. Each successive king *was* Horus, making his acts essentially the acts of the god. The kings of the Old Kingdom (2686–2125 BCE) were each called "Son of Ra," a title that was understood in a literal sense. Ra was believed to impregnate a woman (usually the wife of the king) in the guise of her husband, so that her son was a god in a human body. As we have seen, Ra represents the rising sun, source of life for the cosmos, but is also the heavenly parallel to the king as master of the earth, the king as Horus. Ra was sometimes also depicted as the divine creator who brings order to undifferentiated primordial matter, just as the king establishes sovereign rule over the earth and makes human existence possible. Over time the king's status was reduced to that of a human being in whom the god dwelt and who did the god's will on earth.

The divine honors accorded the king reflect his central importance not only to Egypt, but to the entire cosmic order. The primary role of the king was to establish *maat*—divine order—on earth. *Maat* was the basis for all divine activity. It was the harmony and equilibrium necessary for the proper functioning of the entire cosmos, including both the divine and the human worlds. The concept of *maat* also implies decorum and justice as the motivating force in the king's actions, as the king imitates the divine rule of Horus or Ra.

The king alone as the agent of the gods was responsible for maintaining order, which was understood both as opposition to the forces of disorder and as reconciliation of opposing forces under a divine dispensation. It was the king's role to stave off any incursions of the unexpected into his realm, to repulse any alien power that threatened the harmony of the land, and to oppose and defeat the forces of disorder and evil that constantly threatened to break out and destroy the order the king had imposed. At the same time, the king was to oversee the cycle of the Nile's ebb and flood and generally to ensure that the rhythms of nature necessary for the well-being of the land, its animals, and its people were maintained through his divine power.

The king's divinely given power is exerted not only for the good of humanity, but also for the good of the gods, whose actions, power, and very existence depend on *maat*. Like the gods themselves, each of Egypt's kings was understood to exist in both *neheh* and *djet*, in both the perpetual cycle of divine action and initiative human beings experience as history and the transcendent changelessness of eternity. On the one hand the king was an historical entity who lived, ruled, and died and whose deeds were distinctive to his time and recorded in his tomb and monuments. But on the other hand he was the one divine and eternal King of Upper and Lower Egypt. Each king in turn was identified with Horus on his accession to the throne, ruling the Two Lands just as Horus rules the cosmos. For this reason, the deeds of one king could legitimately be claimed by another, since all royal deeds were the doing of the one divine king. Each king manifested the works of the eternal King of Upper and Lower Egypt through the royal actions he initiated at the gods' command and, in that sense at least, was always regarded as divine.

The king's divine status was confirmed by the various forms of ritual worship devoted to him. The rituals marking the king's coronation recognized that he was the one true divine king, manifesting the royal *ka* inherent in his being. The *ka* is a difficult concept to grasp. Both gods and human beings have *kas*. It is related to a person's conception in the womb, and has to do with the individual identity of a person, his or her character, and the way character determines the shape of a person's life. In the case of the king, the royal *ka* is the presence of the divine within him, the divine character or nature that makes him a god in human form even before his birth. The king's possession of the royal *ka* was acknowledged in an annual ritual at the temple of Amun-Ra at Karnak. Another festival, the *sed*-festival, was observed after about thirty years of the king's rule. The *sed*-festival both celebrated and confirmed the king's divine status. Through the rituals of the festival the king died and was reborn, rejuvenating the king and reinvigorating his power to rule. The initial *sed*-festival would take place after thirty years' reign, but then might be celebrated every three years or so. Rameses II (1279–1213 BCE) would have celebrated the *sed*-festival thirteen times during his sixty-six years of rule over Egypt.

Despite their divine status, during their lifetime the kings of Egypt were worshippers and suppliants of the gods, but after death the king became the object of worship. Kings built funerary temples for themselves, where statues representing the king would serve the same function as a god's cultic statue, as a dwelling place for the royal *ka* after the king's death. The king's death marked the transition from his embodiment of the sort of kingship identified with Horus to his embodiment of the sort of kingship identified with Horus's father Osiris. In addition to the royal tomb, the dead king was honored with a funerary temple where he continued to be worshipped and to receive offerings of food and drink. During the Old and Middle Kingdom the royal tomb complex itself might include a funerary temple. During the New Kingdom,

Partially reconstructed mortuary temple of Hatshepsut (1479–1458 BCE) in Deir el-Bahri. © 2008 Jupiterimages Corporation

when the deceased monarch was buried in the Valley of the Kings, funerary temples were separate from the royal tomb.

The Myth of Kingship: The Death of Osiris

The Egyptian myth of kingship was a means of justifying and legitimizing royal succession in Egypt through a complex tale of sibling rivalry, murder, intrigue, and revenge. The story was both an explanation of "how things got to be the way they are now"—and to that extent a creation story—and the basis and justification for royal succession by the firstborn son. This story appears in or is alluded to in a variety of sources, including the Pyramid Texts of the Old Kingdom, coffin inscriptions in the Middle Kingdom, a Dynasty 18 "Hymn to Osiris," and the New Kingdom story, "The Contendings of Horus and Seth." Plutarch, a Greek philosopher, biographer, and essayist of the late first and early second century CE, includes a Hellenized version of the story in his "Concerning Isis and Osiris." The myth of kingship essentially falls into two parts. The first deals with the death of Osiris at the hands of his brother Seth, and the second with the contest between Horus and Seth to determine who would rule the cosmos as Osiris's successor.

The story begins with Osiris, firstborn son of Geb and Nut, ruling the Two Lands with his sister and consort Isis. Osiris presides over a golden age of peace and prosperity and receives the acclaim of all the gods. But Osiris's younger brother Seth grows jealous and kills Osiris, although the details of the murder are obscure. It appears that after the murder Seth dismembered Osiris's body and scattered the pieces across Egypt. This particular detail of the story may have been intended in part to justify the many places in Egypt that claimed to be the resting place of Osiris. In Plutarch's version of the story, Seth dismembers the dead Osiris only after Isis's initial discovery of his body, and it is Isis's inability to reassemble it after its dismemberment that leads to Osiris's descent into the Underworld.

It should be noted some Egyptian sources decline to depict the death of Osiris since regicide was abhorrent to the ideal of Egyptian kingship. Assassination and usurpation were of course part of the reality of Egyptian kingship over the centuries, but the possibility of regicide made it all the more offensive to the ideal of kingship. In some versions of the story representatives of Seth or other enemies of Osiris are killed instead of him, thereby reinforcing Osiris's power as king. Yet even these versions include Isis's search for the dead body of Osiris, indicating that the death of the god was originally a part of the story that was later obscured.

After the murder Seth assumes the throne as king of the Two Lands with his sister and consort Nephthys. But their sister Isis goes into deep mourning for her lost husband. In her grief Isis weeps day and night until Nephthys finally agrees to help her find Osiris. The sister goddesses search throughout the Two Lands and one by one gather the scattered pieces of Osiris's body. Finally they are able to reassemble it at Abydos, site of the god's primary shrine.

As we will see in detail later, Isis tricks Ra into revealing his secret name, a source of great magical power. Once Osiris's body has been reassembled, through the magic of the secret name of Ra and the power of her erotic love, Isis is able to revive her husband sufficiently to impregnate her and conceive their son Horus. In a depiction of this scene in the tomb of Sety I at Abydos, Osiris has a fully erect phallus and Isis in the form of a sparrow hawk rests on it to receive his sperm. After engendering the son who would avenge his death Osiris departs his earthly domain and enters the Underworld, the domain he will from then on rule over as king. In another version of the story Isis is unable to find Osiris's phallus, which has been eaten by a fish. Without the male vitality necessary for rule over the cosmos of gods and human beings, Osiris descends to the Underworld to rule as monarch over the dead.

This part of the story has some fairly clear symbolic significance. Osiris is a god associated with the power of fertility. The scattering of the pieces of Osiris's body reflects the scattering of seed that leads to a bountiful harvest. In more general terms, the death and new life of Osiris reflects the fertility cycle. It is necessary for the grain to "die" and be scattered before it can return to life as new crops. The new life the grain represents is made possible by the annual flooding of the Nile, sometimes said to be caused by Isis's tears of grief over the death of Osiris. In this way Osiris's death provokes Isis's grief and ensures that Osiris's new life will follow.

The Myth of Kingship: The Contest between Horus and Seth

The second part of the myth of kingship shifts attention to the struggle between Seth and Osiris's son Horus for royal authority over the Two Lands. It is worth noting the difference in the roles played by Osiris and Horus. Osiris plays an entirely passive role in the story. Although as king he presides over a golden age, the only thing he does as king in the story is die. He then is entirely at the disposal of others to be scattered, gathered, revived, and ultimately to descend to the Underworld. He is important only as the father and source of Horus. Horus is active, not only in asserting his right to the throne, but in his struggles and his plots against his uncle Seth.

Seth was the god of disorder and violence. He was represented by a composite animal with a long curved snout, long ears or horns standing up from his head, and in some depictions, a tail with forked tip. Seth is apparently an older god than Osiris, since his iconic creature appears on the mace head of King Scorpion of Dynasty 0 (c. 3000 BCE). Seth was originally associated with Upper Egypt, although his iconic creature is often portrayed wearing the double crown of the Upper and Lower Egypt. The earliest known instance of the name Osiris, by contrast, occurs during Dynasty 5 (c. 2494–2345 BCE), and is associated with an image lacking Osiris's later characteristic attributes.

It is important to emphasize that Seth, despite his violent character, is part of the cosmic order of creation like his siblings and has a proper place within it. He is a counterpart to Horus as representative of the principle of order; Seth is a principle of disorder (*isfet*) and the unexpected in what is otherwise a generally dependable creation. To the extent that disorder is contrary to the will of Horus and threatens well-being, *isfet* can even mean "evil." But Seth is not an evil god nor does he represent the primordial disorder that threatens the divine creation. In fact Seth later serves as Ra's protector against Apophis, a snake-like monster that represents that threatening power of primordial disorder. Horus and Seth in many respects form a duality, not only as divine opponents but also in terms of their identifications and their attributes. Horus of Lower Egypt as a god of order and sound rule struggles with Seth of Upper Egypt as a god of disorder, violence, and the unexpected. But the duality exists within a greater harmony; they are depicted together tying the heraldic plants of Upper and Lower Egypt around the hieroglyph representing unity.

Although the primary characters in this part of the story are Seth and Horus, Horus's mother Isis is almost equally important as she watches out for her son's welfare and intervenes in various ways throughout the contest to assist him. At first she appears as the beleaguered mother of a threatened infant. After Isis gives birth to Horus she must hide the child from Seth in the papyrus marshes. Horus in this part of the story is called Har-pa-khered (Greek: Harpocrates) or "Horus the child," and he is entirely dependent on his mother and her powerful magic to protect him from both natural and divine enemies. Isis's maternal devotion is a major part of her divine identity. It is reflected throughout the myth of kingship but is especially evident while Horus is a child. As a result, the two are often depicted together as divine mother and child, the infant Horus sitting on Isis's lap. This same image is often used to portray the king, the living embodiment of Horus whom Isis protects just as she protected her divine son. Horus's childhood becomes the context for many stories that involve Isis's use of magic spells to cure illnesses or stave off evil.

Once Horus becomes a vigorous youth he is ready to take his rightful place as king. Horus approaches the gods assembled under the authority of Ra and asks for his rights as the legitimate royal successor of his father Osiris. Seth disputes Horus's claim to the throne and seeks it for himself. The central issue in the contest between Horus and Seth is clearly understood to be a legal one, a plea from Horus before a tribunal of the major gods—the Ennead—to recognize his legal rights as Osiris's legitimate heir. The central issue is the royal succession.

Although all the members of the tribunal support Horus's claim, Ra as its head withholds his consent. Ra consistently favors Seth throughout the story, apparently because Ra considers Horus too inexperienced to rule. As a result, the tribunal does not render a judgment and instead refers the matter to the goddess Neith. She was a goddess of hunting and war and the patron goddess of weaving. Neith was also the primeval mother, "creating the seeds of gods and men," and was recognized during the New Kingdom as the mother of Ra. She writes a letter to the tribunal strongly urging the gods to give sovereignty to Horus as his right. But Neith also advises Ra to compensate Seth for his loss of the throne by enriching him and giving him Ra's daughters Anat and Astarte, goddesses with origins in the religious culture of Syria–Palestine.

The tribunal accepts Neith's decision, but again Ra demurs and denounces Horus. The god Bebon berates Ra for favoring Seth and Ra retreats to his pavilion in a sulk. Once again the proceedings come to a halt. Finally Ra's daughter Hathor visits him and moves Ra to laughter by lifting up her skirts and exposing herself. Ra then returns to the divine tribunal and allows the case to continue.

Seth and Horus formally make their respective cases for sovereignty over the Two Lands. Seth bases his case on his virility and his great strength. Horus reiterates his legitimate claim as the son of Osiris, while Isis demands recognition of Horus's rights. Seth refuses to continue with Isis present. Ra agrees and moves the tribunal's proceedings to "the Island in the Middle" where Isis will not be allowed to gain access. Isis, however, disguises herself as an old woman and bribes a ferryman to carry her across the river to the island where the tribunal is in session. Once there, she uses her magic to again disguise herself, this time as a beautiful young woman who excites Seth's lust. In this form Isis approaches Seth as a suppliant. She tells Seth she is a widow whose son's rights and properties have been usurped and asks for his help. Seth is outraged by the injustice she and her son have suffered and by the outrageous behavior of her opponent. At this, Isis changes herself into a kite and tells Seth he has unwittingly condemned himself. Seth complains to Ra about Isis's deception, but Ra offers him no sympathy. He does however move the tribunal's proceedings again, this time to a mountain, and the gods finally agree to award the throne to Horus and crown him king.

The tribunal's decision is rendered moot when Seth challenges Horus to a series of feats of skill, strength, and cunning to decide who will gain the throne. There follows a series of contests between Seth and Horus as the two gods look for ways to outmaneuver and outsmart each other. It soon becomes clear that the idea in each contest is not only for one god to prove himself superior, but also to humiliate and discredit his opponent. Each god tries to shame the other so completely that he will be a totally unacceptable choice for king.

The various contests in this part of the story are strange and even contradictory. Seth, Horus, and Isis are all involved and often at odds with one another, although it is mostly Horus and Isis who work together against Seth. First Seth and Horus turn themselves into hippopotamuses for an endurance contest, to see who can stay submerged for an entire three months. But Isis, believing that Seth will drown Horus, throws a harpoon into the river. The harpoon hits Horus and wounds him, and Isis has to conjure the harpoon's barb out of him. Isis throws her harpoon again and hits Seth, but he cries out to her and she heals his wound as well. This act of kindness toward his opponent infuriates Horus, so he decapitates Isis and carries her head into the desert. The gods agree to take revenge against Horus for this act of violence. Seth finds Horus at an oasis and gouges out Horus's eye. Horus is again magically healed, this time by Hathor. The two eyes of Horus were identified with the sun and the moon. Egyptians would wear a powerful protective amulet representing the Eye of Horus. It took the form of a human eye and was called *wedjat* ("sound one"). It usually depicted the left or "lunar" eye of the god; its wounding and subsequent healing represented the monthly waning and waxing of the moon.

At this point in the story, Ra orders Seth and Horus to make peace. Seth uses the opportunity to invite Horus to a banquet where he attempts to sexually humiliate Horus. But Isis again intervenes; through her magic Seth's trick backfires and Seth is sexually humiliated before the divine tribunal instead. Seth then challenges Horus to a boat race using stone ships. Horus builds a wooden boat and covers it with plaster so it looks like stone. Seth carves a boat out of a mountain top, a boat that promptly sinks. Seth turns into a hippopotamus and scuttles Horus's boat.

The upshot of these contests is a series of victories for Horus and various losses and humiliations for Seth, who uses force and threats when he doesn't get his way in the council of the gods. The problem of the succession is only solved, somewhat surprisingly, through the intervention of Osiris. Prompted by Ra, Thoth writes a letter to Osiris in the Underworld, setting the situation before him. In his reply, Osiris reminds Ra that Osiris is the god responsible for bringing fertility to the earth to provide food for the gods. It is not a good idea to deprive his son Horus of his rightful throne. When Ra is hesitant, Osiris resorts to threats. As god of the Underworld he has powerful demons at his command, and all creatures, gods as well as men, will someday come into his kingdom and be subject to his authority. The gods therefore submit to Osiris's will and award the kingship over the Two Lands to Horus. Seth, now Isis's prisoner, renounces his claim to the throne. Ra compensates Seth for his loss and gives him his daughters Anat and Astarte. He also gives Seth a job worthy of his strength and ability: Seth will stand guard and protect Ra's solar barge from Apophis, the monster of disorder and the unexpected, during Ra's daily voyage across the sky.

If this story seems like a long and difficult journey to an obvious destination, that is part of the point. The proper outcome of the story is never in doubt: Horus is the legitimate son of Osiris and must succeed him as king of the Two Lands. Not only is this the implicit opinion of both the storyteller and his ancient audience, but it is reinforced explicitly throughout the story. The council of gods wants to give the throne to Horus, as does the goddess Neith when she is asked to arbitrate, and even Ra, despite his earlier objections to Horus's youth, finally agrees. When Seth appeals to contests of strength and skill, Horus wins them all. Everything points to the justice and even the inevitability of Horus's victory. Everything that happens in the story to prevent a just outcome to the contest ultimately only confirms it. But what is most important in the story is not Horus's fitness to become king, but his legal and moral right as the firstborn son to inherit his father's throne. Even in all its complications and diversions, the story is a stunning assertion of the right of royal inheritance in the face of assassination, coup, and war.

The story begins in a golden age under Osiris as the rightful king over all creation. After he is murdered, the divine world is in an uproar, and turmoil and conflicts follow. It is only when Horus finally takes the throne as the rightful king and heir that *maat* returns, and with it the order and justice of the golden age. Even the unpredictable power of Seth becomes a part of the daily order of events under the benevolent rule of the legitimate king. The long drama of conflict ends in *maat* that only the true king can provide.

Isis, the Queen of Heaven

The myth of kingship is the basis for many beliefs about Isis and illustrates in part why she is the most important of the Egyptian goddesses. Isis appears in the story in a series of traditional female roles, as lover, wife, widow, and mother. But she fulfills these roles in an entirely nontraditional way by virtue of her powers both as a woman and as a goddess. Isis becomes an ideal ful-fillment of each of the roles she assumes, bringing to each her divine wisdom, her indomitable will, and her fierce loyalty to both the dead Osiris and the living Horus.

Isis is closely associated with the king as his protector. The name Isis means "throne"; the king sits on his throne and enjoys the divine love and protection of Isis just as the infant Horus sits on her lap in depictions of the divine mother and son. In the same way Isis protected Horus against Seth the goddess also protects the king against his enemies throughout his reign, act-ing as his divine patroness and the symbol of his sovereignty. At his death, Isis guides the dead king, now identified with Osiris, through the dangers of the Underworld.

Isis is both wise and clever. She has the gift of discernment that allows her to understand people and situations and possesses knowledge about every-thing in heaven and earth. But she is also cunning. She is able to develop persuasive arguments and successful schemes. It is Isis who argues Horus's case before the assembled gods, and she is persuasive enough as an advocate that Seth demands Isis be banned from the tribunal. It is Isis who tricks Seth into condemning himself. Isis, like both Seth and Horus, appears as a trick-ster figure throughout the story of their contest for the throne, acting on her own initiative and for her own reasons.

Isis's power was expressed not only in cleverness and wisdom, but preem-inently in her power of magic and healing. The goddess was associated with spells that could be used as protection against hostile animals or harmful in-sects. She provided help in all sorts of circumstances to all sorts of people. The belief that Isis was willing to draw upon her divine powers for the prac-tical benefit of her devotees made the goddess as important to the average Egyptian as she was to the king.

According to a myth preserved in a text from Dynasty 19 (c. 1295–1069 BCE), Isis gained the power to heal and cast spells when she learned the se-cret name of Ra. In Egypt as elsewhere in the ancient Near East, the name was believed to be the fullest expression of who a person or a god most truly is, the essence of a person's or a god's deepest hidden being. To know the name was to have a grasp of the most essential nature of a person or a god. Isis devised a plan to make Ra reveal his secret name to her so she could draw on his divine power.

Isis knew there was nothing in the created realm that could harm Ra. So she followed the barge of the sun god on its daily voyage across the sky.

When the sun was high in the sky Ra fell into a doze and began to drool. Isis collected his saliva and mixed it with earth to create a venomous snake. She took the snake and placed it where she knew Ra would pass, and before long the snake bit him. Ra suffered intense burning pain and cried out to the other gods for help. But only Isis had the power to heal the snakebite and relieve his torment. But before she would agree to heal him, Isis demanded to know Ra's secret name. Ra tried various ways to get around her request, but finally he capitulated. Ra knew Isis would share the knowledge of his secret name with Horus, but he exacted a promise from her that she would place Horus under a binding oath not to reveal the name to anyone else. Although our source for this story does not say as much, it is clear Isis agreed. It was the power of Ra's name that allowed Isis to return Osiris's reassembled body to life. Isis's power of magic and spells made her increasingly popular in the later history of Egypt, and contributed to her later status during the Roman era as the patron goddess of a Hellenized mystery religion with devotees throughout the Roman Empire.

The Ideal of the King

The story of the death of Osiris and the contest between Horus and Seth for the kingship is directly relevant to the nature of royal rule in Egypt. Despite Ra's rulings, the legitimacy of Horus's claim to the throne is never in doubt, establishing a firm principle of inherited kingship. Each king of Egypt lived out a life that ideally would mimic the divine model set out in the story of Osiris and Horus, reflecting the eternal nature of the king's divine person and his sovereignty over the people of Egypt. Each king is successively the young and untried Har-pa-khered, then the mature and assured Horus, and finally the venerated Osiris. The deceased king retains his royal identity even as he departs into the Underworld, leaving behind his heir, who assumes the throne and his own royal identity as the new king, the living embodiment of Horus. The king retains in each stage of life both his royal authority and his divinity, while allowing a new king to follow in an historical cycle that does not affect the king's eternal status even as individual kings come and go.

Modern scholars sometimes interpret the contest between Horus and Seth for supremacy as a mythic version of the continuing tension throughout Egypt's history between Lower Egypt, associated with Horus, and Upper Egypt, associated with Seth. On a more fundamental level, however, the story of Horus and Seth may be understood as a mythic account of the more familiar battle between order and disorder, or more specifically, between the virtues of autocratic kingly authority and the threat of social unrest. In the course of the story, Horus is called upon to display all the virtues associated with kingship. He has to be a mighty warrior, an advocate for the cause of right, and a calculating politician. When all else fails, he needs to be a trickster and a deceiver. If Horus is sometimes ruthless in his pursuit of power, ruthlessness is a necessary part of his royal character.

But Horus is also magnanimous in victory, as befits a powerful monarch. Although in some late versions of the story, Seth is destroyed, in most versions he retains a distinctive role within the new order overseen by Horus as king. Seth fulfills a role suited to his skills as a virile warrior, but one that maintains rather than threatens the proper functioning of the cosmos. The king's role in establishing *maat* here finds its fullest symbolic expression. Once he becomes king, Horus finds a fitting place in a well-ordered cosmos for the god whose intemperate actions once threw it into disarray. Horus is master over all created things, even the power of disorder.

The story of Horus's ascension to the throne of the Two Lands provides a model and basis for the power of king. Although the official presentation of the king's power in monuments and other forms of graphic art emphasized the serenity and eternity of his rule, the realities of royal power were dependent on the qualities displayed by Horus. The king's legitimacy depended on primogeniture and the laws of Egypt, understood as the decrees of the gods, although in the long history of Egypt there were frequent cases of usurpation, conquest, and intrigue. But the idea of legitimacy was always maintained. The reigning king was chosen for kingship by the gods, and the royal retainers, administration, priests, and craftsmen all worked to maintain this idea in the minds of his subjects. Of course, the same mechanisms that conferred royal legitimacy could also be used to destroy it; the ideal of the eternal king sometimes required that individual rulers who deviated too sharply from tradition— Akhenaten, for example—had to be purged from historical records in order that the prevailing narrative about the king and the gods might continue without interruption or deviation.

Even during periods of relative peace, a dominant image of the king during the New Kingdom was as a warrior whose power held the Two Lands together as he defended his subjects against their enemies, most notably the foreign nations to the north and south. Royal monuments invariably depicted the king as triumphant over his enemies—whatever the actual outcome might have been—and celebrated his victories in glowing terms. But both the victories and the peace that ensued were understood as divine gifts bestowed on the king as a favored individual and not on the nation at large. The king was the sole direct beneficiary of the gods' gifts to him as ruler. For example, a text survives of a prayer to Amun attributed to Rameses II at the

Tutankhamun between the goddess Sekhmet and Ptah, flanked by Horus as a crowned falcon and Wadjit, goddess of Lower Egypt. © 2008 Jupiterimages Corporation

battle of Qadesh (c. 1275 BCE). In this prayer Rameses chides Amun because the god has not properly requited the king for the many gifts and favors the king has offered him, and more specifically, has not come to Rameses's aid in battle. When the god finally responds and grants Rameses the victory he wanted, this blessing is presented as a divine favor for Rameses, not for his nation. Although the nation benefits from the rule of the divine king and the gifts the gods shower upon him, the gifts are given for the king's sake and not for the sake of the nation.

Two other literary works attributed to kings of the First Intermediate Period and the Middle Kingdom reflect prevailing ideas about the character and characteristics of the ideal Egyptian king. These two works are representative of the wisdom tradition, the systematic compilation of pragmatic advice that is found throughout the ancient Near East. We will deal with the wisdom tradition at greater length later. But these two Egyptian works are worth our consideration now, since they purport to give us the advice of kings to their sons and successors, advice intended to make them successful rulers approved of by their subjects and the gods.

"The Instruction for Merykara" is attributed to Khety III of Dynasty 10 (c. 2160–2025 BCE), one of the regional dynasties that contended for power during the First Intermediate Period. The book is now generally dated to Dynasty 12. The title is appropriate. The book is presented as instruction for Khety's son Merykara, advising him how to conduct himself in personal matters as well as in matters of government. First Merykara must behave in a way that will lead his subjects to admire and respect him. He must be benevolent toward his subjects, and give special attention to providing for those most in need, orphans and widows. He must be just in his rulings, but he should also show mercy when it is appropriate. He should show wisdom in all he says and does. He must be truthful with those who serve him so he will command their respect.

In regard to the gods, the king should build monuments and temples for them and serve faithfully as their priest. "The Instruction for Merykara" reveals a particular concern with the idea of judgment after death and uses it as a motivation for correct behavior in the present life. "As for the (divine) tribunal which judges sinners, you know that they are not indulgent on that day of judging the offender; . . . And existence in the beyond is for eternity . . . but as for him who reaches them having done no wrong, he will exist there like a god, walking proudly like the Lords of eternity" (Simpson, 157–158).

More specifically within the political sphere, the good king must provide for the needs of the nation. This means defending the borders with sufficient troops and fortresses, but also choosing and prizing good officials, promoting the best men without partiality. Khety offers some very specific advice on how to govern Upper and Lower Egypt and how to deal with the perennial threat from the people who live in Syria–Palestine: "He has been fighting ever since the time of Horus. He neither conquers, nor can he be conquered. He does not announce the day of fighting, but is like a thief whom society has expelled" (Simpson, 161).

But Khety saves his most pointed advice for how to deal with a potential traitor. Here ruthlessness is called for. His instruction on how to react if Merykara should find a potential traitor with a cadre of supporters is unequivocal: "Get rid of him, and slay his children, obliterate his name, and destroy his supporters, banish [all] memory of him and of the partisans who respect him" (Simpson, 154). To "obliterate his name," to "banish [all] memory of him and of the partisans who respect him" was the worst kind of punishment. It meant not only death and disgrace for the enemy in the present world, but with the elimination of his name and memory, the loss of any part in the world to come. Those who threaten the legitimate king—and so also the order that prevails in heaven and on earth—must be dealt with in the harshest terms.

"The Testament of Amenemhat," a work from the Middle Kingdom, provides its own model for the good king in words attributed to Amenemhat I

(1985–1956 BCE), founder of Dynasty 12. "The Testament of Amenemhat" is overtly literary, since it is presented as the words of the king to his son Senusret I after Amenemhat had been murdered in a palace coup. It may remind the modern reader of Shakespeare's *Hamlet*, or more specifically with Act 1, Scene 5, of the play, when Hamlet learns the circumstances of his father's death from his ghost. While Senusret was away from the palace, Amenemhat was attacked by armed men while he was sleeping one evening after dinner. His murder prevented him from sharing his thoughts with Senusret while he lived, so now he passes on his advice after death, "risen as a god" (Simpson, 167). Amenemhat tells Senusret the details of his murder, then reviews the many good deeds that distinguished his reign, in the process providing a model for the ideal king.

As king, Amenemhat provided for the poor and served the gods faithfully. He ensured the welfare of the kingdom by promoting talented men without regard to their class or their status at birth. He fearlessly defended the borders of Egypt and conquered and humiliated enemies both to the northeast in Syria–Palestine and to the south in Nubia. But Amenemhat's reign was also distinguished by his oversight and his preparations for the future. During his reign the Nile floods provided abundant grain and prosperity, reflecting the natural harmony enforced by the power of *maat*. He prepared an elaborate tomb for himself, "built for eternity." Finally he provided for Senusret and his succession, ensuring continued peace and good fortune for Egypt.

But the unfortunate circumstances of his death also lead Amenemhat to warn Senusret to be on guard against those around him: "Put no trust in a brother, acknowledge no one as a friend, do not raise up for yourself intimate companions, for nothing is to be gained from them" (Simpson, 168). Despite his ability to choose good ministers and defeat his military enemies, the wise king will put his trust in no one but himself. The greatest threat to the king comes not from his open enemies, but from treacherous friends, since their attacks are unexpected and fall upon the king when he is least prepared.

In both of these works that purport to offer the advice of a king to his son, the thrust of the message is that the king must be just and pious, and must show benevolence both to the gods and to his subjects. He must make the nation secure from its enemies, especially its traditional enemies to the north and south. But ultimately the greatest danger comes from within, and the king must depend on his own abilities to discern who is trustworthy and who is not, and must show ruthlessness in dealing with those who would betray him.

Senusret is the object of lavish praise in *The Tale of Sinuhe*, a story that dates from the end of the Middle Kingdom, but is set at the beginning of Dynasty

12. Sinuhe is a court official who flees Egypt in the aftermath of the palace coup against Amenemhat. Ending up in Syria–Palestine, Sinuhe lists Senusret's virtues in conversation with the ruler of Upper Retenu. "He is a god without peer, no other comes before him; he is lord of knowledge, wise planner, skilled leader, one goes and comes by his will" (Lichtheim, 1:225). But most of Sinuhe's praise focuses on Senusret's prowess in battle, as a warrior whose presence makes the enemy weak and then run away in panic. But he also conquers his own people through his kindness and affection, so all his subjects unite in celebrating his might and the godly power he wields over Egypt.

Similar praises are offered to Senusret (1870–1831 BCE) in a cycle of six songs written in his honor (Simpson, 301–306). His might in battle strikes fear in the hearts of the enemy and brings peace and prosperity to his people. The second song features the recurring phrase, "How jubilant are . . .", listing the beneficiaries of his rule, including the gods whose offerings he has assured (Simpson, 303). The third song includes the refrain, "How great is the Lord for his City!" as a preface for the blessings the king bestows on the land. Here and in the fourth song the benefits the people enjoy at the king's hand are primarily a result of his mighty power in battle, expressed through a series of metaphors depicting domestic peace and well-being.

The impression given by these different literary works—the different versions of the struggle for the kingship, the books offering advice from a royal father to a young king, the praises of particular kings—is that the same traits that are useful in gaining the throne remain useful once it has been gained. In the myth of kingship, Seth's murder of Osiris disrupts the peace and harmony—the *maat*—that had prevailed during his reign, and introduces an era of conflict, when there are no set rules and victory must be gained by any means necessary. The eventual victory of Horus restores the peace and harmony that had previously prevailed under his father's rule. In the same way, once the king is securely on his throne, he must show himself just and wise in governing, benevolent, and peaceful, acting at the behest of the gods to ensure their blessings for all the people of Egypt. If any problems arise to threaten his rule, whether enemies from without or treachery within, the king must act swiftly and decisively—even ruthlessly—to quash the turmoil and ensure that peace and order is restored.

This again is the reason for the impression of peace and serenity, the sense of eternity that one finds in the art and architecture of ancient Egypt. It is a graphic representation of the peace the earthly kings worked so hard to secure. If the history of royal rule in Egypt was sometimes filled with conflict and uncertainty, if the nation sometimes fragmented and could be restored only after decades or centuries of conflict, it was all the more important that royal monuments showed the Two Lands the benefits of the peace that would ultimately prevail. Royal art and architecture reflected the unchanging reality that was believed to lie behind each king's reign, as the tumultuous changes and chances of history were subsumed into a portrayal of the peaceful reign of the eternal divine monarch.

CHAPTER FOUR

Egypt: The World of the Dead

Egyptian Ideas about the Nature of the Person

Egyptian civilization showed more concern with the next life than any other ancient culture known to us. This was true despite the Egyptians' cultural emphasis on the present life and the powers that sustained it: the sun giving life and light, the black earth of the Nile Valley providing abundant crops, and the divine king maintaining order on the earth and in the heavens. But the preoccupation was not a rejection of the pleasures of this life. It was an expression of the wish and the expectation that those pleasures might continue forever in much the same form. The dominant Egyptian ideas about and images of life after death present the afterlife as essentially an idealized version of the life already lived by the elite in the present world, except without the changes brought by illness, calamity, old age, and death. Preparation for death and the afterlife was in many ways the attempt to create an eternal, unchanging version of the present life for the dead to enjoy forever.

To some extent, the Egyptians' apparent preoccupation with preparation for death is the result of using tombs and their furnishings as predominant sources in the work of reconstructing ancient Egyptian culture. Tombs not only provide many of the texts that survive from ancient Egypt but also the artifacts of everyday life, kept in tombs for use by the deceased. Tombs generally reflect the concerns and beliefs of the upper levels of Egyptian society, especially during the earlier periods of Egyptian history, and so inevitably skew our perspective. At the same time, however, the great abundance of material available from Egyptian tombs is generally continuous and consistent with widely spread evidence from Neolithic burials and other ancient Near Eastern cultures. The similarities between these different burial traditions—even though the Egyptian evidence is far more abundant and elaborate than that offered by the other ancient cultures—suggest also similarity in burial practices and beliefs about the situation of the dead. In short, the Egyptian concern with the afterlife and preparation for death is assuredly not just a matter of our perspective based on particular sorts of evidence, but was in fact a central reality of Egyptian religious culture.

Egyptian beliefs about the afterlife depended on ideas about the nature of the human person. How a person's individual identity and existence was expressed and experienced in this world would also determine how it would be expressed and experienced in the world to come. According to the Egyptians, the human person was comprised of five parts: the body, the name, the shadow, the *ba,* and the *ka.*

The name, as we've seen, was an essential expression of the person, both in this life and the afterlife. The name expressed the deepest sense of the self both among human beings and among the gods. The name was so closely tied to the essential reality of the person that it was believed someone could be harmed by writing down his or her name and then destroying it. When someone's name was read aloud or spoken, it was filled with breath or spirit, and to that extent "lived" again. To eradicate someone's name was to prevent the memory of their existence from being preserved, and so also to threaten the very essence of their being.

The idea of the shadow was based on its mundane reality, the shade that the presence of a body creates in direct sunlight. A person's shadow was understood metaphorically as the physical presence of a person distinct from the body. In fact, it was the shadow that determined the physical presence of a person in the body as well. The shadow was the presence—the "thereness"—of a person in both this life and the afterlife.

The *ba* is often understood in the modern sense of "soul," but the two concepts do not really coincide. The *ba* is the impression others receive of the self, but also the activity or spiritual presence of the person perceivable in what he or she does. We might say it is the persona of an individual, that is, what a person projects to others as his or her self. But the *ba* is also something like self-consciousness, since a person can interact with his or her *ba* as with another person, as in The Dispute between a Man and His Ba (Lichtheim, 1:163–169). The *ba* is the primary mode of existence for the dead, often represented as a bird with a human head. It resides in the mummy, but also participates in the afterlife in the kingdom of Osiris during the night. During the day, the *ba* ascends into the heavens to dwell among the "indestructible" stars that circle the North Pole and so never set.

The *ka* is the most complex concept in the Egyptian idea of the person. The *ka* has to do with the individual identity of a person, his or her character, and the way character determines the shape and ultimate nature of a person's life. Khnum is sometimes shown creating the *ka* alongside the body of a particular person, and the *ka* is also related to a person's conception in the womb. It relates to the interaction of the mind and the body from birth, and so might also be characterized in part as the "life force." After death the *ka* remains in the tomb with the body. It is the part of a person that requires nourishment, so offerings are made to the *ka* at the tomb of the deceased by *ka*-priests. The internal *ka* is a sort of spirit of protection and blessing for a person. The external *ka* is any representation of the person in a graphic image. Tomb murals created a *ka* of the world for the deceased's *ka* to live in and enjoy eternally, since the *ka* remains in the tomb after death.

It is necessary to have some idea of the different component parts of a person since Egyptian burial practices, from mummification to tomb decoration, are based on the needs of these different aspects of a person. We tend to think of preparation for death in Egypt as being primarily about the body, but what was done to the body was determined by beliefs about the ways someone participated in the afterlife. The body was preserved so that the entire person—body, name, shadow, *ba*, and *ka*—would survive and enjoy blessedness in the realm of the dead.

Earliest Egyptian Burial Practices

The earliest Egyptian burials are consistent with other burials of the Neolithic era (8300–3000 BCE), reflecting what were apparently common beliefs about the situation of the dead. The people of the Neolithic era in the ancient Near East and Europe generally believed in some sort of afterlife. Death, like birth, was believed to mark a transition from one form of existence to another. The deceased would be separated from the living but would still be "alive" elsewhere and would still require the daily necessities associated with the present life. The dead were buried with great care, often dressed in the clothes and accessories they wore in life, with the body placed in either a contracted position or stretched out full length. The grave would include gifts and offerings apparently intended both to make the dead person happy and to aid the transition to the afterlife. There were different burial practices, including group graves in carefully constructed burial chambers, individual burials in cave-like tombs, and individual burials in the ground covered by heavy stones. Sometimes bodies were later disinterred and the bones reburied in ossuaries. There is also evidence from the Neolithic era of attempts to maintain contact with the dead through communion meals at the burial site. In general, the people of the Neolithic era seem to have been in awe of the dead and wished to keep them well-disposed toward the living, but also wished to facilitate their transition to their new mode of existence.

The earliest Egyptian burials are similar to other Neolithic burials in the ancient Near East. The graves held provisions for the deceased, including pottery, tools, and other items necessary for daily life. The body was buried in a contracted position, lying on its face or on its side, in a shallow round or oval grave. In contrast to general practice during the Neolithic era, in Egypt burials were generally located away from the villages of the Nile Valley, in the desert. There may have been several reasons for this. Desert burial may have indicated the deceased was now separated from the life of the community, or it may simply be that the fertile soil of the valley was so highly valued that it was reserved for agriculture. Desert burial may also have been a way to promote preservation of the body. Some scholars speculate that the Egyptian's distinctive belief in an afterlife closely resembling life among the living was a result of Egypt's arid climate. The hot dry air and sand of the desert have preservative qualities that fostered a natural process of mummification. Since buried bodies did not decay and retained something of the appearance they had during life, the Egyptians may have been encouraged to believe that the existence of the dead was not that different from their previous existence in life. While this is speculation, it is true that the Egyptians subsequently developed techniques that would preserve dead bodies in much the same way they might be naturally preserved by desert burials.

Over time new funereal practices were introduced into Egypt. Each was presumably intended to protect the body and so also the welfare of the deceased, but sometimes new problems arose as a result. Initially these innovations seemed to focus on protecting the body from the earth in which it was buried. The body might be wrapped in skins or cloths, or it might be enclosed in some sort of container, a woven basket or a wooden coffin. The same impulse to protect the body led to burial in rectangular burial pits, sometimes lined with mud brick. The burial pit would then be covered with a flat wooden roof. Unfortunately, wrapping the body to protect it from the desert sand meant the body did not benefit from the sand's natural preservative effects and suffered decomposition. The use of roofs over the burial pit made it easier for grave robbers to gain access to the grave and loot the funeral goods.

After the unification of the Two Lands, two further innovations developed to address these problems. The wealthy began to have their graves dug into rock rather than sand, and covered with stone rather than a wooden roof, with the intention of foiling grave robbers. To ensure the survival of the body after death, artificial methods of mummification were introduced to duplicate natural processes. The intention of mummification was to maintain both the identity and the life essence of the deceased. The body itself was a part of a person's identity and so needed to be preserved, but it also served as a home to both the *ba* and the *ka* of the deceased. Mummification was necessary if the dead person was to survive and gain entry into the afterlife.

The Process of Mummification

Development of an effective means of artificial mummification was slow and results varied. Some mummies from the Old Kingdom retain a remarkably life-like appearance achieved through molding and decoration of a plastered exterior. But beneath the plaster the bodies have almost completely deteriorated. The major innovation in preparation of the body from that time was apparently removal of the vital organs from the abdominal cavity.

From roughly the beginning of the Middle Kingdom (c. 2055 BCE) mummification techniques improved considerably and already included many of the later methods and practices that were typical of the art of mummification at its height. Scientific examination of mummies has told us a great deal about the process of mummification and its development over the centuries. The primary written source from the ancient world for the full development of the mummification process is a portion of the nine-book *History* written by the Greek historian Herodotus in the fifth century BCE. His account probably reflects common mummification practices and techniques of the time. Although mummification practices had already declined from the heights achieved during Dynasty 21 (c. 1069–945 BCE), most of the techniques and practices Herodotus discusses had been in regular use since their initial development during the New Kingdom (c. 1550–1069 BCE).

The process of mummification was both time-consuming and expensive, since it involved an elaborate process carried out over a period of ten weeks. The dead body was turned over to the morticians and washed. The brain was removed through one of the nostrils with a long hook and discarded, but the heart was left in place because it was thought to be the abode of the deceased's *ba*. The *ba* would continue to dwell in the mummy. The other internal organs were removed through incisions in the abdomen. Four groups of organs—the lungs, liver, stomach, and intestines—were then dehydrated with natron (a mixture of sodium bicarbonate, sodium carbonate, sodium sulfate, and sodium chloride, although the formula varied) in the form of a dry powder. The preserved organs were placed in four canopic jars decorated with heads of protective deities, the four sons of Horus. Sometimes the organs were wrapped in linen bands and later placed back into the body once it had been embalmed. The body was then treated with natron powder to dehydrate the body tissues.

After the body was dehydrated it was filled with spices and stuffed with linen soaked in resin to replicate the contours of the living body. The abdominal incision was sewn up and the nostrils plugged, sealing the body's orifices. The body was then coated with resin before it was wrapped in linen bands. The body or its wrapping would include a multitude of amulets intended, along with magic spells memorized from a funerary text, to protect or aid the deceased on the journey through the Underworld to the kingdom of Osiris. The body was often padded in the process of wrapping and then decorated to make it appear as lifelike as possible. Various methods were developed to maintain the physical identity of the deceased and to make the mummy resemble the living form of the person whose *ba* it would house.

This is the most elaborate form of mummification Herodotus describes. He also provides the details of two other techniques. The first technique was to treat the body with natron but to leave the internal organs in the body intact. Oil was then injected into the lower abdomen and released again some time later, theoretically carrying away with it the decomposed remnants of the viscera. The second technique was the simplest and most economical. The body was simply washed and then dehydrated with natron. All the internal organs were left intact and the body was not necessarily wrapped in linen bands. There are mummies extant that reveal evidence of all these methods of mummification. Archaeologists have also determined that even when mortuary techniques were at their height and the most elaborate methods were employed, the process of mummification was still sometimes rather haphazard, depending on the circumstances of a person's death and the skill and honesty of the morticians who prepared the body.

The finished mummy was placed in two or more wooden coffins. These coffins might also be carved and decorated to resemble the deceased. The coffin might be set upright within the tomb or placed flat in a stone sarcophagus. The coffins and sarcophagus would also be decorated with spells and inscriptions to protect the body and speed the journey of the deceased into Duat, the Egyptian Underworld.

The Tomb and Its Decorations

Like the mummy, tomb furniture and decoration were intended to serve the needs of the deceased. Since the *ba*, the *ka*, and the shadow resided in the tomb with the mummified body, various sorts of furniture and decoration were created to accommodate them. A small air vent or passageway led from the burial chamber to the outside to allow the *ba* to travel back and forth between the tomb and the outer world, since the *ba* spent time in the tomb, in Duat, the realm of the dead, and among the stars. The *ka* remained with the mummified body. The shadow resided in the tomb statue of the deceased. Within the tomb the deceased enjoyed the depiction of his or her earthly life in the murals adorning the tomb walls, the *ka*-world.

Food and drink were left in the tomb to provide nourishment for the *ka* of the deceased. The food was commonly presented in the form of a complete meal, including meat, grains, dairy products, bread, beer, and wine. The food was either displayed on dishes or sealed in containers. One such meal could provide the deceased with an eternity of nourishment, as the shadow could magically replenish itself forever from the same food. In time, various sorts of substitutes were made for actual food, since the shadow's needs were provided by magic rather than the substance of the food itself. Sustenance for deceased royalty was also provided by daily food offerings presented by the *ka*-priests in the mortuary chapel that was part of the royal tomb. The offerings were left in front of a stele or false door in the wall of the chapel that provided the *ka* of the deceased with access to the offerings. Nutrition was essential for the *ka*, so food offerings that might end after several generations were supplemented by lists of offerings on the chapel walls, and portrayals of food production, thereby providing food for the *ka* for eternity.

Adjacent to the funerary chapel in royal tombs, usually near the stele or false door, was the *serdab*, an enclosed chamber in which were placed one or more statues of the deceased and his or her family. The only apertures in the chamber were one or more slits cut in the wall, allowing one to see in—or the statues to see out. The *serdab* was already a feature of royal tombs during Dynasty 1 (c. 3000–2890 BCE).

In addition to food, the tomb was provided with household furniture and all the other luxuries and necessities appropriate to the earthly status of the deceased. With the increase in wealth among the elite, there was a proportionate increase in the number, kind, and quality of burial goods included in the tomb. Already by Dynasty 1 tombs for the elite included extensive space for storage rooms in rectangular tombs called "mastabas," made of dried mud bricks. As we have seen, the need to protect funeral goods from plunder led to more elaborate tombs made of stone, with underground chambers dug out or cut from the earth. Rock-cut tombs were built as early as Dynasty 5 (2495–2345 BCE), and possibly before.

Even the decoration of the tomb, notably the wall paintings and reliefs depicting scenes of everyday life, was functional. The wall paintings provided a *ka*-world for the *ka* of the deceased to enter into and enjoy throughout eternity.

For images to be an effective presence for the deceased in the *ka*-world they had to be presented in their most complete characteristic form. This may account in part for the characteristic Egyptian depiction of the human form. The body is shown from the side with the legs apart, so both legs are fully visible. The torso is twisted to show both shoulders and both arms in their entirety. The face is presented in profile to permit a full depiction of the eye, the most important feature of the face. The portrayal is intended to show the deceased in motion, alive and active in the *ka*-world. Similarly, other items were drawn in full even when this violated a naturalistic portrayal of things as they appear in nature. The need to portray things in full led to some interesting stylistic practices; for example, items in boxes were shown hovering over the box so they could be depicted as well as the box that contained them. In the pictorial *ka*-world, only what was fully depicted would be fully present.

Models of items served much the same purpose, providing for the needs of the deceased by representations of items he or she would use in the afterlife. Models ranged from small vases to complete three-dimensional scenes of daily activities or favorite pastimes from the life of the deceased. The use of models reached its height in tombs dating from the Middle Kingdom.

Also left in the tomb were hundreds of models of male and female slaves. These figures varied greatly in size and were intended to serve as the deceased's servants in the afterlife. This was a modification of an earlier practice. During Dynasty 1 the slaves of high officials were put to death and buried with their master. But this practice soon disappeared and models representing slaves were left in tombs instead. Beginning in the Middle Kingdom models of mummified figures were placed in tombs. These figures were called *shabtis*, "answerers." Originally one figure was placed in the tomb to serve as a deputy for the deceased, but later greater numbers were included to serve as slaves. The *shabti* might be inscribed with the duties the figure would be called on to perform, and sometimes they were organized in groups under other figures that were meant to serve as overseers. The *shabti* derives its name from its primary function, to answer when they are called by their master. Their answer was invariably to be "Here I am," indicating the slave's readiness to serve.

Part of the preparation of the tomb, at least from the New Kingdom onward, was the "Opening of the Mouth" ceremony. This ritual was among the most ancient and important in Egypt, since it made it possible for something to live, or in the case of the dead body, to live again. The rituals associated with "Opening of the Mouth" were performed on the *shabtis* and other representations of living beings, including the funerary statue of the deceased.

There are disagreements among scholars about the earliest form of the ritual and its intention. Most forms of the ritual include touching the mouth with something, ranging from the priest's finger to an implement such as an adze, often made of flint; an adze was widely used in such rituals during the New Kingdom. The rituals included purification with water and animal sacrifice, accompanied by the recitation of spells. All of these rituals were intended to enable these things to carry out their specific duties as living creatures, by opening the mouth to receive life. But the most important of the "Opening of the Mouth" rituals was performed on the mummy to restore to it the powers of life, allowing it to see, hear, and speak once again. This ritual was typically performed by the eldest son of the deceased as his heir, and was a central feature of nonelite as well as royal burials. In fact, a tenuous claim to the throne could be bolstered by a new king performing the "Opening of the Mouth" ritual for the mummified body of his predecessor.

The intention of the elaborate preparation of the body, the tomb, and its contents, the rituals that accompanied burial and the offerings placed in the tomb or later provided in the funerary temple, was to ensure a blessed afterlife for the deceased. But it is important to remember that the focus in all of these preparations for death was not on death itself, but on life, the blessed life the dead would continue to live in the Underworld with the help of the living.

Egyptian Concepts of the Underworld

In Egypt the dead were in some ways still very much present in the world of the living. Their monuments and the necropolis in which the dead were entombed ensured a constant awareness of their continued existence and the mighty deeds of their lives. The dead remained alive through the speaking of their names by the living, and rituals continued in their funerary temples long after their deaths. The tomb was designed as an eternal habitation in this world for the deceased, a home it might enjoy forever. But at the same time, it was believed the dead also enjoyed an afterlife elsewhere, a life lived in the company of the gods.

As we've seen, there were competing versions of the major Egyptian myths of creation, and the same is true to some extent of Egyptian conceptions of the afterlife. Egyptian beliefs about the fate of the dead were not systematic or consistent. Different beliefs were dominant at different times and there seems to be considerable evolution in ideas about the afterlife over the centuries. To some extent a person's beliefs about the afterlife depended on the chief god he or she worshipped, as in the case of Ra, although some ideas appear to be constant. For the most part it appears that Egyptian ideas about the afterlife were meant to be evocative and not simply descriptive. By their variety they expressed what were otherwise inexpressible truths.

In addition to archaeological evidence provided by Egyptian burials, tombs, and monuments, we have three primary ancient Egyptian textual sources for information about the situation of the dead. The first, the Pyramid Texts, are texts found inscribed on the walls of pyramids from the Old Kingdom (2686–2125 BCE). The inscriptions include instructions to guide the dead king to the afterlife, and magic spells to assist and protect him. In the afterlife the king will share the role of Osiris, who ruled over the kingdom of the dead. The Pyramid Texts were later collected and edited during the Middle Kingdom (2055–1650 BCE) into a collection called the Coffin Texts. Like the Pyramid Texts, the Coffin Texts take their name from where they were written down or inscribed. The Coffin Texts were inscribed on the interior of coffins belonging to members of the upper classes. This is an indication that during the Middle Kingdom the Egyptian elite in general shared most of the aspirations for the afterlife that during the Old Kingdom had been reserved for the king alone as the beloved of the gods.

During the New Kingdom (1550–1069 BCE) another group of texts collected a great deal of information to guide the deceased into a blessed afterlife. This was *The Book of Going Forth by Day*, often called the *Egyptian Book of the Dead*. It included descriptions of the various situations the deceased would encounter on his or her way to Duat. There were also invocations and spells to allow the deceased to pass through various stages on the journey and to acquire the gifts of breath and speech necessary for the afterlife. Other spells were meant to ward off predatory animals and other dangers that might threaten the deceased's safe passage or the blessed nature of the afterlife. The text might be accompanied by illustrations. One extant version of *The Book of Going Forth by Day*, the Papyrus of Ani, has many illustrations of the royal scribe Ani and his wife making offerings or greeting the gods with gestures of reverence; these illustrations are accompanied by texts praising the god, usually Osiris. In contrast to the beauty of the illustrations, the text is corrupt, with omissions and errors, and Ani's name appears to have been added by a different hand after the manuscript had been compiled from work done by at least three different scribes. All indications are that the Papyrus of Ani was assembled from standard sheets prepared in advance. This is a further indication of the gradual democratization of ideas about the afterlife. During the New Kingdom, entrance into the Underworld was believed to be available even to those who could afford no better than a prefabricated version of *The Book of Going Forth by Day* that was personalized only after its purchase had been arranged.

These collections of texts share a common point of view. They all teach that the way to the kingdom of Osiris was difficult and full of pitfalls. For this reason it was necessary for the deceased to be prepared beforehand with information about the journey, the names of the various entities that would be encountered on the way, and the appropriate magic spells and rituals that would ensure safe passage. These texts were guidebooks, intended to prepare and equip the deceased for the journey through the hazards of the Underworld and to ensure a safe arrival at the final destination.

Predynastic burials in Egypt already show a distinction according to earthly status, and during the Old Kingdom the king in particular was set apart for special treatment in burial and in the afterlife. As the fact that they were inscribed on the inside walls of pyramids indicates, the Pyramid Texts were written solely for the benefit of deceased royalty. They depict the divine king after death essentially continuing his life among the other gods. Early ideas reflected in the Pyramid Texts placed the dead king in the heavens as one of the circumpolar stars that never sets. Other portions of the texts placed the deceased king in the retinue of Ra, following in his own boat the sun god's royal barge as Ra traversed the arch of Nut's body each day on the celestial Nile, the Milky Way.

After the weakening of royal authority at the end of the Old Kingdom (c. 2125 BCE), access to the afterlife was believed to be open to nearly everyone, and texts formerly reserved for the king were more widely distributed. For example, in the Coffin Texts, dating from Dynasties 11 and 12 (c. 2055–1773 BCE), Nut, the sky goddess, admits favored souls into the starry realm, that is, into Nut herself. More commonly, the dead were associated either with Ra or with Osiris, who each represent different aspects of the afterlife. Ra is associated with the sun and so also with the idea of rejuvenation, since Ra is reborn each day. The afterlife associated with Ra is thought of as dramatically different from life on earth. By contrast, Osiris is associated with the chthonic or earthly and the idea of eternal life. Just as Osiris died but continues to be alive in his kingdom of the dead, so also those who die will live in his kingdom forever. The afterlife associated with Osiris is essentially similar to the earthly life of the Egyptian elite, but in an idealized, changeless form and without the tribulations common to life on earth.

The story of Ra's nightly journey through the Underworld was a common subject of funerary texts during the New Kingdom (c 1550–1069 BCE), especially the texts written on the walls of tombs in the Valley of the Kings on the west bank of Thebes. These stories traced the progress of the sun's journey from its setting place in the west to its reappearance at dawn in the east. This is essentially a story of Ra's daily death and resurrection, providing a pattern for the dead king to follow during his travels in the Underworld in order to achieve renewed life. During his travels, Ra is identified with three other gods. Ra is associated with Atum at the setting of the sun, then with Osiris during his journeys through Duat, and finally with Kheprer the divine scarab when Ra rises to life once again as the reborn sun.

There are three major compositions that depict Ra's journey through the Underworld. All three show evidence of the reuse and compilation of earlier texts, including omissions and apparent misreadings. The earliest of these texts is "The Book of Am-Duat" or "The Book of What Is in the Underworld," from Dynasty 18, found in two early complete versions, one in the tomb of Thutmose III (1479–1425 BCE) and the other in the tomb of Amenhotep II (1427–1400 BCE). The prologue makes it clear that the book is a book of knowledge that will allow the deceased to make a safe journey through the perils that lay ahead in the Underworld. The sun's journey is divided into twelve scenarios representing the twelve hours of the night when Ra is "dead" in the Underworld. The sun travels through the Underworld in his royal barge with attendants who protect and help him during his journey. During the night Ra brings life to those in Duat and annihilation to his enemies before he is ultimately reborn as Kheprer at dawn.

Another text of this sort is "The Book of Gates," with its earliest known appearance in the tomb of Horemheb (1323–1295 BCE), the last king of Dynasty 18, with full versions in the tombs of Sety I (1294–1279 BCE) of Dynasty 19 and Rameses VI (1143–1136 BCE) of Dynasty 20. In "The Book of Gates" Ra's journey is again divided into twelve scenarios, each bounded by a gate guarded by gods, guardians, and a fire-spitting cobra. All of these are easily subdued when Ra, here in the form of "Flesh of Ra," says their names. Knowledge of a being's name, as we have seen, ensures power over it. The fifth scenario takes "Flesh of Ra" into the judgment hall of Osiris, then to the expulsion of the primordial monster Apophis while Ra restores his human victims to life. Again there is the pattern of Ra granting life to the blessed while his enemies are annihilated. At the end, Kheprer, the new sun, sits in a boat on Nun, the primeval sea, with the sky goddess Nut stretching over-head while standing on the head of Osiris in Duat.

The third and apparently the latest of the texts devoted to Ra's journey in the Underworld is "The Book of Caverns," also found in the tomb of Rameses VI. The book is divided into six sections, each depicting one of the caverns Ra must pass through on his nightly journey through the Underworld. As in "The Book of Gates," Ra displays his knowledge and power by subduing the guardians and monsters he encounters in the Underworld by speaking their names. As Ra proceeds through the caverns, he brings life and light to the gods and goddesses who lie in oval sarcophagi awaiting revivification from the sun god. At the same time, the text depicts in contrast the punishment of the enemies of the gods in gory detail, leading to their final annihilation. Again at the conclusion Ra appears as Kheprer, god of the rising sun, but this time the image of Ra is a combination of the ram-headed god and the sacred scarab, with the symbol of the sun as a child poised to rise at the imminent dawn.

Each of these stories reflects both the centrality of the sun in the Egyptian worldview and the sun god in the Egyptian pantheon. But these stories also share the conviction that the Underworld is similar to the present world primarily in the sense that it is a realm of divine action, a place where the sun is essential to well-being. Just as Ra follows a twelve-hour passage from east to west across the sky each day, bringing life to the inhabitants of the earth and pronouncing judgment against his enemies, so he also follows a twelve-hour passage from west to east under the earth each night, bringing life to the inhabitants of Duat and pronouncing judgment against his enemies there.

The stories about Ra in the Underworld provide further evidence that Duat as the realm of the dead is not separated from the gods and their life-giving power. The Underworld draws blessings and sustenance from the same god who presides over the earth. Perhaps more important, stories about Ra in Duat emphasize the sun god's indomitable power, based in his wisdom and the magical power at his command. Whatever obstacles may rise up against him, in the heavens or under the earth, Ra is able to overcome them all. Whether his people are among the living on the earth or the dead in the Underworld, he is present to give his light and life and to govern them in peace.

The Kingdom of Osiris

As his prominence in the accounts of Ra's journey through the Underworld indicates, Osiris was from the earliest times identified as the ruler of Duat, the Egyptian Underworld. Beliefs about the Underworld as the kingdom of Osiris are among the oldest beliefs about the abode and situation of the dead. These beliefs were dependent in part on the myth of kingship. The story of Osiris's peaceful rule over the earth, his murder by Seth and his resuscitation by Isis to conceive their son Horus, all connect Osiris's identity as a fertility god with his role as ruler of the dead. Osiris leaves his earthly kingdom to Horus as his successor to rule instead in Duat. Osiris exchanges dominion over the living for dominion over the dead. Osiris is typically depicted with the accoutrements of kingship, the scepter, flail, and the *Atef* crown that combined the white crown of Upper Egypt with two feathers. But Osiris is most often portrayed with his body mummified and wrapped in linen cloths, indicating his royal power as the god of the dead.

Although the abode of the dead was sometimes located in the western desert, the Nile Delta, Syria, or even in the Milky Way, the "Heavenly Nile," Osiris's realm was most commonly associated with the regions under the earth. Befitting Osiris's identity as a fertility god, his kingdom was an abundantly fertile place, an idealized version of the Nile Valley of Egypt where want was unknown. This is where the deceased would live at leisure while slaves—the *shabtis* placed in the tomb and brought to life through the "Opening of the Mouth" ceremony—would work the land and otherwise provide for his or her needs. This is clearly an aristocratic ideal, a vision of an afterlife where everyone lives the life of a king or queen.

Entrance into the kingdom of Osiris was determined by an elaborate process of judgment after death, a process involving confession, judgment, and trial by ordeal. As is so often the case, details of the process of admission differ from one text to another, but we can sketch out a general account of the process. After death, the deceased is guided by Anubis, the jackal-headed god of the dead and of cemeteries, into the kingdom of Osiris. Sometimes the guide is the goddess Hathor. Anubis conducts the deceased into the courtroom of Osiris, the Hall of Truth. As ruler of the Underworld Osiris was also the arbiter of justice, so it is he who oversees the judgment of the dead, the ritual process that would determine their eternal destinies. Osiris sits in state in the Hall of Truth attended by his consort Isis and their sister Nephthys. Together the sister goddesses are responsible for mourning and protecting the dead.

The deceased recites a long list of offenses that he or she has not committed during life in the presence of the three gods. This is in effect a claim to a series of virtues; each time a person does not offend the gods it is because he or she is conforming to a code of behavior made up of the actions the gods approve. Since the list is part of a ritual recitation, it probably reflects the moral standards of a widely recognized—even if unwritten—code of proper behavior. The list of offenses is most likely idealized and was not necessarily an accurate reflection of what the deceased may or may not have done during his or her lifetime.

This recitation is in many ways comparable to the magic spells the deceased uses to open the way into the afterlife. Like the spells, the recitation includes repeated phrases and elements that indicate its essentially ritual function. After reciting it before Osiris, Isis, and Nephthys, the deceased recites the same list before a series of forty-two divine judges, each one presumably representing one of the traditional nomes or regions of Upper and Lower Egypt. Each of these judges must be addressed by name. Similarly, any obstacles encountered on the way to the Underworld must be addressed by name in whole and in part. The progress of the journey through Duat and the names of the entities the deceased encounters along the journey are an important part of the information conveyed by such texts as those found in *The Book of Going Forth by Day*.

Once the recitation of the list of offenses is completed, the deceased is subjected to a ritual that determines his or her eternal fate. This again indicates the confession before Osiris, Isis, Nephthys, and the forty-two divine judges is a formality, since the fate of the deceased is determined by what happens next, the weighing of the heart. The heart of the deceased is placed in a balance opposite the goddess Maat, represented either by a statue or a hieroglyph. The process is overseen by Thoth, the scribe of the gods who is entrusted with recording and announcing the result of the trial. In depictions of this scene, the weighing of the deceased's heart typically takes place in the presence of Osiris, Isis, and Nephthys, sometimes with Anubis in attendance as well.

If the heart of the deceased proves to be heavier than Maat, it is because the heart has been made heavy by evil deeds. This means the heart must be destroyed. According to some versions of the judgment, an evil heart is eaten by a composite beast with the head of a crocodile, the forelegs of a lion, and the hind legs of a hippo. Appropriately enough this monster is called Ammit, "the Gobbler." In other versions of the judgment, the evil heart is destroyed by being thrown into a fire. Either way, it is clear that the evil heart is utterly destroyed. With the destruction of the heart, the unfortunate person to whom it belongs also ceases to exist. Nonexistence appears to have been a difficult concept for ancient people to grasp. From earliest times human beings seem to assume that the dead continued to live on in some way. But the heart being devoured or burned up would mean it could no longer be a source of life to its owner in this world or the next. That person would cease to be. This idea represented one of the deepest fears of the Egyptian, the "second death" that meant that a person who had once lived had been annihilated and was no longer alive in human memory or in Duat.

In fact this disastrous outcome never occurs in the funerary texts or depictions of the judgment, since the whole purpose of such depictions is to prepare the deceased for successful entry into Osiris's kingdom. If the heart is light—as it invariably proves to be in the texts—this is because it has been made light by virtue. In this happy event, Thoth announces the result of the ritual to Osiris, and the deceased is welcomed into Osiris's kingdom to enjoy

The weighing of the heart in the Judgment Hall of Osiris. The ba of the deceased appears to the left of a scale containing the heart on the left and a feather representing maat on the right. Anubis oversees the process while Thoth waits to write down the result, standing next to the composite beast Ammit, "the Gobbler." From the Papyrus of Ani, Dynasty 19. © The Trustees of the British Museum

its benefits for eternity. An appeal to Osiris for the vindicated deceased appears in *The Book of Going Forth by Day*: "May he come in freely, may he go out in peace from the House of Osiris, without being repelled or turned back. May he go in favored, may he come out loved, may he be vindicated, may his commands be done in the House of Osiris, may he go and speak with you, may he be a spirit with you, may no fault be found in him, for the balance is voided of his misdoings" (Faulkner, 30). The reward for those who are found blameless at judgment is freedom to come and go as they will and to have access to the gods whose blessed life they now share.

The Dead and the Living

The eternal welfare of the dead depended very much on the activities of the living. Although a person would order and oversee many of the preparations for his or her burial while still alive, it was the responsibility of those left behind at death to ensure that the preparations were carried out at the proper time and in the proper way to ensure they would have their full effect. It was the responsibility of the living, and especially of those who were closest to the deceased, to perform the proper prayers, spells, and rituals at the time of burial. It was also the responsibility of the living, usually the eldest son or *ka*-servants employed for the purpose, to maintain the offerings at the mortuary temple, where the deceased was nourished by food offerings and held in memory through the continual speaking of his or her name.

An essential part of honoring the dead was to speak their names aloud. Just as the other components that made up the fullness of a person were preserved in various ways to ensure his or her eternal survival, so also the name of the person—the essential expression of who he or she was, the deepest sense of his or her personality—was preserved by writing it in inscriptions to be spoken aloud by the living. By speaking a name, one filled it with breath or spirit, putting "life" into it as Ptah had put life into the gods and the elements of the cosmos when he spoke their names at the beginning of creation. Inscriptions including the name of the deceased would be spoken aloud by those who read them, and this ensured the name would be kept alive in this world. Execration texts were intended to have the opposite effect, by writing down the names of enemies and then destroying what had been written. Once the names had been destroyed, they could no longer be spoken, and those who had those names were symbolically lost to memory and so "died." Memorial inscriptions on tombs might be obliterated to the same effect, to ensure the memory of a disgraced king or queen was destroyed and their name lost forever, never to be spoken again.

The dead were believed to be very much alive, living in their tombs in the same way that they had once lived in their houses, surrounded by the necessities of life. This is clear from tomb furnishings and design, which often imitated the design of Egyptian houses, to the point that they included gardens and lavatories. Necropolises were even in some cases laid out like cities, incorporating blocks of "dwellings" allowing the living easy access to the tombs. We might compare mausoleums in modern cemeteries, which incorporate the model of the home and the temple, including doors and windows, and are set in garden environments with winding suburban streets among trees, bushes, and flowers. In Egypt the dead were also believed to be able to influence some events on earth, so their aid might be sought by letters asking for their intervention in the affairs of the living. Sometimes the dead might move among the living as ghosts, ghosts that might be benevolent or malevolent. Malevolent ghosts might attack those who disturbed their tombs or other offenders against the gods, or even the innocent. On the other hand, there is little evidence that the ancient Egyptians generally feared the dead. This may be because so much care was taken to ensure that the dead would be happy with their situation in the afterlife.

At the same time the dead were present on earth among the living, they were also believed to be in another place, in the kingdom of Osiris or among the stars in the sky. To some extent the ideal of the afterlife was to live like a god, enjoying daily memorial offerings. But in other ways the afterlife was like the life of the elite on earth, overseeing the labor of others in the fields and enjoying rich harvests in a fertile kingdom like the Two Lands. This dichotomy in the situation of the dead, who continue to live both in the tomb on earth and among the gods in Duat, may reflect the distinction between ideas associated with particular gods in *neheh*, the stream of history, and prevailing concepts of the nature of the divine life shared by all the gods in *djet*, the time of eternity. The gods exist in two sorts of time at once. But the dichotomy also arises from the permeability of the distinction between the existence of the gods and that of human beings. The blessed dead essentially attain the status once restricted to the divine king, who also simultaneously exists and acts in both *neheh* and *djet*. Like the divine king, the dead retain a place in the world of human beings but also participate in the life of the gods.

What is most notable, however, is whatever the concept of the existence of the dead might have been, the emphasis was always on a continuation of life on earth in an idealized form. Although there may have been aspects of what we might consider the ethereal among the many Egyptian beliefs about the afterlife, they were heavily outweighed by ideas based in the practical, physical realities of earthly life. The hope for the future was essentially a continuation of the pleasures found in the present life without life's more burdensome aspects. But there was also anxiety over the possibility of a "second death." This might be the result of a negative judgment in the Hall of Truth, followed by the heart's annihilation by fire or in the guts of Ammit, the Gobbler of Evil Hearts. Or it might be the result of one's name no longer being spoken aloud and filled with spirit, or one's former existence being forgotten, no longer "remembered."

Whatever consolations were offered to the ancient Egyptians by their visions of the afterlife, generally the greatest good was still believed to be a long life spent enjoying what pleasures life had to offer on earth while it lasts. The "Song of the Harper" taken from the tomb of King Intef, found among the love poems in Papyrus Harris 500 says in part, "So rejoice your heart! Absence of care is good for you; follow your heart as long as you live . . . Follow your heart and your happiness, conduct your affairs on earth as your heart dictates, for the day of mourning will (surely) come for you" (Simpson, 333). This was a common sentiment shared by other Near Eastern religious cultures that did not share the Egyptians' hopes for a blessed afterlife.

It was the present life that was primary. The Egyptians' apparent concern with death was really a concern with preparing for what would be only a new phase of life that closely resembled life on earth. For them life and death were not two powers at war with one another, but two aspects of the same existence. Life ended in death, but death was the entryway to a new and better life.

CHAPTER FIVE

Egypt: The Human World

The Primacy of Ritual Worship

Egyptian religious concerns were addressed primarily through the daily worship rituals carried out in temples. Much of what people believed about the gods and their powers, their activities, and their relationship with humanity was expressed in the act of worship. As a result, worship was also the primary influence on Egyptian religious sensibilities. When the ancient Egyptians performed rituals, whether public or private, whether formal or informal, they were acting on their deepest concerns and beliefs, hoping to influence the gods in a way that would benefit them in some way. Ritual acts of worship were part of the attempt to maintain harmony and equilibrium—*maat*—between the human world and the divine world. For this reason, everything involved in the performance of ritual worship, from sacred spaces to religious festivals to sacred animals, was essential to the well-being of the human world. And as we will see, religious rituals of various sorts permeated the lives of ancient Egyptians, bringing virtually all of their daily activities, from the exalted to the mundane, into the realm of sacred concern.

The focus of official ritual worship was not only the gods but also living kings and sacred animals, as well as the dead. Some scholars have argued that what sets those beings designated "gods" by the Egyptians apart from other sorts of beings is simply that "gods" are objects of worship. In other words, in ancient Egypt worshipping something makes it a "god." This conclusion may have more to do with connotations of the Egyptian word usually translated "god," *ntr*, than with the ancient Egyptian idea of what a god was. We will find a similar problem reflected in the languages of Mesopotamia. But it is worth noting that ritual worship was not restricted to what we would think of as gods, but to other beings believed to control or be endowed with divine power.

Temple Personnel

The primary location for Egyptian ritual worship was the temple. A temple was usually sacred to several gods, although some were dedicated to worship of a single god. The temple was actually a complex, including the temple building and the precinct immediately surrounding it. An Egyptian temple would be associated with an entire estate that was most often separate from the temple complex. The temple estate—including agricultural land, pens for sacrificial animals, and housing for cultic personnel—provided everything necessary to support the ritual worship performed in the temple sanctuary. The temple was essentially a self-sufficient complex of people and animals, goods and services, workers and overseers, all working toward a single end: the proper worship of the gods through daily rituals and annual festivals.

Although the king was officially the chief cultic official for the nation, hereditary or appointed priests conducted worship on his behalf in temples and other sacred spaces. During the Old and Middle Kingdoms there was no full-time professional class of priests, and holders of the priesthoods usually had other administrative duties as well. There were three general orders of priests responsible for different aspects of worship. The higher order, called "god's servants," performed the rituals focused on caring for the cultic image of the god. The lower order of priests, called "pure ones," carried the shrine containing the god's image during rituals, poured out water offerings, supervised craftsmen and servants, and carried out other duties. There were also lector-priests who were responsible for reciting the texts relating to rituals, including appropriate prayers and spells. There were specific responsibilities assigned to different priests within these orders, either within the context of worship or in the administration of the temple estate.

Priests served in groups, with each group serving in a given temple for one month out of four, or three months altogether each year. The rotation among groups of priests meant an individual priest could serve more than one god or group of gods in more than one temple. Both men and women served as priests during the Old Kingdom, with women of high status serving the goddesses Hathor and Neith. After priesthood became a full-time occupation during the New Kingdom only men served as priests. There were other cultic functionaries besides priests involved in ritual worship, as well as musicians, singers, and dancers, both men and women.

In addition to the religious power inherent in the priesthoods, the priests might enjoy considerable political and financial power as well. There are many instances in Egyptian history of specific priests and priesthoods gaining dominant political power. Probably the best example is the power wielded by the priests of Amun-Ra during Dynasty 18 (1550–1295 BCE) at the beginning of the New Kingdom. It was in part to reclaim political power from the priests of Amun-Ra that Amenhotep IV imposed exclusive worship of Aten. Under the royal name Akhenaten the king served as both the god's chief worshipper and the exclusive means by which Aten conveyed his blessings to the Egyptians. After Akhenaten's death the priests of Amun-Ra regained the upper hand and the names of both Aten and Akhenaten were obliterated from his royal monuments, although the name of Aten continued to occasionally be found elsewhere.

Temple Rituals

The primary temple ritual took place in the early morning, coinciding with the sun's rebirth at dawn. The head priest and other priests would be up before dawn to get ready for the ceremony, cleansing themselves and preparing food and drink offerings for the god. The head priest would unlock and open the doors of the temple just as the sun rose. Inside the temple was a box-like shrine with closed doors; the shrine was the dwelling place for the cultic statue of the temple's god. Once the temple had been purified with water and incense the doors of the god's shrine were opened and the cultic statue removed. Most of these statues were relatively small, around two feet tall on average. The cultic statue might be made of stone, wood, or metal, and was intended to provide an abode for the *ba* and *ka* of the god, the divine presence of the god within the temple. The head priest prostrated himself before the statue and presented it with a small image of Maat, goddess of justice and divine order.

After it had been removed from its shrine, the cultic statue was stripped of the previous day's clothing while the shrine was washed and purified. The statue was then decorated with eye paint and anointed with oil. The priests dressed the statue in fresh ceremonial clothing consisting of four different colored cloth strips, each with a particular function. The statue was also invested with the symbols of the god's power, such as the crown, crook, and flail.

During this ritual the cultic statue was also presented the day's offering, although some modern reconstructions place the offering after the morning ritual of purification. The offerings were meant to allow the statue to nourish itself with the spiritual essence of the food. What was presented to the cult statue was only a small portion of all the offerings prepared. The offerings were usually presented during the day to the different gods worshipped in the temple before finally being divided among the priests.

At the end of the morning ceremony, the priests scattered fresh sand on the floor of the temple. They replaced the cultic statue in its shrine and closed the doors. The priests then left the temple. The head priest was the last to leave, using a broom to smooth the sand behind him before he closed and locked the doors of the temple.

Other rituals were commonly performed as well, both in temples and in other sacred spaces. Daily temple rituals included cleansing rituals and ceremonies meant to drive away the forces of disorder that might threaten the god. Hymns were sung throughout the day and night to ensure the orderly passing of the hours. Priests of the higher order were also responsible for soliciting or interpreting oracles from the god.

Temples also observed annual festivals throughout the year, festivals that might last from one day to almost four weeks. A major feature of these festivals was the transportation of the cultic statue from its temple to another location for a specified length of time and the god's later return to the temple. The ostensive purpose of the festival was to allow the god to visit another god—often a spouse or other relative—in commemoration or reenactment of a mythic event. Since the gods always traveled in boats, the cultic statue would also be transported in a boat or in a bark, a boat-shaped shrine carried by the god's priests.

The transportation of the bark provided one of the few occasions when the temple gods, or at least their shrines, were visible to the majority of their worshippers. Over time and especially during the New Kingdom, festivals became occasions for outpourings of public religious sentiment. Entire villages would turn out to see the divine procession of the god's bark as part of the festival. The appearance of the god outside the precincts of the temple estate also provided an opportunity for people to procure oracles. They would present the god with a question and the god would indicate an answer—either "yes" or "no"—through the movement of the cultic statue as it was carried in its bark. Such festivals provided one of the few opportunities for an encounter between the official religion of the elite and the popular religion of the common people. Some memorial monuments for private individuals mention that the deceased had attended a sacred festival during his or her lifetime.

As the chief cultic official of the Two Lands, the king played the leading role in several annual festivals, particularly those that involved his own royal

Procession of the sun bark of Ra. © 2008 Jupiterimages Corporation

authority or the fertility and well-being of the land. The annual festival of Opet in civil month two, for example, required the king to travel to the temple of Luxor at Thebes to have his royal power renewed by his father Amun-Ra. This festival seems to have arisen during the New Kingdom and celebrated the close ties between the king and Amun-Ra, and expanded to twenty-seven days during Dynasty 20. It was during this festival that Amun granted divine power and authority to the king as his son. The king also played a major role in the harvest festival of Min, a god of fertility, in civil month nine, when the king cut the first sheaf of barley. As we have seen, rituals were celebrated in honor of the divine king both during his life and after his death, including the *sed*-festival that ensured the king's rejuvenation and revitalization after thirty years of his reign, and again every three years or so after that.

Funerary cults provided offerings for all those dead who had been prepared to enter the afterlife through mummification and the ceremony of the Opening of the Mouth. But there were also annual festivals to commemorate the dead. The dead were remembered and honored with offerings on New Year's Day at the beginning of the civil calendar, and during the Wag festival about two weeks later which in time also incorporated the offerings associated with the Thoth festival. The Sokar festival in civil month four was a somber commemoration of the death of Osiris that was first celebrated during the Old Kingdom and came to greater prominence with the relocation of the royal capital to Memphis.

Another commemoration came in civil month ten as part of the Valley Feast at Thebes. During this festival the cultic statues of Amun, his consort Mut, and their son Khonsu would travel from their temple in Karnak to Deir el-Bahri across the Nile. Worshippers would visit the tombs of family members to honor the dead.

The Egyptians also devoted religious cults to animals. Specific sorts of animals could serve essentially the same purpose as a god's cultic statue, as a dwelling place for the *ba* and *ka* of the god they represented. Temples would include a number of animals that were carefully chosen and honored as manifestations of the temple's god or gods. They were believed to be able to give oracles on the god's behalf by making a choice between two possibilities—for example, entering one of two stables—to provide a response to a question that could be answered "yes" or "no." At death the sacred animals were mummified and presented as votive offerings to the god of the temple. Away from the temple estate, animals sacred to the gods were also kept in private homes and honored as the gods' representatives, and buried with honor after their deaths.

Popular Religion in Egypt

The ruling elite and the literate administrators who filled the ranks of the royal bureaucracy made up, with their families, only a small percentage of the population of the Two Lands. The life of most Egyptians was very different from theirs. For the vast majority of ancient Egyptians, life was a constant process of loss—loss from illness, accident, mutilation, poor nutrition, mental disorder, and early death.

A list of common occupations and their trials may be found in a wisdom text from the Middle Kingdom, "The Satire of the Trades." The bulk of this work is a satirical description of the various sorts of skilled and manual labor common in Egypt, written from the perspective of a scribe in the royal bureaucracy. As one might expect, the text emphasizes the intense physical effort required to perform most of their jobs, as well as the filth and stink involved. Even accounting for a scribe's obvious professional prejudices, it is clear the manual labor that supported the vast majority of the Egyptian population was degrading, grueling, unpleasant, unhealthy, and apparently unending.

It is difficult to reconstruct religious culture among the common people in ancient Egypt. Although we have abundant sources over many centuries for the official religious culture of Egypt, there are far fewer sources for what we might call "popular religion." For one thing, traditional concepts of religious propriety reserved any depiction of worship of the gods to those involving the king or members of the royal family. This tradition began to change during the New Kingdom, when religious sentiment and religious activity apparently began to spread to the general population. An increase in expressions of personal piety during this time appears to reflect a belief in a more universal accessibility to the gods. We also find evidence that people looked to particular gods as their patron deities, and trusted those gods to watch out for them and serve as their protectors in the divine realm. During the New Kingdom we also find an increase in devotional items—such as small votive images of gods and goddesses or monument stones—in the homes of common people.

The gods of greatest interest to common Egyptians were those who would hear their complaints and offer them help in their daily lives. Any religious action the average person initiated was most likely motivated at least in part as a response to personal misfortune or as an attempt to gain protection against misfortune in the future. The most immediate religious concerns were practical ones, such as good health or good fortune, or success in legal appeals.

The common people recognized and invoked the major gods of the national cults, but were drawn most notably to those gods who were believed to hear the concerns and fill the needs of their worshippers. Both Amun and Ptah, for example, were said to hear and respond to prayers. Amun's temple at Karnak included a chapel of the Hearing Ear from the reign of Rameses II (1279–1213 BCE). Ears engraved in monuments to a god or in the walls of a temple symbolized the god's willingness to hear and attend to the prayers of the faithful. An image of Ptah Who Hears Prayer appears in a temple built during the reign of Rameses III (1184–1153 BCE). A common motif in the invocation of a god in Egyptian prayers is the god's willingness to hear the prayers of his or her devotees; the god is "one who hears requests" or "one who comes at [the sound of] the voice of him who calls to him" (Redford, 313).

Isis was a popular goddess among people of all sorts, apparently because of the practical assistance she offered to those in need. Among her other titles and attributes, Isis was said to be "powerful in magic." As we have seen, Isis was the source of spells used by her devotees to find relief in various difficult situations. Often these spells had their origin in a story about Isis as the protector of the young Horus. One such story is "Isis and the Seven Scorpions." In it, Isis sends scorpions to sting the child of a woman who has failed to help

Isis and Horus in need, but the goddess later relents and heals the child with a magic spell (Hart, 42–44). The story includes the spell which a hearer can then use to cure the poison sting from a scorpion. Most often the afflicted person would be identified with Horus and the one performing the healing with Isis, placing the use of practical magic within an eternal mythic context.

Minor national gods who appear to have been most popular with the common people were those whose interests were closest to their own, or who would act to help them in need. Imhotep was an historical figure, the architect of the step pyramid of Djoser (2667–2648 BCE) who was later deified and designated "son of Ptah" and became a patron of scribes. During the Ptolemaic period (305–30 BCE) Imhotep was identified with the Greek god Asclepius as a god of healing who could resolve various human ills. Bes was a protective spirit who was usually depicted as a grotesque dwarf. Bes may have been related to an older god, Aha "the fighter." Bes protected human beings at specific times—during childbirth and while asleep, for example— and his image was a popular protective amulet. In addition to worship of national gods, there was also popular worship of local deities, usually older gods associated with particular regions or locations who were believed to be particularly attentive to the people who lived in those places.

These gods and others could be worshipped in private cults, that is, places set aside for rituals, public or private, apart from the temples dedicated to particular gods. In the ruins of Akhetaten, reflecting religious practices during the reign of Akhenaten (1353–1336 BCE), there is evidence of public chapels with a stele or a cult statue representing a god, where food offerings, incense, or libations might be offered. Stelae served as public commemorations of particular occasions when devotees felt they had received divine blessings. As a result, stelae were monuments to the conviction that the gods could heal and show mercy as they chose.

From the reign of Rameses II comes a collection of three penitential hymns that reflect the concerns of common people (Simpson, 284–288). The hymns were inscribed on stelae in public chapels frequented by workmen in western Thebes. In each case, the hymns name specific workmen who praise a god— Amun, the goddess Mertseger, Ptah—for the relief they have gained at the god's hand in a time of trouble. In most cases, the trouble is the result of some offense the petitioner has committed against the god, and the stele serves in part as a warning to others to honor the god in the proper way. These hymns provide another example of the widely spread popular piety that marked the religious culture of Egypt during the New Kingdom.

Household shrines provided the opportunity for ritual worship in the home, either in honor of a god or in commemoration of dead relatives or venerated ancestors. The household shrine was commonly a niche in a wall with a small space in front of it for libations or offerings. Shrines for dead family members usually took the form of household stelae or small busts of the deceased between four and ten inches tall. In either case, household shrines offered the means of expressing personal religious sentiments through ritual worship in the private home.

Other forms of piety and religious activity among common people often focused on gaining divine insight into a problem, or gaining foresight into the future. The primary way to do this was by seeking an oracle. As we have seen, an oracle might be obtained from a sacred temple animal, or during a religious procession. Messages from the gods or other supernatural sources might also be given through portentous dreams that would require interpretation by a priest or some other person who understood the meaning of dreams. Texts providing interpretations of dreams survive, the earliest of them dating to the Middle Kingdom. An inquirer might also consult a "wise woman," a female seer with the gift of foresight, or resort to several of these methods together to gain a comprehensive reply.

Magic and Charms

Despite the popularity of these forms of ritual worship, the most common religious activities among average people in ancient Egypt through most of its history seem to have focused on what we might style "magical" practices and rituals. Although "magic" in our culture carries the taint of illegitimacy, in ancient Egypt magic was part of the divine panoply of power, most notably in the case of Isis. Priests recited spells to subdue the powers of disorder and to otherwise help to maintain divine equilibrium in specific situations. But magic also played an important part in the business of everyday life.

What we might identify as magical practices stood alongside other, more practical, ways of interacting with the natural world, for example in medical procedures. In some cases, a spell alone would be considered sufficient remedy for a specific illness or other medical problem. In other cases, such as a broken bone, a spell would accompany a specific practical procedure such as setting the bone and binding the limb. The spell was intended to ensure the efficacy of the practical procedure. The two forms of treatment were considered complementary and were carried out by the same practitioner, who learned both in the context of his medical education. The situation was the same in other sorts of work. The magic was a means of ensuring that the practical action would have its desired result. An obvious parallel in our own culture is the practice of praying for the sick, when prayers are most often offered in conjunction with, rather than instead of, practical medical procedures.

The most common form of magic among the Egyptians was probably the use of amulets. Amulets were worn by all sorts and classes of people to protect the wearer from malevolent forces. In fact, the gods were believed to wear amulets as well, and amulets were included in the mummy wrappings of the dead. Amulets had many different traditional forms and were made from many different materials. Most often a given material was specified for a particular sort of amulet because of its color, so if necessary other materials of the same color could be substituted. Amulets were already popular in Egypt during the predynastic period.

The most powerful amulet was the *wedjat* ("sound one"), a representation of a left eye lined with kohl and an eyebrow with the markings of a falcon. This amulet was also known as the "Eye of Horus" and was used as early as the Old Kingdom. Its origin is an episode of "The Contendings of Horus and Seth," when Seth tore out one of Horus's eyes. The eye was later restored by Thoth. The *wedjat* usually represents the left ("lunar") eye, although some examples represent the right eye, Horus's uninjured "solar" eye.

There were many different kinds of funerary amulets, each with a specific function. Several hundred amulets might be included in the wrappings of a single mummy, since the effect of the amulets was believed to be cumulative—the more amulets, the greater the protection. Some funerary amulets took the form of various symbols of divine power associated with the king. Originally these amulets were restricted to royal mummies. But after the democratization of the afterlife during the First Intermediate Period (2160–2055 BCE), most of them began to appear in the wrappings of mummies of all sorts and classes. This again points to the privileged status the dead enjoy in the kingdom of Osiris. There every person is blessed with the privileges and prerogatives of a king. The most important funerary amulet was the heart scarab, made from green stone in the shape of the sacred beetle. This amulet protected the heart of the deceased until it could be weighed in the Hall of Truth in the kingdom of Osiris. If the heart of the deceased were somehow to be lost, the heart scarab could serve in its place.

Religious Sentiment in the Egyptian Wisdom Tradition

An important part of religious culture in ancient Egypt and the ancient Near East in general was the wisdom tradition. Wisdom literature was pragmatic, intended to teach how a person might best get along in life, with an emphasis on practical advice. It was meant to be learned and memorized. The most characteristic expression of wisdom in the ancient Near East was the proverb, a pithy expression of one small facet of the truth about life.

Wisdom literature is most often presented as the teaching of a father to a son. The older man shares the benefits of his experience with the boy to ease his path in life. Advice from a king to his heir—a form of wisdom literature we have already discussed—forms a subset of this genre, with its own specific concerns, mostly centered on court life and military action. But the idea of the wiser, more experienced older man instructing the young, inexperienced boy endures.

Egypt has left more wisdom literature than any other ancient Near Eastern culture. Extant examples of wisdom literature from ancient Egypt fall into several categories, indicating both the importance and the variety of the Egyptian wisdom tradition. There are the usual instances of teachings from a father to a son, but the subject matter in a given book might be fairly diverse or it might be narrowly focused to make a specific point. There are also instances of wisdom teaching in unexpected forms, most often expressing the injunction *carpe diem*—seize the day—to enjoy the pleasures of life as it comes. The importance of wisdom literature in the Egyptian tradition is clearly indicated by the careful ascription of wisdom works to specific individuals, whether kings, officials, or scribes. Elsewhere in the ancient Near East works of wisdom literature are most often anonymous.

The Maxims of Ptahhotep is one of the foremost examples of Egyptian wisdom literature, both in its general presentation and its contents. It survives in four copies and has been placed in two distinct historical contexts. Some scholars believe it was written toward the end of Dynasty 6 (2345–2181 BCE) during the Old Kingdom; others support a later date of composition, during Dynasty 12 (1985–1773 BCE) of the Middle Kingdom (cf. Simpson, 129). The work includes thirty-seven "maxims" on different themes, generally running from four to twelve lines, with a prologue and epilogue explaining the origins and purpose of the text. The *Maxims* is presented as the advice of a venerable noble who has spent his long life in service to the king, and the content of the *Maxims* is ostensibly addressed to his son, whom he wishes to succeed him in his post. As a result, his advice is particularly suited to a man in a position of power whose well-being depends on the good opinion of his superiors, but who also wishes to do the right thing for those who depend on him for their welfare, both the members of his family and the people of Egypt.

The general attitude of the work is summarized in part in a passage in the epilogue: "Suppress your impulses and control your mouth, and then your advice

Figure of a scribe, Dynasty 5. © 2008 Jupiterimages Corporation

will be [welcomed] by the officials . . . Be painstaking all the time that you are speaking, so that you may say things of importance. Then the officials who are listening will say: 'How excellent are the words of his mouth!'" (Simpson, 147–148). It is important to listen and speak carefully, always speaking from genuine knowledge in a humble and sincere manner. A wise man is prudent in dealing with those around him, and always behaves in a way that will gain the respect of others. He does his best in his work to bring benefits to those who depend on his efforts, and he is strict but loving with his wife and sons. He does not boast of his good fortune or denigrate those who are less fortunate or who come from humbler origins. He avoids the company of women and is shrewd in legal proceedings, suiting his conduct to the status and behavior of his opponent. Most important, he is aware that the divine principle of *maat* determines the course of life on earth and ensures a balance between a person's deeds and fate: "Great is Maat, and its foundation is firmly established; it has not been shaken since the time of Osiris, and he who violates the laws must be punished" (Simpson, 132). The moderation and self-command enjoined by Ptahhotep—as well as his conviction that proper behavior will have its just reward—finds parallels in other wisdom literature in Egypt and throughout the ancient Near East.

Egypt provides another example of wisdom teaching presented as the instruction of a father to a son in *The Wisdom of Amenemope*, probably written during Dynasty 20, between 1188 and 1075 BCE. The book includes a prologue, thirty chapters of various lengths, and an epilogue. Many of the teachings have to do with the value of wisdom. The book teaches the student to show respect for the great but also advises exhibiting graciousness and mercy toward the lowly. It advises against taking revenge or quarrelling, or complaining about one's lot in the world. The primary values *The Wisdom of Amenemope* teaches are honesty, humility, respect for the gods and rulers, mercy, generosity, a temperate tongue, and good judgment in choosing one's friends. *The Wisdom of Amenemope* was a highly influential work. Parts of it have close parallels in the Hebrew Bible in Proverbs 22:17–24:34, a section subtitled "The Sayings of the Sages."

We find much the same veneration for the wisdom teacher and scribe in "The Satire of the Trades." It was composed during the Middle Kingdom and survives in a number of copies, most of them corrupt. We have already had occasion to mention this work; the father, Kheti, warns his son Pepi to devote himself to his studies so he may avoid the woes suffered by artisans and manual laborers in their daily work. But this book more than any other makes it clear that wisdom literature belongs to the scribe's world. The litany of woes common to laborers is followed by instructions on how a scribe should conduct himself, and praise for the skills of writing and speech the scribe commands. Kheti's disdain for manual labor, his limited perspective, and his advice to Pepi are all based on his pride in being a scribe. "It's the greatest of all the callings," he boasts, "there's none like it in the land" (Lichtheim, 1:185). Like other examples of wisdom literature, "The Satire of the Trades" reflects belief in an orderly hierarchical creation with the gods above and humanity in their places below. Integrity and diligence can lead to a happy life, but one's ultimate fate lies in the hands of the in-scrutable gods.

A wisdom text from Dynasty 12 (c. 1936–1759 BCE), *The Dispute between a Man and His Ba* (Lichtheim, 1:163–169), reveals a complex relationship to prevailing Egyptian attitudes toward life and death. In it a man who finds his life intolerable wishes to die, but his *ba* encourages him to instead stand fast against his troubles and embrace life. It is ultimately about the advisability of suicide, although the idea of suicide is often implicit rather than openly stated. This is a familiar theme in the ancient world, with parallels in the Greco-Roman tradition and in the early Jesus movement. In this case the debate is sharpened by the expectation of a blessed afterlife in the West. Why, the man asks his *ba*, should he have to endure disrepute and the evils common in this world when he can expect happiness in the company of the gods in Duat after death? He yearns for death and sees it as a release from all his tribulations. The man's *ba* offers several responses. The *ba* tells him he should play the man and be steadfast in his troubles. He is only making himself miserable when he does not appreciate the life he has now. The man's lot is not as bad as those some others have to bear. Finally, the *ba* argues on the basis of life itself: it has value that should not be cast aside. There is much to be enjoyed in the present life, and the pleasures of the afterlife can be enjoyed in due time, when one's life on earth is over. The arguments are not entirely persuasive, especially in comparison to the eloquence of the man's complaints. But the *ba*'s arguments support the idea that the ancient Egyptian concern with the afterlife is less about death than it is about life, the continuation after death of a life that offers many pleasures that one must grasp even in the midst of troubles.

The Instruction of Any is a late wisdom work of the Third Intermediate Period, dating from Dynasty 21 or 22 (1069–715 BCE). The text survives in incomplete corrupted copies and fragments, and much of it is difficult to understand, let alone translate. The contents of *The Instruction of Any* reflect the democratization of the wisdom tradition in Egypt. Although it is ostensibly directed to Any's son, the scribe Khonshotep, its advice is more broadly applicable, and useful for any person with the intelligence and will to heed its words. Such a person is advised to honor the gods with pious actions, but more especially through offerings, being careful to keep accounts of what he has given the god (Lichtheim, 2:136). One should provide for the future by preparing a tomb, no matter what one's age. A man should be courteous toward neighbors and respect his superiors and should avoid associating with women, drinking beer, and revealing confidences. He should be aware that fortunes can change, and be generous in sharing food with the needy, and be moderate in all things.

Notably *The Instruction of Any* includes an epilogue featuring a debate—almost an argument—between Khonshotep and his father. Khonshotep repeatedly insists that Any's teaching is too much to master and in any event does not take into account a person's specific character. Any responds each time that any person can attend to the teaching and conform to it, whatever his natural bent. Although Any has the final word, it is clear that the author at least considers the possibility that wisdom teaching must find a receptive heart if it is to be useful. Significantly it is Any's own son who questions the value of his father's instruction, and argues that human character is not entirely the result of a person's own concentrated efforts.

In the last centuries before the Common Era, we find an increased skepticism here and elsewhere in Near Eastern wisdom literature that a human being is entirely free to determine the course of his or her own life. This skepticism arose not only on the basis of observation in daily life—the good did not always prosper, the wicked did not always suffer—but also from an increased awareness of the inscrutability of the gods and their treatment of human beings.

Religious Sentiment in Other Egyptian Literature

Despite the scribal origins of wisdom, we find some of its themes and ideas echoed in other forms of literature that purport to express the ideas and sentiments of "common people" associated in some way with the court. One example is provided by the poems identified as "Harpers' Songs" because they are inscribed in tombs as songs sung by harp players who performed for the king's entertainment. These songs reflect uncertainty about the fate of the dead or perhaps prefer the joys of the present life to the uncertain pleasures that may await some in Duat. One such song copied in antiquity from the tomb of King Intef reviews the fate of all humanity including the great and the wise: "A generation passes, another stays, since the time of the ancestors . . . [yet] those who built tombs, their places are gone, what has become of them?" (Lichtheim, 1:196). The harper then gives this advice: "Make holiday, do not weary of it! Lo, none is allowed to take his good with him, lo, none who departs comes back again" (Lichtheim, 1:197). Another of the Harpers' Songs from the tomb of an official of Dynasty 20, Inherkhawy (c. 1160 BCE), reviews the austere facts of life in a way that recalls the book of Ecclesiastes in the Hebrew Bible: "All who come into being as flesh pass on, and have since God walked the earth; and young blood mounts to their places" (Foster, 181). The advice given too is similar: Since life must come to an end, seize the day and enjoy life's pleasures while it lasts. The emphasis in these songs on enjoying life as it passes may reflect the harp player's general concern with the pleasures and travails of the present world, or at least what the elite believed the attitudes of common people like harp players to be. Although there are nods toward traditional piety and an expectation of life after death "in the West," these songs present a contrast to the prevailing attitudes of the ruling elite through the words of a commoner serving in the court.

Another Egyptian text, "The Prophecy of Neferty" (Simpson, 214–220), reflects a social background similar to wisdom literature and celebrates the Egyptian king as the source of all blessings. "The Prophecy of Neferty," as the title indicates, is presented as a prophecy, but it is in fact a literary work that depends on a tradition of written prophetic oracles. The text purports to recount a prophecy given during the reign of Sneferu (2613–2589 BCE), but its contents suggest it is in fact much later, probably from the reign of Amenemhat I during the Middle Kingdom. In the story the text tells, the prophet Neferty offers to entertain the pharaoh by looking either into the past or into the future. Neferty's ability to look into the past as well as the future indicates his gift is some sort of mystic insight that allows him to "see" across the spectrum of time. True prophecy, by contrast, is usually understood as the proclamation of a message sent by a god to the prophet. Prophecy is explicitly attributed to the god and not to some inherent ability belonging to the human agent. Neferty's "prophecy" is a poetic foretelling of a catastrophe when the Asiatics will overrun Egypt, as they did during the First Intermediate Period (c. 2160–2055 BCE). But Neferty also says the nation will be saved by a king from the south, Ameny, who will drive the Asiatics out of Egypt and establish peace and prosperity in a renewed kingdom. The narrative is in fact a review of history presented under the guise of prophecy, that is, it describes past events from the perspective of a prophet who lived in an earlier era, who "foresees" the unfolding of history as if it were the future. The intention of the book seems to be to extol the pharaoh (probably Amenemhat I) as the gods' champion for Egypt. In the process the author presents the events of Amenemhat's reign not merely as the history of a king, but as the fulfillment of divine prophecy, and reaffirms both the gods' control of history and the divine power of the king.

We find a similar veneration of the king, as well as the expression of deep love for Egypt itself, in *The Tale of Sinuhe* (Simpson, 54–66). The story is set in the Middle Kingdom at the beginning of Dynasty 12 and recounts the adventures of a courtier who flees Egypt in the aftermath of a rebellion. It begins with the death of the first dynast, Amenemhat I, in 1956 BCE, in a palace coup. This is the same king celebrated in "The Prophecy of Neferty" and "The Testament of Amenemhat." Whether the intention is to honor Amenemhat as an individual or to honor him as the founder of Dynasty 12 is open to question. The praise lavished on Amenemhat's son Senusret I in *The Tale of Sinuhe* suggests it was the dynasty rather than the man who was being celebrated in this case.

At the beginning of the story Sinuhe, a harem official under Amenemhat, flees Egypt after Amenemhat's assassination. To escape the political and social strife he sees coming Sinuhe enters Syria–Palestine, where he is made welcome by a Bedouin chieftain friendly to Egypt. Sinuhe becomes one of several native Egyptians in service to Amusinenshi, the Syrian ruler of the province of Upper Retenu. Amusinenshi is full of praise for Egypt and its king, and takes Sinuhe into his family by giving one of his daughters to Sinuhe as a wife.

The Lord of Upper Retenu also gives Sinuhe authority over a district of his domain called Yaa, which Sinuhe praises as a fertile and prosperous territory. There Sinuhe is able to live happily for many years with his Syrian wife and sons, who grow to adulthood during his sojourn. Sinuhe also serves Amusinenshi as a general, protecting his territory against the "Asian hordes." He even engages in single combat with another chief of Retenu and defeats him handily. By the grace of his god Sinuhe prospers in Retenu, but his thoughts are always on Egypt and its king.

Ultimately Sinuhe is summoned back to Egypt by Senusret, who succeeded his father after suppressing the coup against him. Sinuhe puts his authority in the hands of his Syrian sons and disposes of his property. He returns to Egypt to be honored by the king and the royal family, and happily lives out the rest of his days in his native land enjoying the king's benevolence and the blessings of living under his authority in Egypt.

The Tale of Sinuhe is most likely a fictional work, but it provides a vivid portrait of the attitudes, aspirations, and yearnings of a member of the Egyptian elite at the time it was written. Most notable is the attitude Sinuhe displays toward the king, who is presented as a divine figure who is the source of all blessings for his subjects as well as the sum of all virtues. Sinuhe praises Senusret in a long panegyric delivered to Amusinenshi as "a God, indeed, without peer . . . He is a master of knowledge, excellent in planning and efficient in commanding, one by whose command one comes forth and goes down" (Simpson, 57). Senusret is a god himself, but also the gods' gift to Egypt. The king is fierce in battle and scatters his enemies, but he is beloved by his people who take joy in his rule. He also assures many children for his subjects, presumably since the *maat* he imposes within his domain promotes the fertility of his subjects as well as the fertility of their land and domestic animals. When Sinuhe refers to the king, he often includes a list of his honors and titles that were most likely traditional, but here also reflect the regard that a courtier has for his lord and master, whom he sees as the source of all blessings for the Two Lands.

Throughout *The Tale of Sinuhe* Sinuhe repeatedly refers to "god" in the singular, but he also prominently mentions the many gods and goddesses of the Egyptian pantheon, notably in enumerating the honorifics of the king. His references to a single god appear mostly in context of the divine influence that guides and protects him. This most probably refers to the god Sinuhe worships as his patron deity, the one god he looks to for protection and support while in exile from Egypt. His references to other gods appear in blessings and references to people, places, and events in Egypt under the protection or patronage of particular gods. Sinuhe clearly acknowledges all the gods of Egypt and knows how each fits into the divine hierarchy, but he seems to place his trust primarily in the mercy and power of his patron god. Sinuhe addresses his patron god in prayer after his defeat of the chief of Retenu, thanking his god for protecting him as an exile and giving him prosperity in a foreign land, but also asking him to bring an end to Sinuhe's exile and return him to Egypt.

What is especially striking in *The Tale of Sinuhe*, however, is Sinuhe's continual longing for his home, for the gods and goddesses, the rulers and people, the customs and comforts of Egypt. Although he finds a home and prosperity among the Bedouins, Sinuhe's description of their way of life reflects an apparent Egyptian disdain for their uncivilized manners and customs. Such disdain might be expected from the members of the Egyptian royal court, and it is evident in Senusret's summons to Sinuhe to return from Syria–Palestine. But Sinuhe shares the Egyptian disdain for the people of Syria–Palestine and sometimes even reveals it to his Asian host. Sinuhe boasts to Amusinenshi how Senusret shows his power in smiting Asiatics and subduing those who dwell in the desert. After Sinuhe returns to the comforts of Egypt, pharaoh says in jest that he has become an Asiatic, nurtured by the Bedouin. But soon Sinuhe has been stripped of his foreign garb and bathed, groomed, and clothed as a noble Egyptian. Once again in his proper place, Sinuhe disdainfully consigns the trappings of his recent way of life to those who were bred to it. For Sinuhe, Egypt is home, Egypt's king is the gods' intended master of the earth, and Egypt's customs and comforts are the best the world has to offer.

Apparently one of the greatest benefits that fall to Sinuhe upon his return to Egypt is the prospect of proper funerary rituals after his death. In his summons to Sinuhe the king offers him all the trappings of an Egyptian burial: a linen shroud, a golden coffin, a limestone tomb, and all the Egyptian mourning rites and funerary offerings. This stands in contrast to what he might expect after his death in Retenu, where his body would be wrapped in a sheepskin and buried in the earth. After Sinuhe's return, the king reassures him that he will have a proper burial, overseen and attended by Egyptians instead of Bedouin bowmen. Indeed, the preparation of Sinuhe's pyramid tomb, its gardens, and its elaborate furnishings is described in some detail as the last of the blessings bestowed on him by pharaoh at the end of the story (Simpson, 66).

The Tale of Sinuhe was originally told among the elite of ancient Egypt and eventually written down for their entertainment. But the love Sinuhe expresses for his country, his king, and his gods arguably reflects the spirit of Egyptian religious culture as it was experienced not just by the elite, but by all the people of the Two Lands.

So we find essentially two different facets to religious practice in ancient Egypt, each a valid representation of the culture that engendered it, but each also only part of the true picture of Egyptian experience and spiritual aspirations. One is the official religious culture, centered in the temple and the tomb, dependent on the divine king's power to impose order on the cosmos. The other is popular religious culture, centered in the home or local shrine, where people would commemorate their ancestors and intercede with the gods through prayers and votive offerings. Worship in popular religious culture was primarily concerned with provoking divine responses to the inevitable losses of a difficult life, and protection against such losses. At the same time, participation in the festivals associated with official religion created a bond between common people and the religious culture promoted by the elite, uniting them in a common veneration of the nation's king and the nation's gods.

There is not a clear distinction between these two facets of Egyptian religious culture, since it was largely homogenous, with popular elements integrated into and discernible in "official" religious culture and vice versa. Perhaps it is better to say that while one of these facets of ancient Egyptian religious culture is prominent in the extant archaeological evidence and the other is more difficult to discern, both represent the spirit of Egyptian religion as it was experienced by its devotees.

SECTION TWO

MESOPOTAMIA

CHAPTER SIX

Mesopotamia: Historical Survey

The Beginnings of Mesopotamian Civilization

Ancient Mesopotamia was roughly equivalent to the territory that makes up the modern nations of Iraq and eastern Syria. The name *Mesopotamia* is Greek, meaning "between the rivers," referring to the Tigris and the Euphrates. Mesopotamia was defined by those two rivers just as Egypt was defined by the Nile. In ancient times Mesopotamia's people called it only "the land" or by the names of a succession of kingdoms. Assyria comprised upper Mesopotamia, in the northern Tigris River valley, while Babylonia was essentially lower Mesopotamia to the south, including the delta formed as the Tigris and Euphrates reach the Persian Gulf. The southern part of Mesopotamia was home to the early kingdoms of Sumer and Akkad.

Mesopotamia is a diverse territory with broad stretches of fertile land around the rivers, but foothills, marshes, steppes, and desert within close proximity. The climate is semiarid, with rainfall in inhabited areas ranging from seven to fifteen inches annually. While in Egypt the Nile's regular flooding ensured the fertility of the surrounding valley, in Mesopotamia the flooding of the Tigris and Euphrates do not coincide with the growing season. Consequently successful agriculture in Mesopotamia has always depended on carefully managed irrigation.

The fifth millennium BCE saw the first homogenous culture in Mesopotamia, represented today by physical remains throughout the territory, although predominantly in the southeast. These physical remains from the Chalcolithic era represent a material culture that is now identified as

Ubaid, after Tell al-Ubaid, the archaeological site in lower Mesopotamia where its characteristic remains were first discovered. Earlier settlers in Mesopotamia did not leave enough material evidence to provide much information about them. But we know both agriculture and the raising of domesticated animals for food, as well as the sort of settlements that benefitted from them, were established in Mesopotamia by the eighth millennium BCE, and still formed the basis of the economy at the beginning of the Ubaid period (c. 5000–4000 BCE). People of the Ubaid period settled primarily in the south, around the river delta near the Persian Gulf, in agricultural villages and, over time, in small cities of several thousand. These small cities featured substantial mud-brick houses and large, well-built temple complexes. Within Ubaid villages, the largest and most elaborate building was always the temple, a sign of its importance as a center of worship, commerce, and trade. There is substantial evidence of trade along the Tigris and Euphrates and beyond during the Ubaid period.

The political nature of Ubaid villages and cities is a matter of some dispute among scholars. Some believe Ubaid society was composed of families and households roughly equal in status and wealth, engaged in the work necessary to provide for its members. Others maintain that the priests of the temples combined political with religious authority, giving as evidence the priests' capacity to impress laborers to build and maintain the temples the priests served. In either case, it appears that political power and leadership was nonmilitary.

The Sumerians and Akkadians

Most of the fourth millennium BCE represents the Uruk period in Mesopotamia (c. 4000–3100 BCE). During this era there was a substantial growth in the number of settlements and the beginnings of a massive shift from agricultural villages to urban centers, a shift that reached its height by the mid-third millennium BCE. There was a variety of reasons for this population shift, reasons having to do both with ecological problems involved in farming and the perceived advantages of cities as centers of commerce and administration.

The distinctive culture of the people later known as the Sumerians appears in southern Mesopotamia in the second half of the fourth millennium BCE, probably as a development of the cultures of indigenous peoples. During the Early Dynastic period (c. 2900–2350 BCE) the Sumerians established a flourishing civilization with the rise of a series of powerful city-states. A city-state included one or more cities surrounded by fortified walls and the adjacent irrigated agricultural settlements that provided food. It was ruled by a hereditary king (Sumerian *lugal*, "big man"). The city-state was a hub for trade and the production of various sorts of goods as well as the political and religious center of the area, with a coterie of functionaries to serve its administration. A city and its king might enter into a confederation with another city either as its vassal or its master, but political unity of different cities under a single king was a relatively late development.

Writing first developed in Mesopotamia about 3300 BCE among the Sumerians. Writing grew primarily out of a need for accurate accounting methods, as a means of keeping track of goods and contractual obligations. The writing system was cuneiform (from Latin, "wedge-shaped"), created by the use of a short reed with a tip cut at an angle, allowing a scribe to make both triangular and round impressions in a wet clay tablet. Cuneiform began as a pictographic system that represented objects with schematic drawings. But over time it developed into a phonetic system based on the sound associated with the name of the object depicted. The sounds represented by the symbols could then be used to form the syllables of a word. Cuneiform writing was widely adopted and became the means by which Sumerian and Akkadian oral poetry and wisdom traditions were written down and preserved. A large body of Sumerian literature has survived recorded on clay tablets, providing information not only about the Sumerian way of life, but also about the Sumerian gods, their mythology, and religious rituals.

Struggles for hegemony among the Sumerian city-states over agricultural land led to warfare and conquest. A series of Sumerian cities in the far south—including Kish, Uruk, and Ur—were politically dominant in lower Mesopotamia at different times during the fourth millennium BCE. At the end of the Early Dynastic period, Lugalzagesi (c. 2340–2316 BCE), a king of Umma, conquered Ur and Uruk and in his inscriptions claimed dominion over all of southern Babylonia.

The Akkadians were descendants of Semitic groups who had migrated into central Mesopotamia, at the northern extension of Babylonia, and settled there in the early fourth millennium. The Akkadian king Sargon the Great (2334–2279 BCE) united the Mesopotamian city-states under his own rule to create a large territorial kingdom. Establishing a precedent that would be followed for centuries, Sargon would destroy the walls of the cities he conquered and compel the loyalty of the local king or replace him with a governor of Sargon's own choosing. Sargon was the first Mesopotamian king to have a standing army instead of depending on a muster of troops from the general population. He established military outposts throughout his realm to enforce loyalty and order. Sargon became the model for Mesopotamian kingship in later generations, although toward the end of his long reign he had to deal with periodic uprisings of subject peoples among his vast holdings. His grandson Naram-Sin (2254–2218 BCE) was also a powerful general, but without Sargon's talents for leadership. He ultimately was unable to halt the erosion of Akkadian power in the territories. The Akkadian Empire lasted a little more than a century before its fall. Its capital Agade quickly sank into obscurity and Mesopotamia was left in near anarchy for a time.

Sumerian supremacy was reestablished by Ur-Nammu (2112–2095 BCE), who founded the Third Dynasty of Ur (2112–2004 BCE), shifting the center of political and military power from north to south. Like Sargon, Ur-Nammu appointed governors for his subject cities. He created an effective centralized administration and promoted the rebuilding of the nation after the destruction resulting from warfare. Either Ur-Nammu or his son Shulgi enforced the first known law code in history, a code notable because it substituted monetary compensation for physical punishment. Ur-Nammu is also significant as a builder of ziggurats. Ziggurats were massive stepped brick pyramids, square at the base, with steep stairways to provide access to their various levels. Ziggurats were topped with a temple or shrine and were built of baked mud bricks covered with a layer of glazed fired bricks. Ziggurats apparently represented the sacred mountain where the gods resided and where their worshippers might encounter them. One ziggurat built in Ur by Ur-Nammu and dedicated to the Sumerian moon god Nanna measured about 64 by 46 meters at the base and was originally about twenty meters high.

Ur-Nammu's son Shulgi (2094–2047 BCE) ruled peacefully for most of his reign and provided for the preservation of his nation's literary tradition through his establishment of scribal schools in the cities of Ur and Nippur. These schools provided the government with men who could read, write, and calculate to serve as bureaucrats. Shulgi mounted a war against a people known as the Hurrians in territories neighboring his kingdom to the north about 2070 BCE, probably to protect Sumerian trade routes. He expanded his domain both through military conquest and diplomacy. Under both Shulgi and his son Amar-Suen (2046–2038 BCE) Sumerian power was maintained over a vast region of Mesopotamia through military power and effective royal administration.

The Third Dynasty of Ur lasted about seventy years, ending in the kingdom's disintegration from internal and external forces on all sides. The kingdom was attacked by a people called the Amorites from the west and another people called the Elamites from the east. Elam came under the control of Shimashki, one of Ur's major enemies, and under its leader the Elamites devastated the city of Ur in 2004 BCE. Mesopotamia fragmented into a collection of small kingdoms that replaced the earlier city-states. Notable among these kingdoms were Isin and Larsa in the south, and Asshur and Eshnunna in the north. They contended for regional dominance over the next two centuries.

During this same time new groups of nomadic and sedentary Semitic peoples appear in Mesopotamia. Nomadic herders of sheep and goats appear in historical records only to the extent that they came to the attention of the city-states' governments, or interacted with them in friendly or hostile ways. An archive from the nineteenth and eighteenth centuries from the city of Mari on the Euphrates in Syria provides some information about such nomadic groups, reflecting Mari's place as a primary point of contact between Babylon and Syria. These Semitic groups were given the general name "Amorites," a name associating them with the west. Although Amorites had held positions of power in the courts of Ur, they were generally regarded as enemies of the Third Dynasty. After the fall of Ur, one man who identified himself as "king of the Amorites" would establish a new center of power in Babylon.

The Babylonians

From the beginning of the second millennium BCE, the focus of Mesopotamian power for centuries was either Babylon to the south (in what is consequently called Babylonia) or Asshur to the north (in the territory known as Assyria). Babylon was initially established as a Semitic city-state in the area of Akkad. The Babylonians were Amorites who took over much of Sumerian culture, including its religious culture, although it gave the gods and goddesses Akkadian names. In the early second millennium Akkadian displaced Sumerian as the dominant language of Mesopotamia.

Babylon came to prominence in the eighteenth century BCE under the rule of its first great king, Hammurabi (1792–1750 BCE), the "king of the Amorites" who made Babylon the seat of Mesopotamian kingship. As a young king Hammurabi was drawn into regional conflicts, first acting through diplomacy and later through military force. He gradually increased his domain by conquest. Between 1766 and 1761 BCE Hammurabi defeated a series of enemies, eventually establishing dominion over all of southern Mesopotamia, although he never gained complete dominion over northern Mesopotamia. Like Sargon of Agade, Hammurabi either placed governors over his new possessions or made their kings his vassals.

Hammurabi is remembered today primarily because of his law code. The Code of Hammurabi addressed a wide range of human activities and was notable for combining mercy and mitigation with capital or corporal punishment.

Babylonian society was divided into free men, dependents, and slaves, and punishments were meted out according to the status of both offender and victim. But the intention of the stele that preserves the law code is to present Hammurabi as a king who establishes justice in his domain, and shows him standing before Shamash, the sun god who was responsible for overseeing the administration of divine justice.

Despite his attempts to create a central administration, Hammurabi's large, diverse kingdom was held together primarily by his personal power. During the reign of his son Samsuiluna (1749–1712 BCE) Babylon began to lose territories, some major cities were depopulated, and there was a general emigration toward northern Mesopotamia. Hammurabi's successors continued to rule for a century and a half after him, maintaining the old traditions, but they ruled over a depopulated realm from which real power seems to have departed. Babylon finally fell in 1595 BCE to Mursili I (1620–1590 BCE), king of the Hittites.

During the period from about 1590 to 1390 BCE the Near East and much of the rest of the eastern Mediterranean basin was in turmoil. The lack of documentation for the historian has made this a "dark age." Some states ceased to exist, while others continued in seriously diminished circumstances, and many cities were abandoned. These two centuries were a period of general political unrest in Mesopotamia. Between 2300 and 2000 BCE the territories surrounding Mesopotamia had seen large migrations of people sharing a common language tradition that is now called Indo-European. These peoples entered the Near East from central Asia. They included the Hittites, who founded a large kingdom in Asia Minor, and possibly the people who became the ruling classes in the Hurrian kingdom of Mitanni and among the Kassites. The Hurrians established Mitanni in an area encompassing large parts of northern Syria and Mesopotamia. Hurrian is neither Semitic nor Indo-European, but the kings and some of the gods included in royal inscriptions and letters are given Indo-European names. The Hurrians campaigned to the west and southwest, invading the Hittite kingdom several times, and extending their power into Syria–Palestine, where Hurrian names are found among the regional kings.

Similarly, the Kassites, an Iranian people, spoke an unknown language, but it also was neither Semitic nor Indo-European. The Kassites founded a dynasty that ruled Mesopotamia for over four centuries after the fall of Babylon. Remarkably little is known about this long period in Mesopotamian history because of the lack of documentation. Once they had established their authority, the Kassites apparently ruled in peace and adopted the customs and Akkadian language of the Babylonians, including Babylonian religious culture. Notably it was also about this time that Aramaic, an alphabetic Semitic language, began to replace Akkadian as the dominant language in Mesopotamia.

The Assyrians

Assyria, a Semitic kingdom of the upper Tigris valley, was the dominant kingdom in Mesopotamia by the mid-fourteenth century BCE and later became a world empire extending in an arch over the Arabian Desert from Media and Elam in the east to Lower Egypt to the south. Assyria's boundary to the north was high mountains, but to the west there was a broad plain leading to Syria and to the south the river delta and the cities located there. Assyria was dominated by the kingdom of Mitanni during much of the fifteenth and fourteenth centuries BCE, but became independent under Assur-uballit I (1363–1328 BCE). He initiated campaigns on all three of the nation's frontiers, to the northeast, west, and south. For a century or so, relations between Assyria and Kassite Babylonia were peaceful, but the Assyrian king Tukulti-Ninurta I (1243–1207 BCE) conquered and sacked Babylon in 1235 BCE to assert his sovereignty over the south. He gained renown beyond Mesopotamia, appearing in Genesis 10 as Nimrod and in Greek legend as King Ninos. But his successors were unable to maintain control over Babylon. A revived Kassite dynasty ruled in Babylon until the city fell to the Elamites in 1157 BCE.

Historical records are scanty throughout the upper Near East for the twelfth century BCE. This was a period of renewed ethnic migration, arising in part from the fall of the Hittite Empire in Asia Minor and the collapse of Mycenaean Greece at the end of the Bronze Age, events that coincided with the influx of the so-called "Sea Peoples." Assyria initially managed to survive with its power intact. Tiglath-Pileser I (1114–1076 BCE) increased the size of his kingdom to an unprecedented extent, but after his death Assyria appears to have been affected by the greater unrest, and only fragmentary records of those years remain. Toward the close of the tenth century BCE Assyria had been reduced to its central territories. Although embattled, it remained an independent kingdom with a strong army. Adad-nirari II (911–891 BCE) freed Assyria from the encroachments of its enemies and regained some of Assyria's lost territory, preparing it for an age of empire.

Further growth of Assyrian power came in the ninth century, when the kingdom's reach was extended to the Mediterranean under Assurnasirpal II (883–859 BCE). With Assurnasirpal and his successors, the Assyrian desire for security and self-preservation developed into a drive for conquest, as its kings defeated their enemies and put down internal rebellions to consolidate their power. Assurnasirpal could show extraordinary cruelty against rebels, but he was also a builder—notably of the new capital of Kalhu (modern Nimrud)— and a naturalist. His son, Shalmaneser III (858–824 BCE) campaigned across the Near East but met with only limited success. In Syria–Palestine Shalmaneser was opposed by some states and became allied with others, as each regional state sought its own advantage among its neighbors. Shalmaneser made Israel an Assyrian vassal under the Israelite king Jehu (842–814 BCE). For nearly a century after Shalmaneser's death, Assyria was bogged down in internal revolts and political instability. The situation was made worse by a series of relatively weak kings who were unable to assert their authority even as other forces in the Near East consolidated their power.

The Assyrian Empire revived and achieved its greatest size under Tiglath-pileser III (744–727 BCE), soon stretching from Gaza in the southwest to the Persian Gulf to the south and into Asia Minor. Tiglath-pileser subdued his enemies and conquered new territories, but also reformed the army and the royal administration to make both more efficient instruments of his power. Conquered territories no longer retained their kings as vassals, but were now placed under the control of Assyrian overseers while retaining their existing administration. To further minimize the possibility of revolt, Tiglath-pileser instituted mass deportation of native populations from conquered territories to other parts of his empire. This practice effectively eliminated the native ruling class as a potential source of leaders for revolts against the Assyrian king. There was continuing warfare during Tiglath-Pileser's reign, with the Babylonians and Elamites to the south and east, as well as conflicts among Assyria's vassals and enemies in Syria–Palestine, who would form and dissolve alliances as their own interests dictated.

Tiglath-pileser was succeeded by his son Shalmaneser V (726–722 BCE) who died after ruling for only a short time. His brother, Sargon II (722–705 BCE), devoted most of his reign to quelling revolts and dealing with Assyria's enemies, notably Elam, Egypt, and Urartu, a nation to Assyria's north. By the end of Sargon's reign, Assyria controlled the entire Fertile Crescent, from the border of Media, a portion of modern Iran northeast of Assyria, to Egypt. Sargon's successors were mostly kept occupied defending their possessions, fighting to regain territory Assyria had lost, or confronting old enemies. Sennacherib (704–681 BCE) had to suppress rebellions in Syria–Palestine and Babylon after Sargon's death. He laid siege to Hezekiah, king of Judah, in Jerusalem and made him a vassal, and captured and destroyed the city of Babylon. His youngest son Esarhaddon (680–669 BCE) rebuilt Babylon and secured peace to the south, then campaigned in Syria–Palestine and to the northeast. He also mounted a full-scale assault on Egypt, where he established sovereignty over the Nile Delta as far south as Memphis.

Esarhaddon's son Assur-bannipal (668–627 BCE) was the last great king of Assyria. His brother Shamash-shum-ukin became viceroy in Babylon, which he governed as an essentially autonomous nation. Assur-bannipal put

Sargon II (722–705 BCE) and the Tree of Life. © 2008 Jupiterimages Corporation

down a revolt in Egypt and destroyed Thebes, but later lost his Egyptian possessions while his armies were occupied fighting the Elamites. In Babylon Shamash-shum-ukin revolted against Assyrian authority but was defeated by his brother. Assur-bannipal also defeated rebels among the Arabs and finally subdued Elam, which had been an enemy of Mesopotamia for over three thousand years. But Assur-bannipal overextended his power and resources. Revolts broke out after his death, and the Assyrian Empire was dismantled by the Medes, an Iranian people from the northeast of Assyria, and by the Neo-Babylonians in the south.

The Neo-Babylonians

During the period of Assyrian hegemony, Babylon had come under the control of a new Semitic people, the Chaldeans. After Assur-bannipal died in Nineveh, one of his sons, Sin-shar-ishkun, made himself king of Babylon. But riots in the city led him to escape to safety in Nineveh. The Chaldean Nabopolassar took control of Babylon and fought against Sin-shar-ishkun (622–612 BCE) after he had become king of Assyria following his brother's death. The Babylonians made common cause with the Medes. Together they attacked Assyria and laid siege to its capital Nineveh, which they captured and destroyed in 612 BCE.

Nabopolassar (626–605 BCE) continued to rule in Babylon, but increasingly left military campaigning to the crown prince Nebuchadnezzar. Nebuchadnezzar secured a major victory against the Egyptians in Syria–Palestine at Carchemish in 605 BCE. When Nabopolassar died his son returned to Babylon to become king as Nebuchadnezzar II (604–562 BCE). Several of the states in Syria–Palestine, including Judah, withheld tribute from Nebuchadnezzar, inspired in part by the hope that Egypt would assist them in throwing off the yoke of Babylon. Once his throne was secure, Nebuchadnezzar continued his military campaign in Syria and dealt harshly with those states that had rebelled against him. Nebuchadnezzar deported Jehoiachin of Judah to Babylon with three thousand of the leading citizens of Jerusalem and Judah. After a later revolt Nebuchadnezzar laid siege to Jerusalem and captured the city after eighteen months, leading to a second wave of exiles. Nebuchadnezzar sacked the city and destroyed its walls to prevent another revolt. From that time he maintained Babylonian control over Syria–Palestine and thwarted Egyptian ambitions there while strengthening his eastern borders against the Medes.

Nebuchadnezzar left behind a secure and prosperous empire, but it was soon thrown into political chaos. Nebuchadnezzar's son Evil-Merodach

(561–560 BCE) was killed and succeeded by his brother-in-law Neriglissar (559–556 BCE). Neriglissar's son Labashi-Marduk (556 BCE) was overthrown after ruling only nine months. One of the conspirators who had plotted against him, Nabonidus, became king in June 555 BCE.

Weakened by misrule and threatened by Media, the Babylonian Empire was running out of time. Nabonidus (555–539 BCE) exalted the moon god Sin over Marduk, the traditional chief god of Babylon. Nabonidus abandoned his capital to live in Teima, an Arabian oasis. He appointed his son Belshazzar to be his regent in Babylon, where he presided over a worsening economic and military situation. Media gained control of the major trade routes between east and west. Nabonidus asked Cyrus II of Persia (559–530 BCE) to campaign against the Medes, in part because Nabonidus was determined to rebuild a temple devoted to Sin in Harran, a territory the Medes controlled. Cyrus's campaign ended with his complete control over the Medes. As king of both Persia and Media, Cyrus united the two major peoples inhabiting the territory of Iran. Cyrus then initiated a ten-year military campaign that ultimately brought under his control the largest Near Eastern empire the world had yet known.

Cyrus and the Persians invaded Babylon in 539 BCE. A revolt by the priests of Marduk toppled Nabonidus and Belshazzar, who subsequently disappeared from history. The priests of Marduk, the chief god of Babylon, essentially handed power to the Persians under Cyrus. From that point on, Mesopotamia, the home of empire, itself came under the control of the rulers of a series of world empires—the Persians, the Macedonians, the Romans—and remained a subject territory for the rest of the ancient era.

CHAPTER SEVEN

Mesopotamia: The Gods and the World They Made

The Nature of the Gods

There is a fundamental problem in discussing the gods of Mesopotamia: We are not entirely sure what the terms used to refer to the gods are supposed to mean. The term for "god" is *dingir* in Sumerian and *ilu* in Akkadian, but the etymology of both words is unknown. The cuneiform ideograms used to represent the words in each language associate the idea of a god with the heavens. This implies that the term is essentially spatial, that the idea of a god in Mesopotamia originally had more to do with location than with essence. The gods are those beings that live in heaven, not on earth where human beings live.

In this spatial sense, the primary attribute of the gods appears to be superiority, that is, superiority to earth-bound human beings. But that idea clearly evolved to mean any sort of superiority that exalts a divine being over a human being, or sets one human being apart from the mass of humanity. This might include, for example, the superhuman abilities of a hero or the extraordinary wisdom of a sage. To the extent that those abilities set the hero apart from the rest of humanity, to the extent that wisdom makes the sage superior to other human beings, the hero may be said to be divine or the sage to be god-like. So the line between the gods and exceptional human beings is not entirely clear. Both are superior, "above" the mass of humanity, but the superiority of the gods seems to differ from that of the hero or the sage by orders of magnitude. But at some point, the distinction between gods and even the most exalted human beings does come down to essence or nature: The gods are immortal and heroes are not, so heroes—no matter how great—are ultimately relegated to the status of human beings. In Mesopotamian mythology, the only human beings to attain (or retain) immortality are the sage and his wife who survive the Great Flood. But supernatural strength does not erase the distinction between the gods and even the greatest heroes among human beings. We will see how the distinction between the immortal gods and the inevitably mortal hero becomes a central concern in the stories told about ancient Mesopotamia's epic hero Gilgamesh.

In addition to their place in heaven (or under the earth, the domain of the gods of the Underworld), the gods also had at their command the mysterious power called the *me* (pronounced "may") that seems to have combined divine authority and supernatural power. The *me* in essence comprised everything that makes the gods superior to human beings. At the same time, the gods have specific divine gifts and powers that can be taken on, stripped off, or given away, much in the same way that clothing and jewelry can. In fact, these powers may be identified with the gods' garments, personal adornments, or armaments. In one story about the goddess Inanna she contrives to gain all of Enki's divine powers as gifts in the aftermath of a drinking contest and runs off with them before he can sober up. In another story, Inanna is progressively stripped of her garments and the divine powers they represent one by one as she descends into the Underworld. The gods' power is not only symbolized by the clothing, jewelry, and weapons they wear or carry, but the power also seems to reside within those things as well. The symbols of divine power are so potent that when they are taken up or surrendered, the power they represent is taken up or surrendered as well.

This seems be the case especially with the divine symbols of sovereign or royal power. In the Babylonian creation story, before Ea kills the elemental father god Apsu, he first removes Apsu's belt and crown and puts on Apsu's mantle of radiance, effectively stealing his royal power and authority. When Apsu's consort Tiamat takes a new lover after his death, she invests her lover with leadership over the army, puts him on a throne, and gives him the Tablet of Destinies which insures his word will be law. Later, after Marduk defeats this god in battle, he takes the Tablet of Destinies from him as both a sign and an embodiment of the sovereign power Marduk will wield over the other gods from then on. The divine power is seized when its symbol is seized.

The gods' divine power can also be augmented and protected by various means, especially by magic. The mighty warrior Marduk prepares for his battle with Tiamat not only with weapons, armor, and a chariot drawn by four monsters, but with a magic spell on his lips and an herb held in his hand to protect him against poison. A spell can also grant power to a god. When Tiamat makes her new consort leader of the army, she casts a magical spell for him that will make him greatest among the gods. This does not mean that the ancient Mesopotamians believed the gods' power depended on magic; it means that divine or sovereign power was aided and abetted by rituals, including the recitation of formulas and the performance of acts we might consider magical.

As was also the case in Egypt, spells and other aspects of "magic" were a practical and necessary part of many activities, both sacred and profane, and complemented other aspects of those activities. At the same time, spells also appear in stories about the gods in their more "magical" sense, as a means of affecting someone's feelings or actions. Before Ea strips Apsu of his symbols of sovereignty, for example, he uses a spell to put Apsu into a deep sleep. Obviously spells, even in these few examples, can be seen to serve different functions—providing protection, granting authority, causing sleep—that in ancient Mesopotamia were considered a normal part of the gods' divine power. As was also the case with Isis in Egypt, the divine power wielded by the gods and goddesses of Mesopotamia included the use of effective spells and other aspects of magic to do or achieve certain goals—but their power was not dependent on magic nor was their power itself merely magical.

We will probably not go too far wrong if we think of the Mesopotamian gods as much like the overlords in an ancient earthly political hierarchy. They rule over their subjects with a mixture of kindness and severity, and their power is thought of primarily in terms of military prowess and the authority to execute justice. They can gain power or lose it, and they wear or carry the outward symbols of power they possess. But unlike earthly overlords, the gods are endowed with a divine authority and power that elevates them far above the capabilities of human beings. The symbols of their power embody that power and confer it upon their owner. They have strength, knowledge, and skills that surpass those of human beings, but they are still recognizably human in their emotions, their desires, and their ambitions.

The model of a political hierarchy is particularly suitable for the Mesopotamian gods. There are clear distinctions of rank among them. One of these distinctions is between the gods who reside in the heavens and the gods who reside on earth and in the Underworld. In earlier sources the first group of gods is the Anunnaki, and the second is the Igigi. But in later sources—why and when the change came about is unknown—the Igigi are identified as heavenly gods and the Anunnaki as gods of the Underworld. Under the authority of the chief gods and the other leading gods of the Mesopotamian pantheon, the multitude of lesser gods fills ranks and offices like those of a royal administration. At the bottom of the hierarchy are those gods who are relegated to manual labor, whose ultimate rebellion against their lot led to the creation of human beings to assume their more arduous tasks.

At the same time, although the Mesopotamian pantheon is clearly hierarchical, it is difficult to arrange it in a systematic way. As was the case in Egypt, the Mesopotamians had major and minor gods, and were most likely to worship the gods who had some sort of direct influence over their daily lives. But apparently they were not concerned about assigning gods (other than their chief gods) specific places in the divine hierarchy. The other gods each played their part in divine governance, but their relative rank was of little concern to the Mesopotamians.

The Mesopotamian Pantheon

The earliest surviving list of Mesopotamian gods was compiled around 2600 BCE. It lists 560 gods by their Sumerian names, with the chief gods listed first: An, Enlil, Inanna, Enki, Nanna, and Utu. An (Akkadian, Anu), "Sky," as his name suggests, was god of the sky. An was the chief god in the Mesopotamian pantheon until he was later displaced by the chief gods of Asshur and Babylon when those cities became dominant over the rest of Mesopotamia. An was identified with and inhabited the highest of the three heavens. Again, location is an indication of superiority. An lived far above the other gods and so was superior to them just as they were superior to human beings. An's original consort was Urash, the earth goddess, although later it was Ki, whose name also means "Earth." In either case, An and his consort form an elemental couple of sky and earth, like Nut and Geb in Egypt. But in this case, the marital intercourse between An and his consort does not produce divine offspring. Instead their sexual activity produces abundant vegetation on earth. The fertility overtones of the union of sky and earth are obvious, as the rain that falls from the sky enables the fertile earth to bring forth crops and other vegetation.

Enlil (Akkadian, Ellil, "Lord Lil"), "Wind," was the moist wind. Enlil was the chief god of Sumer, the god who ruled over human affairs and carried the Tablet of Destinies that dictated the course of human and world history. Enlil was among the greatest gods and was honored with titles that exalted him over other gods, either as their ruler or as the source of their being. His consort was Ninlil ("Lady Lil"), whose primary identity, as her name indicates, was as the consort of Enlil. In some sources this goddess was originally named Sud. The children of Enlil and Ninlil included the gods Ishkur, Nergal, Ninurta, Urash (not to be confused with the goddess of the same name), Nanna, and the goddess Inanna. In other sources these gods have other parents, and Nergal in particular is sometimes designated the son of Inanna rather than her brother. Like other members of the older generation of gods, Enlil was later superceded by other, younger gods as their patron cities or peoples became dominant.

Inanna (Akkadian, Ishtar), "Lady of Heaven," was originally a fertility goddess who gathered a wide range of associations and powers, and eventually became a dominant goddess styled "Queen of Heaven and Earth." Inanna's consort was Dumuzi, a pastoral god identified with bountiful clusters of dates. All Inanna's divine attributes derived in some way from her primary association with fertility. We will consider the evolution of Inanna's divine character, as well as several of the stories about her, in some depth later.

Enki (Akkadian, Ea), "Manager of the Soil," was god of sweet (as opposed to salt) water, the water that makes agriculture and human life possible. He was usually portrayed as humanity's primary benefactor among the gods, the source of knowledge, especially knowledge of magic. Enki was the god of the fresh water under the earth that produced springs and rivers. It was the effective management of these sources of fresh water through man-made canals and irrigation that made life in ancient Mesopotamia possible. Enki's wife was Damgalnuna or Damkina. Together they were the parents of Marduk, the chief god of Babylon, as well as the ancient human sage Adapa of the city of Eridu, who inadvertently fated human beings to die.

Nanna or Nanna-Suen (Akkadian, Sin) was god of the moon. Nanna was associated with the passing of time as the guardian of the night. Mesopotamians followed a lunar calendar, so the appearance of Nanna as the moon waxed and waned was the primary means of marking the passing of the months and years. Nanna sailed across the sky each night in a bark, what human beings recognized as the crescent moon. His consort was the goddess Ningal. Together they were the parents of Utu, the sun god, and in some traditions they were also the parents of Inanna.

Utu (Akkadian, Shamash), "Sun," drove his chariot across the sky daily and, like the Egyptian sun god Ra, traveled through the Underworld each night to return to the east. Part way along his nightly path through the Underworld was the garden of the sun god, with trees that bore gems like fruit. Because he cast light on the earth and made everything visible, Utu was also a god of truth and justice who was involved in human affairs, generally as a benefactor. Utu's consort was Sherida (Akkadian, Aya), the goddess of light. Sherida was also a goddess of fertility and sexual love, perhaps because of the inherent beauty of light, or because of the role the light of the sun plays in making the earth fertile. The children of Utu and Sherida were the goddess Kittu ("Truth") and the god Misharu ("Justice").

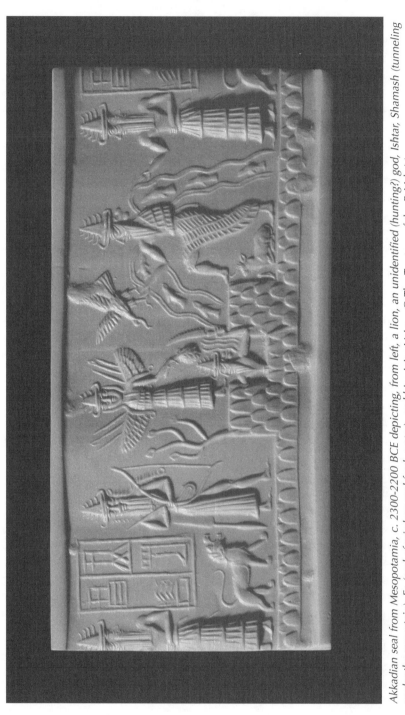

Akkadian seal from Mesopotamia, c. 2300–2200 BCE depicting, from left, a lion, an unidentified (hunting?) god, Ishtar, Shamash (tunneling under the mountain), Ea (god of wisdom and fresh water), and his vizier Usimu. © The Trustees of the British Museum.

Other gods of the cosmic and political order were also prominent in the Mesopotamian pantheon. Ishkur was a Sumerian god of storms, hail, and lightning. In his Akkadian form as Adad, he was also a more benevolent god of rain and mountain streams. The goddess Ninmah was said to be a consort of Enki. She was midwife to the mother goddess Nammu during the creation of humanity, and the goddess who protected women in childbirth. She had a contentious relationship with Enki because the god had raped their daughter and other female members of his family. In one story, Enki and Ninmah had a drunken contest to determine which one could devise a creature that the other could not give either a good or bad destiny. Enki finally devised a creature so utterly wretched that it could not be given a good destiny, and would not be the worse for a bad destiny. As a result Enki won the contest, much to Ninmah's chagrin. The Mesopotamians were among the first people to brew beer, and their gods apparently also enjoyed its intoxicating effects.

Ninurta was the son of Enki and Ninmah. Ninurta had a double nature as both a god of war and a god of agriculture. Ninurta taught farmers how to prepare and cultivate the earth to ensure plentiful harvests and he kept a watchful eye on their activities throughout the agricultural year. Ninurta also appears as a defender and champion of the gods, fighting both against the enemies of Sumer and the supernatural beings that threatened the gods and the well-being of the cosmos. In one story recounted in the Sumerian poem "Lugale," Ninurta fought against the demon Asag, a composite monster that caused disease and made fish boil in the rivers. Ninurta overcame Asag as well as a horde of stone warriors who had fought against Ninurta alongside Asag. To celebrate his victory Ninurta built a mountain with the corpses of the stone warriors, thereby enhancing the flow of water into the Tigris and Euphrates. He also gave his mother Ninmah a new name, Ninhursaga, "Lady of the Mountains." As Ninhursaga, the goddess was the mother of eight gods and goddesses that bestowed benefits on humanity.

The god Nergal and his consort Ereshkigal were the deities of the Underworld, rulers and guardians over the realm of the dead. Nergal was closely associated with two similar gods, Erra and Lugal-irra. He was also associated with deadly forces that harm humanity, including plagues and forest fires. Ereshkigal ("Lady of the Great Earth") was a sister of Inanna ("Lady of Heaven"). She initially ruled alone over the Underworld. Her first husband was a god named Gugal-ana, "canal inspector of An." He may have been equivalent to the god Ennugi, one of the sons of Enlil. Gugal-ana died, leaving Ereshkigal a widow. When Inanna descends to the Underworld, she disguises her true intention by claiming she has come to attend the funeral rites for Gugal-ana. We will consider stories about Inanna's descent and Nergal's conquest of the Underworld and his subsequent marriage to Ereshkigal in detail later.

Two of the chief gods of Mesopotamia were originally the patron gods of cities that gained preeminence over the rest of the territory through conquest. Since these gods were able to deliver all of Mesopotamia into the hands of the kings who worshipped them, they were obviously more powerful than the other gods whose worshippers were conquered. More important, the kings who served them were able to exalt them over the other gods and grant them priority in worship and divine honor. Asshur, the war god of Assyria, was identified with the city that bore his name and gained ascendancy as a result of Assyria's rise to power in the ninth century BCE. The Assyrians identified Asshur with other chief gods, including the Babylonian Marduk, and with the primordial creator god Anshar. Asshur was the protector of the Assyrian people and ruled over them through their king as his viceroy, but otherwise Asshur's character is fairly indistinct.

Marduk, the patron god of Babylon, became the head of the Mesopotamian pantheon during the period of the Neo-Babylonian expansion and empire under the Chaldeans. Marduk is attested as early as the Third Dynasty of Ur as the patron god of Babylon and later was also known by his title Bel, "Lord." We may compare this title to the name of Baal ("Lord"), a chief god of Syria–Palestine. As Babylonian power increased, Marduk became more important, assuming several attributes of both An and Enlil. As we will see, in the Babylonian creation story *Enuma elish,* Marduk is made king of the gods of Mesopotamia by acclamation, and also is responsible for the creation of the inhabited world. In an appendix to the creation story, "The Fifty Names of Marduk," the names of several other gods are attributed to Marduk, apparently making those gods essentially no more than aspects of the chief god. At the same time, however, as far as we can determine Marduk was never worshipped to the exclusion of other gods or goddesses.

The Accumulation of Divine Attributes: Inanna

The evolution of the Mesopotamian fertility goddess Inanna provides an example of how a god could grow in importance by a gradual accumulation of titles and powers related—sometimes only tangentially—to the god's original identity. Inanna was worshipped in Sumer for three thousand years, from at least the beginning of its civilization around 4000 BCE to around 1000 BCE. Under her Akkadian name Ishtar the goddess was worshipped in Babylon for another thousand years beyond that, until the dawn of the Common Era.

The earliest references to Inanna pair her with her consort Dumuzi, whose name means "the faithful son." Dumuzi is a pastoral god who is usually represented as a shepherd. As a god of the open countryside, Dumuzi was often in conflict with Enkimdu, a god of canals and irrigated land, who was a patron of farmers. In association with Inanna, Dumuzi represented the large ripe clusters of dates that hung from the date palm. In this aspect Dumuzi bore the title Ama-ushumgal-anna, "the one great source of the date clusters." Inanna in turn was identified with the storehouse where the date harvest was kept, and so also with the idea of material abundance and plentiful yields of produce. Inanna was also associated more generally with the fertile earth and its mysterious powers of generation. Inanna's presence brought life and vitality to human beings and animals. She provoked and inspired them to engage in sexual intercourse, and made the plants of the earth plentiful and fruitful.

The beneficial power of fertility inspired by Inanna and Dumuzi was celebrated in an annual rite of sacred marriage. Although the details are not clear, the ritual apparently involved sexual intercourse between the priestess of Inanna and the king of the city, probably in Inanna's temple. The sacred marriage (known technically by the Greek term *hieros gamos*) was essentially a symbolic ritual act. Sexual intercourse between the priestess and the king imitated but also evoked the intercourse between Inanna and Dumuzi as an earthly reenactment of a timeless event. The intention of the ritual was to ensure the fertility of both the land and the animals within the kingdom. It is worth noting that this was not a private act but a public religious ritual, a means of assuring the people that the gods of fertility would continue to provide for their needs.

As this ritual indicates, Inanna's association with fertility in connection with Dumuzi was expressed primarily in terms of sexual activity and active sexuality. In literature devoted to the goddess, Inanna openly expresses her eagerness for sex, especially with Dumuzi, and their sexual activity always retains at least vestiges of ideas and language associated with fertility. The poetry about Inanna and Dumuzi is heavily and frankly erotic. In one extant hymn, "The Courtship of Inanna and Dumuzi," Dumuzi's role of shepherd is clear as she asks him to give her fresh goat milk to drink and to "fill my holy churn with honey cheese" (Wolkstein and Kramer, 39). In the same poem, Inanna begs Dumuzi to plow her vulva just as the farmer plows the fertile earth, a somewhat unexpected image for the pastoral god who was by his nature opposed to agriculture. But it becomes apparent that the intercourse between Inanna and Dumuzi embraces all aspects of fertility and generates all forms of produce, despite Dumuzi's specific divine identity. So it appears that

Inanna's role as the instigator of fertility is dominant and the specific role of Dumuzi as her consort becomes overshadowed, especially since the goddess retains her associations with fertility even when seeking or engaged in sexual intercourse with lovers other than Dumuzi.

But Inanna's sexuality also has overtones of danger. She is sexually voracious, and this poses a threat to her various lovers. At the conclusion of "The Courtship of Inanna and Dumuzi," for example, after the couple have had intercourse fifty times, an exhausted Dumuzi pleads, "Set me free, my sister, set me free" (Wolkstein and Kramer, 48). But Inanna is also dangerous because she often dismisses her lovers by ruining them. In the *Epic of Gilgamesh*, Gilgamesh spurns Ishtar's advances and lists the various lovers she has had and the tragic fates that have befallen them after she tired of them. She broke the wing of the *allallu*-bird, she turned her herdsman lover into a wolf, and she sentenced the horse to perpetual servitude under human masters. Even Dumuzi suffered her wrath, as we will see, and as a result was required to spend half of each year in the darkness of the Mesopotamian Underworld.

Inanna is connected with all the different aspects of human sexuality, such as the female beauty that inspires sexual desire in men and the skills associated with its enjoyment. The goddess is noted for her own beauty but more especially for the beauty of her robes and adornments. Not only are they beautiful, but like other symbols of divine characteristics they represent and even embody different aspects of her godly power. Inanna is associated with the arts and the amatory skills practiced by courtesans, but even more with the sexual pleasure they provide. Inanna is a goddess of prostitutes and is identified with the evening star that illuminates their nightly activities. That "star" even today retains its sexual connotations as the planet Venus, named for the Roman goddess of erotic love. Inanna is sometimes depicted as a prostitute herself, soliciting men in the alehouse or calling to them from a bedroom window overlooking the street, inviting them to come in and share the delights of her bed.

Inanna's many different associations with sexual desire arise from the fact that she essentially *is* sexual desire in all its forms, and without her there cannot be human or animal procreation, or the continuation of human or animal life. If Inanna is sometimes threatening and predatory that is because the power of sexual desire can be seen as a threat to civilized life, as a force of deep, churning emotion that seems to lie beyond human control. Ancient civilizations found it necessary to domesticate erotic desire through the institution of marriage, but even marriage, as human beings throughout the ages have come to understand, cannot contain the unruly power of sexuality Inanna represents.

Inanna is restless and impetuous, and this makes her dangerous and un-predictable. Her deep emotions are expressed through natural phenomena such as lightning, flood, storm, and wind—all sudden, violent eruptions of nature that have no discernible cause. Inanna also loved the heat of battle in war. Unlike the Greek goddess Athena, Inanna did not love war as a contest of wits, a strategic engagement between armies, or for the military skill or cunning displayed by the warriors. Inanna was not even particularly concerned with war as a means of conquest or exacting divine vengeance on humanity. Instead Inanna loved war for the deep passions—anger, hate, fear, revenge—war provokes. The Sumerians called battle "the dance of Inanna." They believed she loved the exhilaration of combat and the shedding of blood. She could be found in the thick of the fighting, encouraging the warriors to attack and kill the enemy, goading stragglers to close with the enemy, and swooping down on the unfortunate warriors who tried to flee the carnage.

But Inanna has another important identity that may seem to stand in contrast to her associations with sexuality, war, and natural disasters. Inanna is also "Queen of Heaven and Earth," the preeminent goddess in the Mesopotamian pantheon. In this role Inanna is depicted as the ruler of the gods in heaven and the director of human affairs on earth, with an interest in the welfare of her people that stood in tension with her more volatile characteristics. But her role as Queen of Heaven and Earth also derived from her primary identity as a goddess of fertility. Inanna's association with the cycle of fertility and heavenly bodies such as the evening star gave her power to regulate the movements of the planets and stars that control the cycles that govern all life on earth. In this more benevolent connection Inanna is also the guardian of the social order, including kingship and culture, as well as the overseer of judgment in legal matters.

Inanna's rise to power was presented in mythic terms in a story that reveals both her cleverness and her ruthlessness. In the story Inanna one day put on all her adornments and her robes of power—the source of her dazzling beauty as well as her divine sovereignty—and went to visit Enki, the god of wisdom. Enki welcomed her into his house. The two talked and began to drink strong beer together, and before long they were in a drinking bout, matching each other drink for drink—but only Enki got drunk. Soon Enki began trying to impress Inanna by offering her various gifts, the powers he used to rule over creation. Once he'd offered all his powers to her, Inanna took them and left. Once Enki was sober again he tried to regain his divine powers from Inanna. But the goddess refused to return them and instead taunted him with a song praising herself and the wonderful gifts she had received from him. This story may remind us of how Isis gained magical power from an aged Ra by employing another kind of trickery. On the one hand, these seem to be traditional stories about old men who foolishly allow themselves to be taken advantage of by attractive young women. On the other, these stories seem to argue that the only way a female might wield power is if she has misappropriated it from its genuine, male source. One of the things that makes Inanna (like Isis) threatening is her willingness to appropriate male prerogatives and male power and to use them for her own ends, even against the wishes of the male gods. In her hands male power is supplemented by female cunning and becomes that much more powerful. Mesopotamians were wary of the power of the gods that might lash out at them in unexpected and violent ways, but they believed even the other gods feared Inanna.

It should be clear by now why one of Inanna's traditional epithets is "lady of myriad offices." But all the different aspects of Inanna's divine nature are based on a few fundamental characteristics. We might best identify Inanna with the force and energy of life, an energy that is sometimes calm and predictable but at other times chaotic and frightening. Inanna's role as Queen of Heaven and Earth appears to arise at least in part from the recognition that she embodies in herself the full range of human activity, both constructive and destructive, and lifts them into the realm of the divine.

Mesopotamian Stories of Creation

The origins of the gods, the relationships among them, and the relationship between the gods and their creation, are all subjects of the Mesopotamian cosmogonies. Cosmogony, as we've seen, considers the origins of all things in mythic terms, that is, in terms of how the gods are involved in bringing the cosmos and all it contains into being. This means that cosmogony is concerned not just with *how* creation comes about but also, and more centrally, *why* the cosmos is created and *who* among the gods (or other beings) is responsible for its origins.

As we have seen, most sorts of creation stories assume some form of existence before the creative action begins. Creation by making, creation by combat, and creation by sexual intercourse require the presence of at least one god and something else (the potential material for making the world, or a monster to be defeated, or a god or goddess to serve as a partner in sexual intercourse). Most often what exists before creation is some sort of undifferentiated matter from which the gods somehow emerge. In Egyptian mythology, this undifferentiated matter was the sea of Nun. In Mesopotamian mythology the undifferentiated matter is contained in the sea of chaos that fills the unlimited depths, the Apsu. But here—unlike in Egypt—the force of chaos is personified in elemental gods who will become the stuff from which the cosmos and all it contains will be made.

The Babylonian creation story *Enuma elish* (Akkadian, "When above," the first words of the story) was probably composed around the twelfth century BCE. The date of its composition remains open, but in any event the poem no doubt existed and evolved for centuries before it achieved the form in which it was ultimately written down. The divine hero of the poem is Marduk, the chief god of Babylon, and the climax of the poem is the construction of the city of Babylon as his royal home. There is some question whether Marduk was the original hero of the poem or if the hero was originally an Amorite god Marduk later displaced. If that were the case the poem would reflect an origin among the Semitic ancestors of the Akkadians, and there could conceivably be ties to creation myths found in Syria–Palestine.

As we have seen, it is common for a god to gain the attributes, titles, and even names of another, and this is certainly true of Marduk during the process that led to him becoming the chief god of Babylon. In the second part of the poem listing the fifty names of Marduk, the last name given him is *Bel Matati*, "Lord of the World." Since this is also a title of Enlil, this may indicate Enlil was the original hero of the creation story. The poem in its current form was probably composed to be performed during the New Year's festival celebrated during the first days of the month of Nisan at the beginning of spring. This was when the world was renewed, an appropriate time to celebrate Marduk's victory over the gods of chaos and the establishment of the divine order that also regulated the succession of the seasons.

The drama of *Enuma elish* begins with three uncreated elemental beings, the primordial god Apsu ("Depths"), his divine consort Tiamat ("Waters"), and Apsu's vizier and counselor Mummu. Apsu is the depthless abyss that contains the underground seas that embody chaos. But he also represents the principle of separation, the marking off and distinction of one thing from another. Although Apsu has divine power, his energy is dissipated in unfocused activity and does nothing—it has no intention and no goal. In the poem, Apsu's unfocused activity is likened to sleep, the unconscious expenditure of minimal energy without purpose. Apsu's consort Tiamat is the mass of waters. She is both the bitter sea waters that support the earth from below and the heavenly waters that threaten humanity in the form of storms and floods. Tiamat "fills" Apsu and is formless in the same way water is. Like Apsu, Tiamat exerts unfocused energy without purpose. Tiamat too wishes to sleep, but unlike Apsu she is dangerous when she is roused; then her chaotic forces break out into blind, violent turmoil, like a sudden storm at sea. The third primordial being, Mummu ("Maker"), is subordinate to Apsu and Tiamat and abets their lethargy. He is characterized as their "vizier," their chief attendant and functionary who carries out their wishes. In that respect, Mummu seems to represent the forces that oppose the expenditure of creative energy in focused activity. We might best characterize him as a principle of entropy.

Creation initially proceeds without intention or purpose as Apsu and Tiamat sleep. Without intention, different forces and elements within the waters of the depths mingle together to create new substantial cosmic elements and the gods associated with them. First the sweet water of the abyss mingles with the bitter water of the seas, creating the gods Lahmu and Lahamu. Both names mean "silt" and their creation is a mythic version of a natural process: Freshwater rivers create silt where they enter salt water seas or oceans. Next Anshar and Kishar, the two horizons, are created when they are separated by the birth of Anu, "Sky," whose wide expanse pushes them apart. Anu in turn engenders Ea-Nudimmud, god of the sweet waters of the earth and of wisdom.

But the divine energy and self-assertion that is typical of the newly created gods cannot be contained. The new gods, unlike their parents, are active, full of dynamic energy as the expression of their divine power. The gods soon disagree with each other and come into conflict, disrupting their parents' sleep. They create an uproar in Tiamat's belly, the womb that has given them birth, and the noise they make keeps Apsu awake. So Apsu and Mummu together over Tiamat's motherly objections decide to kill the gods, so they may again have peace and return to their slumbers. But the gods learn of their plan and wise Ea thwarts them by casting a spell on Apsu, putting him into a deep sleep. Ea kills Apsu and steals his crown, and then binds Mummu and imprisons him in the depths. Ea and his consort Damkina establish their thrones at the top of the depths (Apsu), and it is in the depths that new gods are born.

The poem next describes the birth of the son of Ea and Damkina, Marduk, the great god who will become the hero of the story of creation. Marduk is created far superior to all the other gods. The poem describes his divinity in terms of multiples to indicate how far he surpasses other gods. He is endowed with a double portion of divinity, his height is enormous, he has four eyes and four ears, and is clothed in the mantle—the *me* or divine power—of ten gods. The birth of Marduk stirs up Tiamat and apparently prompts a group of the lesser gods to prod her into action against Anu and Ea, because Marduk by his very existence makes sleep impossible. These lesser gods seem to share Apsu's and Tiamat's preference for unconscious and unfocused activity, perhaps indicating they are gods of chaos. By contrast, the other gods, especially

Marduk, represent the divine activity and especially the divine principle of order that will ultimately triumph and make the created world possible.

Stirred to action and revenge for the death of Apsu, Tiamat takes a new husband, Qingu, a god called "the clumsy laborer." Tiamat makes Qingu general over an army of monsters she has created to fight the gods, who still reside in Apsu. She also gives Qingu the Tablet of Destinies, the ultimate token of his divine authority. Anshar, father of the gods, apparently tells the other gods about Tiamat's army of gods and monsters, and he instructs Ea to finish what he started when he killed Apsu. But Ea turns back after seeing Tiamat's army, since he knows he is not powerful enough to defeat her. Anshar next sends Anu to placate Tiamat, but he too turns back in fear of Tiamat and her army. Finally Anshar calls the gods into council to find another god to deal with Tiamat, and Ea summons Marduk to fight as the gods' champion. Marduk accepts on the condition that all the gods will acknowledge him as their king. Anshar makes sure all the gods are informed of the situation— apparently some were not even aware of the threat from Tiamat and her army—and they all agree to accept Marduk as their champion and their king. The assembled gods set up a royal throne for Marduk, and together hail him and proclaim, "Marduk is king!"

Marduk makes careful preparations before setting out to find Tiamat to fight and destroy her. Marduk arms himself with bow and arrow, a mace and net, as well as natural forces, the four winds and lightning. He mounts a chariot pulled by four monsters, carries a healing plant, and has a magic spell ready to augment his power. Marduk and Tiamat meet and exchange taunts before engaging in single combat. When Tiamat opens her mouth to devour Marduk, the tempest wind roars into her body and blows her up like a balloon while Marduk shoots an arrow into her belly. The lesser gods in Tiamat's army fly away in a panic and Marduk quickly subdues them. He places Tiamat's monsters in chains, and binds her consort Qingu, taking from him the Tablet of Destinies. Finally, Marduk smashes Tiamat's head and splits her body in two, using half to form the firmament of the heavens and the other half to form the dry earth. So the forces of chaos, Apsu, Tiamat, and Mummu become part of the order of creation, set into their proper places in the cosmos by Marduk's creative power.

To finish off the work of creation, Marduk also brings order to the divine world. He builds temples and cult centers on earth, and assigns the gods their places in the firmament, thereby creating the calendar and establishing the orderly passage of time. All the gods pay homage to Marduk, who puts on his kingly robes, fastens the Tablet of Destinies to his chest, and assumes his entire kingly array. To relieve the lesser gods of manual labor, Marduk kills his captive Qingu and uses a clot of his blood to create humanity, whose role is to work hard and serve the gods. Finally, Marduk builds the city of Babylon as his dwelling place and the crown of his work of creation, after he has brought peace and order to all parts and aspects of the cosmos. The poem closes with a recitation and explanation of the fifty names of Marduk, an act of homage to the power of Marduk as king of the gods.

This story, or some earlier version of it, was the Mesopotamians' explanation of the origins of all things, the cosmos and the gods that rule over it. But mythic creation stories, of course, are not just about the origins of gods and the cosmos, but more broadly about how things got to be the way they are now. "How things are now" involves preeminently the problem of humanity's status before the gods and the tribulations of human existence in general. Mesopotamian mythology gives considerable attention to the human situation, but most of the stories of creation do not deal with it directly. It almost seems as if human beings are of too little importance to the gods for them to devote much divine energy to them. Instead, Mesopotamian mythology traces the origins of the human situation back to choices made by primeval human beings who were in some way superior to other people and privileged by the gods. But even so the human situation arises not only from their choices in the earliest ages, but also from the essential nature of humanity itself.

Enuma elish includes an account of the creation of human beings from the blood of Qingu, a rebellious god. This says something about the nature of human beings, but whatever it says is only implicit and does not really explain the human situation. Such an explanation may be found instead in the story of Adapa. The story is preserved in two versions, one found in Egypt dating to the fifteenth or fourteenth century BCE, and the other in Asshur, the capital of Assyria, dating to the late second millennium BCE. Both versions are fragmentary, but enough of the text survives to provide us with the main points of the story.

Adapa of Eridu was one of seven sages sent to humanity by the god Ea before the Flood. Ea, in keeping with his role as humanity's benefactor, sent the seven sages to teach human beings the skills necessary for civilized life. As a sage, Adapa is clever and "super wise" (*atrahasis*). Adapa was also a priest of Ea in Eridu, traditionally believed to be the oldest city in Mesopotamia. As a priest, it was Adapa's job to provide offerings for the god, to conduct rituals in Ea's temple, and to teach people the proper way to honor and worship the gods.

Apparently one of Adapa's duties is catching fish as offerings for the god. One day while he is fishing, Adapa is thwarted in some way by the South

Wind (the relevant text is missing). In retaliation he breaks the South Wind's wing, effectively preventing her from blowing. When Ea finds out what Adapa has done, he realizes Adapa's action is an offense against the gods. Ea summons Adapa and advises him to appear before Anu, king of the gods, to receive forgiveness for what he has done.

But before he appears before the gods, Adapa must know how to behave in the gods' presence. Ea tells him how to conduct himself in Anu's court if he wants to avoid further offense. But Ea also tells him how to protect himself from any harm Anu may wish to do to him. Ea gives Adapa the proper replies to the questions Anu will ask him and tells him how to act in such a way as to win Anu's favor. But Ea also warns Adapa not to eat the Bread of Death or to drink the Water of Death Anu will offer him.

When Adapa appears in Anu's heavenly court the gods Dumuzi and Gizzada intercede with Anu on his behalf. Adapa refuses the bread and water Anu offers him, just as Ea instructed him. But it turns out that what Anu offered to him is in fact the Bread and Water of Life (i.e., of immortality). When Adapa refuses them, Anu send Adapa back to earth. Because of his refusal, human beings lose their chance at immortality and all humanity is doomed to die.

The key to the story appears to be a play on the words "bread of heaven" (*shamuti*) and "bread of death" (*sha muti*). But it is not clear whether Ea intended to deceive Adapa or not, or whether he meant to deprive humanity of immortality. The story also involves rules for giving and accepting hospitality, with incidental information about the appropriate garb and behavior for those mourning the dead, since it is about the occasion that made death—and mourning—inevitable. We will find a somewhat different explanation for the human situation later in the story of Atrahasis, whose name—"Super Sage"—suggests a close association with the primeval wise man Adapa.

There are several themes at work in both *Enuma elish* and *Adapa*, and these have as much to say about Mesopotamian ideas about how the world works as do the events of the stories. As was the case in Egyptian cosmogonies, in *Enuma elish* the order and harmony that reign over creation are seen as the work of the gods fighting against and prevailing over the forces of disorder. What sets the younger gods apart from the older gods associated with the chaos that reigned before creation is specifically their dynamic energy focused in divine activity. In *Enuma elish* chaos is not a hostile force *per se*; it is instead an anticreative force, power expended aimlessly and without effect. Like entropy it moves toward dissolution and destruction unless it is opposed by the power of divine energy and order. Marduk, as the champion of the younger gods, represents focused divine energy in its most powerful form, which enables him to overcome chaos and bring creation into being. In the human world, the anticreative force of chaos might be identified with the destructive forces of nature as they were known in Mesopotamia, including flood, wind, and scorching heat. Or it might be associated with human threats of war, invasion, and conquest, all forces that threatened the worldly order human beings work to create.

In *Enuma elish* human beings are almost an afterthought in the work of creation, and they are created specifically to labor and serve the gods, reflecting their origins in a clot of blood taken from the rebellious god Qingu. But at the same time, Marduk as a creator god in part represents the power of civilization, itself the result of human activity and creative reason. As Marduk must overcome the forces of chaos to create, so human beings must work against the power of chaos—nature's irrational power as it was known in Mesopotamia, human conflict, and opposition—to build a city that was a monument to human achievement and aspiration. As patron god of the capital Babylon, Marduk was allied with its king who also exerted power on earth, in the form of order, justice, and peace. This is an apparent paradox: Marduk is king of the gods but also a champion of the results of human activity while human beings themselves have little or no status in the eyes of the gods.

The paradox is resolved at the mythic level, since in *Enuma elish* it is in fact Marduk himself who builds Babylon as his habitation, and not human beings. In other words, what the poet sees as the premier city of the world, the center of Mesopotamian civilization, is something that Marduk himself made in his own honor and for his own enjoyment. In the same way, any notable human achievements were likely to be attributed to the work either of the gods or of supernaturally gifted human beings, either heroes or sages. So there is the vast mass of humanity and far above them the gods, and in between are a few supernaturally gifted human beings who act as agents of the gods in some capacity and as a result stand above the rest of humanity. This idea is in keeping with the spatial meanings of *dingir* in Sumerian and *ilu* in Akkadian. Both imply the primary divine attribute is any sort of superiority over the human, including the superhuman ability of a hero or the superhuman wisdom of a sage.

In the story of Adapa, even the wisest human sage is somehow led astray by the explicit directions of a god, with the result that all humanity must face death and the shadowy existence of the Underworld. Through no fault of their own, all human beings are condemned to death. Both *Enuma elish* and the story of Adapa extol the greatness and incomparability of the gods and their mighty deeds of power, but these works also place humanity at the very bottom of the cosmic hierarchy, at the mercy of the gods who made them.

These creation stories reveal the Mesopotamians' uneasiness in the face of the gods' power, similar to the uneasiness a person might feel about the vast power of an absolute but unpredictable king. Certainly the people of Mesopotamia honored and worshipped their gods with the expectation that the gods would listen to their requests and bless their endeavors. But there is a strong sense in the surviving literature that they did so with a certain amount of fear and trepidation. They were at the gods' command and under their control, and the ways of the gods were not only mysterious but often arbitrary. Even in their acts of worship, the Mesopotamians seem always to have harbored both a fear of the gods and some doubt that the gods would in fact deal kindly with their human subjects.

CHAPTER EIGHT

Mesopotamia: The World of Kings and Heroes

Kings and Heroes in Mesopotamia

There were significant differences between the historical experiences of ancient Egypt and the historical experiences of ancient Mesopotamia, and these differences are reflected in their political cultures. The histories of both nations were full of internal and external conflicts, and both were ruled by a succession of dynasties interspersed with periods of civil unrest. But there is no doubt that Egyptian culture was much more homogeneous than Mesopotamian culture. Although Egypt was sometimes ruled by dynasties whose kings came from Libya, Nubia, or Syria–Palestine, these dynasties were generally short-lived and gained political legitimacy by assimilating the prevailing traditions of Egyptian kingship—the titles, symbols, and religious ideas that had been associated with the king since the earliest days of the union of the Two Lands. Mesopotamia, on the other hand, was ruled by different peoples throughout its long history. The dominant languages in Mesopotamia over the centuries were first Sumerian, then Akkadian, and finally Aramaic, representing the political and cultural influence of successive ruling peoples. All the different groups that came to power over Mesopotamia—Sumerians, Akkadians, Babylonians, Kassites, Assyrians, Chaldeans—identified themselves with the heritage of the Mesopotamian cultures that had preceded them, but most of these groups also introduced at the same time significant changes and modifications to that heritage.

These changes, of course, extended into religious culture as new peoples adapted the practices and mythology of earlier Mesopotamian religious traditions to suit their own needs, interests, and theological ideas. We have already seen evidence of these changes in the two names, Sumerian and Akkadian, by which most of the gods of ancient Mesopotamia were known. More significantly, stories about the gods evolved as new gods were incorporated into them and new stories were created to explain how the new gods stood in relation to older ones—for example, how Marduk stood in relation to Anu and Enlil as king over the gods, or how Nergal stood in relation to Ereshkigal as ruler over the realm of the dead. The evolution of Mesopotamian religious culture was determined much more by the dominance of a succession of different ethnic and regional dynasties than it was by any king's personal preference for a patron god or the influence of a body of priests, both major determinants for religious development in Egypt. The influence of different peoples and dynasties on the evolution of Mesopotamian religious culture is evident in the monuments, buildings, and art of ancient Mesopotamia as well as in its literary tradition.

The reality of continual warfare and the awareness of threatening external forces may also have contributed to the Mesopotamian ideal of the hero. The hero is a man endowed by the gods with exceptional strength, skill, and intelligence who uses these gifts to battle against enemies who would disrupt the peace and well-being of civilized humanity. Like the vigilante, the hero is not bound by the rules and restrictions of the civilization he defends, and he is rarely entirely at home in the civilized world. But the hero represents everything that makes civilization possible. For this reason, the hero as well as the king embodies and displays the virtues the Mesopotamians associated with the job of defending, leading, and governing the nation. The king was a focus of public veneration and as such played an important role in Mesopotamian religion, but the hero was the focus of legends and played an important role in the shaping not only of Mesopotamian cultural identity but of Western literature as well.

The Place of the King in Mesopotamian Culture

Although there were originally different forms of leadership in Mesopotamian city-states, military kingship ultimately became the dominant form of government. The king's primary responsibility was to command the nation's armies in the field during campaigns of conquest as well as defensive wars. To a large extent the king's legitimacy as monarch was based on his military prowess. But in addition to his responsibilities as commander and chief strategist, the king oversaw all aspects of government. Most governmental functions were in fact directly supervised by chief ministers under the king's authority. These ministers resided in the royal palace complex and each con-trolled an extensive bureaucracy. They were responsible to the king, and the king in turn was responsible for ensuring they fulfilled their duties properly.

Like an ancient temple complex, the royal palace complex included the means for supplying all the workers and material support necessary for its daily functioning. The palace was both the center of government, the residence, and workplace for myriads of state officials of different ranks. The palace in-cluded facilities for the king's court, including rooms of state such as a throne room and audience chamber. But there were also other, smaller courts for the crown prince, the queen mother, and other members of the royal family who wielded political or administrative power in their own rights. At the opposite end of the social ladder, the palace complex included housing for the king's household servants, workshops and housing for craftsmen, and extensive fa-cilities devoted to storing and preparing food to feed them all.

The king would keep a watchful eye on all the functions and expenditures of his government, and his was the final voice of authority in all matters of governance. As king he was responsible for ensuring the welfare of the land and all his subjects. This meant first that he was to ensure external and in-ternal security. But the king was also expected to ensure the fertility and pro-ductivity of the land through irrigation projects. He was obliged to provide for his people's material needs and to protect those who had no other means of protection. The king was the chief judicial official, responsible for pro-moting justice and ensuring the proper administration of law within his realm. The primary institutions of justice in Mesopotamia were found in the city, where crimes were punished, legal decisions rendered, births recorded, disputes adjudicated, and fines and penalties exacted according to the judg-ments made. But once decisions had been made at the local level, appeals could be made to the king. The king would hear cases brought to him, and he had the power to grant clemency or pardon if he felt a situation called for it. The king was also the chief lawgiver. He would issue royal edicts to cover specific situations that might arise during his reign, and collect and dissemi-nate law codes. Mesopotamian law codes, including the best known, the Code of Hammurabi, primarily reiterated existing laws while instituting some new ones. In this way the legal tradition was both preserved and ac-commodated to new circumstances.

The King and His Relationship to the Gods

The concept of kingship as it developed in ancient Mesopotamia was always based on the king's close relationship with the gods and the idea that he served as the gods' viceroy on earth. The king was also a central figure in Mesopotamian religious culture as both patron and chief worshipper. Mesopotamian kings built new temples and renovated existing temples as a means of ensuring the goodwill of the gods the temples honored. Kings also provided generously for the performance of religious rituals and the support of cultic personnel. The king took part in worship and festivals, although in some cases other people served as his representatives, including other members of the royal family.

In Babylon the king played his primary religious role during the New Year's festival, submitting to the authority of Marduk by confessing his transgressions and undergoing ritual humiliation by the high priest before being reinvested with the symbols of his power for another year. Although the elaborate ceremony was in part a commemoration of Marduk's triumph over the primordial monster Tiamat and his creation of the cosmos, the festival was primarily a ritual of kingship. It is likely that the Chaldeans adopted this festival from other peoples in Mesopotamia. Just as the story of creation in *Enuma elish* probably existed in earlier forms with other gods than Marduk as hero, so it also seems likely that the New Year's festival had likewise originally been devoted to another god or gods before being taken over and adapted by the Chaldeans to honor Marduk. Whether the New Year's festival had always included the annual renewal of the king's divinely given authority to rule, or whether the focus on the king as the gods' chosen was a Neo-Babylonian addition, is an open question. We will examine the New Year's festival in detail later.

The king was sometimes subjected to religious strictures arising from his preeminent place in the nation and before the gods. If an omen portended trouble for the nation, the priests might require the king to carry out specific actions to turn the evil away. But the king was also the beneficiary of special blessings. The king usually had a close relationship with one god as a patron or patroness, and Mesopotamian religious literature reflects the idea that a particular god or goddess might have special regard for the king and guarantee his well-being. The names given to Mesopotamian kings, for example, include the names of the gods their fathers worshipped. The names of many Babylonian kings include the name of Nabu, the scribe of the gods and patron of writing, and others incorporate the name of Marduk, while the names of many kings of Assyria include the name of Asshur. Although a name often revealed the god worshipped by a person's father, it would not necessarily coincide with a person's own religious preferences. For example Nabonidus (Nabu-naid, "the god Nabu has exalted [him]"), despite his name, was a devoted worshipper of the moon god Sin. He named his own son Bel-shal-usur (most often known as Belshazzar), "Bel protect the king," invoking Bel, one of the names of Marduk. Since the name Bel can also mean simply "Lord," there is at least the possibility that Nabonidus had his own patron god in mind when he gave his son the name.

But kings were also claimed by specific gods as their favorites through oracles delivered to the king. For example, an oracle of Ishtar was given to the Assyrian king Esarhaddon (680–669 BCE), in which the goddess declares herself to have been the divine midwife at his birth as well as his wet nurse. In an oracle given to Esarhaddon's son Assur-bannipal (668–627 BCE) in a dream, Ishtar speaks in the voice of an over-indulgent mother. She tells Assur-bannipal to remain in his palace, eating and making merry, while she goes out to deal with his enemies. All he must do is praise the goddess and she will grant him his heart's desire, without the trouble of enduring the strains of battle. Nabonidus's devotion to the moon god Sin led him to abandon kingly rule in Babylon to his son and live in an Arabian oasis. All indications are that these special bonds between particular patron gods and goddesses and the king were not merely a formality of royal theology, but deeply felt spiritual relationships that led the king to give special honor and devotion to his patron in the divine realm.

The king's relationship with the gods was of course of greatest importance when he went campaigning, since it was their protection that assured his military victories. The theological consequences of the sort of military kingship found in ancient Mesopotamia were substantial. Although in Egypt the king was expected to show his military prowess in protecting the kingdom from external enemies, for the most part he was not primarily a war leader. But throughout most of the history of Mesopotamia the dominant kingdom or people remained in power by using military power either to extend hegemony to include new people and territories or to defend its own territory successfully against the incursions of hostile outsiders. As it was in Egypt, in Mesopotamia the person of the king was the guarantor of the nation's material and spiritual welfare, but in Mesopotamia he fulfilled this role first by being a successful military leader. The king enjoyed the favor of the gods, but their favor was exhibited preeminently when they granted the king and his armies victory over the enemies that threatened his realm.

In the business of governing, all political and social goods from the gods were mediated to the people through the king as the divine instrument through which all earthly blessings might be received. The king stood apart as superior to the rest of humanity by virtue of his role as the agent of the gods, governing at the gods' behest to dispense their blessings. Unlike in Egypt, where the king himself as Horus was considered divine, in Mesopotamia the king was the gods' agent but remained human. There were some exceptions when Mesopotamian kings were afforded divine honors and worshipped in their own temples, but such cases were rare. Naram-Sin (2254–2218 BCE), grandson of Sargon, was the first Mesopotamian king to declare himself a god. More commonly, Mesopotamian kings were regarded as human beings whose unique gifts raised them above the rest of humanity. They were honored and obeyed as political leaders but they were also venerated as superior beings comparable to the legendary heroes and sages of old who had used their divine gifts for the welfare of a struggling humanity.

The permeability of the boundary between human kings and mythic heroes is illustrated by the monarchs in the Sumerian King List, which includes the names of both legendary and historical figures, and some that combine aspects of both. The Sumerian King List was compiled by modern scholars from partial versions found in several fragmentary sources. It is a list of a succession of kings from the earliest monarchs to kings who ruled during the eighteenth century BCE. The list includes the names of legendary Mesopotamian kings who were renowned for their mighty deeds. These clearly legendary kings include those who ruled before the Great Flood, whose reigns are said to have lasted thousands of years. But the cities where these legendary kings supposedly ruled are themselves historical, making it difficult to determine where in the Sumerian King List legend ends and some sort of history begins. The first kings after the Flood are still said to have reigned for hundreds of years, but their names reflect the ethnic diversity typical of Mesopotamia in the second millennium BCE. Poetic accounts of some of these kings also survive, recounting their mighty deeds. These stories reflect a continuing political tension between the city of Uruk and a nation called Aratta, probably located to the northeast of Uruk in the territory of Iran.

Later kings included in the Sumerian King List have reigns of more reasonable lengths, and the historical reality of many of them has been confirmed by archaeological discoveries. The Sumerian King List is considered a valuable resource for reconstructing the history of Sumer, but obviously it needs to be used with some caution. The dominant idea that the list represents—that the king enjoys a special status as someone less than divine but more than human—endured throughout the subsequent history of Mesopotamia. It is an idea that finds literary expression preeminently in the poetic account of the career of the greatest of the legendary kings to appear in the Sumerian King List, the *Epic of Gilgamesh*.

The *Epic of Gilgamesh*

The *Epic of Gilgamesh* focuses on a specific legendary king, but it reveals a great deal about Mesopotamian beliefs about the hero and the ideal king through the adventures of its titular hero. The *Epic of Gilgamesh* is the earliest surviving example of an epic poem. An epic poem presents a hero who undertakes a series of adventures, usually as part of a journey. The hero lives explicitly in relationship to the divine world, and gods and goddesses are major actors in the stories of his adventures. The gods act to encourage or discourage the hero, to help or harm him, and the hero in turn acts toward the gods much as he would act toward a human sovereign or overlord. The most familiar examples of epic poems in the Western tradition are Homer's *Iliad* and *Odyssey*, both products of early Greece, and Virgil's *Aeneid*, written in the early years of imperial Rome.

The adventures in an epic poem usually include feats of derring-do beyond the capacity of ordinary human beings. The hero is able to do them either by virtue of unusual skill, strength, or cleverness. Although the epic hero is under the control of the gods and sometimes interacts with the gods directly, his journey and adventures are an assertion of human capability and free will, and their final result is the accumulation of wisdom. In the case of Gilgamesh, he is in part an example of the exalted status of the king over other human beings in ancient Mesopotamia. But Gilgamesh appears in the *Epic* primarily as a hero, a mighty man of valor, rather than as a king. Like other epic heroes Gilgamesh strains at humanity's limitations, pushing against the barriers between the human and the divine, while remaining unmistakably human.

Gilgamesh appears in the Sumerian King List as a king of the city of Uruk, with the dates of his reign placed somewhere between 2800 and 2500 BCE. He appears to have been an historical figure whose exploits and renown quickly turned him into the stuff of legends. The *Epic of Gilgamesh* was written down in Akkadian, but the individual incidents circulated in oral form for generations—probably centuries—in both Sumerian and Akkadian versions. Different versions of the story are found throughout Mesopotamia, ranging from schoolboy copies to carefully collated and copied texts for royal archives. The definitive text of the *Epic of Gilgamesh* is the version found in the Assyrian capital city of Nineveh, from the seventh century BCE, authored by a master scribe at royal command. Modern scholars sometimes supplement the Assyrian version with an Old Babylonian version found in Ur that dates from the early second millennium BCE.

In the ancient world, putting a story into writing didn't mean that it had reached its final form. The story would continue to be told and to grow in the telling according to the intentions of different storytellers and the particular interests of their various audiences. It is a recurring motif in literary renditions of the lives of famous individuals, whether historical or legendary, for the author to note that his written account is only a glimpse into the words, deeds, and character of the person who is the subject of his work. In contrast to the limited scope of a literary work, it is implied, the living memory always has something more to add—more stories, more details, more insights—to reveal a person's life in all its fullness. This is especially true with the sort of story contained in an epic, a story made up of a variety of individual incidents, not all of them immediately necessary to the narrative arc of the poem. The written account is explicitly only one (incomplete) version of the whole story, with its incidents chosen (from the many available) to say something about the hero and his world to a particular audience.

In the case of Gilgamesh, there are many stories about him that were not included in the epic but appear in different written versions, stories that reflect the diversity of the underlying oral traditions about him. Preserving some of those stories by writing them down in the *Epic of Gilgamesh* did not affect the continued retelling of those or other stories about Gilgamesh in oral performances, either in Mesopotamia or elsewhere. We find versions of stories about Gilgamesh reappearing in other oral traditions from other eastern Mediterranean cultures, testifying to the importance of the storyteller's art, the fertility of narrative imagination, and the continuing human interest in the exploits of heroes who are larger than life.

Gilgamesh the King

The epic begins with a prologue that extols both Gilgamesh's heroic deeds and his accomplishments as king of Uruk, granting him a place of honor among both heroes and kings. Gilgamesh is a paragon of both strength and beauty, superior to all other men in the same way Marduk is superior to the other gods. His father is a man, the king Lugalbanda, but his mother is Ninsun, the goddess "Wild Cow." But it is not just his parents who are responsible for his remarkable abilities. Gilgamesh was specially created by the gods for heroism and kingship, and they combined in him human and divine characteristics that reflect his mixed parentage. More than once we are told that Gilgamesh is two-thirds divine and one-third mortal, nearer to the gods than he is to other human beings. But if his semidivine status foreshadows his mighty deeds of valor, it also foreshadows the central drama of the epic, Gilgamesh's rejection of death, the common fate of all humanity.

Although a list of his heroic accomplishments is placed first and his deeds as a hero later become the substance of the epic, as king of Uruk Gilgamesh also does the sorts of things that make civilized life possible. Gilgamesh fortified Uruk and built its temples to Anu and Ishtar out of baked brick, essentially making Uruk a city. Gilgamesh is also responsible for the first record of his own deeds, engraved in stone; through writing and monumental architecture, Gilgamesh gives Uruk an historical memory, an essential part of the life of civilized people. Gilgamesh is both a hero and a king, both a warrior whose battles against the forces of chaos make civilized life possible, and a king who presides over the civilization he has created and oversees the dispensing of its blessings.

Clearly Gilgamesh exhibited many of the skills the Mesopotamians considered essential for successful kingship, including courage and intelligence. But with the beginning of the story proper, it becomes clear that Gilgamesh has his faults as a king as well, most of them arising from his unbridled appetites. His appetites are part of his heroic character but are ill-suited for the responsibilities of a king. His appetite for battle meant constant warfare for the young men of Uruk, leaving its families bereft of their male children, their chief means of support. Gilgamesh's sexual appetite apparently has led him to exercise continually the so-called *droît de seigneur*, the royal prerogative found in some cultures that allows the king to deflower all virgin brides within his realm. Gilgamesh does as he likes as king of Uruk until his subjects finally complain to the gods about him. Their complaints are less a protest against their king's capricious behavior than they are a plea for the welfare of the city. The gods hear their pleas and in turn complain to Anu, the chief god of Uruk. Anu devises a way to neutralize Gilgamesh, to deter or distract him from further abuse of his city and his subjects.

In the description of Gilgamesh's kingly deeds and the complaints his subjects make against him, we find clues that grant us some insight into the Mesopotamian ideal of kingship. Power in Mesopotamian city-states resided primarily in the person of the king, appointed by the gods as their representative on earth to provide for the needs of their people. As in Egypt, the king was also the people's representative before the gods, making offerings to the gods on their behalf as chief worshipper for the city. The gods' acceptance of the king's offerings not only brought blessings for the city but certified the legitimacy of the king's reign and royal power. The welfare of the city's population was ensured in part by the military protection the king and his armies provided, but also by economic security and the administration of justice, especially for the poor. The king served to some extent at the people's pleasure. If the king did not serve the interests of people, rebellion and usurpation might follow. At the very least, the people might pray for the gods to replace him, as the citizens of Uruk do in the *Epic of Gilgamesh*.

The gods' solution to the problem posed by Gilgamesh is perhaps surprising: They decide to neutralize him by creating his equal, Enkidu. The gods call on Aruru, the goddess credited with creating Gilgamesh, to make "another Gilgamesh" who will match him in size and strength. Aruru creates Enkidu the warrior out of clay and places him in the wilderness, away from human habitations and the influence of civilization. He is essentially the anti-Gilgamesh, his equal in size and strength but his opposite in his place in the world. Enkidu's home is in the wilderness where he lives as a companion to animals, in stark contrast to Gilgamesh's home in the city, where he lives as a ruler over men and women. Enkidu is a primitive man untouched by civilization. Shaggy hair covers his body while the hair on his head is long and uncut, like the hair of a woman. He eats grass and drinks from forest pools like an animal. From the civilized perspective Enkidu is more beast than man.

Enkidu comes to the notice of a hunter, because he frees animals from the hunter's traps and protects them from the depredations of human beings. The hunter complains about Enkidu to his father, who sends him to Uruk to consult with Gilgamesh. Gilgamesh tells the hunter to take a prostitute named Shamhat to the place where Enkidu lives so that she may entice him to have sexual intercourse with her. In the wilderness Shamhat uses her charms to attract Enkidu. In due course he spends six days and seven nights making love with her, and in the process becomes "civilized." Sexual intercourse with Shamhat cuts Enkidu off from nature and the company of the animals, who now flee from him in fear. He is no longer able to run fast enough to keep up with them. According to the narration of the poem Enkidu has been separated from nature because he has become "weak." But Shamhat tells Enkidu that because of their lovemaking "the thoughts of a man" now inhabit him and he has become "wise." In fact, she says, he is like a god, superior to other men by virtue of the supernatural strength and skill the gods have given him.

Shamhat teaches Enkidu the ways of civilized people. He learns to eat bread and drink strong wine, both "civilized" foods whose preparation requires a combination of natural ingredients and human ingenuity. Enkidu also rubs down his body hair and anoints himself with oil, both ways civilized men of ancient Mesopotamia enhanced their appearance. As the poet of the *Epic* puts it briefly, "Enkidu had become a man" (Sandars, 67). Once Enkidu surrenders his old way of interacting with nature and its animals, and embraces the forms of interaction with nature and his own body that are typical of civilized people and societies, he becomes a "man" and is no longer a "beast."

Shamhat tells Enkidu about Gilgamesh, and Enkidu soon comes to the city of Uruk to challenge Gilgamesh and determine which of them is the stronger man. Enkidu confronts Gilgamesh at the door to his father-in-law's house and will not allow him to pass. Soon the two men grapple with each other and wrestle in the street. They are evenly matched and their struggle sends tremors through the city. Unfortunately, the part of the Akkadian version describing the end of the contest is lost. When the text resumes, Enkidu is listening to Gilgamesh and begins to cry. The Old Babylonian text is complete but still unclear; it seems to suggest that Gilgamesh uses some sort of wrestling trick to subdue Enkidu, throwing him to the ground. Whatever has happened, the two men become friends, as foretold to Gilgamesh in a dream. Now "they grasped one another, and embraced and held hands" (Dalley, 61)—the gestures of their friendship ironically mimicking those of their initial struggle. The friendship between Gilgamesh and Enkidu in the Akkadian stories about their exploits stands in contrast to their relationship in the Sumerian stories, where they appear essentially as master and servant.

This fast (in both senses) friendship between Gilgamesh and Enkidu exemplifies an ideal of friendship that we find not only in Mesopotamia but elsewhere in the ancient Mediterranean world. The ancient ideal of friendship is based on the idea of a friend as the "other self," someone whose background, intelligence, skills, interests, and pleasures mirror those of his friend. This ideal finds almost literal fulfillment in the case of Gilgamesh and Enkidu, since Aruru created Enkidu to be "another Gilgamesh" at the gods' insistence. The resemblance between the two men is emphasized repeatedly in the first part of the poem. The only difference between them is that Gilgamesh lives in the very center of civilized life while Enkidu is a "primitive man" who lives in the wilderness. Once Enkidu has been "civilized" through his contact with Shamhat and has "become a man" in diet and appearance, he essentially becomes Gilgamesh's twin. But as his twin, he also has become a fit companion for Gilgamesh, his ideal friend. Gilgamesh and Enkidu are essentially two sides of the same personality; the hero finds his ideal companion and perfect comrade in the mirror image of his twin.

In the extant versions of the *Epic*, the encounter with Enkidu marks the beginning of the stories about Gilgamesh's adventures as a hero, as he leaves the city of Uruk behind to wander in the wilderness. This reverses the usual course of events, when the crown of a hero's career is to become a king. That line of development follows the more usual historical circumstances, when a man becomes king by virtue of his military prowess. In the case of Gilgamesh, there are already indications he does not fit easily into the role of king, and in fact he continues to expect his heroic prerogatives (inciting battles, bedding many women) in spite of his royal obligations. The advent of Enkidu as "another Gilgamesh" initiates Gilgamesh's shift to heroic adventuring, leaving Uruk to its own devices while its king and his companion wander the world.

Gilgamesh the Hero

After their friendship is sealed, Enkidu tells Gilgamesh about Humbaba (Akkadian; the Old Babylonian equivalent is Huwawa), a monster in the forest who terrorizes anyone who attempts to enter it. The great god Enlil has made Humbaba guardian of the forest and its animals, but essentially Humbaba is an elemental monster who represents all the dangers of the forest that threaten civilized people who enter it in pursuit of game or in search of lumber. Gilgamesh is determined to destroy Humbaba, although there is no clear reason why. The episode is fragmentary, so the reason may be lost, but it may be enough that Gilgamesh has decided to do it. On one level, we might see Gilgamesh's decision reflecting the human desire to conquer nature and submit it to the needs of humanity, especially the needs of human civilization. On another level, it is simply the role of the hero to fight and overcome monsters, to rid the world of the evil that threatens humanity. Humbaba is "something evil."

Once Gilgamesh has decided on his course, he is equipped for the perilous combat in various ways, gaining assistance from both human beings and the gods. First Gilgamesh must rely upon Enkidu, who knows the way to the forest and will give him tactical advice, protect him during the fight, and bring him home. Next Gilgamesh goes to the palace of his mother Ninsun for advice. She makes offerings to the sun god Shamash, who put "a restless spirit" in Gilgamesh. Finally, Gilgamesh and Enkidu themselves make offerings to the gods, and apparently promise Enlil a pine door for his temple if they are able to defeat Humbaba. All these preparations are practical, since success in any mythic endeavor requires both preparation with the necessary arms and skills and the help of the gods. But such preparations are also a common motif in stories about heroes combating monsters, an opportunity for the storyteller to build suspense by allowing the audience to consider just how perilous the hero's mission will be.

Gilgamesh and Enkidu make the long journey to Lebanon and the great Pine Forest in a section of the poem marked by repeated actions, words, and motifs. Each day Gilgamesh and Enkidu travel fifty leagues. Each day they dig a well in honor of Shamash, and each evening Gilgamesh asks for a favorable dream. Each night Gilgamesh instead has a troubling dream that Enkidu interprets favorably for him. This motif of travel and dreaming recurs three times, reflecting the ancient conviction that a genuine dream message was confirmed by three repetitions. Gilgamesh's three dreams confirm that the heroes will overcome Humbaba.

Gilgamesh and Enkidu enter the Pine Forest and soon face Humbaba, who derides and mocks them. Gilgamesh is unnerved at the sight of the monster, a giant with a face like coiled intestines, so it falls to Enkidu to rally his spirits. The account of the battle is fragmentary, but it is won by a combination of the heroes' efforts and thirteen winds sent by Shamash that prevent Humbaba from mounting an effective counterattack and make it impossible for him to escape Gilgamesh's blows. Humbaba begs Gilgamesh for his life, offering bribes and promises. The nature of the bribes—luxuriant growth for his groves of trees and lumber for his palace—suggest that Humbaba may have originally been a god of the forest, demoted in the *Epic* to a forest guardian appointed by Enlil. Enkidu warns Gilgamesh to ignore Humbaba's pleas and destroy him, both to eliminate the threat the monster poses to humanity and to gain everlasting fame as his conqueror. Gilgamesh is persuaded and kills Humbaba. The heroes cut down pine trees to make a door for Enlil's temple in Nippur as they have promised, as compensation for the death of Humbaba.

Although in many ways this story is a typical tale of a hero overcoming an elemental monster, it includes touches of irony and foreshadowing of events

Humbaba or Huwawa, a clay mask from Sippar in southern Mesopotamia, c. 1800–1600 BCE. © The Trustees of the British Museum

to come later. Most intriguing is the relationship between Humbaba, the guardian of the Pine Forest, and Enkidu, the former "primitive" man who has embraced civilization. Humbaba is essentially a monstrous version of what Enkidu once was, a protector and companion of wild beasts living far away from where human beings make their homes. Yet it is Enkidu who urges Gilgamesh to kill Humbaba despite his pleas and promises, and it is Enkidu that Humbaba threatens and curses before his death. The story is filled with forebodings of death for Enkidu, who has abandoned the wilderness and adopted human ways. At the same time, the recklessness Gilgamesh displays in this episode shows how he is straining at the limits of human destiny and wishes to become "immortal." These motifs intertwine in the second half of the epic, a melancholy counterpoint to the heroic friendship and adventures of the first half.

The Death of Enkidu

After his victory over Humbaba, Gilgamesh returns to Uruk, where he washes and puts on his royal raiment. His manly beauty attracts the attention of Ishtar, the powerful goddess of erotic love. Here Ishtar appears in her role as an insatiable sexual predator, a dangerous woman who attempts to seduce Gilgamesh through tempting promises. Just as Humbaba's attempts at bribery revealed his roots as a god of the forest, Ishtar's promises reflect her divine character as a goddess of fertility. She promises Gilgamesh gifts fit for a god, but also plentiful crops from his fields and multiple births among his livestock. But Gilgamesh resists Ishtar's advances, proving he is no more vulnerable to the beauty than he was to the beast. But he adds insult to injury, and rebukes Ishtar with an account of her many lovers and the sad fates she decreed for them once she had tired of them. His words apparently reflect a series of origin myths related to Ishtar, explaining some aspect of "the way things are now"—the strange cry of a bird, why horses must serve human beings, the changing seasons—as the result of Ishtar's mistreatment of one of her former lovers. Here again we are reminded that we have access to only a small part of the rich tradition of Mesopotamian mythology that developed over a period of two millennia.

Ishtar is infuriated both by Gilgamesh's refusal and his recapitulation of the suffering she has inflicted on her spurned lovers. Ishtar flees to her father Anu and asks him to send "the Bull of Heaven" to destroy Gilgamesh and Enkidu. Her lust for revenge of course only confirms everything Gilgamesh has said about her. The Bull of Heaven wreaks havoc in Uruk, but Gilgamesh slaughters it and gives its entrails as an offering to Shamash. Ishtar appears on the walls of Uruk in a fury and Enkidu throws a haunch of the bull in her face, threatening the goddess with physical harm. She retreats and gathers the prostitutes of Uruk—the women who acknowledge her as both patroness and protector—to mourn the Bull of Heaven while Gilgamesh and Enkidu celebrate their triumph.

Soon afterwards Enkidu has a prophetic dream. The dream makes it clear Enkidu must die to recompense the gods for the deaths of Humbaba and the Bull of Heaven. In a rage Enkidu beseeches Shamash to curse the hunter and Shamhat the prostitute, the two people responsible for taking him from the wilderness and bringing him to an evil destiny. But Shamash rebukes Enkidu because what Shamhat did has led to Enkidu gaining glory and renown as Gilgamesh's companion. Enkidu relents and blesses Shamhat, although his blessing is a wish that she may seduce many men who will shower her with riches and leave the mothers of their children for her. After another prophetic dream Enkidu becomes deathly ill and soon dies, but Gilgamesh refuses to surrender his friend to death until his body begins to decompose. Gilgamesh recites a long poem of lamentation for his friend, strips off his royal finery, and orders a statue of Enkidu to be made of precious stones and metals for display in Uruk.

The death of Enkidu marks the turning point of the *Epic of Gilgamesh*, the transition between the stories of Gilgamesh's heroics and the beginning of his quest for wisdom. There is a certain logic to the development of the narrative to this point that is appropriate for a story about an adventuring hero and his companion. The epic has so far followed a discernible narrative arc, beginning with a story about Gilgamesh fighting with a man who is his (near) equal, then moving on to a story about Gilgamesh fighting against a more formidable opponent, an elemental monster, and then to a story about him fighting against supernatural opponents, the goddess Ishtar and the Bull of Heaven. Gilgamesh has reached the limits of what a human hero can do in terms of mighty acts of strength and cunning. He must now turn to other sorts of trials.

The Search for Eternal Life

The death of Enkidu, his friend, brother, and twin, confronts Gilgamesh with the inevitability of his own death, the ultimate and final fact of his human identity. It is the fear of death that drives Gilgamesh on a new quest to find a way of overcoming the limitations of humanity: the quest for eternal life. Gilgamesh is a hero, a mighty man of valor who suppresses the forces of chaos and makes civilized human life possible. He stands apart from other human beings by virtue of the divinely bestowed gifts that make him superior to them. But Enkidu's death reveals the human limitations even heroes share with the rest of humanity, and unmans Gilgamesh, since death belies the superiority the hero enjoys over other human beings.

Gilgamesh has expressed fear before, before and during his contest with Humbaba, but that appears to have been the fear not of death, but of defeat and disgrace. Gilgamesh and Enkidu explicitly share the idea that a heroic death brings with it everlasting fame, and everlasting fame is the most important thing for a hero. But Enkidu dies of a wasting illness, and his death is all the more bitter because he is denied the glory of dying a hero's death in combat. There is a clear connection between Gilgamesh's fear of death and his role as a hero who deals out death to others—men, animals, and monsters. When he searches for eternal life, he is searching for a way to prolong his fame as well as his life, so that he may triumph over death (and the human condition) just as he has triumphed over all his other enemies. But Gilgamesh's quest is also a search for wisdom and the meaning of life, for what makes human life worth living despite its troubles and its inevitable conclusion in death.

Gilgamesh's search for everlasting life again takes him far from civilization into the wilderness. Gilgamesh forsakes his royal status, the trappings of civilization, and even the role of the hero, turning to a life in the wild. He wears animal skins and his face is weathered by heat and cold. He survives by hunting. Gilgamesh roams the open country to find the way to the home of Utnapishtim, the only man who has gained the gift of everlasting life from the gods.

His quest takes Gilgamesh under the mountain Mashu, along the subterranean path the sun god Shamash travels each night from west to east, to return to where he will rise in the morning. Gilgamesh finds his way blocked by scorpion monsters who recognize Gilgamesh as a mighty hero, but still insist that no mortal can follow the path of Shamash. Regardless, Gilgamesh plunges into the darkness and after ten leagues emerges into the light again in the garden of the sun god, where the plants bear gemstones in place of fruit.

In the garden of Shamash the change in Gilgamesh's situation comes clearly into focus during a conversation with Siduri the alewife. An alewife was a businesswoman, a woman who sold beer to travelers, usually without any connection to a male relative who might serve as her guardian. She was free to do business and interact with men as something like an equal. When Siduri first spots Gilgamesh, his appearance is so weathered and grief-stricken she thinks he is an assassin. When she learns that he is Gilgamesh she asks why he is so changed in appearance and wretched. Gilgamesh replies at length; he not only grieves for his friend Enkidu, but he grieves because he knows that he too must die.

Siduri in reply tells Gilgamesh to enjoy whatever pleasures life has to offer as long as it lasts and one has the capacity to enjoy them. These words of advice clearly recall the Harpers' Songs from Egypt, as well as similar words of consolation found elsewhere in ancient wisdom literature. Gilgamesh asks Siduri for directions to the home of Ut-napishtim and learns he lives across the "waters of death," the open sea Mesopotamians feared to cross. Gilgamesh seeks out Ur-shanabi the ferryman, whose boat can carry him to the dwelling place of Ut-napishtim.

Gilgamesh's journey in search of Ut-napishtim the Faraway is essentially a search for a revered ancient ancestor from whom to learn the meaning of human life in the face of death. Ut-napishtim, like Noah, has survived a worldwide flood, and he appears in the poem as a repository of ancient wisdom from the earliest ages. But Ut-napishtim has no wisdom to offer Gilgamesh, except that like other men he must live life as the gods have decreed it, with an appointed time for its fated end. Like Siduri the alewife, Ut-napishtim urges Gilgamesh to enjoy what pleasures life has to offer while it lasts, rather than making his life miserable through his fear of death.

For his part, Gilgamesh is surprised that Ut-napishtim is a man like any other, not a hero. Ut-napishtim seems to lack that superiority of strength and ability over other human beings that might justify the gods' decision to exempt him from the universal human fate of death. In fact, Ut-napishtim does share Gilgamesh's superiority over other human beings, but in his case it is the superiority of the sage who possesses a divine wisdom not available to the rest of humanity. Ut-napishtim tells Gilgamesh the story of the primeval flood, in a portion of the poem with close parallels to the Mesopotamian story of Atrahasis and the Israelite story of Noah. We will consider the Mesopotamian story of the great flood in some detail later. But at the end of Ut-napishtim's tale, Gilgamesh is still in despair, for death seems to haunt him and dog his steps.

Ut-napishtim orders Ur-shanabi to return with Gilgamesh to Uruk and civilization. Ut-napishtim also tells Gilgamesh a secret. Although there is no way for a human being to escape death, there is a plant in the depths of the abyss that has the power to restore a person's youth. Gilgamesh manages to get the plant, but on the journey back to Uruk it is stolen by a snake. The snake then immediately sheds its skin. This part of the story seems to be in part an explanation of why snakes are able to shed their skin and so be "rejuvenated." Gilgamesh weeps at his loss, but there is nothing to be done, so he and Ur-shanabi continue their journey to Uruk. When they arrive, Gilgamesh tells Ur-shanabi to inspect the city, using words that echo the beginning of the poem. The story of Gilgamesh has come full circle.

By the end of the epic, Gilgamesh has come to understand how things are, and why they are the way they are, even for a hero who is two-thirds god and one-third man. He seems to come to terms with his ultimate fate. Once back home in Uruk, Gilgamesh resumes his kingly rule and devotes himself to those works celebrated at the beginning of the epic. He takes pride in his accomplishments and sets out the details of his works in words engraved on a stone monument, making Gilgamesh's own writing—his literary work—the ultimate source of all the stories later told about him. Gilgamesh finally makes peace with the civilized world and accepts his human destiny as both king and hero. Presumably his rule over Uruk after his return will be tempered by the wisdom he has gained from his experiences.

By taking up the responsibilities of royal rule once again, Gilgamesh confirms that kingship is the highest aspiration—and the fittest duty—for the man who has been blessed in so many ways by the gods. Gilgamesh was already a king at the beginning of the story, and possessed many of the virtues that a king must possess, but he was still driven by the same forces that drove him as a hero—a desire for glory in battle, a wide-ranging lust for women and adventure, and the self-centeredness that led him to gratify his desires at the expense of his subjects and his realm. But in the course of his adventures, Gilgamesh learns to temper his desires. His fight with Enkidu ends not in victory but in friendship. He overcomes Humbaba and the Bull of Heaven, but his friend Enkidu has to die to recompense the gods for their deaths. His knowledge and a new self-restraint help him overcome his sexual desire for Ishtar and save his life. He undertakes a quest that leads him to forsake the comforts of life to travel to the ends of the earth and the depths of Apsu, but in spite of his sacrifices he ultimately fails to gain what he sought. At the end of his trials he is still a mighty man of valor, but he has been tempered and proven by the trials he has experienced and the wisdom he has gained. In the process of seeking adventure and eternal life, he has gained knowledge and self-discipline, and so become an ideal Mesopotamian king. At the end of the story, Gilgamesh appears at last to see the wisdom of the advice he has been offered by both Siduri and Ut-napishtim, to enjoy what duties and pleasures human life has to offer while it lasts, "for this too is the work of man."

CHAPTER NINE

Mesopotamia: The World of the Dead

The Realm of the Dead in the Ancient Mediterranean World

Ancient Mesopotamian beliefs about the afterlife and the situation of the dead were very different from the optimistic ideas about the kingdom of Osiris or other forms of blessedness in Egyptian religious culture. But Mesopotamian beliefs were in this respect entirely consistent with the prevailing visions of the afterlife in ancient Mediterranean religious cultures in general. Although there seems to have been little doubt in those religious cultures that the dead continued to exist, and that their continued existence resembled life on earth in some sense, the world of the dead was decidedly not like the world of the living, and the dead there did not enjoy the blessings bestowed on the living on earth.

The prevailing beliefs about the fate of the dead in ancient Mediterranean religious cultures reflect the common practice of burying or entombing dead bodies. The realm of the dead, for example, was located beneath the earth's surface. The dead were for the most part buried in the earth or entombed either below its surface or in caves or cave-like structures, so it followed that the eternal dwelling place of the dead must be in the regions beneath the surface of the earth, in the Underworld. Most often the Underworld was believed to lie deep in the earth, under the foundations of the mountains but above the waters of the abyss, at the farthest possible remove from the gods in heaven. Because it was beneath the surface of the earth, the Underworld was associated first with darkness, but also with dust, dryness, and thirst. The dead were deprived of the light of the sun and moon and were cut off from contact with the great gods who lived in heaven. In this dark realm the dead continued to exist, but there they could exist only in a shadowy, semiconscious state devoid of the vitality of life in its earthly form.

Despite the fact that the dead were cut off from the source of life—the sun and the gods in heaven—there are no indications of any belief in the ancient Mediterranean world that the dead simply ceased to exist. The evidence from the prehistoric and later ancient burials—burials that include the tools and goods of everyday life—instead unanimously support the contrary belief that the dead continued to "live" in some sense. This evidence and the evidence provided by later literary works dealing with the fate of the dead argue persuasively that there was a near-universal expectation that life on earth was followed by another, comparable life elsewhere.

From the evidence it seems clear that the concept of nonexistence was simply unimaginable to the people of the ancient Mediterranean world. What was alive would continue to live, even if what they experienced was life only in a degraded and limited sense. The concept that something that once existed no longer did could apparently only be understood by people in the ancient Near East in terms of utter physical destruction, as when a person is devoured by fire or an animal. As it happens, these two forms of physical annihilation were the fate assigned to the souls of the wicked in the kingdom of Osiris in Egyptian religious culture. Once the souls of the wicked were devoured by Ammit "the Gobbler," or burned up, the wicked lost their place in the kingdom of Osiris and ceased to be. Similarly, there is a Sumerian story about Gilgamesh in which Enkidu's spirit describes to Gilgamesh what he has seen in the Underworld. Gilgamesh asks him about the fate of "him who was set on fire." Enkidu replies, "His ghost is not there. His smoke went up to the sky" (Dalley, 135). Annihilation or consumption of the body meant the person too had been destroyed and found no place in the Underworld. However gloomy the fate of the dead in the Underworld, it was far worse to simply cease to exist.

This belief obviously encouraged the proper treatment and disposal of the bodies of the dead to ensure that their shades could enter the Underworld. Although no other people devoted the time and expense the Egyptians did to preparing bodies for their entombment, graves and tombs throughout the ancient Mediterranean show concern with the details of burial. The quality and kind of grave goods included in burials throughout the ancient Near East indicate belief in some status distinctions among the shades of the dead in the Underworld, although the details of those distinctions are difficult to discern.

The realm of the dead was separated by a great gulf from the land of the living, not only by virtue of its location, but because of deliberate physical and legal barriers between the two. A fierce guardian or a series of guardians protected the entrance, both to keep the living out of the land of the dead and to keep the dead in. A river is often said to run through or to surround the realm of the dead, to serve as a further barrier between its inhabitants and the living. The realm of the dead is bound by divine laws, as is the land of the living, and those laws are particularly harsh. Anyone from among the living who might venture into the Underworld was in danger of becoming trapped there, subject to the laws of the Underworld and unable to return to the land of the living. The realm of the dead was ruled by a god with a royal court. But the gods there are bound by the laws of the Underworld just as the dead are, and generally are believed to be unable to leave their realm. They live in darkness like their subjects, separated from the company of the gods in heaven and the pleasures they enjoy there.

Mesopotamian Ideas about the Realm of the Dead

Ideas about death and afterlife in Mesopotamia are fairly consistent with those found throughout most ancient Mediterranean religious cultures. Burials from the Ubaid period and later are usually in cemeteries, plots of land devoted exclusively to the dead. Graves might be holes dug in the ground or brick or stone tombs. They included pottery and various sorts of tools and goods for the deceased to use in the afterlife, although the number and the nature of grave goods varied over time. There is an obvious concern with "proper" burial, in regard both to the furnishings of the grave and the disposition of the body.

The most exceptional burials from the Sumerian period are found in the Royal Cemetery of Ur. The two thousand or so graves that have been excavated there represent a span of at least five hundred years. The most significant are the so-called Royal Tombs, which date from around 2600 BCE, during the Early Dynastic period. These are sixteen chambers built of stone and brick, some accessible through shafts, that include a vast quantity of grave goods of very fine quality, testifying to the great wealth of the principal person buried there. Who these people were is not clear, although they were obviously of great importance socially, politically, religiously, or most likely, all three. What is perhaps most significant, however, is that in some burial chambers the body of the principal person is accompanied by as many as seventy-four others who were buried at the same time. These other people were most probably attendants, whose lives were sacrificed to allow them to accompany their masters or mistresses in death. As we have seen, in Egypt such a practice may have been the basis for the later inclusion of *shabtis* in tombs, to serve the deceased as servants in the afterlife.

As the parallel to Egyptian burials suggests, the Royal Tombs at Ur seem to reflect a belief in an active, even luxurious life for their chief inhabitants in the Underworld. Although the vast majority of ancient Mesopotamian burials reflect an essential equality in the preparation of the dead—and therefore also expectations about their equal lot in the afterlife—the Royal Tombs reflect the expectation that the exalted social status that the principal person (or people) buried in them had in this world would also be theirs for eternity. Sacrificing servants to attend to their needs, piling up luxury goods for future use, the elaborate dress of the bodies themselves, all suggest a belief in this period that at least some people would enjoy a god-like existence after death, similar to what Egyptians expected to enjoy in the kingdom of Osiris. But if this was indeed the case, such beliefs did not long endure in Mesopotamian culture. The vast majority of burials, as well as the almost unanimous testimony of the surviving literature, present a more somber view of the lot of the dead in the afterlife. The Underworld was a place of lamentation that was the common destiny of all the dead, with no differentiation in their fate according to their status or their deeds.

At the same time there is repeated reference to punishment of the wicked, whose sojourn in the realm of woe is punctuated by acute suffering. "The Sumerian Underworld," a poetic fragment of uncertain date, provides some further impressions of Mesopotamian ideas about the Underworld. The fragment comes from a poem in which a Sumerian god praises himself and his divine majesty, and reveals some ambiguity about the situation of the dead. Although all the dead are destined to a common dark fate in the Underworld, there is also a distinction there between the fate of the good and the evil.

In this fragment and elsewhere, there is repeated reference to punishment of the wicked, whose sojourn in the realm of woe is punctuated by acute suffering. We also find the idea—already familiar from Egypt—that only the good experience the afterlife, while the wicked perish. But just how the wicked "die" after death is not clear. At the same time, the idea of punishment of the wicked does not seem to be balanced by an idea of blessing for the good. Even for them, darkness and dust is their lot. As a result, the general impression left by these early glimpses into the Mesopotamian Underworld is that the lot of all the dead is grim, but the fate of the evil is worse— especially so if that fate is nonexistence.

In Mesopotamia the realm of the dead was the domain of a god, as were all other aspects of existence in the cosmic order. But the situation of those gods was similar to that of most of the other gods of the dead in ancient Mediterranean religious cultures apart from Egypt. Because the abode of the dead lay under the earth, the Mesopotamian gods of the Underworld—like its human inhabitants—were separated from the gods of heaven and earth, those gods who oversaw daily human life. The gods of the Underworld with few exceptions are trapped there just as their subjects are, and they cannot travel to the earth or into the heavens to associate with the gods of heaven and earth.

Among the courtiers and servants in Ereshkigal's court were the Seven Judges who passed sentence on the dead when they entered the Underworld. But at least some of the lower gods resident in the Underworld are portrayed in the surviving literature as grotesques, much like the demons in medieval Christian concepts of Hell. In some stories—notably the story of Nergal and Ereshkigal—the goddess's court in the Underworld is apparently comparable to the courts of the gods in heaven, with its ministers and courtiers, a place where the goddess lives in comfort and splendor. But for the most part Ereshkigal's realm is portrayed as dark and cheerless, a melancholy place filled with the fleeting shades of the dead.

Gilgamesh's Fear of Death

This is the concept of the Underworld that evokes the dread of Gilgamesh, when he considers the fate of Enkidu that will in time be his own as well. When he and Enkidu face their combat with Humbaba, Gilgamesh attempts to encourage his friend with the idea that while death is inevitable, an honorable death will bring a person a sort of immortality. If they are killed by Humbaba, people will remember their courage and their noble birth. But later events undermine the reassurance Gilgamesh once found in the idea of renown as a mighty hero after his death. After Enkidu dies, Gilgamesh cannot accept the separation from his friend that death so definitively imposes. He initially refuses to allow Enkidu to be buried, hoping somehow to hold on to his friend in spite of death. He relents only after a week has passed, when it becomes clear that Enkidu's body is decomposing. After performing all the appropriate funerary rituals and prayers for his friend—a means of ensuring the perpetuation of his name and memory—Gilgamesh erects a statue of Enkidu made of precious metals, recreating his physical presence in defiance of the forced separation between the two friends imposed by Enkidu's death.

Still Gilgamesh cannot find peace. But it soon becomes clear what drives him to seek eternal life is not just his grief over the death of Enkidu or his separation from his "twin," but also—despite his brave words when the heroes fought Humbaba—the specter of his own death. It is the fear of death that presses him to become a wanderer and ultimately to seek out Ut-napishtim the Faraway at the very ends of the earth. But he is not driven only by fear. Now Gilgamesh regards all the pleasures and glories of his past life as nothing because they will find their end in the same death that comes to all people—king, hero, or slave.

In the Old Babylonian version of the *Epic of Gilgamesh*, Gilgamesh seems at times to serve as the voice of humanity in the face of death. When Gilgamesh first enters the garden of the sun god, he is met by Shamash, who has been his protector throughout his adventures. The sun god is concerned about Gilgamesh, but he also tells him his quest is futile, since he can never hope to find the eternal life he seeks.

But Gilgamesh rejects the finality of death. In the presence of Shamash, what Gilgamesh fears most acutely is the never-ending darkness beneath the earth that is the fate of the dead. Darkness epitomizes the separation of the dead from the heavenly gods who will never again bring them to mind.

As the story is told in the Old Babylonian version, Gilgamesh next encounters Siduri the alewife. She seems to function here as a voice of human experience and wisdom, in contrast to the divine wisdom of Shamash. Yet Siduri repeats the words of Shamash; she asks Gilgamesh the point of his quest when the gods have reserved eternal life for themselves and decreed death for humanity. The repetition of these words verifies their validity and common sense, especially since they are spoken both by a god and by a woman of humble origins. Despite the fact that Gilgamesh is only one-third human and two-thirds divine, he is bound by the same conditions that bind all humanity, and must accept that he someday will die.

But unlike Shamash, Siduri also offers Gilgamesh advice on how a human being may still find meaning in life, even in light of the finality of death. He may find pleasure in what life has to offer—not only pleasures of the body, but the love one shares with his wife and children. All the things a person can enjoy during life are also part of human fate, just as much a part of humanity's lot as death. Life should be enjoyed to its fullest while it lasts.

These words of advice—*carpe diem*—recall the Harpers' Songs from Egypt, as well as similar words of consolation found elsewhere in ancient wisdom literature. Siduri appears in an Akkadian list as "Ishtar of wisdom," a manifestation of the goddess who is a source of wise counsel. This may explain why Siduri appears in Shamash's garden, and her role as a voice of wisdom in the Old Babylonian version. Although Gilgamesh continues his search for eternal life, ultimately he returns to Uruk and the pleasures and burdens of kingship. At the end of his travels he seems at last to see the wisdom of Siduri's words and to come to terms with his fate.

The Descent of Ishtar to the Underworld

The relationship between the Mesopotamian Underworld and the realm of the gods of heaven and earth is explored in two different stories about heavenly gods who descend into the realm of the dead to conquer it. A story about Inanna/Ishtar reveals a great deal about the goddess's personality and powers as well as the laws that govern the Underworld and those relegated to its depths. The poem is extant in two versions. The earlier, longer Sumerian version featuring Inanna has been assembled from a collection of fragments. Most of these fragments of text were found at Nippur and date from the eighteenth century BCE. The later, shorter Akkadian version featuring Ishtar has been recovered from the library of the palace in Nineveh, the capital of the Assyrian Empire, and dates from the eighth or seventh century BCE. Scholars suggest recitation of the poem may have been part of the celebration of the *taklimtu*, an annual ritual performed in late June or early July to mourn the death of Dumuzi. Other scholars place the performance of the poem in the context of the festival marking the annual journey of the cult statue of the goddess from its temple in Uruk to Kutha, a city that was home to the shrines of the gods of the Underworld.

In the story, Inanna's journey to the Underworld appears to be an attempt to extend her sovereignty over heaven and earth to include the third realm. The Underworld is ruled by Inanna's elder sister, Ereshkigal. The Sumerian version of the poem makes it clear from the beginning that although she rules in the heights of heaven, Inanna's heart is set on conquering the Underworld—her ambition is insatiable. Inanna's insatiability is one of her dominant characteristics, and the idea will reappear later in this version of the poem. Inanna prepares to go down into the pit by adorning herself in her vestments and the insignia of her divine power, each a physical sign of her sovereignty as well as a source of her beauty. But in the Sumerian version there is an early indication that Inanna's campaign into the depths may not turn out as she hopes. Here the goddess takes the precaution of telling her minister Ninshubar what to do if she should become trapped in the Underworld. In that event he must go to the high gods and beg them to help her, moving on to another if one refuses to rescue her. This portion of the Sumerian version is marked by the repetition of actions and words typical of storytelling as well as ritual practice. The same pattern will appear later when the anticipated disaster comes to pass and the gods behave as Inanna has predicted.

In the Akkadian version, Ishtar shouts a threat at the gates of the Underworld: She will smash the door and allow the dead to overrun the world and eat the living. This echoes Ishtar's threat in the episode of the *Epic of Gilgamesh* when she asked the high gods to unleash the Bull of Heaven against Gilgamesh and Enkidu. The force of the threat is that Ishtar will upset the cosmic balance and unleash chaos on creation by violating the boundaries that the gods have established between the realms of heaven, earth, and the Underworld

The focus of the story then shifts to Ereshkigal in her dark realm. As Inanna descends into the Underworld, her sister Ereshkigal sees her and vents her anger at Inanna's ambition and presumption. "What brings her to me? What has incited her against me? Surely not because I drink water with the Anunnaki, I eat clay for bread, I drink muddy water for beer?" (Dalley, 156). Her lot is miserable in comparison to Inanna's, yet her sister wishes to take even the little she has away from her. Ereshkigal sends her gatekeeper to allow Inanna to enter her kingdom, but stipulates that Inanna must lay aside one of her adornments at each of the seven gates that lead to the Underworld. So it happens. As Inanna enters each gate, she loses one of her adornments and with it the divine power it represents. Once again there is a repetition of words and actions at each of the gates: Inanna asks the gatekeeper why he has taken one of her adornments, and the gatekeeper tells her to be quiet and submit to the rites of the Underworld. When Inanna passes through the final gate and enters the Underworld, she has been stripped of all the symbols of her power, and left naked and vulnerable.

At this point in the Akkadian version, Ishtar threatens Ereshkigal, who cowers before her. But Ereshkigal summons her vizier to send sixty diseases against Ishtar, to attack each part of her body. The scene then shifts back to earth and it is never entirely clear what has happened to Ishtar. There is the suggestion later that she has died in the Underworld, but it may be that the idea of one of the great gods dying had become unmentionable, as it had in Egypt in the later versions of the death of Osiris at the hands of Seth. The earlier Sumerian version shows no such qualms. In that version, Inanna is condemned by the Seven Judges of the dead, presumably for her presumption in attempting to conquer the Underworld. Immediately the goddess sickens and dies, and her corpse is hung on a spike. The impaling is apparently a public display of Inanna's dead body—a punishment set aside for those who threaten the queen and her kingdom, a warning to others not to follow her example—and not the common fate of the dead in the Underworld.

At this point the Sumerian and Akkadian versions diverge considerably on how the gods of heaven are alerted to Inanna's death in the Underworld. In the earlier Sumerian version, Inanna has carefully prepared her minister Ninshubar for this eventuality. He carries out her instructions and goes to Enlil, Nanna, and Enki in turn, each time making the same plea in the same words. First Enlil and then Nanna give him the same reply, saying Inanna is "insatiable" and responsible for her own plight. But when Ninshubar goes to

Enki, the god of wisdom, he is struck with grief and quickly devises a plan to set the goddess free.

In the Akkadian version the situation is much more straightforward. Papsukkal, the gods' vizier, sees that in Ishtar's absence the people and animals of the earth have lost all interest in sexual intercourse and are suffering a kind of sterile lethargy. Papsukkal goes into mourning and beseeches Ea (the Akkadian equivalent to Enki) to bring Ishtar out of the Underworld and return her to earth. As befits his role as the god's vizier, their chief overseer, Papsukkal's concern is with the welfare of creation, not with Ishtar's personal plight or even the power dynamics among the gods. The world is suffering from the lack of fertility because Ishtar is trapped in the Underworld, so it is imperative to rescue her and restore the order of creation.

In both versions of the story, the goddess's rescue is brought about when the god of wisdom creates special beings to bring her out of the Underworld against Ereshkigal's will. These creatures are for some reason not subject to the laws of the Underworld and so are able to enter Ereshkigal's realm with impunity. In the Sumerian version, Enki makes two creatures, Kurgarru and Kalaturru, from the dirt under his fingernails. Since they are neither gods who belong to the heavens nor human beings who belong to the earth— because they are made of something that is neither heavenly nor earthly— they are not subject to the laws that bind gods and human beings. Yet even so Enki warns Kurgarru and Kalaturru not to eat or drink anything while they are in the Underworld, since this would mean accepting the obligations implicit in receiving hospitality. Enki also gives the two creatures the bread of life and the water of life to revive Inanna. These are divine gifts we also find in the story of Adapa the sage, where Adapa's well-intentioned refusal of the bread of life and the water of life leads to human beings being subjected to death.

When Kurgarru and Kalaturru arrive in the Underworld, they find Ereshkigal in some sort of physical distress. It may be that she is experiencing the pangs of a false labor brought on by the presence of Inanna, who even dead embodies the power of fertility and sexuality. In any event, the two creatures bring Ereshkigal relief, and in return ask for the body of Inanna. They then restore Inanna to life with the bread and water of life.

In the Akkadian version, the creature Ea creates is "His appearance is bright" or "Good-looks," a handsome fellow who is apparently a eunuch. He is to entice Ereshkigal and bend her to his will, but it seems he can do so without being in any danger of being seduced by her charms in turn. Ea instructs Good-looks to go down into Ereshkigal's realm and ask her for the water-skin so that he may drink from it. The meaning of this instruction is unclear, as is the reason why it provokes Ereshkigal to fury. It may be that "water-skin" in this instance refers to Ishtar's corpse. Ereshkigal curses Goodlooks for his request but summons her vizier Namtar and orders him to revive Ishtar. Namtar sprinkles the goddess with the water of life and restores her. He presents her to Ereshkigal, and Ishtar departs through the seven gates of the Underworld. As she goes through each gate, she again takes up each of her adornments until she returns to earth, once again fully clothed in her divine authority and power.

In both versions of the story, Inanna must also find someone to take her place in the Underworld. This is a common motif in stories about the Underworld and the abode of the dead. Once a place has been made and filled among the dead, it cannot be left vacant. In the Akkadian version of the story, Ereshkigal demands a ransom from Ishtar; her replacement is to be her lover and consort Dumuzi. In the Sumerian version, Inanna leaves the Underworld with a coterie of grotesque demons who attempt to take away one after another of Inanna's courtiers. But in each case she prevents them because the courtier had honored her by going into mourning during her imprisonment in the Underworld. But when Inanna discovers that her husband Dumuzi alone of all her entourage had not gone into mourning—in fact, it seems that he has been enjoying himself during his consort's travails—she consigns him to her place in the Underworld and orders the demons to take him away.

At this point the extant Sumerian version becomes fragmentary. There is the suggestion, however, that Dumuzi is not relegated to the Underworld for all time. Instead, he apparently alternates stays in the Underworld with his sister Geshtinanna, each of them residing there for half the year. This allows Dumuzi to return to the earth for six months each year and continue his marital and sexual relationship with Inanna and so provide for a season of fertility on earth before he again descends to the dark realm.

In the Akkadian version of the story Dumuzi's sister Belili rebels against the unjust sentence that dooms her brother to confinement in the Underworld. She pleads (although with whom is not clear) that Dumuzi be allowed to return to the land of the living periodically. When Dumuzi goes into the Underworld, a period of mourning begins and the earth does not produce crops and its animals do not produce offspring. But when Dumuzi returns to the earth, fertility is restored and the earth produces abundantly. Both the mourning and the celebration reflect Mesopotamian religious rituals to mourn the end of the agricultural year and to celebrate the beginning of a new season of growth and harvest. In both versions of the story Inanna/Ishtar's imprisonment in the Underworld gives way to the imprisonment of her consort Dumuzi in her place. In this way the story provides a connection between the mythic life of the goddess of fertility and the agricultural cycle while still freeing Inanna from the realm of the dead to reign as Queen of Heaven and Earth.

Apart from the concern with the cycle of the agricultural year, another intention of the story seems to have been to clarify the balance between the roles played in creation by Inanna on the one hand and Ereshkigal on the other. Although Inanna is Queen of Heaven and Earth, there is a third realm that lies beyond her control. This is the Underworld where the dead reside, ruled over by her sister. In that realm Ereshkigal holds the power and even Inanna is unable to overcome her. But by the same token, Ereshkigal as ruler of the Underworld cannot fully contain or suppress the power of dynamic life, fertility, and abundance that Inanna embodies and represents. Even when she has been stripped of her divine power and authority, Inanna by her very nature radiates the power of life. Life may be momentarily subjected to the power of death—as happens when the life of each person comes to an end—but life itself and the power of life continues and cannot be stopped by death. Even the goddess who rules over the kingdom of the dead must depend on the power of life and the continual process of life beginning and ending if her reign is to continue. The story seems to recognize a connection between the power of fertility and the role of death in allowing new life to appear. There is a balance between the two: Death ends life, but life grows out of death.

The story may also be in part an answer to the question, "Why is there suffering and death?" This is a less pressing question in a polytheistic religious culture like that of ancient Mesopotamia than it is in a monotheistic religious culture, but it is still a question that must be addressed. In the story of Inanna and Ereshkigal, the answer seems to be that some things are beyond the power of even the greatest of the gods. Even Inanna cannot overcome the power of death, and even Ereshkigal cannot resist the laws inherent in creation. Some things are beyond the power of the gods, and that's simply the way things are. There is certainly no connection implied between Inanna's escape from death in the Underworld and any possibility of a human escape from death. In fact the story makes quite the opposite point. Inanna does not "conquer" death, but is instead conquered by it. She escapes only through the intervention of Enki, who saves her less for her own sake than for the sake of the world that needs the power of fertility and sexuality in order to survive. Even so, Enki is able to rescue Inanna only through a clever stratagem that somehow circumvents the proper order of things in the Underworld. Inanna is presented in the story as a very special case that exempts her from the usual rules of the divine order. Her special status serves only to emphasize the uniqueness of her case, and the otherwise inescapable and final nature of death.

Nergal and Ereshkigal

There is a second story from ancient Mesopotamia about a heavenly deity attempting to usurp Ereshkigal's power as ruler over the Underworld, but it has a considerably different plot and outcome. In this case, the deity is Nergal, the Mesopotamian god of pestilence and destruction. There are again two divergent versions of the story. The earlier, shorter version was found at Tel Armana in Egypt, and dates from 1500–1300 BCE. The later version was found in texts from Sultantepe near Harran in northwestern Mesopotamia, dating from 700–600 BCE, and from Uruk in southeastern Mesopotamia, dating from the Late Babylonian period, 600–540 BCE. The story has its humorous aspects, and may have been created to reconcile conflicting traditions about which god controlled the Underworld by postulating a marriage between the two divine contenders.

The story begins with a banquet in heaven for the gods, a banquet that Ereshkigal cannot attend because she cannot cross the unbridgeable gulf between the realm of the higher gods in heaven and her kingdom in the Underworld. Anu's message to the goddess about the banquet says explicitly that it is impossible for Ereshkigal to come up into heaven, just as it is impossible for the heavenly gods to descend into the Underworld. These restrictions, however, apparently do not apply to the gods' ministers, or at least not to those who function as heralds or ambassadors between the two realms. Anu sends his message to Ereshkigal by the hand of his minister Kakka who carries it down to the Underworld, and the gods invite Ereshkigal to send her vizier Namtar up to heaven to attend their banquet in her place. After Anu's minister Kakka passes through the gates of the Underworld he is received with due courtesy by Ereshkigal, who pronounces peace on all the highest gods. She orders Namtar to attend the banquet, and he ascends the long pathway leading to heaven.

When Namtar arrives in heaven he is honored by all the gods except one, Nergal, who ostentatiously offends him. Although there is no explanation for his behavior, Nergal's rudeness is apparently meant to provide a pretext for his later descent to the Underworld with the intention of conquering it. When Ereshkigal learns how Namtar has been treated, she demands the offending god be sent down to her in the Underworld. So Ea, the god of wisdom, instructs Nergal on how to enter the Underworld without becoming trapped there and being subjected to its laws. Ea tells Nergal to make an ornamented chair to take with him when he goes down to the Underworld. Once there, he is to sit only in this chair and is not to take anything Ereshkigal might offer him, or he will be accepting her hospitality and so place himself under the laws of the Underworld. If he does that, he will have to remain there. Fully prepared, Nergal marches down to the gates of the Underworld. Namtar hears a report of his approach and carries the news to Ereshkigal. At her command Namtar admits Nergal through each of the seven gates of the Underworld and into Ereshkigal's presence.

Once in the Underworld, Nergal is careful to follow all of Ea's instructions. He refuses to accept anything offered by Ereshkigal's servants or to do anything that might involve accepting her hospitality. But Nergal is the son of Ishtar, and while Ereshkigal is bathing she allows him to catch a glimpse of her naked body. Nergal is smitten and succumbs to her charms, embracing her passionately and carrying her off to bed. The two engage in sexual intercourse over the course of a week, until finally Nergal asks Ereshkigal to allow him to leave. He promises he will return to her later and departs, leaving Ereshkigal bereft and pregnant with his child. Nergal bluffs his way past the gatekeepers and returns to heaven.

When Ereshkigal learns that Nergal has left the Underworld she is inconsolable, lamenting that she had not had her fill of making love with him before he left. Namtar asks to be sent to heaven so that he may ask Anu, Enlil, and Ea to send Nergal back to her. Ereshkigal sends him on his way to demand the great gods send Nergal to her, echoing the threat of Ishtar in the "Descent," "If you do not send that god to me, I shall raise up the dead, and they will eat the living. I shall make the dead outnumber the living!" (Dalley, 173). But Ea has anticipated this turn of events, and he transforms Nergal to prevent Namtar from recognizing him. When Namtar arrives in heaven he is unable to recognize Nergal, who sits "bareheaded, blinking and cringing at the assembly of all the gods" (Dalley, 174).

Despite the success of his subterfuge, Nergal soon returns to the Underworld, this time with the overt intention of conquering it. As he descends once again, he strikes down each of the gatekeepers in turn, but asserts his preemptive power by not deigning to engage in physical combat with any of them. When Nergal enters the Underworld where Ereshkigal is holding court, he laughs at her and pulls her off her throne by her hair. At this point, there is a break in the text. When the story resumes, the two gods once again embrace passionately and go off to bed, where they again remain for seven days. Ereshkigal is apparently content to submit to Nergal's authority and rule with him as his consort, and the passion (and sexual intercourse) between them continues unabated.

Clearly this story, like that of Inanna's journey into the Underworld, is meant to explain and clarify the role Nergal and Ereshkigal each play in the governance of the Underworld. The usual assumption is that the story was intended to justify Nergal's role as the ruler of the Underworld, a role originally filled by Ereshkigal. Nergal has the unusual divine power to cross the gulf between heaven and the Underworld and to pass freely across the different realms. He twice travels back and forth between heaven and the Underworld, something that no other of the major gods is apparently capable of doing, although the minor gods who serve as their ministers—gods such as Namtar—are able to due so while fulfilling their duties. Nergal's unusual ability may indicate that as a god of pestilence and destruction he already has an affinity for the realm of the dead that motivates his attempt to seize its throne. It is also notable that although Nergal takes her throne by force, Ereshkigal seems content to submit to his authority. Here too there seems to be a natural association—here expressed as sexual attraction—between pestilence and destruction on the one hand and the forces of death on the other.

As a son of Ishtar, Nergal represents what we might call the "active" work of death, putting into motion those forces that lead to death. Ishtar herself represents and embodies the destructive force of natural disasters and the heat of battle, and Nergal shares that vigorous aspect of destruction. Just as Ereshkigal depends on Ishtar's power of life to maintain and replenish the kingdom of the dead, so she also depends on Nergal's power of destruction and pestilence to kill human beings and bring them into her dark realm. But this idea is also expressed in terms of the sexual relationship between Nergal and Ereshkigal. The goddess who has formerly been solitary and barren as she ruled over the Underworld in this story finds vigor and happiness in Nergal's embrace. At the very least, the story recognizes a harmony and mutuality between the dynamic forces of destruction and the passive forces of death. Since the Mesopotamians thought of their gods as much like human beings, it may also be that it seemed wrong to leave even the Queen of the Underworld without the pleasures of sexual activity and romantic companionship.

Stories about the Underworld as Creation Myths

Mesopotamian stories having to do with the Underworld are for the most part stories about the gods. They form part of the creation narrative, the explanation of "how things got to be the way they are now." In this respect, the Mesopotamian stories stand in contrast to literature dedicated to the Underworld in Egyptian religious culture, which is primarily concerned with the fate of the dead themselves. Although the Egyptian literature includes stories about the origins of Osiris's dominion over the realm of the dead, these stories are subsidiary to the myth of kingship. In the myth, Osiris serves as a model for the dead king who continues to "rule" even as he is succeeded by his legitimate heir on earth. Similarly, the other Egyptian gods involved in the fate of the dead—including Ra and Nut, both of whom provide eternal habitations for the dead distinct from the kingdom of Osiris—are part of an established order in which the deceased may find a place. But again the emphasis is on the fate and the hopes of the dead. The primary Egyptian texts that have to do with the nature of the Underworld—collected in *The Book of Going Forth by Day*—are instructions for the deceased on what to expect and what to do to successfully gain a place of blessedness in the afterlife. In short, information about the Underworld in Egyptian religious culture is primarily intended to reassure and instruct the living so they may find a place of rest after they die.

The Mesopotamian stories about the Underworld, on the other hand, have little or nothing to do with human beings or their fate after death and everything to do with the gods. The stories are concerned with the actions of the gods in the "beginning times," when things were not yet the way they are now, either among the gods or upon the earth. The divine conflicts among the gods in these stories in fact lead to things being the way they are now for both the gods and human beings. Now Nergal and Ereshkigal rule the Underworld together because of the events that are described in their story. Now Dumuzi and his sister Geshtinanna (or Belili) alternate sojourns in the Underworld, thereby creating the cycle of fertility, because of the events surrounding Inanna/Ishtar's descent into the Underworld in an attempt to conquer it. These are stories about the gods and the nature of the cosmos, not about human beings or their fate in the Underworld.

Still, the situation of the dead in the Underworld is occasionally reflected in the gods' words, actions, and circumstances in these stories. For example, when Ereshkigal complains in the "Descent" about the miserable circumstances in which she rules over the kingdom of the dead, her words reflect the gloomy fate of the dead, confined in darkness under the earth with only clay to eat and muddy water to drink. In the same story, once Inanna/Ishtar enters the Underworld she is stripped of her adornments, the symbols of her power over heaven and earth. This reflects the belief in ancient Mesopotamian religious culture that death is the great leveler, bringing the same fate to a king or a demigod like Gilgamesh as it brings to the most humble of human beings. There are no distinctions of rank among the dead, except perhaps the distinction between the good and the wicked. When

Inanna's corpse is stuck on a spike in the Sumerian version of the story of her descent into the Underworld, her punishment is consistent with the idea that the Underworld involves judgment and punishment for the wicked. In the stories about both Ishtar and Nergal, there is a pronounced concern with becoming trapped in the Underworld. Ishtar in fact becomes trapped and must be rescued, while Nergal goes to great lengths to avoid becoming trapped. In both stories it is clear that Ereshkigal herself is trapped in the Underworld and unable to ascend to the realm of the gods of heaven. This again is also the fate of human beings, for whom the road to the Underworld is one-way only.

It is worth noting that both Ishtar and Ereshkigal threaten in different situations to bring the dead up from the Underworld to overrun the world of the living and eat the living, so there will be more of the dead than the living on earth. Ishtar makes this threat at the beginning of her "Descent" in the Akkadian version to get the gatekeeper to open way for her, but also in the *Epic of Gilgamesh* when she asks Anu to send the Bull of Heaven to kill Gilgamesh and Enkidu after they have insulted her. Ereshkigal makes the same threat in *Nergal and Ereshkigal* in the message she gives Namtar to deliver to the gods of heaven after Nergal has left her. In each case, the threat seems to have the same implications: It is a threat to undo the proper order of the cosmos, to break down the set boundaries of ordered existence and bring chaos into creation to destroy it. In each case too the threat is heeded and the goddess given what she wants; the threat of chaos is a threat the gods must respect so the created order may be preserved.

But the threat also reflects the dread and fear the living feel toward the dead, and have felt apparently since the prehistoric era: the fear that the dead will, if they can, somehow return and take revenge on the living. Especially pertinent and revealing is the fear that the dead will eat the living. This reflects the unanimous belief in the ancient Mediterranean world that blood—human or animal—is the source of life. This belief and the fear of the vengeful dead persist in the modern era in the figure of the vampire or the zombie, the undead who feed on the blood or flesh of the living. There is some irony in the persistent human fear of the dead preying on the living. Throughout the history of human existence, living human beings have sometimes survived by eating their dead, but however much the contrary situation has been feared it has never come to pass.

In these Mesopotamian stories about the Underworld, unlike Egyptian stories, the human dead and their fate are not really a matter of concern. The human dead are at best ignored and at worst portrayed as a ravening horde at the command of a vengeful goddess, threatening to escape from their confinement in the Underworld to overrun the land of the living. In this respect the dead are comparable to the demonic lower orders of gods who serve the goddess of the Underworld, who are unremittingly hostile to living humanity. To find some consideration of the human fate of death in Mesopotamian religious culture, we must turn elsewhere. We may find some explanations about the reasons human beings must die in a story about Adapa or Atrahasis, primeval sages whose actions served to determine the fate of human beings for all subsequent generations. Or we may find consolation in the face of death in the ruminations that shape the second half of the *Epic of Gilgamesh*, in the course of the hero's quest for everlasting life. Significantly, these are not stories about the Underworld and the gods who rule or would rule there. These instead are stories written to address and sympathize with the lot of human beings, stories that belong to the land of the living rather than to the realm of the dead.

CHAPTER TEN

Mesopotamia: The Human World

The Gods and Humanity in Ancient Mesopotamia

Much of the surviving religious literature from ancient Mesopotamia depicts the activities of the gods only during the period between creation and the primordial Flood, the period when their actions and interactions determined "how things came to be the way they are now." In stories about the gods we most often find them pursuing their own interests and fighting, loving, deceiving, and helping only one another. The human beings that appear in these stories are for the most part men who are superior to the common mass of humanity—heroes or sages—and they interact with the gods much as they might interact with human overlords to whom they owe fealty. Average people for the most part do not appear in these stories, except perhaps as members of undifferentiated crowds who benefit from a hero's victory or suffer from a god's anger.

The shape of a nation's religious culture reflects its historical situation. Ancient Mesopotamia's history was a history of war, uncertainty, natural disaster, political upheaval, social unrest, and the ever-present threat of chaos. This turbulent history was the inevitable result of Mesopotamia's geographical situation, placed as it was in the fertile plains between two major rivers that linked the East with the West. Lying in valleys between the mountains and the desert, Mesopotamia was the natural pathway for successive waves of migrating peoples slowly moving from central Asia toward the Mediterranean coast. At the same time, the various indigenous peoples fought for hegemony among their neighbors. Asserting effective royal dominion over

Mesopotamia required imposing some sort of harmony among its different ethnic and political factions while preventing incursions by hostile outsiders. Each of the regional groups that came to dominance in Mesopotamia over its long history was originally only one in a collection of diverse peoples.

As a product of this history, a certain anxiety seems to lie beneath Mesopotamian religious culture and its literature. If there is not a sense of actual distrust of the gods, there is at least a sense that the gods are not particularly concerned with the needs and well-being of most of humanity. Hope that the gods might prove benevolent toward their human worshippers is combined with a keen sense of humanity's low status in the eyes of the gods and in the great order of creation. As we have seen, the creation of humanity in *Enuma elish* appears as almost an afterthought to the main drama of the story, when Marduk makes human beings from the blood of Qingu, "the clumsy laborer." Humanity is created to relieve the lower divinities from the burdensome work of providing for the needs of the higher gods. Even at that, human beings often prove a nuisance, since they are noisy and tend to reproduce in numbers that make them bothersome. In short, in Mesopotamian mythology the gods regard "the dark-haired people" under their dominion in much the same way as human overlords might regard their slaves. They are necessary to the gods' well-being but they are also a constant source of trouble. Human beings are both the abettors and disrupters of a quiet life for the gods.

In contrast to the ambivalent attitude toward the gods that seems to permeate the Mesopotamian religious narratives that have survived to the present day, Mesopotamian religious practice was based on the conviction that the people's divine masters could and often would choose to be benevolent, provided their human servants fulfilled their duties. The primary duty of a servant or slave (the two were largely equivalent in the ancient Mediterranean world) was faithful service. Human beings served the gods not only through formal public religious activity such as offerings and worship in the temple, but also through the observance of all sorts of daily prayers, rituals, and practices to invoke or placate the gods. Much as slaves tend to look up to and praise the master on whom their well-being depends, the Mesopotamians admired and glorified their gods, praising them for their benevolence and mercy while seeking help and blessings from them. And like human masters, the gods offered favors to those who pleased them.

As is virtually always the case in a polytheistic religious culture, in Mesopotamia there was a full array of gods to provide for the particular necessities of a person's life. The national gods were responsible for the well-being of the nation and its people, with particular concern for the king as the nation's ruler and guardian. In addition to worshipping the national gods, most people would also worship the god most closely associated with their livelihood, the god whose daily goodwill was necessary for their safety and well-being. Other gods might be invoked in specific situations relevant to their particular divine concerns. Some minor gods were invoked primarily as protective deities who could drive away threatening demons or evil spirits. The benevolence of any or all of these gods might be invoked by actions or words, rituals or incantations. Their goodwill might be enhanced by wearing amulets, or their intentions sought out by means of oracles, revelations through which the gods would speak to their people.

Most important among the array of gods was one's "personal god," a benevolent god who took particular interest in an individual's life and welfare. The personal god guarded a person as a protective deity from the moment of birth, and was in fact often credited as the god who oversaw the person's conception. The personal god was usually anonymous, or at least was not referred to by name by the person he or she protected. Other people however might refer to a personal god in conversation as "N., your god." There was a possibility that a personal god might withdraw favor if a person was not attentive to his or her religious duties, and those who suffered particular misfortune were believed to have been abandoned by their personal god.

The ideal for human life in Mesopotamia, as elsewhere in the ancient Near East, was to enjoy good health and prosperity throughout a long life. The reality of course was that life, then as now, was unpredictable and could often be harsh or violent. Even the longest and most pleasant of human lives inevitably ended in death. All of Mesopotamian religious practice, from the national cult and temple worship to personal and household devotions, from prophecy and divination to the discipline of wisdom, was concerned with making the best of the human condition in the world as the gods had created and shaped it.

Places and Forms of Worship

The place of worship most often associated with ancient Mesopotamian religious culture is the ziggurat. Mesopotamians built ziggurats from about 2200 BCE during the Akkadian domination until about 550 BCE and the Persian conquest. Unlike the Egyptian pyramids, which were essentially monumental tombs, ziggurats were intended solely for religious rituals. They were solid except for accommodations for drainage, with external stairways to allow access to the summit. Ziggurats were usually surrounded by extensive courtyards with towered walls. In addition to a temple at the summit dedicated to the

Partial reconstruction of the Great Ziggurat at Ur, originally built by Ur-Nammu, founder of the Third Dynasty of Ur (2112–2004 BCE). Wiki-media Commons

chief god, ziggurats often incorporated worship spaces devoted to other gods along their terraces. Ziggurats might also in some cases provide a space for the ritual of sacred marriage. Apparently access to a ziggurat was restricted to cultic personnel, with the common people relegated to standing in the surrounding courtyard during worship rituals. But most public worship took place in temples.

In Mesopotamian cities the most important building was usually not the palace of the city's king but the temple. The temple was the dwelling-place of the city's patron god where the daily rituals of worship and sacrifice took place. Both the Mesopotamian temple complex and the daily rituals conducted in its sanctuary recall in many ways the temples and rituals of Egypt, reflecting a general homogeneity of beliefs and practices in regard to the gods in the ancient Near East. The typical Mesopotamian city temple was large and imposing, with extensive decoration and multiple entrances and courtyards. There was both public worship space and more exclusive space reserved for the work and worship of temple priests and servants. The temple complex included everything that was needed for ritual worship, including living space for cultic personnel, storehouses, pens and housing for animals, and workshops for craftsmen. In some cases these facilities might instead be located outside of the temple, in other parts of the city.

A wide array of cultic personnel worked in the temple complex. Both men and women served gods of both sexes. The ranks of priestesses were in some cases filled by daughters of the royal family. The temple offices ranged from the chief priest or priestess to a series of lower priests and priestesses with specialized duties, to musicians and diviners, to magicians and dream interpreters, to cooks and others charged with the practical tasks necessary for the everyday business of the temple. Cultic personnel lived off the goods and monetary income of the temple as their share of the offerings made to the gods they served. Some but not all the cultic personnel lived in the temple complex. Some temples changed cultic personnel regularly, usually according to an annual schedule, while in others positions as priests and other temple functionaries were held for life and handed down from a father to his eldest son. Later, after many of the traditional temple offices had been eliminated, the income customarily due to them from the temple's coffers was still distributed to those who had the hereditary right to claim them. At the lower levels, the cultic personnel included slaves. Often slaves were orphans or poor children who were given to the temple by their parents or other relatives. Despite the relative prosperity and independence of some slaves in service to the temple, in general their lot in life was similar to that of other slaves, burdensome and harsh.

The temple was obviously the center of a city's worship, but because of the goods and other revenue that flowed into the temple complex it was also an important center of a city's trade and commerce. The temple was the house (Akkadian, *bitu*) of the god or goddess who was responsible for the well-being of the city and its people and who presided over the city's daily life. As a result, the temple was also a center of power and authority in legal agreements and disputes.

The primary rituals of the temple focused on the cultic statue of the god, which was presented with food offerings twice daily. The cultic statue was more than a representation of the god; it was believed to embody and insure the actual presence of the god in the temple. Accordingly it was accorded divine honors by the priests. The cultic statue was usually placed in a niche in one wall of the temple, opposite the entrance. It was washed at the start of each day and dressed in fresh clothes. The priests would present food offerings to the cultic statue first thing in the morning after the temple doors were opened, and again last thing in the evening before the temple doors were closed and locked for the night. Offerings were placed on a table with dishes, utensils, and the other necessities for a meal. The food was intended to represent the best meat and produce available as a fitting repast for the god. After the offering had been presented, linen curtains were drawn to allow the god to partake of the food in discreet privacy. Musicians would provide music while temple attendants burned incense. After the god had consumed the spiritual essence of the food offering, the curtains were opened so the table could be cleared, then drawn again to allow the god to wash up. The food remaining from the twice-daily ritual offering provided the daily meals for the priests, their families, and other cultic personnel who served in the temple.

In addition to the cultic statue of the temple's primary god or goddess, the temple would often include statues representing worshippers standing in rapt attention. Through these concrete representations, both god and worshippers were forever in the temple, the one dispensing blessings and the others perpetually engaged in the act of worship, together maintaining and enhancing the relationship between the god and the god's people.

Another important Mesopotamian religious ritual was the *hieros gamos* or "sacred marriage," symbolic intercourse between a city's king and a priestess representing the goddess Inanna or Ishtar. As we have noted before, the *hieros gamos* was both symbolic and imitative. The priestess and the king represented Inanna and Dumuzi. The intention of the ritual was to ensure the fertility of the kingdom by imitating the sexual intercourse between Inanna and Dumuzi that was believed to be the source of fertility for the earth and sexual vitality for both animals and human beings. It is probably within the context of this ritual of sacred marriage that much of the love poetry celebrating the erotic love between Inanna and Dumuzi was performed. The sacred marriage is also related to what is often called "sacred prostitution" in the temples of Ishtar, when priestesses of the goddess would have intercourse with male worshippers in return for a monetary donation to the temple. Both the Greek historian Herodotus and various authors of works found in the Hebrew Bible condemned this practice as immoral and, indeed, cited it as a prime example of the decadence they thought was typical of Mesopotamia. The taint of decadence and illicit sexuality lingers around the name of Babylon even today.

Religious Festivals

As in Egypt, religious festivals in Mesopotamia celebrated the relationship between the gods and humanity and provided a way for common people to experience the presence of the gods among them. The public display of the cultic statue took place in annual festivals when the god of the temple celebrated his or her New Year or when the god would "visit" another god in the other god's temple. The cultic statue was placed in a portable shrine that was carried in procession or transported in some other way. Some temple complexes included a dock for boats that were used to transport the temple's cultic statue to the shrines of other gods. A cultic procession during a religious festival provided one of the few opportunities for common people to see the cultic statue, and in that way to experience the "presence" of the god among them. Stories that describe the visit of one god to another—or even stories about attempted conquests like "The Descent of Ishtar to the Underworld"— are usually interpreted by scholars as cultic myths that initiated or justified festivals of visitation.

There were various regional festivals dedicated to different gods throughout ancient Mesopotamia, although most of these were similar in terms of the rituals and personnel involved. The major agricultural festivals at Ur in the early second millennium BCE were a Feast of Sowing in the autumn, during late October or early November and another, Cutting the Grain, in late April or early May. These festivals marked the beginning of sowing and reaping, respectively. The city's king would plow the first furrow during the Feast of Sowing in front of the gathered population before the actual work of sowing began. Similarly Cutting the Grain initiated the work of gathering the produce of the fields, with the city's king once again acting as the ceremonial representative of his subjects.

The major festival in Mesopotamian religious culture was the New Year's festival (*Akitu*) that celebrated the triumph of divine order over chaos in the gods' act of creation. This festival was both a celebration of the triumph of creative energy over chaos and an appeal to the gods to ensure the continued well-being of the nation for the coming year. But at least in its later form in Babylon, the elaborate ceremony was primarily a renewal of kingship through the renewal and reauthorization of the reigning king as the gods' chosen viceroy on earth. The central act of renewal was surrounded with elaborate preparatory prayers and ceremonies involving the king as the primary participant.

The major source of information about the New Year's festival comes from the first millennium BCE, during the Neo-Babylonian period. At that time the new year was celebrated in honor of Marduk during the first days of the month of Nisan at the beginning of spring (March/April). The first several days of the festival were devoted to preparatory purification through ritual cleansing and prayer, and the construction of two "statues of evil." The fourth day began with prayers to Marduk and his consort Sarpanitum, the chief goddess of Babylon. During the evening of the same day the creation story *Enuma elish* was recited or performed. This ritual performance placed the other events of the festival in the context of the (re)creation of divine order through the triumphant power of Marduk as the patron god of Babylon. The connection between Marduk and the king of Babylon clarified the king's key role as Marduk's agent in holding back the powers of chaos that continually threatened to devastate Mesopotamia. The parallel to the king of Egypt as the one who insures *maat* on earth is clear. In the context of the *Akitu* festival, as in Mesopotamian religious culture generally, whatever stability the nation might enjoy was solely the result of the gods' divine favor toward the king and the king's reciprocal actions that fulfilled divine directives for the prosperity, peace, and well-being of the city and the empire it controlled.

The early part of the fifth festival day involved the purification of the temple of Marduk. This was followed by sacrifice of a sheep that was then dragged through the temple and finally thrown into the river. The sheep carried with it the sins committed during the old year, sins that were wiped away by its death. In Israelite Yahwism, much the same purpose was served by the scapegoat that carried the sins of the people into the wilderness on the Day of Atonement, as described in Leviticus 16:8–22. The symbolic elimination of sin from the community is often an important part of new year rituals, allowing the people to renew their relationship with the gods as they move from the old year into the new.

In the evening of the fifth day came what was arguably the central act of the New Year's festival, the ritual humiliation of the king and his subsequent reinstatement as the chosen instrument of Marduk. First the king was stripped of his royal regalia before he entered the inner sanctuary of the temple. There the priest slapped the king's face and pulled his ears, presumably to remind him of his unworthiness and his subordinate place as the servant of Marduk. The king would then kneel before the cult statue of Marduk and recite a list of the wrongs he had not committed during the previous year. The priest of Marduk then reassured the king of the god's favor and returned his royal regalia. Finally the priest would again slap the king's face. If tears came to his eyes, this was taken as a sign of Marduk's favor toward him. Clothed again in his royal regalia and restored to his place in the divine order, the king took part in other rituals during the night, including the sacrificial burning of a white bull.

On the sixth day, the two "statues of evil" that had been made during the first days of the festival were beheaded. This act was intended to defeat and banish the powers of evil from the kingdom for the coming year. Later days of the festival saw the arrival in Babylon of the cultic statues of gods from other important cities to honor Marduk as their king and to share in the general festivities. The festival apparently concluded with a ritual procession. The king himself led the chariot bearing the cultic statue of Marduk along the city's chief thoroughfare, out the Ishtar Gate to the New Year's house (*bit akitu*), with the cultic statues of the other gods following in procession. The crowds on either side of the street knelt in adoration of the gods. The cultic statues remained in the *bit akitu* for several days before returning to Esagil, the temple of Marduk, and on the twelfth day of the festival they returned to their own cities.

From the temple of Marduk the destiny of the city was proclaimed, probably taking the form of reassurance that the gods would continue to protect the city during the coming year. The final day of the festival was marked with banquets and celebration. It may also have been at this time the king ensured the fertility of the land for the coming year through the ritual of sacred marriage, engaging in sexual intercourse with a priestess of Ishtar.

The New Year's festival reinforced the king's authority through its annual renewal but also served to remind the people of the nation's dependence on the goodwill of the gods, which was mediated through the king. The people in turn could please the gods through their individual acts of worship, but also preeminently through their loyalty and reverence toward the king.

Reconstruction of the Ishtar Gate of the city of Babylon, originally built by Nebuchad-nezzar II (604-562 BCE). © 2008 Jupiterimages Corporation

Popular Religion

Apart from official religious cultic practices and festivals, there were other ways that religious ideas and sentiment permeated ancient Mesopotamian culture. The common person could make connections with the gods in a variety of ways, both communal and personal. Like religious people of all times and places, ancient Mesopotamians offered their gods hymns of praise, enumerating the gods' many virtues and emphasizing in particular their sovereignty over the earth and its creatures. In Mesopotamia these praises tend to be full of stereotyped images and phrases that might vary little from one god to another or one hymn to another. On the other hand, it is from such hymns that we gain a better sense of what traits were prized in which gods, and what powers each god was believed to control and exert.

Often, of course, praise of a god served as a prelude to requests. These requests might be general appeals for the god's continued help and goodwill, or specific pleas for help in distress, as the petitioner abased himself or herself before the god, seeking divine favor. Here again we may see the similarity between human attitudes toward the gods and a slave's attitude toward his or her master. In both cases, the petitioner's fear of the master's power and unchecked emotion create a cautious reverence that tends to glorify the master and see him or her as the source of all benefits the petitioner might receive.

Much of daily human interaction with the gods was essentially pragmatic and formalized. Many of these interactions were essentially part of everyday activities, actions, and procedures undertaken with the intention of getting something done. The religious ritual was intertwined with a practical action to bring about the desired result, whether building a house or giving birth or undertaking a journey. Particular gods were invoked in matters that related to their sphere of power and influence. People in different occupations invoked different patron gods, just as people in different situations invoked the different gods who were known for being of assistance under those circumstances.

The gods were also invoked in rituals meant to ensure health or prosperity, spark sexual love, bring misfortune upon others, or ward off misfortune sent by others. Most of these rituals are usually classified as "magical" by scholars rather than as religious, in part because they are concerned with immediate practical results and do not appear to reflect religious sentiment. But in fact the distinction between religious and magical practices is ambiguous, and it is doubtful that ancient Mesopotamians themselves would have recognized such a distinction or found it useful. Yet the distinction may prove useful in some ways for modern readers.

Essentially, the difference between "religious" ritual and "magical" ritual depends on the intended result of the words a person speaks or the actions a person undertakes. If the words or actions are meant to please a god or other supernatural figure with the intention of persuading the god to do what the person concerned wishes, then the actions are considered religious. But if the words or actions are meant to force or compel a god or other supernatural figure to do what the person wishes, then the actions are considered magical. At issue is the intended effect on the gods, whether the god's response is voluntary or involuntary.

In ancient Mesopotamia there were both approved and disapproved forms of what we might call magical practice. For the most part, magical rituals meant to benefit a person were accepted as legitimate, while those aimed at harming others were rejected. At the same time, there is little evidence that those who practiced rituals harmful to others—what is usually called "black" magic—were subjected to legal prosecution very often.

One acceptable and popular form of magic was protective magic involving the use of amulets or talismans. These tokens were believed to ward off evil or to bring good luck. Their effect depended either on what the amulet or talisman was made of, how it was created, or what it was fashioned to represent. Particular materials were believed to have inherent properties that would turn away evil beings or power. The images of specific gods or demons were believed to be effective in warding off certain evils, particularly in situations of notable peril such as childbirth. Personal seals apparently also served their users as amulets in some cases. Both seals and amulets were sometimes very closely identified with the person who used or wore them, becoming essentially the person's stand-in in the spiritual realm. Magic was apparently practiced by all sorts and classes of people in ancient Mesopotamia. It was legitimized by its association with the god of wisdom, Ea/Enki, and his consort Damkina, who also supervised its use. Later their son Marduk became a patron of magic as well.

Discerning the Will of the Gods

Obedience to the gods was the proper foundation of all human behavior, both personal and social, since it was necessary to please the gods with faithful service if one were to receive benefits from them. For the most part, the Mesopotamians saw a clear cause-and-effect relationship between human behavior on the one hand and the divine response on the other. Whatever might happen to a person each day or over the course of his or her life was a reflection and result of his or her behavior. As a result, ancient Mesopotamians tended to understand sudden strokes of good fortune as a reward from the gods for a person's record of obedience and good behavior. In Sumerian and Akkadian, the only term to express the idea of enjoying good luck is "to acquire a god" (Jacobsen, 155). This implies not only that the lucky person has pleased the gods but also that he or she has gained a divine ally through a consistent pattern of obedience. Conversely, bad luck was most often understood as divine punishment for a person's disobedience and evil behavior. The idea of suffering bad luck is expressed by the phrase "not to acquire a god." The luckless person was left bereft, without a helper or advocate in the divine realm.

Misfortune of various kinds was not generally attributed to the influence of demons until the first millennium BCE, when they became a major cause of concern. Demons were initially thought of as supernatural beings who acted solely at the behest of the gods to do good or evil toward humanity as divine agents. An example appears in the Sumerian version of the story of Inanna's descent into the Underworld. When the goddess leaves the Underworld after her rescue, she is accompanied by grotesque creatures from Ereshkigal's realm, creatures that later carry Dumuzi off at Inanna's command. Belief in independent action against human beings by malevolent demons arose about the same time as belief in comparable supernatural beings who guard humanity against them, around 1000 BCE. Surprisingly enough, such protective spirits might include other demons. The most notable example is Pazuzu, who provided protection against the evil brought in by ill winds. Amulets of Pazuzu also protected women in childbirth. Exorcists were believed to be able to expel evil demons from a person, especially those demons that caused disease. Exorcism was often associated with other, more practical forms of medical intervention, a primary example of the intertwining of the magical and the practical.

In cases of personal misfortune, it became imperative to discover what offense against the gods had provoked it if some solution were to be found. Often the investigation required the use of magical practices that could both identify the cause of the misfortune and propose an appropriate remedy. If the misfortune arose from some form of personal misbehavior, there were spells that could remove the effects of the sin and purify the one afflicted. Other magical procedures might include burning a symbolic carrier of sin, comparable to the sheep that bore the sins of the people during the New Year's festival. If someone's misfortune arose from the machinations of an enemy, there were magical remedies available, as well as the more forceful response imposed by laws against witchcraft.

Since it was imperative to obey the gods, discerning divine intentions was a matter of major concern. Divine revelations might be sought out through human intermediaries, but they were often offered spontaneously by the gods in various ways. Whatever the case, such revelations were carefully analyzed to determine what message the gods meant to convey.

Omens were striking events of various sorts that were recognized as intentional divine communications that required interpretation if they were to be properly understood. Omens included unusual or unexpected events in the private or public realm. Events in nature such as earthquakes or lightning strikes might be taken as omens. Apparently coincidental events, such as the appearance of certain animals under certain circumstances, might also be taken as omens. Omens might also be discerned in more unusual events, such as unusual natural phenomena or the birth of malformed babies or animals. Any given omen might be intended for a person, a family, a city, or for the entire nation. Omens might be either good or bad. They might be forewarnings of impending disaster that might still be averted through ritual or magical actions. They might be forecasts of good fortune to come that would encourage the people in times of need or uncertainty. But communication from the gods was often mysterious or equivocal. Omens had to be interpreted by qualified spiritual authorities, and those authorities would also know what actions it was appropriate to take in response to a given omen. Thousands of texts from ancient Mesopotamia list how different unusual occurrences are to be interpreted, usually by tying particular ominous events to very specific meanings for the future.

Divine revelations could also be solicited by another sort of diviners, spiritual adepts who would discover the will of the gods through the use of a special ritual procedure or apparatus. In such cases, the diviner sought a revelation on behalf of a client and created a situation in which the gods could convey an answer of "yes" or "no" according to the outcome. This would make the gods' reply relatively easy to understand, provided the question itself was clear.

Diviners might also interpret specific phenomena such as the casting of lots or the appearance of the dregs from a cup of wine. A major form of divination in Mesopotamia was extispicy, divining the future by examining the viscera of sacrificed animals. There are hundreds of accounts of how diviners read the entrails of sheep or poultry to learn the future. There are also many surviving models of livers to serve as a reference and guide in the work of divination. Such divination took place under the aegis of the gods—notably Shamash and Adad—who were invoked at the beginning of the procedure to ensure that what the diviner found would be an accurate account of what was to come. Despite its technical character, divination was still a deeply religious business. Similarly, omens given to someone in dreams would be interpreted by diviners who were believed to be able to do so only because they were inspired through a divinely given gift for such interpretation.

Information about divine intentions in the present or for the future could also be gained through observation of the movement of the stars. Astrology was a major rival to extispicy as a divinatory technique, and during the first millennium BCE some practitioners would combine the techniques to substantiate their insights. The "science" of astrology was developed by the Chaldeans, the dominant people of the Neo-Babylonian Empire. Astrology was based on the belief that events on earth were the result of the influence of divine powers determining human actions and emotions according to the essential nature of those powers. Each divine power was identified with an astral sphere, one of the multiple concentric layers of stars then believed to lie between the earth and the highest heaven. The movement of the stars in the astral sphere paralleled the waxing and waning of the influence of the power of the god identified with that sphere. This meant that the future actions of the divine powers could be anticipated, since the nature of each power's influence was always the same, but its intensity and balance in relation to other powers was always changing with the position of the stars. Since the stars have a regular pattern of movement, the pattern of divine influence could always be calculated. Divine actions in the future—not only the immediate future, but over hundreds of years—could be calculated on the basis of the unchanging patterns of the movement of the stars, revealing their present and future influence on individuals, nations, and peoples. Astrology became a highly popular form of divination in the West, and over many centuries finally evolved into the science of astronomy.

Another important source for divine revelation was prophecy, when an inspired person proclaimed a message sent by one of the gods in regard to the past, present, or future. Prophecies were proclaimed in the name of a particular god, and might be based on a vision—something seen by the prophet— or on an audition—something heard by the prophet—either while in a state of ecstasy or in a dream. Prophecies were usually presented in poetic form, and in the Mesopotamian context might include interpretation of the vision by the prophet. The meaning of some prophecies that survive from ancient Mesopotamia are obscure, but this is usually because they are general, vague, or so widely applicable as to be meaningless. Some prophecies that have survived in literary form appear to be inventions after the fact, presenting a vision of the "future" in vague or ambiguous terms. We have considered an Egyptian example of such a prophecy after the fact, "The Prophecy of Neferty." The ambiguity in some of the surviving Mesopotamian prophecies may reflect the sort of obscurity found in genuine prophecies or may be a contrived attempt to add an element of mystery. Surviving examples of such oracles usually, but not always, identify the prophet and the god who speaks through him or her. Mesopotamian prophets included both men and women, and their prophecies were often communicated to those in authority as important insights into the will of the gods for the king, the nation, or the people. But prophecy was never as important in Mesopotamian (or Egyptian) religious culture as it would be in Israelite religious culture.

Wisdom in Mesopotamia

As it did elsewhere in the ancient Near East, in Mesopotamia wisdom literature formed an important part of the human response to the world the gods had made. Part of the extant Mesopotamian wisdom literature is of the pragmatic, optimistic sort, emphasizing "how to get things done." Wisdom literature of this kind comes from different periods, including a very old collection of Sumerian wisdom, "The Instructions of Shuruppak," whose earliest versions date from around 2500 BCE. This same tradition is represented by an Akkadian work, "Counsels of Wisdom" and an Aramaic work from around the late sixth century BCE, "The Words of Ahiqar."

Another form of Mesopotamian wisdom literature is what scholars call "fables" or "contest literature." It had its place in the scribal schools, where students learned debating skills. Fables were fictional debates between contrasting characters representing some dichotomy in the world, such as the Akkadian "Dispute between the Tamarisk and the Date Palm." Each of the two characters debates its usefulness or virtue in contrast to the other. The contest is judged by a king or god and ends in reconciliation between the two parties with the recognition that each has its place and function in the created order.

Another, more unusual Akkadian work is "A Pessimistic Dialogue between Master and Servant," an example of wisdom literature that might be taken a number of different ways. In the dialogue the master proposes a series of actions, first proposing to do something and then proposing not to do it. In each case, the servant first gives good reasons for doing what the master proposes, then after his master changes his mind, immediately gives equally good reasons for not doing it. The work might be understood as an illustration of the duplicity of servants and their advice, the limited usefulness of proverbial wisdom, or perhaps the folly of too much debate. At the very least, it is clear that the intention of the work is satirical, even if it is not entirely clear who or what is being satirized.

We have already considered examples of pessimistic reflections on the limits imposed on human existence in the *Epic of Gilgamesh*, specifically the words of Shamash and Siduri in the Old Babylonian version of the story. Like *Gilgamesh*, the most prominent of the surviving works of Mesopotamian wisdom reflect a more nuanced view of human life as it is lived in relationship to the gods than is provided by more optimistic examples of wisdom literature. For example, one Sumerian text, "Man and His God," presents a situation familiar from Job: A man who appears to be suffering without reason complains to his god, asking for deliverance and vindication. The god in this case is the man's personal god, the deity who is supposed to represent his interests and speak on his behalf in the divine assembly. The fragmentary text begins with a lamentation, as the man bemoans his unjust suffering at the hands of both enemies and friends. He asks others to plead to the god for him, and details his various afflictions. But the man also acknowledges the wisdom of the sages who insist that all human beings are guilty of sin, and he confesses his sins to his god. As in Job, the ending is happy. The god heeds the man's words and drives away the demons that afflict him. The god restores his health and joy, and the man praises his god in return.

An Akkadian work probably dating from the end of the second millennium BCE, *Ludlul bel nemeqi*, "I Will Praise the Lord of Wisdom," is the most famous work of Babylonian wisdom. It also recalls Job, but in the sense that it focuses on the inability of human beings to know what motivates divine action. The poet laments his situation. He is beset by the wicked on every side and must hide himself and his shame from the scornful eyes of his neighbors. He seeks help from the gods, but his prayers and lamentations provoke no reply. Even the efforts of diviners do him no good, while the wicked who ignore the gods seem to prosper. The poet then recounts a series of revelatory dreams that promise the gods will soon help him. These dreams are followed by an exhaustive recounting of all the good the god Marduk did to restore the poet's health and good fortune, in part by driving away the demons that plagued him. The poet then praises Marduk and his consort Sarpanitum and recounts his visit to Marduk's temple Esagil ("the lofty house"). The poem ends with a description of the gifts and offerings the poet gave at the temple Esagil in thanksgiving for the mercy he had received at Marduk's hands.

A third work also dating from the end of the second millennium, "The Babylonian Theodicy," resembles the book of Job in yet another way. "The Babylonian Theodicy" (that is, a justification of the gods' behavior toward humanity) is an acrostic dialogue between a man who is suffering misfortune and a pious friend who offers him reassurances that the gods care about and provide for humanity. The poem alternates between the complaints of the sufferer on a number of issues and the wise, comforting words of the friend in reply. This dialogue recalls the debate between Job and his friends that makes up the bulk of the book of Job. Here again, the primary problem is the prosperity of the wicked; the sufferer complains that the wicked do well while he is afflicted despite his obedience to the gods. The friend replies that the wicked are doomed, though they may prosper for a moment. No matter what, the just person must not turn away from obedience. The friend accuses the suffering man of being led astray from wisdom by his misfortune. The primary problem, both agree, is that the will of the gods is inscrutable. The poem ends with the sufferer, apparently resigned, humbly petitioning the gods, though his words retain the sting of his complaints: He asks that the gods who have forsaken him may now finally show him mercy.

The Great Flood

There are other meditations on the human situation expressed through Mesopotamian literature, most notably the story of the Great Flood. The Mesopotamian version of the story has come down to us in two related but distinct versions: the story of Ut-napishtim that forms part of the *Epic of Gilgamesh* and the free-standing story of the sage Atrahasis.

Ut-napishtim's account of the Flood stands apart from the rest of the *Epic of Gilgamesh* by virtue of its focus on Ut-napishtim and its parallels to similar stories. Although Ut-napishtim tells the story in the first person, narrative omniscience allows him to describe the gods' plans and their words to each other when they gather in council in heaven. In fact Ut-napishtim speaks throughout the narrative more as a traditional storyteller than as a participant in the events he describes. This may reflect his role as a sage, a source of ancestral wisdom, a role consistent with his earlier Sumerian incarnation as Ziusudra, the son Shuruppak addresses in "The Instructions of Shuruppak." Ut-napishtim describes the story he tells as "the secret of the gods" (Dalley, 109), again indicating the divine origins of his knowledge.

The story begins "in those days" in the city of Sharuppak on the Euphrates. The gods of the city decide among themselves that the great gods should send a flood. No reason is given for the flood, nor do we know whether the flood was meant to affect only Sharuppak or the entire world, as the rest of the story seems to assume. There is no debate among the high gods involved. Anu, Enlil, Ninurta, Ennugi who oversees irrigation canals, and Ea all agree to send a flood. Ea reveals the gods' plan to Ut-napishtim, although again we are not told why. But since Ea has sworn an oath of secrecy, he reveals the plan to the house where Ut-napishtim lives, and Ut-napishtim only "overhears" the god's words.

Cuneiform tablet containing part of the Flood narrative from the Akkadian version of the Epic of Gilgamesh, *7th century BCE, part of the library of Assur-bannipal (reigned 669–631 BCE).* © 2008 Jupiterimages Corporation

Ea gives Ut-napishtim a plan of escape from the Flood by building a boat, and gives him all the instructions he needs to carry out the plan successfully. The story details the building of the boat by a group of workmen. Finally Ut-napishtim loads the boat with all his gold and silver, his family, all the animals on earth, and "all kinds of craftsmen," the artisans who have mastered the skills necessary for human civilization.

The mechanics of the storm and the Flood are described with a wealth of detail, as the story shows an interest in implicating all the gods in the destruction caused by the Flood. The Flood is caused not only by a prolonged storm but also by the unleashing of the waters of the abyss, as the forces of chaos are let loose to overwhelm the earth. The gods themselves are frightened by the

Flood and ascend to the heaven of Anu, the highest heaven, where they cower against the dome of the firmament.

The Flood lasts six days and nights before the waters slowly begin to recede. Ut-napishtim's boat runs aground on Mount Nimush, the only mountain high enough not to be covered by the waters of the flood. Ut-napishtim sends out a series of birds—a dove, a swallow, a raven—to see if dry land has appeared. When the raven doesn't return to the boat, Ut-napishtim lets the people and animals out of the boat and offers a sacrifice. The gods smell the sweet savor and gather around the sacrifice. This leads to a conflict among the gods. Ishtar blames Enlil for instigating the Flood; Enlil is angry Ut-napishtim has survived; Ninurta accuses Ea of revealing the god's plan; and Ea argues that the flood was too devastating and indiscriminate a way to deal with the problems humanity poses. Instead he introduces the idea of proportionate justice, so that only the guilty are punished for their crimes. Enlil relents and blesses Ut-napishtim and his wife. He grants them life like the life of the gods and moves them far away from the places other human beings live, near the mouths of the two rivers.

In "Atrahasis," by contrast, the story of the Flood is the climax of a much longer story about the creation of human beings and "how things got to be the way they are now." The story also includes some overlaps and parallels to the creation story in *Enuma elish*, but the focus is on human beings and the acts that established the human situation as it now exists. As in *Enuma elish* there is an account of how the divine hierarchy was established, with the high gods assigning different roles in governing the cosmos among themselves. At first the lower gods must do all work in the world, including grueling physical labor. But after 3600 years the lower gods revolt and take up arms against the high gods. In the face of the rebellion Anu, Enlil, and Ninurta decide to create human beings to do the work the lower gods find too burdensome. Also as in *Enuma elish*, human beings are made in part from a sacrificed god. The gods sacrifice one of their own, Ilawela. Nintu, goddess of the womb, Mami, midwife of the gods, and Enki mix clay with Ilawela's flesh and blood to create humanity. They also provide for the continuation of the human species through sexual intercourse and establish ten months as the period of human gestation. Human beings take up their duties and all appears to be well.

But in the beginning, human beings are immortal just as the gods are, dying only when they are killed by someone or something. As they reproduce the population grows until after six hundred years there are too many people and the noise they make becomes too much for the gods to bear. So the gods decide to send a wasting disease to afflict and kill human beings, and so reduce their numbers. But the wise man Atrahasis ("Super-sage") beseeches his lord Enki, god of wisdom, to tell him how to save humanity. Enki complies and humanity survives the calamity.

But the human population continues to grow. As the story tells it, every six hundred years the gods become fed up with the number of human beings and the noise they make. Enlil repeatedly complains to the gods that humanity's noise is keeping him awake. We may see a parallel with *Enuma elish*, except there it is the younger gods (including Enlil) who cause the uproar and the older gods Apsu and Tiamat who wish to destroy them. So the gods send a series of ills: wasting illness; two drought-induced famines; another plague; and another, six-year-long famine that leaves only two families alive. But each time the gods try to destroy humanity Atrahasis seeks help from Enki, and each time Enki replies with a strategy to bring an end to the calamity. Finally, the gods agree to send a great flood to wipe humanity off the face of the earth.

The account of Atrahasis's preparation for the Flood and the coming of the Flood itself is very much like the corresponding parts of the story of Ut-napishtim as it appears in the *Epic of Gilgamesh*. In the story of Atrahasis, the command to save all the animals is muted, and Enki tells Atrahasis that he has a week to build the boat before the Flood comes. There is an emphasis on Atrahasis's anxiety as he waits for the boat to be completed. It is also clear that the gods suffer hunger and thirst during the Flood, since they no longer receive sacrifices from human beings. When Atrahasis offers a sacrifice after the Flood, Nintu, the goddess who created humanity, blames Anu and Enlil for the disaster and the near-destruction of humanity.

At the end of the story, Atrahasis and his wife do not gain immortality, as do Ut-napishtim and his wife. Instead they retain the immortality that all human beings have shared up to that point. But after the Flood all other human beings are subjected to a limited lifespan to control the number of people on the earth. The gods also devise other means to limit the growth of the human population. Two of these methods survive in the extant text. The gods may punish with death those people who oppose them, and one-third of women giving birth will lose their babies.

These stories convey in narrative terms fundamental ideas about humanity's relationship to the gods that were current in ancient Mesopotamian religious culture. In the Mesopotamian stories, the Flood is not divine vengeance taken against human beings for their wickedness. It is not an act of divine justice. Instead it is the last in a series of attempts to deal with a persistent nuisance, the noise human beings make, noise loud enough to interrupt the gods' sleep. After other attempts fail, the gods finally resort to a drastic plan to wipe out humanity entirely. But even this plan is carried out without any consideration of the severity of the calamity the gods are unleashing or its very real consequences for the gods themselves. Although they are united in their disdain for human beings, the gods squabble among themselves. The gods change their minds and display a series of human failings: fearfulness, short-sightedness, denial, and the desire to escape responsibility for their failures. In general, throughout both of the Mesopotamian versions of the Flood story we have considered, the gods are depicted as very much like human beings, with competing desires and a bull-headedness that can easily lead to disaster for themselves and for humanity.

Notably what changes at the end of the story is the human condition, not the character of the gods. The story of the great Flood is part of Mesopotamian creation mythology, part of the story of "how things came to be the way they are now." But part of "the way things are now" in the ancient Mesopotamian way of thinking is that human beings are subject to the whims of capricious gods, whose actions are motivated by a host of personal reasons, very few of which have to do with the welfare of their human subjects. Although at the end of the story the gods come to see the Flood was a mistake, there is no guarantee that chaos will not break out again and once more threaten humanity. At the end of each of these two versions of the story of the great Flood, one of the goddesses takes a stand against a recurrence of the devastation it has brought upon humanity, vowing to remember and never forget what has happened. In the story of Atrahasis, the goddess is Nintu. But in the story of Ut-napishtim in the *Epic of Gilgamesh*, the goddess is Ishtar, the most unpredictable and vengeful of the goddesses. She is a goddess who is both benevolent and threatening, one who shows little respect for vows and promises, and there is no way to predict or determine how she will act in the future. Ishtar's promise to remember the disastrous results of the great Flood is a slender thread on which to hang the hopes of the human race. This ambivalent ending to the story of the greatest calamity to ever afflict humankind reflects the essential uncertainty about the human predicament in the hands of unreliable gods that is the hallmark of Mesopotamian religious culture.

SYRIA–PALESTINE

CHAPTER ELEVEN

Syria–Palestine: Historical Survey

The Beginnings of Civilization in Syria–Palestine

The area designated Syria–Palestine comprises the western arm of the Fertile Crescent, extending from northwestern Mesopotamia to the northern Sinai Peninsula. Lying east of the Mediterranean and west of the Arabian Desert, Syria–Palestine is a strip of fertile land suitable for cultivation and settlement. This strip generally narrows from north to south, from as wide as two hundred kilometers to as narrow as seventy kilometers or so. It is the natural passageway between Egypt to the south and Mesopotamia and Asia Minor to the north, three centers of ancient empires. As a result, most of the history of Syria–Palestine is a story of trade, migration, warfare, and conquest. This area has never been ethnically or culturally unified, but there has always been a basic similarity among the interrelated cultures and states located there.

The early history of Syria–Palestine can be reconstructed from a number of sources, but these sources are more abundant for some periods than others, and some periods remain entirely undocumented. The major sources are the physical remains recovered by archaeological digs in the area. Other sources include inscriptions, writings, and annals of the Mesopotamians and Egyptians that include references to Syria–Palestine and its peoples, such as the Egyptian *Tale of Sinuhe*. In addition, there is the religious literature of Israel and Judah, the Hebrew Bible and other writings preserved in Hebrew and Aramaic. These biblical and extrabiblical texts must be used with caution, since they were collected in something like their current form only after the Babylonian exile (587 BCE) or later, and they were preserved for their religious content rather than their historical value. However, the Hebrew and Aramaic texts remain major sources for the history of Syria–Palestine in the era from about 1100 to 150 BCE, from the beginning of the Israelite kingdoms to the re-assertion of national identity during the Hellenistic era.

Although the earliest human remains in Syria–Palestine date from the Pa-leolithic era, a break in the archaeological record indicates the region was es-sentially desolate for a millennium near the end of the Neolithic era. But during the Chalcolithic era (c. 4000–3150 BCE) peoples apparently unre-lated to earlier inhabitants built unfortified settlements in Syria–Palestine, sometimes on the ruins of earlier settlements, but often in virgin territory. Their material culture, however, does shows points of continuity with that of earlier inhabitants. The pottery produced by these settlers shows innovations in production and design. They had different burial customs than their Ne-olithic predecessors, and they produced a variety of ceramic figurines with obvious fertility associations. The material culture of Syria–Palestine during this time shows no signs of either Mesopotamian or Egyptian influence, in-dicating that it is indigenous, the product of the ingenuity and needs of the people living there at the time.

The Bronze Age in Syria–Palestine

The Bronze Age (further divided into early, middle, and late periods) saw the rise of cities and states with highly developed cultures throughout the Near East. There is evidence of Egyptian influence in Syria–Palestine during the first part of the Early Bronze Age (c. 3150–2200 BCE), but it disappears from the material culture for the rest of that era. During the latter part of the Early Bronze Age, from about 2850 to 2200 BCE, what is now identified as Canaanite material culture first appears in Palestine west of the Jordan River, in most of Lebanon, and in southern coastal Syria. This homogeneous cul-ture united the different city-states of the region even while Syria–Palestine continued to be subject to dynamic change as the result of both the migra-tion of new peoples of various ethnic backgrounds and languages into the area in addition to innovations and cultural development among the peoples long resident in the area.

The Early Bronze Age in Syria–Palestine was characterized by urbaniza-tion, trade, and development of distinctive forms of material culture, reli-gious practice, and art. From about 2500 BCE a number of major cities ap-pear in northern Syria, rivaling in size the cities of southwestern Mesopotamia. These cities managed to hold their own against a series of Sumerian and Akkadian military campaigns against them. But a wave of political and economic collapse swept away most of the cities of Syria—Palestine toward the end of the Early Bronze Age around 2300 BCE. This catastrophe anticipated by a century or so the end of the Akkadian Empire in Mesopotamia (c. 2193 BCE) and the fall of the Old Kingdom in Egypt (c. 2125 BCE).

The Middle Bronze Age (c. 2200–1550 BCE) was initially an era characterized by seminomadic life in Syria. Later the population again gathered in large numbers as cities began to reappear around the turn of the millennium, about 2000 BCE. At least some cities in northern Syria survived the general depopulation at the end of the Early Bronze Age, and Mesopotamian trade with them continued throughout the Middle Bronze Age.

The Middle Bronze Age in Palestine, as in Syria, began with seminomadic culture followed by a period of urbanization and strong influence from a resurgent Egypt. Pastoral nomads were the primary inhabitants of Palestine for about three centuries, from 2300 to 2000 BCE, before the area saw a revival of city life. Around the beginning of the second millennium old cities were once again inhabited and new cities were founded. Most of these cities were heavily fortified, attesting to the political insecurity of the era. Egyptian influence in Syria–Palestine revived during the Middle Kingdom of Egypt (2055–1650 BCE), with Byblos on the Phoenician coast as Egypt's principal trading partner, although there was also considerable overland trade by donkey caravan. At some time around 1700 BCE, scribes in Syria–Palestine developed a linear alphabet that could be written on flat surfaces, vastly simplifying the process of writing and storing texts.

More significantly, various ethnic groups from Palestine began to extend southward into Egypt, building their own cities in the Nile Delta. Among these was Avaris, the city that became the capital of Egypt under the "Asian" Hyksos Dynasty 15 (1650–1550 BCE). With the return to native Egyptian rule with Dynasty 17, Egyptian dominion over the territory of Canaan was reestablished, marking the end of the Middle Bronze Age in Palestine.

The Late Bronze Age (1550–1200 BCE) saw the rise of new imperial powers in the Near East. Syria–Palestine became the primary battleground between various northern states and the resurgent power of Egypt, beginning with Dynasty 18 (1550–1295 BCE). In the mid-second millennium the Hurrian kingdom of Mitani was dominant over Syria, but the Egyptians gained power over Palestine and some of Mitani's vassal cities, including Ugarit and Qadesh. The kings of many cities in Syria–Palestine became vassals to Egypt as a result of the campaigns of Thutmose III (1479–1425 BCE), including his victory over a coalition of cities at Megiddo in 1468 BCE. Egypt's possessions in Syria–Palestine were divided into three provinces, although native kings generally retained their power as Egyptian vassals. Among the Amarna letters discovered in the archives of Akhenaten (1352–1336 BCE) are letters from vassal kings in Syria–Palestine, asking for the Egyptian king's assistance against the rulers of other cities who have "rebelled." These letters also mention kings turning their land over to people called the Apiru, apparently stateless groups living in the Palestinian countryside as bandits.

Mitanni submitted to the power of the Hittite state of Hatti about 1341 BCE. Despite some substantial Egyptian victories against them, the Hittites gained and held control not only of northern Syrian cities, but also the Egyptian province of Amurru, a vassal kingdom in the territory of what is now northern Lebanon and southern Syria. Rameses II (1279–1213 BCE) regained Amurru for a period, but after the decisive battle of Qadesh in 1274 when Rameses was defeated by Muwatalli II of Hatti (1295–1272 BCE), Amurru remained under Hittite control until the fall of their empire at the end of the thirteenth century BCE.

The Late Bronze Age ended with a general implosion of the civilizations of the eastern Mediterranean basin around 1200 BCE, destroying some states and forcing others to turn inward in order to survive. There was a general economic collapse that may have been triggered by severe droughts in the late thirteenth and early twelfth centuries BCE throughout the eastern Mediterranean basin. The economic collapse led in turn to the fall of the kingdoms of Mycenaean Greece, Minoan Crete, and the Hittite Empire, and initiated incursions of new peoples into the Near East, most notably those known as the Sea Peoples. The fall or neutralization of Near Eastern imperial power at the end of the Late Bronze Age set the stage for the rise of independent states in Syria–Palestine.

Independent Kingdoms in Syria–Palestine

The Phoenician cities of the Lebanon coast survived the economic collapse, although as centers of trade they were inevitably affected by it. Cities such as Tyre, Sidon, Arwad, and Byblos were centers of seaborne trade that extended across the Mediterranean to Spain and Morocco. There were Phoenician colonies along the seacoast of both southern Europe and northern Africa, most notably in the west. These cities were centers of trade in luxury goods, and became synonymous among their neighbors for wealth and its attendant vices.

Israel first appears in Near Eastern history in an inscription on an Egyptian stele of Merneptah (1213–1203 BCE) commemorating a military campaign in Syria–Palestine during the fifth year of his reign. The stele says "Israel lies desolate" in a context that suggests the Israelites had established a presence in Palestine but had not yet formed a state. According to their own traditions, the Israelites first entered Syria–Palestine as nomadic herders of sheep and goats, living in autonomous family groups united by blood and a common allegiance to their god. The people later settled into agricultural communities and fortified cities, primarily in the central hill country of Palestine and in the Jordan Valley, away from trade routes controlled by the Philistines and the Canaanite cities. During the first century or so of Israel's settled life in Palestine its people were ruled by charismatic war leaders and city princes.

The dominant power in Palestine during this time was the Philistines, who had settled in the coastal plain of southwestern Palestine in the early to mid-twelfth century BCE. The Philistines probably came to the Palestinian coast from the Aegean Sea. They were one of the Sea Peoples, a term used by Egyptians to refer to different groups of seafaring peoples who first entered their territories during the reign of Rameses III (1184–1153 BCE). The Sea Peoples were apparently refugees from the collapsed Mycenaean, Minoan, and Hittite kingdoms. Around 1180 BCE, toward the beginning of Iron Age I (1200–1000 BCE), the Philistines arrived in Palestine from the sea and conquered a territory along the central coast. They destroyed many of the cities there and founded five major cities of their own: Ashdod, Ashkelon, Ekron, Gaza, and Gath. The trade routes between Egypt and the north ran along the coastal plain of Palestine through Philistine territory, increasing the Philistines' influence. They shared a common culture with the other Sea Peoples that set them apart from the previous inhabitants of the area as well as from their Canaanite neighbors. In the second half of the twelfth century BCE, with the waning of Egyptian power in Palestine, the Philistines expanded their territory to the north, east, and south, and solidified their control of Palestine in the eleventh century BCE.

The states of Syria–Palestine at this time ranged from loose tribal confederations to royal city-states, representing different peoples and cultures. The cities and territories of Syria–Palestine during Iron Age I had ill-defined borders and to a large extent shared common languages and a common culture. The kingdoms of Israel and Judah occupied territory in central Palestine, between the region of Philistine hegemony along the coast and the highlands to the east along the western boundaries of the Arabian Desert, extending from the Negev in the south to the Phoenician cities in the north. Ammon, Moab, and Edom, to the east and south of Israel and Judah, were thinly settled territories during this era and apparently had not yet coalesced into kingdoms at the time the Israelite kingdoms were founded. All these territories included some major cities and spoke a variation of the language of Canaan, a cognate language of Phoenician and Hebrew.

In the territory of Syria were the states of the Aramaeans, with Damascus the most important of their cities. The Aramaeans were originally a seminomadic people who apparently entered Syria in the Late Bronze Age from the wilderness on the fringes of the Arabian Desert. They only coalesced as an independent people around 1200 BCE, during a decline of Assyrian power. The kings of Aram fought against Israel before and during the reign of Saul, and were for a time incorporated into Israel's sphere of power before the Aramaeans regained autonomy in their own kingdoms in the wake of the death of Solomon of Israel.

After the death of Saul, his military commander David fought Saul's son Ishbaal to gain control over Israel, becoming king about 1000 BCE. David was already king of Judah, the territory south of Israel, and he became king of Israel by covenant with its leaders after Ishbaal's death. David established his capital in the Jebusite city Jerusalem, in the center of his newly united kingdom. David campaigned successfully against the Philistines and other peoples and states of Syria–Palestine. He left a prosperous and secure kingdom to his son Solomon, but Solomon alienated his Israelite subjects by forcing them to provide labor for his extensive building projects while exempting his subjects in Judah. Israel rebelled several times against the Davidic dynasty, finally breaking away during the reign of Solomon's son Rehoboam (922–915 BCE), who remained as king over Judah. From that time on, Israel and Judah were often at war with each other until the reign of Omri of Israel (876-869 BCE) who united his kingdom and essentially reduced Judah to a vassal state.

The various states in Syria–Palestine fought or formed alliances among themselves repeatedly over a period of two centuries or so, generally preserving their independence until the encroachment of the Assyrian Empire into Syria–Palestine in the ninth century. From that time on, the political fortunes of all the states of Syria–Palestine depended on the actions of the Assyrian kings as either allies, opponents, or conquerors.

An Israelite general, Jehu (842–815 BCE), slaughtered all the princes of Omri's dynasty, made himself king and initiated an alliance with Assyria against Aram–Damascus. The Assyrian alliance led to a period of peace and prosperity under Jeroboam II (786–746 BCE), but a series of usurpations and short reigns subsequently weakened Israel. Israel turned against Assyria and allied itself with Aram–Damascus in 734 BCE, but Israel was forced to submit and Damascus was destroyed by Tiglath-pileser III. After Tiglath-pileser died in 727 BCE, Israel rebelled again. Assyrian armies conquered Israel and Sargon II captured its capital Samaria in 721 BCE after three years' siege. About 27,900 Israelites from the top layers of society were deported and replaced by nobility from Assyria's other conquests to serve as imperial administrators.

Judah had a similar history of obedience and rebellion with Assyria and its imperial successor, Babylon, throughout the seventh century BCE. Ahaz of Judah (735–715 BCE) voluntarily submitted to Assyria when Israel and Aram–Damascus fought a war against Judah to force Ahaz to join their alliance against Assyria in 734 BCE. Hezekiah of Judah rebelled after the death of Sargon II in 705 BCE, but the Assyrians retaliated and reduced the kingdom to the rump state of Jerusalem. Hezekiah's son Manasseh (687–642 BCE) restored the alliance with Assyria and enjoyed a long and prosperous reign as an Assyrian vassal. Judah rebelled against Assyria again under Josiah (640–609 BCE), who was killed when Egypt moved into Judah to defend a faltering Assyrian Empire against Babylonian attack. With the fall of Assyrian power, Judah shifted loyalties between Egypt and Babylon six times during the last twenty years of its existence. In 589 BCE, Nebuchadnezzar laid siege to Jerusalem and took the city in 587 BCE. Nebuchadnezzar deported the aristocracy of Judah to Babylon even as many of Judah's people fled to Egypt.

Syria–Palestine under Imperial Power

After Nebuchadnezzar, as we have seen, the fortunes of the Babylonian Empire rapidly declined until it was dismantled by the Medes and Persians. The Persians and their king, Cyrus, invaded and gained control over Babylon and much of its empire in 539 BCE. Persian policies toward subject peoples were considerably more enlightened than those of the Assyrians and Babylonians. The Persians respected native political and religious traditions and allowed native aristocracies to reside in their own territories under the rule of Persian political authorities, with the understanding that any attempts at rebellion against their overlords would be ruthlessly suppressed. The Persians also allowed their subjects to worship their own gods according to their ancestral traditions, provided they would also entreat their gods for the welfare of the Persian king. The exiled people of Judah were allowed to return to their own country and to reestablish their ancestral worship there, as were the exiles of other nations of Syria–Palestine. This often led to conflict between the returned exiles, taken primarily from the aristocracy, and the majority of the native population that had remained in the country during the Babylonian period. Persian dominion led to a process of national self-definition, most often based on ancestry, language, and religious culture. Peoples once unified as territorial political entities became, under Persian dominion, communities defined instead by their ethnic and religious identities.

The Persian Empire's major rival for power in the eastern Mediterranean was Greece. In the late fourth century BCE, Greece was united under the leadership of Philip of Macedon (359–336 BCE), who ruled as a military monarch. His son Alexander the Great (336–323 BCE) defeated the Persians and went on to conquer the eastern Mediterranean basin and the Near East in thirteen years, building a vast empire that extended from Macedonia in the west to the Indus River in the east, from Armenia and Bactria in the north to Egypt and Arabia in the south.

After Alexander's death in Babylon at the age of 32 in 323 BCE, his empire was divided among his generals. Two of them gained control over much of the Near East and eventually each declared himself king over his domain: Ptolemy ruled over Egypt (305–282 BCE) and Seleucus over the territory of Syria (306–281 BCE). Both Ptolemy and Seleucus founded dynasties that continued to hold power until the Roman conquest. Both dynasties, the Ptolemies and the Seleucids, claimed sovereignty over Palestine, the territory between their two domains. After several battles, the Ptolemies took control of Palestine and held it for most of the third century BCE. The Seleucids gained dominion over Palestine in 198 BCE and retained control until the Roman conquest in 63 BCE. But their subject peoples in Syria–Palestine retained their national identity in spite of imperial rule, and in some cases initiated rebellions in attempts to regain the autonomy their ancestors had once enjoyed before the age of empires.

CHAPTER TWELVE

Syria–Palestine: The Gods and the World They Made

Ideas about the Gods in Syria–Palestine

The religious cultures of the peoples and states of Syria–Palestine all shared some ideas in common about the gods and the ritual means of honoring them. The religious communities in Syria–Palestine, like those of Egypt and Mesopotamia, were "natural" religious communities, that is, the religious community was coterminous with the secular community. In Syria–Palestine, the secular community might be as small as a clan or tribe; in Mesopotamia or Egypt, it might be as large as a city-state or a nation. The equivalence of the political and religious community meant the head of the political entity— whether a patriarch, a clan or tribal leader, a civic magistrate, or a king—was also the chief cultic official, representing his subordinates and dependents before the gods. Priests and other religious officials were also officials of the political order as members of the administration, and served as official advisors to the leader. There was no division between the sacred and the secular, since all of life's pursuits fell under divine jurisdiction.

The common religion of Syria–Palestine was polytheistic, with the gods arranged in a royal hierarchy that reflected the political hierarchy of the city-state. The name and identity of the chief god would vary depending on the territory or the ethnic identity of the worshippers. The variety of religious cultures in relatively close proximity in Syria–Palestine led to syncretism, the combination of one system of gods, myths, and rituals with another. We have already seen examples of syncretism with the gradual accumulation of divine attributes and associations by gods such as Amun or Marduk, but also in the identification of one god with another, similar god, such as the identification of the Sumerian goddess Inanna with the Babylonian Ishtar. Syncretism reflects the universalizing tendencies of polytheism, as the system expands to accommodate or assimilate gods, myths, and rituals from different traditions.

Syncretism is most apparent in Syria–Palestine among states that had extensive contact with either Egypt or Mesopotamia, usually through trade or military conquest. Byblos on the Phoenician coast, for example, had a long history of trade with Egypt from at least the first dynasties of the Old Kingdom. But there are indications of inclusion of some aspects of Egyptian ritual offering practices in Byblos dating from this early era as well. The people of Byblos worshipped Baalat ("the Lady"), a goddess who was often represented with attributes that identify her with Hathor. Baalat was sometimes depicted with two long horns and the solar disk between them. Egyptian religious culture, in turn, acknowledged the gods of Syria–Palestine as manifestations of their own deities under such titles as "Ra of Foreign Lands." In the story of the contest between Horus and Seth, two goddesses of Syria–Palestine, Anat and Astarte, appear as daughters of Ra who are given to Seth as wives. Syncretism of this sort is a result of cultural interaction that acknowledges the legitimacy of different religious cultures by synthesizing many of their primary features. It is one aspect of ancient cosmopolitanism. But it is also a form of cultural hegemony in which all gods are identified as no more than variant identities of one's own gods, whom one knows by their "true" names.

In addition to polytheistic systems, in Syria–Palestine we also find both henotheistic and monotheistic religious cultures. Henotheism (from Greek, "one god [among many]"), like polytheism ("many gods"), assumes a multitude of gods exist. But in a henotheistic religious culture only one out of the many gods that exist should be honored and worshipped. Usually the single god worshipped is assumed to be supreme over other gods in both power and influence. The single god also has moral character—that is, he or she is expected to adhere to what is good and just—at least to the extent that the god is expected to assume responsibility for his or her worshippers and to provide for their welfare. As a result, the favor of this one god determines how a person or a community fares in the world, and adverse events can be blamed on improper behavior that has somehow offended the god. Henotheistic worship differs from the worship of a dominant god in a polytheistic religious culture because in henotheistic systems the god who is worshipped is worshipped exclusively, to the exclusion of all other gods. Usually in a henotheistic system, "other gods" means the gods of other, usually hostile, peoples, and their gods are assumed to be hostile to one's own god. In a henotheistic system other lesser gods may also be associated with the primary god, but any such gods are strictly subordinate. In fact they are usually understood to be lesser spiritual beings, not gods in the same sense as the one god who receives worship. The moral character of the god in a henotheistic system sometimes creates problems for his or her worshippers, especially in situations where the god has failed to protect or provide for them despite their efforts to please the god. But this is also generally true of the specific god a person worships in a polytheistic system, the personal god. In cases where the personal god or the god of a henotheistic religious culture fails in his or her obligations, it becomes necessary to justify or explain the god's actions as somehow consistent both with the god's power and with his or her responsibility to promote the welfare of worshippers.

A monotheistic religious culture also offers worship and devotion to only one god, but his or her worshippers believe their god is the one and only god that truly exists. The devotees of the god maintain that all other beings called "gods" and worshipped by other people are not really gods at all. Either they are some other sort of spiritual being inferior to the one true god, or they do not exist at all and their worshippers are in thrall to an illusion. In a monotheistic system (from Greek "one [and only one] god"), the one god worshipped is all-powerful and responsible for creating and maintaining all things that exist. But the god him- or herself is a different sort of being. The god is the source and creator of the cosmos, but not subject to its laws or limitations. The god is also the absolute moral arbiter of right and wrong, and as such is absolutely righteous. The distance between this god and creation is not just a physical and substantive distance, but a moral distance as well.

If the moral character of a god in a henotheistic religious culture sometimes creates the need to justify the god's treatment of his or her people, this is even more the case with the god of a monotheistic religious culture. The god is believed to be both perfectly righteous and all-powerful, fully capable of doing whatever he or she wishes. But if a righteous god is also all-powerful, how can there be injustice or evil within the created order? Here again the need to justify the god's deeds in human history arises and must be addressed.

Monotheism is the most familiar concept of the divine in the modern West, but the idea runs counter to humanity's historical experience of both nature and human society. Nature does not seem to reflect a single power at work; instead it seems to be the domain of a combination of powers, some benevolent and some hostile, often working in apparent opposition to each other: water and fire, sun and rain, heat and cold. Similarly, human beings exist in community and are social animals. Human cultures and civilizations depend on the work done by a variety of people as individuals or in groups every day for the common good. Sometimes human beings too seem to work at cross-purposes and conflicts are common among them. The natural assumption is that the forces controlling creation are also many and diverse. As we have seen, this is the assumption behind polytheistic religious cultures in Egypt and Mesopotamia, where a host of gods and goddesses govern creation. By contrast, the idea that the cosmos is under the direct control of a single all-powerful deity working in solitude is more the product of theological reflection than direct observation of either nature or human beings.

Although there is no necessary evolution in religious cultures from polytheism toward monotheism, henotheistic religious cultures generally tend toward monotheism. But the demarcation between the two is difficult to identify in any given historical example. In a henotheistic system the claims made for the one god worshipped by the community to the exclusion of all others tend to become more and more absolute. We have seen an example of this in the worship of Aten in Egypt during the reign of Akhenaten. This one god is worshipped because he or she is the most powerful of gods, the wisest, the most faithful, and so on. At some point such claims tend to elevate the worshipped god to a higher plane or state of existence than any other gods, to the extent that the others cease to be "gods" in the same sense as the one god the community worships. This apparently did not happen in the case of the worship of Aten, but when it does happen, at that point a henotheistic religious culture becomes monotheistic.

The Gods of Syria–Palestine: El, Baal, and Others

The peoples of ancient Syria–Palestine worshipped a myriad of gods. The royal archive at Ebla, a city in northwestern Syria, dating from around 2350 BCE, includes lists of offerings (mostly bread and mutton) offered to the many gods worshipped there. Some of the gods whose names appear in the Ebla archives are known to us from other religious cultures—including both Mesopotamia and Egypt—while others were apparently unique to the region. Since Ebla was something of a cultural crossroads, the archive's tablets offer a good indication of the number and diversity of gods worshipped in Syria–Palestine during the mid-third millennium BCE. There is no reason to believe that the pantheon became any smaller or less complex during succeeding centuries.

The chief god of the pantheon of most peoples in ancient Syria–Palestine was El, the creator of all things and father of the gods, whose name became the generic Semitic term for any god (cp. Akkadian, *ilu*). El was the oldest of the gods and head of the divine council, well-respected by the other gods for his wisdom in judgment. In texts dating to the late twelfth and early eleventh centuries BCE from Ugarit, an ancient city on the Syrian coast, El unfailingly appears as a benevolent deity. He was more of a chief among equals than a king over the other gods. El's home was in the mountains to the far north. These same mountains were the source of the waters of the cosmos, and this was where the other gods would go when they wished to consult El or to ask him to grant their requests.

El's most significant epithet, found in the Ugaritic texts, is "the Bull El," an indication not only of his power and strength, but also his male potency as a qualification for his primacy among the gods. El appears in different stories and contexts enjoying the recreations and prerogatives of a patriarch—hunting and feasting, but especially enjoying sexual intercourse with his mistresses, who respond with cries of delight. His consort Asherah is also his sister and the mother of the gods. His mistresses include another of his sisters, Astarte, and his daughter Anat, who is also the wife of his son Baal. As we have seen in Mesopotamia and Egypt, incestuous sexual relationships are typical of polytheistic divine patriarchies. El's relationships with his mistresses appear in a text that seems to be the basis for a *hieros gamos*, the sacred rite of sexual intercourse between the political leader and a priestess representing a fertility goddess to ensure an abundance of crops and animals. There are other indications that the *hieros gamos* was a religious ritual in Syria–Palestine as well as Mesopotamia, primarily denunciations of sacred prostitution preserved in the Hebrew Bible.

El also appears as a divine warrior, but only in the context of gaining supremacy over the other gods. In other stories it is El's son Baal who appears as a divine warrior and who sits at El's right hand in council as his chief advisor. Both gods are given titles or epithets that identify their attributes and associations, such as "the Bull El" or El Shaddai, "El of the Mountains."

Baal became identified with the dominant gods of many of the peoples of Syria–Palestine, where he was worshipped for centuries under various divine names. The name Baal means "Lord" or "Master." He was identified with Hadad, the god of storms. Like El, Baal became a generic identification for all gods or a secondary title for regional gods ("Baal of Peor" in Numbers 25:3), each of whom were also known by their own name. In some cases, however, the word "Baal" refers not to the god, but is merely an honorific title. For example, the familiar name Baal-zebub, should probably be translated "Lord of the Small Vermin" or more loosely "Lord of the Flies." Assuming it is a genuine title for a god, it suggests not a divine warrior like Baal, but a god more similar to Nergal, a god of pestilence, in this case the pestilence brought on humanity by insects and mice.

Baal's title "Rider of the Clouds" reflects his original identity as a storm god whose showers allow the earth to become fertile. Baal's identity as a fertility deity is dominant in stories involving his consort Anat. The epithet "mighty Baal" appears throughout the stories about the god, reflecting his role as a divine warrior and his frequent use of brute force to achieve his ends.

A number of stories about Baal dating from the mid-fourteenth century BCE survive in Ugaritic texts. The texts are fragmentary and the relationship between one and another is not clear, so they may form a collection of separate stories or a single epic tale. In one story, El commands Baal to serve Prince Yamm ("Sea") as his slave. El has apparently chosen to favor Yamm over Baal and has built a temple for him. Yamm sends envoys to the assembly of the gods, envoys who refuse to kneel before El and demand the gods kneel to them as Yamm's envoys instead. El gives them Baal as a slave to serve Prince Yamm, but Baal clubs Yamm repeatedly with cudgels, subduing him. Baal kills Yamm and seizes his royal power. Yamm's "death" apparently excludes him from the company of the other gods and restricts him to his proper place in his watery realm, the sea. Next Baal laments the fact that he has no temple like the other gods, leading to a series of intercessions and divine actions. Baal and his sister Anat visit Asherah, "Lady Asherah of the Sea," apparently intending to seek her intercession with El on Baal's behalf. El ultimately assents and a house is built for Baal by Kother the craftsman according to Baal's specifications. At the end of the story the gods gather at a feast to celebrate the new temple of Baal.

In another story that has clear parallels to Inanna's descent to the Underworld, Baal descends to do battle with Mot ("Death"), god of sterility and ruler of the Underworld. Mot, like Yamm, is El's favorite in preference to Baal. But both Mot and Yamm are also Baal's natural enemies, enemies he must overcome if the earth is to emerge from the sea and become fertile. Baal sends his messengers to Mot to announce the building of Baal's temple, but somehow Baal comes under Mot's power and makes himself Mot's slave. Baal's messengers tell El that Baal is dead. El mourns and seeks a successor among his sons, but neither Yadi Yalhan nor Ashtar is a fit replacement for Baal.

Baal's consort Anat goes into mourning and gives sacrifices for Baal's death-offering. But she then descends to Mot's realm to force him to give up her brother. Anat defeats Mot and treats his body in the same ways farmers treat seed and grain. She winnows Mot's body, then burns it, and finally grinds it up before scattering his body in the fields. Anat tells El about a dream she has had about abundant rain and the dry river beds flowing with honey—this is a clear sign that Baal has returned to life and the earth has become fertile

Bronze Canaanite figure of Baal, c. 1400–1200 BCE. © The
Trustees of the British Museum

once again. Baal also does combat with Mot before resuming his proper place on earth. The fertility overtones in this story are obvious, as Baal dies and returns to life again with the help of Anat, and Mot's body is scattered like grain to give rise to new life on earth.

In some of the surviving texts praising Baal there are apparent references to another story. In this story Baal and Anat fight against a primordial sea monster, Lothan, a minion of Prince Yamm. Lothan is also related to the biblical Leviathan and other monstrous sea serpents, such as the Egyptian Apophis, referred to in other ancient Near Eastern religious mythology.

As her role in the story of Baal and Prince Yamm suggests, Asherah was a significant goddess in her own right, in addition to her identity as El's consort. She appears in the Ugaritic texts as Athirat. Her name also appears forty times in the Hebrew Bible. Most of these references are to a cult object identified with the goddess, but others clearly refer to the goddess herself (cf. 2 Kings 21:7; 23:4). Asherah was a fertility goddess, particularly in connection with her consort, and she appears to have been popular throughout Syria–Palestine, including Israel and Judah. She is probably the goddess depicted by figurines found in houses dating to the eighth and seventh centuries BCE in Judah. This goddess is depicted holding her breasts, a posture that emphasizes her associations with fertility. The cultic objects sacred to Asherah, of which there were many in Israel and Judah, appear to have been stylized trees made of wood. This again would reflect Asherah's connections with fertility, especially given the phallic implications of trees.

Although scholarly opinion is divided on the matter, it seems likely that at least during some periods in the history of Israel and Judah that Asherah was believed to be the consort of Yahweh, the god of Israel. Her cultic objects were placed in worship spaces sacred to Yahweh, even near the altar (cf. Deuteronomy 16:21). Yahweh is often identified with El, and it is reasonable to assume that he would then have appropriated El's consort as well. Such an association between Yahweh and Asherah would go a long way toward explaining the stubborn persistence of the goddess and the stylized sacred tree that bore her name in the worship of Israel and Judah.

Astarte is a sister of El as well as one of his mistresses, and she appears in the Ugaritic texts as a consort of Baal. Her niece Anat shares both roles with her, although in stories about Baal Anat is dominant as his wife. Astarte was chief goddess of the Phoenician city of Sidon (cf. 1 Kings 11:5, 33), although she was worshipped in other Phoenician cities and throughout the Mediterranean basin where Phoenician influence was strong. It is also possible that Astarte is the "Queen of Heaven" mentioned as an object of Judah's worship in Jeremiah (7:18; 44:17–19, 25), and we know from Egyptian sources from the New Kingdom that she was also a goddess of war. This is true also of the goddess Anat, as is clear in the stories in which she appears in the Ugaritic texts. Both Astarte and Anat were known beyond Syria–Palestine. They appear in "The Contendings of Horus and Seth" as the daughters of Ra whom Neith tells the sun god to give to Seth as compensation for his loss of the throne to Horus.

The god of the Phoenician city of Tyre was Melqart ("king of the city"). Baal was worshipped in Tyre and the other Phoenician cities, and Melqart was sometimes called "Baal Melqart" or "the Tyrian Baal." But here again the name of Baal should be understood instead as the title "Lord," so Melqart is identified in these names as "Lord Melqart" or "the Tyrian lord." Melqart was a different sort of god than the warrior Baal. Melqart was instead a god of the Underworld, comparable to Nergal in Mesopotamia.

As should be clear, the traditions preserved in the Hebrew Bible provide a major—although often biased—source of information about some of the other gods of Syria–Palestine. Ideally this information should be augmented or clarified by evidence from other texts or archaeological discoveries. For example, on the basis of information in the Hebrew Bible, the Jebusites apparently had a chief god called Salim (SLM). The Jebusites inhabited the part of the southern portion of Palestine at the time Israel was founded as a kingdom. Their territory included a large part of what later became Judah. The name of Salim is incorporated into the name of the Jebusite capital, Jerusalem ("foundation of Salim") and into names given to the children of his worshippers, such as Absalom ("father Salim"), one of the sons of David.

The Hebrew Bible also includes references to the gods Chemosh and Molech, and claims that both gods demanded human sacrifice. Chemosh was the chief god of Moab and was also worshipped at Ugarit. Sources such at the Moabite stone (ninth century BCE) depict him as a god who could be both angry and loving toward his people, much like Yahweh. The claim that he required human sacrifice may be a slur against the Moabites. "Molech," on the other hand, may be understood as an insulting form of *melekh* (Hebrew, "king") employing the vowel sounds of *bosheth* ("shameful"). It is a general reference to a chief god but does not indicate which specific god is intended. 1 Kings 11:7 identifies Molech as the chief god of the Ammonites. He was considered powerful enough that ritual practices associated with Molech were incorporated into the royal cult in Israel under Solomon (961–922 BCE), and later again in Judah, notably under Manasseh (687–642 BCE). Molech may well have been a god of the Underworld, like Melqart or Nergal. According to 2 Kings 23:10, in Judah worshippers would "make a son or daughter pass through the fire as an offering to Molech" at a shrine, the

Topheth, near Jerusalem in the valley of Hinnom. If historically accurate, this would most likely be a reference to human sacrifice. The practice was outlawed during the cultic reform under Josiah (640–609 BCE).

Dagon is identified as the chief god of the Philistines in the Hebrew Bible (cf. Judges 15:41; 1 Samuel 5:1–7), but we know little about him. He might be the same god as the Canaanite god identified in some Ugaritic texts as the father of Baal, a god who appears to have been associated with the storm and fertility. But if so, we also know little about the Canaanite Dagon, except that his divine functions seem to have been usurped by Baal and El.

The Gods of Syria–Palestine: Yahweh

Israel's worship of Yahweh stands apart to some extent from the worship of other gods among its neighbors in Syria–Palestine, although in some respects the forms and rituals of worship have much in common. The name of the god of Israel appears in texts of the Hebrew Bible and elsewhere as four unvocalized consonants, equivalent to YHWH. It is unclear how the name was pronounced, since in ancient written Hebrew there were no indications of vowel sounds and in Jewish tradition the name is never spoken. In most English translations of the Hebrew Bible the divine name is replaced by "the LORD," following the tradition of using "Adonai" ("Lord") as a substitution. "Yahweh" is the reconstructed pronunciation of YHWH.

The four consonants of the divine name appear both standing alone and as a theophoric (i.e., "god-bearing") element in names such as Jonathan ("gift of Yahweh") or Jehoshaphat ("Yahweh judges") in both Israelite and non-Israelite sources. So it is probable that the name of the God of Israel also existed outside of Israelite religious culture. The origins of the name are Semitic. Most scholars agree that the root of the name is the three Hebrew consonants—roughly equivalent to the letters HWY—that form the infinitive "to be." The name YHWH would then be the finite form of the verb— "He is"—a meaning consistent with the revelation of the divine name to Moses in Exodus 3:14.

The original traits and associations of Yahweh are difficult to determine, although some scholars have speculated he was a god of the storm or of the mountain. Yahweh is identified with El in many respects and shares his age, his wisdom, and his role as creator. An alternative designation for Yahweh in the Hebrew Bible in Elohim, a plural form of El, usually translated as "God" in English. Yahweh is also sometimes identified with El Shaddai, "God [or El] of the Mountain," but this may only be a secondary syncretistic identification with El. Yahweh's associations with storms may also be indirect, arising from similar terminology used to refer to attributes shared by Yahweh and his divine rival Baal.

What does seem clear is that Yahweh was always associated with the wilderness, with the "no man's land" far away from the human habitations of villages and cities. Throughout the history of Israelite religion, even when Yahweh was worshipped in a temple, he continued to be encountered in the wilderness, the marginal scrubland that makes up much of Syria–Palestine. Yahweh's association with the wilderness is in keeping with the idea that the people of Israel were originally nomadic herders of sheep and goats, wandering in the wilderness in search of pasture. The earliest religious observances connected to Israelite worship of Yahweh are Sabbath observance and the Passover, both appropriate festivals for nomadic herders. Both are observed within the family setting with no need for priest or temple.

According to Israelite tradition, the initial association between Yahweh and the people of Israel was established through the patriarchal father, Abraham, so a primary identification of Yahweh is as "the God of Abraham, Isaac, and Jacob" (cf. Exodus 3:15). This identification has parallels elsewhere in ancient Syria–Palestine, where a god is designated "the god of [Name]," indicating a personal connection. There are also parallels to the Mesopotamian idea of a "personal god" who serves as a person's advocate and defender in the heavenly council. The association between a god and an individual also seems to acknowledge the diversity of religious allegiance in polytheistic Syria–Palestine, as in the biblical formula, "Blessed be Yahweh your God" (1 Kings 10:9). The connection between a particular god and a particular person or group of people was to some extent a matter of choice. Out of the many gods one might worship in a polytheistic religious culture, one formed an allegiance with a particular god on the basis of personal interest and recognition of the god's sovereignty and power. But there was mutual interest as well, since both the god and the worshipper benefited from the relationship.

This was certainly believed to be the case with the relationship between Yahweh and the people of Israel. The traditional Israelite understanding was that Yahweh had chosen Abraham and his descendants as his own people, and Abraham had responded with faith and trust in Yahweh. The relationship was voluntary on both sides, but it took the form of a covenant, a legal agreement binding on both parties. In the Hebrew Bible, the covenant between Yahweh and Abraham is presented as a covenant of grant, based on Yahweh's unconditional promise to Abraham: "I will make of you a great nation, and I will bless you, and make your name great, so that you will be a blessing" (Genesis 12:2). A corollary of this promise is the pledge that Abraham's multitude of descendants would possess Canaan, the same place where the biblical tradition claims Abraham had sojourned as a nomad (Genesis 12:7).

The idea of a voluntary covenantal relationship is dominant in Israelite religious and historical traditions, although the nature of the covenantal agreement changes. In Exodus, after Israel's escape from Egypt the covenantal relationship established with Abraham is renewed in a form of legal agreement in which each party assumes specific responsibilities toward the other. The covenant between Yahweh and Israel at Sinai is presented in Exodus and the following books as the primary lawgiving occasion for Israel, governing both its religious and its civil life. The Sinai covenant imposes stipulations on both parties, obligating Yahweh to protect and govern his people Israel, and the people to obey Yahweh's commands. By so doing, the people pledge themselves to follow a way of life that will set them apart from the other peoples and states of Syria–Palestine and the rest of the ancient Near East. This distinctive way of life—exemplified by cultural practices, appearance, and diet as well as more overtly religious behavior—is understood in terms of the people's allegiance to Yahweh. In other words, observance of the covenantal stipulations is the means by which the people affirm their allegiance to Yahweh as their God. Their allegiance is intended to produce *shalom*, a state of harmony and equilibrium between the human world of Israel and the divine world ruled by Yahweh. This state of harmony and equilibrium is essentially the goal of all religious yearning and action. In the Hebrew Bible the ideal of the covenantal relationship is summed up in the prophetic declaration, "You shall be my people, and I shall be your God" (cf. Jeremiah 30:22; Ezekiel 36:28b).

Divine Rivalry in Syria–Palestine

The conflict between rival gods in Syria–Palestine is illustrated by stories in the Hebrew Bible about the people of Israel encountering other religious cultures in Canaan. Most of the stories reflect the idea that Yahweh alone is the god of Israel with an exclusive claim on the people's loyalty. In the Pentateuch (the first five books of the Hebrew Bible) this exclusive claim is understood in terms of Yahweh bringing Israel out of Egypt and establishing the covenant with Israel at Sinai. In some parts of the tradition as it survives in the Hebrew Bible, the subsequent period when Israel wandered in the wilderness is seen as a "honeymoon" when Israel was faithful to its covenant with Yahweh. But in other parts of the tradition, the people desert Yahweh to worship other gods from the very beginning, even at the foot of Sinai while Moses is receiving the covenant (Exodus 32). Both parts of the tradition are likely to be to some extent retrojections into Israel's early history, either of problems that in fact arose only after settlement in Canaan or of idealizations of the earlier nomadic life of Israel, created in contrast to those problems. In any event, as the tradition has been retained in the texts of the Hebrew Bible, Israel's religious history reflects an almost continuous struggle between the exclusivist claims of the worship of Yahweh and the allure of the gods of the polytheistic religious cultures of the other peoples of Syria–Palestine.

The process through which the people later identified as Israel came to settle in Canaan is open to question, but it is the case that Israelite religious culture—if it was originally a religious culture suited to the needs of nomadic herders—was necessarily transformed by the people's new association with settled agricultural village and city life in Syria–Palestine. The needs and concerns of farmers and villagers and city dwellers—artisans, merchants, soldiers, and state functionaries—are different from those of wandering herders of sheep and goats. Once they had settled in Canaan, the religious interests of the Israelites would have come to resemble those of other settled peoples, whose religious activities formed a seamless part of their mode of life. As we have seen, religious rituals performed as part of planting or harvesting the crops were considered a necessary part of the process, and the Israelites would have taken these practices over from their neighbors. As a result, the people of Israel would almost inevitably have participated in the rituals associated with the various gods of Syria–Palestine other than Yahweh. Preeminent among these gods was Baal, whose worship was not only ubiquitous among the peoples of Syria–Palestine, but was specifically intended in part to ensure the land's fertility. Any worshippers of Yahweh who were or became settled farmers would have combined their worship of Yahweh with at least ritual recognition of other gods in particular circumstances. But doing so would violate the idea of a henotheistic covenant, if that was indeed one of the original characteristics of Yahwistic worship. For those who believed Israel should worship Yahweh alone, the question was whether the people would worship Yahweh exclusively or would consider Yahweh their chief god while offering worship to other gods as well.

This is the question at issue in the story about the contest between the prophet Elijah and the Tyrian priests of Baal on Mt. Carmel in 1 Kings 18:20–40 to determine which god should be worshipped on the mountain. At its core, the story is about a jurisdictional dispute between Yahweh and Baal at the overlapping boundaries of their power. In the ancient Near East, gods were assumed to have local authority, that is, they manifested their divine power in the places where they were worshipped. The god was "present"—and so also most active and effective—in his or her temple, where the god's cult statue was located. The god's power radiated out from the temple but dissipated over a distance, like a radio signal fading away the farther one goes from the transmitter. The more shrines a god had, the larger his or her realm of operation and the greater the god's power and ability to act in response to the prayers and offerings of worshippers. Destroying a god's temple was believed to destroy the god's ability to operate effectively in the area where the temple had stood. According to this way of thinking—which was ubiquitous in the ancient Near East—when worship of Yahweh was restricted exclusively to the temple in Jerusalem under Hezekiah (and again later under Josiah), the net result was that the LORD's power to act was diminished (cf. 2 Kings 18:22). What Hezekiah did effectively limited Yahweh's divine influence to the immediate vicinity of Jerusalem. Ironically, Jerusalem was the only part of Hezekiah's kingdom that did not fall to the power of the Assyrian king Sennacherib.

In the case of Mt. Carmel, the mountain was roughly equidistant from Tyre, the home of Jezebel and her god Baal, and the city of Samaria, capital of Ahab and cultic home of Yahweh, who was worshipped in a temple there. In the story, Elijah and the priests of Baal prepare identical altars with identical sacrifices, then call upon their gods to send down fire from heaven to ignite the wood on the altar and consume the sacrifice. The priests of Baal cry out to Baal while gashing themselves with swords and spears to produce a flow of blood; "but there was no voice, no answer, and no response" (1 Kings 18:29b). By contrast, when Elijah invokes his god, Yahweh reacts immediately and sends fire from heaven to consume the sacrifice and the altar as well.

It is important to note that although Elijah in this story and others works for exclusive worship of Yahweh in Israel, he does not represent monotheistic worship of Yahweh of the sort promoted by the author of Kings or the later prophets of Judah. During their contest, Elijah taunts the priests of Baal by suggesting various things that might prevent Baal from hearing their cries to him (1 Kings 18:27) when in fact it was only distance. The god who lived in Tyre was too far away to respond to his worshippers on Mt. Carmel.

Creation Stories in Syria–Palestine

The surviving creation stories from Syria–Palestine present some characteristics familiar from other creation stories, but also reflect the concerns of their specific religious cultures. El was a creator god, although stories of his creative activity have failed to survive in anything other than his divine epithets or titles, such as "El, creator of earth." It is not clear what sort of creative activity El engages in, although other of his titles would suggest creation by sexual generation and by combat. For example, El is given the title "father of the gods." As the father of the gods he is their creator, the origin of their being, much like Atum or Ptah. El is also specifically the father of Baal, "Bull El his father, King El who created him" (Cross, 15). El's consort Asherah has the title "Creatress of the gods." These epithets suggest that El and Asherah bring creation into being by conceiving and giving birth to the gods who represent the various elements of creation, as happens in the creation stories we have considered from Egypt and Mesopotamia. This is an example of creation through sexual generation.

El is also a divine warrior, although in the surviving literature this role has for the most part been taken over by his son Baal. But the battles fought by El or Baal suggest some sort of creation by combat as well. Stories about Baal's combat with Prince Yamm and with Mot may be considered creation stories in the broad sense, since they are about the process of imposing order on the cosmos, as the sea and death are restricted to their proper places in the divine order. Similarly Baal and Anat's battle with the sea serpent Lothan may also be a creation myth, similar to Marduk's world-creating battle with Tiamat.

The Hebrew Bible retains some evidence that Leviathan was originally a chaos monster comparable to Lothan, specifically in Psalms and Job in their reflections on creation. In Psalm 74 the destruction of Leviathan is recalled in what is apparently a metaphor for Elohim's work in the Exodus (Psalm 74:13–14), but in Psalm 104 Leviathan is merely a plaything for Yahweh (Psalm 104:26). In Job the sea monster the divine warrior defeats is called Rahab (Job 26:12–13). Both ideas—Leviathan as cosmic menace and Leviathan as divine pet—are present in Job 41, when Yahweh asks Job whether he is able to control the beast as Yahweh does (Job 41:1–5). These references probably recall a tradition in which Yahweh battled Leviathan as part of the process of creation and, once he had subdued the sea monster, made it a part of the divine order.

The book of Genesis in the Hebrew Bible includes two distinct accounts of the work of creation, one a small-scale creation Yahweh Elohim brought into being by making, the other a large-scale creation Elohim brought into being by the speaking of a word. The small-scale creation found in Genesis 2 is part of a longer narrative tradition intended to explain Israel's origins that now forms part of the Pentateuch, the first five books of the Hebrew Bible. The small-scale account of creation may have originated during the period of the Israelite kingdoms. It was later incorporated into a more extensive narrative tradition about "how things came to be the way they are now" that may be identified in several books of the Pentateuch.

The small-scale story of creation is apparently the earlier of the two accounts in the Hebrew Bible and it reflects many of the elements and concerns of popular folklore. The story is anthropocentric, primarily concerned with human beings and their situation in the world, standing in contrast to the creation stories of Egypt and Mesopotamia, which are concerned almost exclusively with the activities of the gods. The story begins in Genesis 2:4b and presents a creation centered on humanity and its needs. But it also provides an explanation for the difficulties human beings face in life despite the goodness of the divine creation.

In this story the work of creation appears to be limited to a single day. In this story the Yahweh Elohim creates by making: "In the day that [Yahweh Elohim] made the earth and the heavens . . . [Yahweh Elohim] formed man." (Genesis 2:4b, 7a). Humanity is the first of Yahweh Elohim's creatures, formed by his own hands out of dust. Apart from the heavens and the earth that provide the foundation for the god's creative work, everything else—including all plants and animals—seem to be brought into being only for the benefit of the first human being, Adam. The Garden of Eden is created as a home for Adam, with all the plants that are good to eat, while Adam is given the job of tending the garden. All the animals are made in an attempt to provide companionship for the human being, and Adam shares the divine creative function by giving names to the animals, that is, by identifying their essential nature. Finally, even the first woman is made for Adam to serve as his companion. In this story of creation, Yahweh Elohim makes almost everything that exists for Adam, to feed or please him.

What follows on the first part of this story of creation (that centers on providing for the needs of the first man) is the account of the first man's "fall," that is, his expulsion from the Garden of Eden and the explanation of "how things came to be the way they are now" for all human beings. This is an integral part of the story of creation rather than its sequel. The events of the fall are foreshadowed by the planting of the tree of life and "the tree of the knowledge of good and evil" in the garden (Genesis 2:9) and the divine order to the human being not to eat the fruit of that tree (Genesis 2:16–17) in the first part of the story. But Yahweh Elohim's order is joined to a threat that if Adam eats fruit from the tree he will die. The threat makes it clear that the second part of the story is not about the origin of sin, if sin is understood as the capacity to disobey divine commands. If Adam were not already capable of disobeying Yahweh Elohim's command when the tree was planted, there would be no reason to threaten him with death should he disobey. Adam's ability to disobey or obey what Yahweh Elohim commands—to sin or not to sin—is assumed by the story from the start. Instead the story is an explanation of "how things came to be the way they are now," why human life is so difficult if everything in creation was created good and beneficial for humanity. The reason is, human beings disobeyed Yahweh Elohim and so are to blame for the current sad state of affairs.

The reason why first Eve and then Adam disobey the divine command is their desire to "be like [Elohim], knowing both good and evil" (Genesis 3:5b). After they eat the fruit, the first knowledge they gain is the realization they are "naked," uncovered and vulnerable before the judgment of Yahweh Elohim. The first evil they know is the evil they have done by disobeying him. Neither the sin Adam and Eve commit nor the "knowledge" they gain is sexual in nature—that idea is largely the creation of the Christian theologian Augustine of Hippo.

The punishments imposed on the man and woman are painful reminders of the distance between their desire to "be like Elohim" and their actual fate as fallen human beings. The man can create new life from the ground as Yahweh Elohim did when he formed the plants and animals, but the man can only do so through the daily labor of tending the ground so plants may grow and provide him with food. The woman can create human life by means of a human body as Yahweh Elohim did when he created her from Adam's rib, but Eve can only do so through (sexual) submission to her husband and the painful process of childbirth. The "labor" Adam and Eve must endure to create new life stands in distinct contrast to Yahweh Elohim's ability to make things effortlessly, just as their eventual deaths stand in contrast to his immortality.

The second creation story that now provides the opening of the Hebrew Bible (Genesis 1:1–2:4a) takes a cosmological approach to the story, but still remains traditional in many ways. "In the beginning" there is the "formless void" of chaos and the waters of "the deep." As in *Enuma elish*, the initial elements before creation are the waters of chaos and the abyss where the waters churn. But here something else is present as well: the divine *ruakh*, the wind, or breath, or spirit of Elohim—one Hebrew word means all three. The *ruakh* is the force Elohim uses to give voice to his intentions and to initiate the work of creation. As was also the case in *Enuma elish*, the process of creation is a process of imposing divine order on chaos. Here, however, order is imposed not by divine combat between a god and the personified forces of chaos, but by Elohim voicing his divine intention as the spirit breathes life into his thought and makes it active. The parallel to the creation story from Memphis, of Ptah creating by "speaking" the gods into being, is obvious.

Elohim's first creation is light, but light is created to allow the creation of "day" through the separation of light and darkness into separate, specifically temporal, "spaces." The creation of light is in other words a necessary preliminary to the ordering of time itself as the primary means of imposing order on material creation. The measurement of time is the first principle of order in creation. This idea is what guides and organizes the progress of creation in this account as it proceeds through a series of "days" marked by the passing of evening and morning.

The second act of creation is another sort of separation, the separation of the waters by the creation of the firmament, the (literal) sphere of the created order, setting creation apart from the surrounding chaos. As we have seen, the usual Near Eastern view of the cosmos was that the earth was protected by the dome of the sky that held back the waters above the earth. The firmament was supported by the mountains of the earth, which itself floated above the waters of the abyss under the earth. The abyss was the source of the waters on the earth's surface, oceans, lakes, rivers, and springs. The creation of the firmament provides the basis for further earthly creation.

On the third day Elohim establishes boundaries for the waters of the earth to allow dry land to appear, and creates the plants that cover the earth. Here dry land is created not for its own sake but to allow for the abundant growth of plants, especially those that provide food for animals and human beings. Perhaps surprisingly, the fourth day returns from the earthly scale to the cosmological scale. Elohim apparently finishes the work of the first day by localizing the light of day in the orb of the sun, with the moon and stars to provide a subtler light during the night. Relegating the creation of the heavenly bodies to the fourth day may represent an attempt to reduce the sun and moon to cosmic lamps, in rebuttal to the worship of solar and lunar deities among some of Israel's neighbors. More important, the creation of sun, moon, and stars is carried out in service to the ordering of time "for seasons and for days and years" (Genesis 1:14b) which affect the fertility cycle, and only secondarily "to give light upon the earth" (Genesis 1:15).

With the earthly stage prepared, animal life finally appears. The fifth day sees the creation of aquatic life and birds, filling the seas and the air, the two realms of earthly life not hospitable to human beings. Here "the great sea monsters" are part of the divine creation, not representatives of the powers of chaos as they are in other ancient mythologies; we may contrast Tiamat, Apophis, and Lothan. With the first creation of animate, sentient creatures comes also the idea of divine command, as Elohim delivers his first order: "Be fruitful and multiply" (Genesis 1:22). This order is a commission for all the earth's creatures to continue God's work of creation through natural means, to propagate their own species by sexual reproduction.

The sixth day sees the creation of animal life on the earth itself, including the creation of human beings. This is another indication that the author is more concerned with spheres of created life (sea, air, earth) than with the specific types of life involved. Still the focus here is on humanity, created in Elohim's own image to serve as stewards over the earth and its creatures. As in the earlier creation story in Genesis 2–3, there is an emphasis on humanity's similarity to its creator, but that similarity is itself a function of the divine creative power which human beings do not entirely share. Human beings are also commanded to create new life, but they must do so through sexual reproduction, like the animals. It should be noted that the animals and humanity are given use of the plants for food; eating meat is a later reward to humanity for Noah's rescue of the animals in Genesis 9:1–5.

The work of creation apparently comes to an end on the sixth day, since at that point Elohim reviews all he has made and the repeated motif appears for the final time: "[Elohim] saw everything that he had made, and indeed, it was very good. And there was evening and there was morning, the sixth day" (Genesis 1:31).

But after the cosmos is complete, one final work of creation remains. Significantly the final work of creation is the result of Elohim *not* working. This is the Sabbath, the day of rest in Israelite religious culture, "created" by Elohim's own day of rest. The final work of creation is not humanity but the Sabbath, the weekly religious festival whose importance surpasses the human need for rest; it is presented here as part of the very fabric of the cosmos. The Sabbath was the primary festival of Israelite religion and is the end of creation in both senses; it is the final work, but it is also its goal, the point toward which Elohim has directed all the work of creation from the first day. We may compare Marduk's creation of the festival calendar toward the conclusion of *Enuma elish*, but here the Sabbath is even more important. It is what has determined the progressive course of the entire process of creation.

So there is a complete transformation of cosmogonic myth in this account of creation. The story of creation is no longer about the political or social order imposed by a divine conqueror; instead it is about the sacred order of religious observance imposed through the divine subjection of all creatures to the orderly passage of time. The creator god is less one whose power is to be feared and obeyed than one who is to be properly revered and worshipped, because reverence and worship are part and parcel of the very fabric of creation, from the cosmic to the earthly level.

The difference in the content of these two Israelite creation stories in comparison to the other creation stories we have considered should not blind us to another important difference the Israelite stories represent. The other creation stories we have considered have for the most part been expressions of divine hierarchies that mimic and justify human royal hierarchies on earth. They are stories of how the divine order was imposed over the cosmos and the gods themselves, as each god found a place in the divine hierarchy established through the work of creation. Such stories served to justify the way things are in the world, not only the order of creation but also the political order among human beings. The message was that the gods had done their work and put everything—and everyone—in their place. Only the king was of real importance to the gods. The place for most human beings was at the bottom of the divine order, serving the gods and waiting on their good graces to provide for their servants' needs.

This is not the case in the creation stories in the Israelite tradition. In both of the surviving stories, human beings are granted an important place in creation, either as the reason why most of the rest of creation came into being, or as the stewards and protectors of what has been created. But here there is no political hierarchy among human beings in creation, only the authority that arises from (patriarchal) family relationships, husband and wife, parent and child. Here perhaps the creation stories already anticipate the later history of humanity as it unfolds in Genesis, where Yahweh makes covenant not with kings, but with family leaders, heads of households, through whom divine blessings flow to their families and their descendants.

CHAPTER THIRTEEN

Syria–Palestine: Kings and Prophets

The King and the Gods in Syria–Palestine

In the kingdoms of Syria–Palestine, as elsewhere in the ancient Near East, the king was understood to be chosen by the gods to rule over the people as their viceroy and the mediator of divine blessings to the people. Kingship was a gift from the patron god of the city or state, first of all to the king himself but also to the people who benefited from the king's rule on the patron god's behalf. The patron god or goddess was also credited with any military victories the king might enjoy. A tangible expression of this idea was the portion of the spoils given to the god as a thanksgiving offering after a military victory. The king built and maintained temples for the patron god, with the god's chief temple in the royal capital, in close proximity to the king's palace. The king was often depicted as a "son" of the patron god, and the god acted as a mother or father to the king, shielding him from harm and ensuring the well-being of his kingdom.

Because of the close, sometimes filial relationship between the king and the patron god or goddess of the nation, the king was also the chief sacral official who oversaw operation of the cult by priests and other functionaries. For the most part the actual work of sacrifice and temple worship was carried out by the priests on the king's behalf. But as we have seen in Egypt and Mesopotamia, in some cases the king himself and even members of his family offered sacrifices and performed other cultic duties. The king also determined the course of the nation's religious policy. Each king inherited the traditions of the national religious culture, but the king would decide which gods in the pantheon were to be accorded the most attention and worship, and could raise the status of a god through construction of a new temple complex or a restoration of neglected rituals. For the most part such changes in religious culture were gradual and evolutionary, but in some cases they reflected decisive shifts in religious policies or political alliances, since virtually all political change had religious significance and vice versa.

Religious policy became a particular point of concern once the independent states of Syria–Palestine came under the influence or control of other states. A ruler might introduce the worship of new or foreign gods in response to an alliance or a desired alliance with the ruler of another state—for example, as the result of a dynastic marriage. When one state became dominant over another, its king would most often impose mandatory worship of its patron gods in the context of the subject state's official ritual cult. Recognition and worship of a dominant state's gods by a subject people produced a wealth of divine benefits for the dominant state, and so became an essential expression of political loyalty. Conversely, one of the first expressions of a subject king's intention to rebel against his overlord might be expulsion of the overlord's gods and the cultic personnel who served them from the state cult, coupled with a renewed emphasis on exclusive worship of the patron gods of the subject nation. In short, in Syria–Palestine as elsewhere in the states of the ancient Near East, religious culture was largely a function of royal policy aimed at enhancing or legitimizing the political power of the king, and reflecting the rise and fall of the kingdom's fortunes among the surrounding nations.

The King and Yahweh in Israel and Judah

Israel and Judah present the clearest examples from Syria–Palestine of the various factors that might play into the development of the religious culture of an independent state in Syria–Palestine during the first millennium BCE, primarily because of the abundance of their surviving religious literature. But the beginning point is hard to identify, since it is difficult to reconstruct the religious culture of the territorial state of Israel at the birth of the monarchy. The author of the theological history found in the biblical books of Samuel and Kings notes that before the ministry of the prophet Samuel who oversaw Israel's transition to a monarchy, "the word of [Yahweh] was rare" (1 Samuel 3:1). Although this is a comment based on a later theological assessment, it seems likely that worship of Yahweh was overshadowed by worship of other gods on the eve of the birth of the kingdom of Israel. Although Yahweh apparently had a place as the patron god of the kingdom, its first kings worshipped other gods as well. The evidence is the names of early royal princes. Saul worshipped both Yahweh and Baal, as indicated by the names of his sons Jonathan ("gift of Yahweh") and Ishbaal ("man of Baal"). David worshipped Yahweh and Salim, the god of the Jebusites who were dominant in Judah, David's native territory. David named some of his sons for Yahweh, such as Adonijah ("Yahweh is my lord") and others after Salim, such as Absalom ("Father Salim"). David's eventual successor had both a Jebusite name, Solomon, and an alternative Yahwistic name, Jedidiah ("Yahweh's beloved," 2 Samuel 12:24–25). This may reflect an attempt to reconcile the two parts of David's kingdom, Israel to the north and Judah to the south, through the acknowledgement of the patron gods of both states. David's loyalty to Yahweh may have arisen in part from his need to legitimate himself as a successor to Saul, since he was not an Israelite by birth. David's long struggle with Saul's son Ishbaal for control over Israel after Saul's death indicates this attempt was not entirely successful (2 Samuel 3:1; 5:5).

The Jebusite character of Jerusalem and David's own association with Bethlehem, a city under Jebusite dominion, had a formative influence on the conduct of the worship of Yahweh in the royal capital. David was able to capture Jerusalem because he had an insider's knowledge of its defenses (2 Samuel 5:8), and the city seems to have retained much of its Jebusite population and identity after David claimed it as his own. The Jebusites worshipped Salim, El-Elyon ("El the Highest") and possibly an agricultural god named Lehem ("Bread") since the name of the Jebusite town of Bethlehem apparently means "house of [the god] Lehem" (cp. 1 Chronicles 4:22).

Traditional Israelite religion seems to have been favored in the north. The religious ideas and rituals of the ancestral religious culture were not associated with either temples or monarchy, but instead with charismatic leaders like the "judges," military leaders and city rulers whose rule intertwined political and religious authority. Once he became king over both Judah and Israel, David and his priests modified Israelite religion in the light of Jebusite practice. David passed over the Yahwistic priest Abiathar, who had accompanied him during his military campaigns, to choose the Jerusalemite Zadok as his high priest. Under Zadok the worship of Yahweh was, apparently for the first time, associated with a city in the midst of settled territory rather than with a mountain top in the wilderness. Later Israelite revolts in the northern territory against David and his dynasty were in part rejections of the Jerusalem version of Israelite religion and Yahweh's close association with David's dynasty and the temple in Jerusalem.

The temple was the fullest expression of the Davidic accommodation of Israelite worship to the situation of the united kingdom of Israel and Judah.

Solomon built a temple that, like his two royal names, represented an attempt at synthesis between the urban religious culture of the Jebusites and the pastoral religious culture of the Israelites. Up to this time Yahweh had been worshipped in a tent or tabernacle that reflected the nomadic life of Israel, or at local shrines. Although Yahweh had a dwelling place on the mountain named either Sinai or Horeb, his presence was in the midst of his wandering people, represented by the portable Ark of the Covenant. David moved the Ark into Jerusalem and gave it a permanent place in close proximity to his own palace. Several sites in the north in the territory of Israel, including Bethel and Shiloh, had far better claims to legitimacy and long histories as cultic sites for Yahwistic ritual worship. But once Jerusalem became the political center of Israel under David, the city became Israel's cultic center as well. Both the king and the god made the royal capital their abode, symbolizing the close collaboration between them.

There were other national shrines devoted to the worship of Yahweh in both Judah and Israel, the so-called "high places" (bamoth). The "high places" were not necessarily pagan altars, since the word bamoth simply means "altars" and often refers to sites that are clearly devoted to the worship of Yahweh. Some of these national shrines may have also been dedicated to the worship of gods other than Yahweh as well—just as other gods were sometimes worshipped in the Jerusalem temple—but for the most part the shrines continued to be served by the Levites, members of the official national priesthood, throughout the history of the two kingdoms.

After David's kingdom again divided into the two kingdoms of Israel and Judah around 928 BCE, the subjects of both kingdoms continued to worship Yahweh in their own territories according to their own traditions. The author of Samuel and Kings, who was himself a Judahite, identifies Israel's rebellion against David's dynasty with a rebellion against Yahweh, since the kings of Israel authorized worship sites in Israel instead of worshipping at the temple in Jerusalem (cf. 1 Kings 2:25–30). But it was unthinkable that any ancient king or his people would worship the national god outside the boundaries of his own kingdom, since the god resided among his people. Once Israel broke away from Judah, its kings reinstated the traditional cultic sites devoted to Yahweh at Bethel and Dan. The kings of Israel used figures of calves to localize the god's presence at the shrine. The calf may have served as a "footstool" before Yahweh's throne as the place Yahweh's presence "rested" or "abided," just as his presence was also supposed to abide between the wings of the cherubim on the lid of the Ark of the Covenant in Jerusalem (cf. 1 Samuel 4:4; Psalm 80:1). On the other hand, the calf or calves may have been representations of the god himself, symbolizing his divine power and virility (cp. "the Bull El"). Later Ahab's father Omri established a new royal capital in Samaria and built a temple of Yahweh there, much as Solomon built the temple in Jerusalem. Both kings followed the standard ancient practice of providing a place for the god and the king to live as neighbors.

After the kingdoms split, Judah continued to worship at the Jerusalem temple, but also at other altars dedicated to Yahwistic worship elsewhere. Both Israel and Judah incorporated the worship of foreign gods into the national cult in various ways, such as through the inclusion of the *ashteroth* as cultic representations of the goddess Asherah. There were also unofficial religious practices not sanctioned by either nation's kings or priesthood, as expressions of folk religion and foreign religious influences. It is important to remember that religious "orthodoxy" at any given point in the history of a people or state was determined by the presiding political and religious authorities as custodians of the religious culture. In Israel and Judah, however, an unusual question arose: Who truly speaks for Yahweh?

Political and Religious Authority in Israel and Judah

This problem was a difficult one, because by the time of the early kingdom, political power among the people of Israel was identified in its dominant tradition with religious authority manifested in essentially nonmilitary forms of leadership. The preeminent example is Moses, whose authority as leader of Israel was solely derived from his role as Yahweh's chosen mediator of divine revelation. In the traditions preserved in the Pentateuch, Moses's power and authority are political as well as religious, both subsumed under the title of "prophet" (cf. Deuteronomy 34:10). Moses's role is clearly distinguished from the role of his brother Aaron as high priest (Exodus 4:10–16). Aaron takes the lead in honoring Yahweh in ritual worship, but he receives his instructions from Moses and operates under his authority. When Moses later delegates some of his authority to the elders of Israel, the authority he grants them is political authority exercised as judgment in disputes (Exodus 18:13–27). Moses ultimately commissions Joshua to succeed him as leader of Israel (Numbers 27:18–23), conferring on Joshua both his religious and his political authority. Joshua served in tandem with the priest Eleazer just as Moses served with Aaron, but like Moses, Joshua remained Yahweh's primary instrument for leading and governing his people.

The tradition that leadership in Israel was a combination of religious and political authority continues in the stories of the conquest of Canaan under Joshua. After the people become settled inhabitants of Palestine, they live under the authority of regional political leaders from about 1200 to 1020

BCE. These are the leaders called "judges" in English translations of the Bible. The Hebrew word translated "judge" (*shophet*) derives from a verb meaning "to rule"; the judges were men and women who ruled over some part of the people of Israel by virtue of their possession of the "spirit of Yahweh" (*ruakh YHWH*).

The author of the biblical book of Judges gives the impression that individual rulers arose in times of crisis to lead armies or take other action to renew the people's fidelity to Yahweh, providing charismatic leadership akin to that provided by Moses or Joshua. The stories about these rulers are a mixed lot. Some of the judges survive only as names; others are military leaders or rulers over cities, like Gideon, who ruled over Shechem. At least one, Samson, is a mighty man of valor, who like Gilgamesh exhibits an unbridled sexual appetite and a reckless impetuosity, and experiences a series of improbable adventures. Samson never leads an army or functions as a political leader in any apparent way, so his inclusion among the judges is something of a puzzle. His primary contribution to Israel's welfare is killing large numbers of Philistines, primarily as a result of his romantic involvements with Philistine women.

Stories about the Israelite judges seem to reflect accurately the relatively unsettled religious practices of Israel at the time, when Yahweh was perhaps recognized as the patron god of Israel while other gods, notably Baal, were worshipped as well. The author of Judges several times notes apologetically, "In those days there was no king in Israel; all people did what was right in their own eyes" (cf. Judges 21:25). As we have seen, this unsettled religious situation extended at least into the early years of the Israelite kingdoms.

The last of the regional charismatic rulers was Samuel. As judge over Israel Samuel combined the roles of prophet, priest, and magistrate at a time when the people were living in the northern highlands of Palestine. Samuel, like Moses, is presented in terms of the Israelite ideal of leadership as someone who is both a political and a religious leader, acting at the behest of Yahweh to rule the god's people. As we have seen, in the ancient Near East this was an idea more usually associated with the king than with a priest-ruler. Samuel followed a regional circuit in carrying out his duties, traveling from Bethel to Gilgal to Mizpah (1 Samuel 7:15–17). These cities were probably the major religious and administrative centers for Israel at the time, and mark roughly the extent of Samuel's jurisdiction. Samuel's two sons were potential successors to their father as leaders over Israel, but they were rejected by the people, who were clamoring for a military leader to protect them against their primary enemies, the Philistines and the Amorites.

The people's rejection of Samuel in favor of Saul is presented in the book of Samuel as a rejection of Yahweh's leadership over Israel, another instance of the people of Israel wishing to be "like the nations" (1 Samuel 8:4–9, 19–22). In fact it represents the historical transition from one kind of political leadership to another, from the government of a regional administrator or city leader supported by a muster of troops gathered from the general populace to a centralized military monarchy supported by a professional standing army. It is worth noting that the transition from the rule of "judges" to the rule of kings does not represent a shift from "charismatic" to "dynastic" leadership. Some of the "charismatic" leaders among the judges established dynasties or attempted to (cf. Gideon, Eli, Samuel) and the kings of Israel and Judah were believed to be granted the spiritual gifts (i.e., the *charismata*) necessary to rule Yahweh's people as his regent on earth.

In any event, the tradition that survives in the Hebrew Bible exalts religious authority over political authority, or rather presents Yahweh investing those to whom he give religious authority with political authority as well. Elsewhere in the ancient Near East the assumption was that anyone who is born to or who gains political authority has been chosen by the gods to rule over their people—in short, that political authority entails religious authority. The contrary tradition in the Hebrew Bible may be a result of later conflict between kings as political authorities and prophets as religious authorities, based on the idea that Yahweh chose the prophets and inspired them to proclaim divine revelations, "the word of Yahweh," to the people. In any event, the authors of the books preserved in the Hebrew Bible for the most part exalt the authority of prophets over that of kings, to the extent that the vast majority of the kings of Israel and Judah are condemned for deviating from the proper worship of Yahweh.

Although Samuel was a political leader, he is presented in the book of Samuel preeminently as a prophet, someone endowed by Yahweh with different sorts of spiritual power to provide for the people's welfare. This may be why the passing of political power in Israel from Samuel to Saul is presented in the tradition as Israel's rejection not of Samuel, but of Yahweh as leader over them (cf. 1 Samuel 8:4–9). Despite the fact that the transition from Samuel's rule to Saul's was in traditional religious terms not that great—since both were charismatic figures believed to be Yahweh's choice to rule over Israel—the shift from spiritual power to military power as the basis of political authority was significant. It was a major change in the way that the people of Israel understood their relationship to Yahweh, and it became the basis for the later conflict between the kings of Israel and Judah and the prophets.

Kings and Prophets in Israel and Judah

The most common source of conflict between the kings and priests of Israel and Judah on the one hand and the prophets on the other was the question of religious authority: Did Yahweh direct the religious behavior of his people through the decisions of the king as his viceroy, or by speaking through the prophets as his messengers? The king and other political leaders were concerned with practical management of the nation's affairs—how best to respond to internal and external threats, and what wars to fight or alliances to form to ensure the nation's security. The priests and Levites, notably the high priests, served at the king's pleasure as government functionaries and generally shared the concerns and the point of view of the political leaders. The priests believed their primary responsibility was the proper maintenance of the temple cult and the supervision of cultic worship of Yahweh (and perhaps other gods) in shrines elsewhere in the state, in support of the king. Cultic worship was after all the means of maintaining and enhancing the relationship between Israel or Judah and its god. It was ritual sacrifice that compensated for the religious violations the people committed and restored Yahweh's goodwill toward them. Like most of their contemporaries in the ancient Near East, official religious authorities in Israel and Judah believed the religious duty of the people at large was simply to obey the king and support the cult.

The prophets of Israel and Judah, however, generally spoke from a different point of view. They believed the primary duty of king, priests, and people was to be obedient to Yahweh through specific moral, social, and political actions as well as proper worship. Although some prophets were part of the official religious establishment in connection with ritual worship, there were men and women who were apparently widely recognized as prophets who had no connection with the religious establishment at all. In general the prophets represented an independent, self-authenticating voice of religious authority not beholden to the interests of the king or the priesthood. They were a distinct, and often dissenting, voice for Yahweh's will for the country and its people.

The problem of religious authority was made more difficult by the fact that the prophets often tended to represent a nonconforming view of Yahwistic religion, based either in a traditional rejection of royal authority in favor of divine authority or in a strict henotheism or evolving monotheism. As we have seen, the notion that Yahweh alone should rule over Israel seems to have been older than the monarchy, and was generally represented in terms of political leadership under a religious figure Yahweh had endowed with spiritual authority. After the establishment of the kingdom under Saul and

David, this ideal of political authority mediated by a spiritual figure came to represent dissatisfaction with the reality of the political and religious policies and compromises that are a necessary part of statehood. This central belief informing this ideal was "Yahweh alone," but included the idea of an authoritative religious figure governing Israel or Judah on Yahweh's behalf, acting as an intermediary between Yahweh and the people as Moses had.

"Yahweh alone" as sole monarch over his people Israel also meant "Yahweh alone" as the one and only god for Israel to worship. Henotheistic belief in Israel and Judah was most often expressed in terms of Yahweh's incomparability and strength as his people's defender, and led in time to a nascent monotheism. Although henotheism is a religious principle, it would have very real consequences for the way Israel and Judah conducted their political affairs. If Yahweh alone was the only god for the people to worship, there could be no accommodation to other religious cultures, either in allowing their adherents to worship according to their own traditions in Israel and Judah—as Solomon allowed his foreign wives to do in Jerusalem (1 Kings 11:1–8)—or in worshipping the gods of the nations that made vassals of Israel or Judah.

The ideal of "Yahweh alone" also tended to make the prophets theological idealists, claiming in any and all circumstances that the best policy was adherence to the word of Yahweh as they proclaimed it and trust in Yahweh to deliver Israel or Judah from their enemies. An example is the conflict between King Ahaz of Judah and the prophet Isaiah of Jerusalem during the Syro-Ephraimite War, over the question of whether or not to seek an alliance with Assyria against Israel and Aram-Damascus. Isaiah was probably an official prophet who carried out his prophetic ministry in the context of the Jerusalem temple and the official cult of ritual sacrifice. He provided Ahaz with repeated assurances from Yahweh that Judah would prevail if Ahaz would trust in the promises Yahweh had made to David (Isaiah 7:1–17). But Ahaz was driven by the more practical considerations of royal politics, and ultimately decided to turn to Assyria for protection. The conflict between political realities and theological idealism in the history of Israel and Judah almost always resulted in a defeat for idealism, although the idealists wrote the histories that have survived.

An example of an independent prophet without any official standing in the official ritual cult is Elijah, who appears in 1 Kings as a champion for "Yahweh alone," exclusive Yahwistic worship in Israel. In the Hebrew Bible Elijah is the first major independent prophet of the period of the Hebrew kingdoms. In the book of Kings Elijah finds himself in opposition to Ahab of Israel (c. 871–851 BCE) and his wife, Jezebel, a daughter of Ethbaal, a priest of Astarte who seized power in Tyre about the same time that Omri deposed the usurper Zimri in Israel. All the stories about Elijah in 1 Kings have the same essential point: Yahweh, not Baal, is the giver of all good things and the only god for Israel to worship. Elijah is presented in Kings as a model of prophetic ministry—including proclamation, prophetic action, and the working of miracles—a model that was followed by many of the prophets who came after him.

Independent prophecy did not inevitably lead to conflict with the king and the official representatives of the state cult. Some prophets—notably Obadiah, Nahum, and Habakkuk—focused on the offenses committed by the enemies that oppressed Yahweh's people and not the failings or faithlessness of the kings or the people themselves. But this was not a case of prophetic authority bowing to royal authority, but instead the two acting and speaking in concert. Later, after the fall of Jerusalem and the exile of Judah's aristocracy, prophets both in exile and in Judah would take the lead in helping those who worshipped Yahweh to survive and redefine their community in light of the disaster that had befallen them.

Religious and Political Leadership under Foreign Dominion

The fall of Jerusalem to the Babylonians in 587 BCE was an unparalleled calamity in the history of Judah, one without apparent remedy. It demanded a theological response because the fall of Jerusalem was not only a political and military disaster, but a killing blow to many of the primary ideas informing Judah's religious culture. The fall of Samaria and the nation of Israel to the Assyrians in 721 BCE had seemed to vindicate Judah, the Davidic dynasty, and the religious rituals and worship that centered on the Jerusalem temple. Those in Judah could readily conclude that Samaria had fallen because of its wickedness—including its rebellion against David and his descendants as Yahweh's chosen rulers over his people. But the fall of Jerusalem and the Babylonian conquest of Judah swept away all the benefits the people of Judah believed Yahweh had conferred on them through the covenants: the land, the Davidic king, and the temple. Worst of all, there was no discernible way of renewing the covenantal relationship, since the stipulated means of doing so, ritual sacrifice in the temple, had come to an end when the temple was destroyed.

In the face of this catastrophe, there were two possible theological conclusions. Either the gods of Babylon had overseen the destruction of Judah and Yahweh had been powerless to prevent it, or Yahweh had himself brought about the disaster. If the people were to adhere to their ancestral traditions and continue to worship Yahweh, the second option was the only viable one. They had to accept the idea that their own failure to obey the covenantal stipulations had led Yahweh to allow the Babylonians to conquer Judah as punishment for his people's offenses. It seemed that events had validated the call to repentance proclaimed by prophets such as Isaiah of Jerusalem, Ezekiel, and Jeremiah, demanding the people recognize their responsibilities under the covenant. It now fell to the prophets to make sense of the experience of exile as a prologue to leading the people to reconciliation with Yahweh.

In fact, that work had already been part of the prophetic proclamation in Judah. Isaiah of Jerusalem looked forward to a new era when Yahweh would be reconciled with his people, a time Isaiah envisioned as a return to the conditions in the Garden of Eden under the rule of an idealized Davidic king (cf. Isaiah 9:1–7, 11:1–16). The last part of the prophecies of Ezekiel recounts Ezekiel's vision after the fall of Jerusalem of the city restored and rebuilt according to a new, idealized model (Ezekiel 40–48). Even Jeremiah leavened his prophecies of doom and destruction with reassurances after those prophecies had been fulfilled that Yahweh would make a new covenant with his people that would become the basis of a renewed community (Jeremiah 31:31–40). Each of these prophets combined the message of impending disaster as the inevitable outcome of Judah's disobedience with a message of hope and reconciliation with Yahweh, who they said would remain faithful to his covenantal promises despite the faithlessness of his people.

Chapters 40 through 54 of the book of Isaiah reflect a different historical situation and a different prophetic voice than the earlier chapters of the book. Scholars refer to the prophet of this later portion of the book as "Second Isaiah," a disciple of Isaiah of Jerusalem who was also a prophet in his own right and carried out his prophetic ministry during the Babylonian exile. In the prophecies of Second Isaiah we find for the first time a clear and manifest monotheism proclaimed in direct rejection of polytheism and more specifically the worship of cultic statues.

The prophecies of Second Isaiah promote monotheistic ideas in part by the ways they present Yahweh displaying his sovereignty over the cosmos. They portray Yahweh creating and counseling human beings, revealing himself in history, helping those in need, and declaring his intentions through the prophets and later fulfilling those prophecies with his mighty deeds. But Second Isaiah also includes satires on the worship of cultic statues that equates the cultic statue with the god it represents (Isaiah 40:18–20; 41:6–7, 29; 42:17; 44:9–20; 45:20). These satires mock the idea of worshipping something made by human beings, a thing that can rot or topple over, something that has no power of its own to see or hear its suppliants or to do them any good. This is of course a misrepresentation of the use of cult statues in ancient Near Eastern religious cultures, since the statues were meant to localize the presence of the god—much as the Ark of the Covenant localized the presence of Yahweh in the Jerusalem temple—but were not themselves considered to *be* the god. But the prophet is not interested in such theological niceties. It is sufficient for his purposes that the worshippers of other gods treat their cultic statues with the respect due to the gods they represent, washing, dressing, and feeding them and addressing them with their prayers and supplications.

Second Isaiah's portrayal of the impotence of cultic statues and the gods they represent stands in clear contrast to his descriptions of the power of Yahweh as god of the whole world. The prophet also embraces the logical corollary of his belief that Yahweh is the one true god. If Yahweh alone is god, then he is lord not just over Israel or Judah, but over all the peoples and regions of the world and he directs and uses them for his own purposes. The prophet proclaims that Yahweh used the Babylonians to punish the king and people of Judah; now he will use the Persians to punish Babylon for the evil they have inflicted on his people. Second Isaiah identified the Persian king Cyrus as Yahweh's anointed, chosen like David to fulfill a particular role in accomplishing Yahweh's will among his people (Isaiah 45:1). In short, Second Isaiah presents Yahweh as the one who rules over his people, and all the kings of the earth merely as his instruments to carry out his divine intentions. Even though Yahweh's people were under foreign dominion, they were still also under their god's care and could live out their covenantal relationship with him. In Second Isaiah's prophecies, the entire world is Yahweh's domain and all people serve his purposes.

As we have seen, Persian imperial policies toward subject peoples were relatively enlightened in regard to native political and religious traditions. The Persians allowed native aristocracies to reside in their own territories under the authority of Persian political officials, provided they remained loyal. The Persians also allowed subject peoples to worship their own gods according to their ancestral traditions, provided they would also entreat their gods for the Persian king. In Second Isaiah's oracles, the day when the leaders of Judah would return from exile would be Yahweh's "day of salvation" (Isaiah 49:8), when Yahweh would set right the destruction of his "day of wrath" and reestablish his covenant with the people in peace.

But in fact, the return to Judah was considerably less glorious for those who had lived in exile. They found themselves in a ruined land most of them had never seen before. Only the leading citizens of Judah had been sent into exile, and "the people of the land" who had been left behind by the Babylonians—the vast majority of Judah's population—had continued to live as they always had. They had good reason to see the exile as a judgment on their former political leaders, while they, the common people, had remained to live in the land Yahweh had given them. Now the children of those disgraced exiles wanted to reassume leadership over the community in their ancestral homeland. Tensions quickly developed between the returned exiles and those who had been left behind. Soon important theological questions arose: What sort of community could Yahweh's people now become? What would hold them together? And in light of their troubles, what had become of the promises Yahweh had made through Second Isaiah?

The prophet Haggai addressed these questions in the context of Yahweh's continuing covenantal relationship with his people. We have no way of knowing whether Haggai was one of the exiles who returned to Jerusalem in 520 BCE or someone who had lived in Judah all his life. His prophecy reflects temple traditions, especially those psalms that idealize and celebrate temple worship, and the idea of the temple and its rituals as Judah's link with its god. Haggai was confident that reconciliation with Yahweh and the restoration of the community could be precipitated by a single act: the reconstruction of the temple in Jerusalem. The people had put off rebuilding the temple until their economic situation improved, but Haggai maintained only a rebuilt temple could ensure the community's prosperity, since it was Yahweh's abiding presence in the temple that was the source of all blessings (Haggai 1:7–11). But Haggai also warned that the temple alone would not ensure the community's well-being. He called the people to obey the covenantal stipulations so that both their worship and their lives would be pleasing to Yahweh. In this respect Haggai's message is consistent with the message proclaimed by the prophets before the exile, that sacrifices offered in the temple would be ineffective if the people were not obedient to their covenantal obligations (Haggai 2:10–14). Ritual worship and proper moral behavior were two different aspects of the covenantal relationship with Yahweh.

After the return from exile, a new model of community leadership arose. With real political power in the hands of foreign empires, the community's leaders had to use their secular authority for an essentially religious purpose: ensuring the national identity of the people as the people of Israel by enforcing their obedience to the covenantal relationship with Yahweh. The prophetic mandate became a political mandate as the people ceased to be defined by the boundaries or government of a state, to be defined instead by the boundaries and behavior of an ethnic and religious community, the Jews. Nehemiah served as governor of Jerusalem under Persian authority, for example, and according to the book bearing his name worked to establish and enforce the covenantal law in Jerusalem against great odds, and over two terms of service largely succeeded in doing so. The most difficult problem in the community, one addressed by Nehemiah as governor and later by the priest Ezra, appears to have been intermarriage between Jewish men and women who were not Jews. This was a particularly important issue, since so many of the covenantal stipulations that were believed to determine Jewish practice and identity were focused on what happened in the household and so were dependent on the religious duties of women. The solution imposed first by Nehemiah and later again by Ezra was to force Jewish men to divorce wives who were not Jewish, and to renounce any children who had been born as a result of the marriage. These may strike us as drastic measures, but at the time the political and religious leaders of the community believed such measures were the only means of ensuring the survival of the Jews' distinctive religious culture.

Ezra more than Nehemiah represents the enduring model of specifically religious leadership over the Jews. For most of the following few centuries the Jerusalem community and the surrounding countryside were under the direct authority of the high priests while political leadership remained in the hands of foreign rulers, whether Persian, Macedonian, or Roman.

Israel's History as Covenantal History

The presentation of Israel's history in the Hebrew Bible as a history of its interactions with Yahweh is very much the result of the work of the prophets of Israel and Judah. It was the prophets who emphasized obedience to Israel's covenantal obligations as the source of its historical well-being, and disobedience as the cause of its many trials. In Judah the idea of covenantal obedience was often understood primarily in terms of support for the Davidic dynasty and ritual worship exclusively in the temple in Jerusalem, ideas that survive in the biblical books of Samuel and Kings. But the idea of Israel's history as a history lived out in covenantal relationship to Yahweh, an idea that shapes and informs all of the books of the Hebrew Bible, is a prophetic idea that subjects all the exigencies of history to the judgment of an eternal ideal, the idea of Israel as Yahweh's chosen people.

Other ancient Near Eastern religious cultures, of course, also understood their history as being under the dominion of the gods and of the patron god in particular. The gods had a special relationship with the people, but that relationship was mediated through the king as the gods' viceroy on earth. Every people maintains an oral tradition about its origins, not only as human beings but as members of a particular group with a distinctive history. But what we find in Israel is the development and refining of the idea of Israel as "the people of Yahweh" in virtually all of its extant literature, from history to poetry to wisdom. In the history presented by the texts of the Hebrew Bible, this identity begins long before Israel's history as a nation and continues after it. It is not dependent on kings or priests as mediators, but only on Yahweh's covenantal promise and the people's fulfillment of the covenantal stipulations their ancestors accepted at Sinai. If the books of the Hebrew Bible continually present the leaders of Israel—kings or not—as men and women who serve as mediators between the people and Yahweh, it is because their authors believed the relationship between the people and their god was the key to and the meaning of their history as a community. While other ancient Near Eastern religious cultures were concerned with the work of the gods in the past in creation of the world as it now exists, and in support of the king as the source of blessings in the present, the religious culture of Israel was concerned with how the mutual obligations between Israel and Yahweh had been manifested in the past as a guide to how his people should live in the present. The prevailing belief was that Yahweh was active among his people in the present, not only to hear prayers and receive sacrifices, but to shape and guide the people's history according to their obedience to the covenant he had made with them.

The narratives of the Hebrew Bible that recount this history are the product of a long process of oral storytelling and story modification in response to historical events and evolving ideas about Yahweh and his people. These stories are rooted in a conviction that Yahweh has always been at work in Israel's history, a history understood in light of a triad of specific events: the Exodus from Egypt, the establishment of the covenant at Sinai, and the entry into the land of Canaan. This is true even of stories that take place prior to these key events, since the stories were preserved and passed along in a community shaped by the consequences of those events.

Over time, stories of individual events and heroes combined into narrative traditions, collections of stories that shared a common point of view about Yahweh, humanity, and how humanity can (or should) live in harmony with Yahweh. Ultimately those stories were collected and written down, with each author presenting the stories from a particular point of view. We have already seen the contrast between the two versions of creation in Genesis 1–3, for example. But all the authors of the books of the Hebrew Bible are united in their conviction that the primary reality about the people of Israel is that they are Yahweh's chosen people whose lives should be directed by their covenantal relationship with their god.

Following on the creation stories of "how things came to be the way they are now" in Genesis 1–11, the rest of the historical narrative focuses on the history of the people of Israel, beginning with Abraham and his descendants. The stories about the ancestors in Genesis are primarily that—stories—with literary and theological intentions not related to whatever value they may or may not have as historical reminiscences. The stories are in some ways comparable to creation stories, since they trace the origins of the people of Israel and explain in part "how things got to be the way they are now" for the people of Israel.

The history of the people of Israel begins when Yahweh picks out Abraham (then named Abram) from among all humanity to make a covenantal promise to him (Genesis 12:1–3). No justification is offered for Yahweh's choice of Abraham, but Abraham's subsequent behavior in response to Yahweh's promise seems to justify it. His trust in Yahweh leads Abraham to live as a nomad in Syria–Palestine, the land his descendants will eventually inherit. His trust leads him not only to believe that he will have a son with Sarah despite her age, but also to sacrifice that son at Yahweh's command. Finally, Yahweh declares, "Now I know that you fear [Elohim], seeing you have not withheld your son, your only son, from me" (Genesis 22:12b).

Abraham's son Isaac inherits the covenantal promise, which then passes to his younger son Jacob. The story of Jacob and Esau emphasizes Yahweh's freedom in deciding whom he will benefit by bestowing his favor, when he chooses Jacob as "covenant-bearer." Previously Yahweh had chosen Isaac, the son of Abraham by his wife Sarah, over Ishmael, Abraham's son by Sarah's Egyptian maid Hagar. In Genesis 28, Yahweh chooses the younger twin, Jacob, over Esau after Esau forfeits his inheritance rights and Jacob gains Isaac's blessing by trickery (Genesis 25:29–34; 27:1–40). Here the story in Genesis makes it clear that the moral status of human beings does not determine how Yahweh chooses to direct events on earth. Like Abram before him, Jacob later acquires a new name, "Israel"—translated as something like "he who contends with El" in Genesis 32:22–32—as a symbol of the difficulties of his new life lived in covenantal relationship with Yahweh (who is identified with El), although the name should probably be interpreted "El will rule."

The history of Abraham's family in Genesis is not only an explanation of the origins of the Israelites, but also of many of the other nations and peoples among whom the Israelites lived. The story explains the relationships among nations in terms of family relationship among eponymous ancestors. Isaac's half-brother Ishmael, for example, became the ancestor of nomadic Bedouin tribes while Jacob's brother Esau became ancestor of the nation of

Edom (cf. Genesis 37:25, 36:9). Such supposed family relationships among the different peoples of Syria–Palestine reflect an awareness that some neighboring peoples were more like the Israelites than others, especially those others "driven out" or destroyed by the Israelites, such as the Canaanites.

The transition between the story of Abraham's family and Israel as a nation is marked by the sojourn in Egypt and a shift of focus to Moses as Yahweh's designated mediator. Jacob and his family move down into Egypt to escape a famine in Canaan, and remain there under the protection of Jacob's son Joseph, who has gained an exalted position in Egypt's government through the king's favor. But later the situation of the Israelites deteriorates and they are reduced to the status of slaves. At Yahweh's instigation, Moses leads the people out of Egypt, their escape from Egypt's army made possible by a miracle at the sea. In Exodus, this miraculous escape becomes the basis for Yahweh's covenant with Israel at Sinai.

As the story is presented in Exodus, the covenant confirms Yahweh's status as Israel's national god, and makes it clear Israel has chosen to serve Yahweh out of all the gods believed to exist: "You shall have no other gods before [or beside] me; you shall not make for yourself an idol . . . you shall not bow down to them and worship them; for I [Yahweh] your god am a jealous god" (Exodus 20:2, 4–5). Yahweh's "jealousy" is the jealousy of a henotheistic deity, who demands exclusive worship from his people. Israel accepts the covenant with Yahweh because he has already demonstrated his power by saving them from the Egyptians (Exodus 19:3–6). While it is true that Yahweh chooses Israel, it is also true that Israel chooses Yahweh. By choosing Yahweh Israel places itself under the authority of his chosen leaders. The subsequent history of Israel is presented in the Hebrew Bible as a history of rebellion and repentance, both acceptance and rejection of Yahweh and his designated leaders for Israel. The struggle between kings and prophets over how the nation may best do Yahweh's will is merely a continuation of this history.

After Israel enters Canaan, the people are ruled by the regional city rulers, magistrates, and war-leaders called the judges. The monarchy begins with a successful war-leader named Saul who comes to power when the kingdoms of Syria–Palestine are under military pressure from the Philistines. Because he becomes king as a consequence of his military prowess, Saul is later threatened by the successes of his military commander David. Although the author of Samuel depicts Saul's jealousy toward David as a sort of madness, he also portrays David taking steps to place himself in the line of royal succession, such as marrying Saul's daughter Michal (1 Samuel 18:20–29). In the story Saul goes mad as the result of his awareness that he has lost Yahweh's favor and David has gained it. The author makes it clear that David has been chosen by Yahweh through Samuel and is beloved by the people of Israel. After the deaths of Saul and his son Jonathan at the hands of the Philistines, all of David's rivals for Saul's throne are eliminated, although never as a result of David's own actions. Instead the throne is Yahweh's gift to David.

In the book of Samuel David's reign is further legitimated by the "Davidic covenant," a covenant of grant from Yahweh promising unconditionally to maintain David's dynasty forever (2 Samuel 7). As a result, the fate of Israel is from then on tied to a specific royal "house" and the divine plan for its governance is defined in terms of Davidic kingship. Although any Near Eastern king was believed to be chosen by the gods of the nation, here the choice of David becomes an eternal condition of history.

At the same time, the narrative motif of "David the blessed" is balanced by a contrasting motif of "David the cursed," the latter precipitated by David's marriage to Bathsheba after he has arranged the death of her husband Uriah the Hittite (2 Samuel 11:1–12:14). The primary result of David's crime is the struggle among his sons over the succession to his throne and rebellions that foreshadow the later split in the kingdom. At the same time, the struggle for the succession ultimately places Solomon, the son of David and Bathsheba, on his father's throne. Solomon's reign is presented in the book of Kings as a golden age for Judah and Israel, with a king who reigns wisely and fairly over his people, who enjoy unparalleled peace and prosperity. At the same time, as in the succession narrative during David's reign, there are clear indications during Solomon's reign that the rebellion against the Davidic dynasty continued. Ultimately the rebellion will lead to the division of the kingdom into the two nations of Israel and Judah.

The history of the two kingdoms as it appears in the books of Kings and Chronicles is a continuation of the people's history of repeated rebellion against Yahweh. After the reign of Solomon, the north rebelled against his son Rehoboam and abrogated the covenant the people of Israel had made with David. The kingdom divides into its two component parts, Israel to the north and Judah to the south. Judah remained loyal to David's dynasty and the Jerusalem temple as the central location for ritual sacrifice. Still the authors of Kings and Chronicles depict the kings of Judah as chronically unwilling to restrict the worship of Yahweh to the rituals of the Jerusalem temple.

Meanwhile the northern nation of Israel rejected the covenantal agreement it had made with David (cf. 1 Kings 2:16–20) and is ruled by a succession of kings and dynasties during its history, many of them short-lived. The author of Kings approves of none of the rulers of Israel, not only because they rebelled against Yahweh's chosen dynasty, but also because they established and authorized cultic sites in Israel rather than worshipping in the temple in Jerusalem. The author of Kings attributes the ultimate fall of the northern kingdom to the Assyrian Empire to Yahweh's anger at Israel's rebellion against his chosen king and worship in the Jerusalem temple. Similarly, the author of Kings attributes the later fall of Judah to the Babylonians to the repeated refusal of its king and its people to obey what Yahweh commanded. In the book of Kings, all the kings of Judah with two notable exceptions—Hezekiah and Josiah—are guilty of violating the covenantal relationship with Yahweh by allowing worship outside of the Jerusalem temple. In time their offenses lead to the fall of Judah and Jerusalem to the power of the Babylonians.

In writing their history in these terms, the biblical authors are guided by a theological ideal that is in fact largely the creation of the prophets of Israel and Judah. It is the prophets who repeatedly called for trust in Yahweh rather than in military alliances with foreign nations. It is the prophets who proclaimed Yahweh alone was the god for Israel and Judah to worship. It is the prophets whose vision of Yahweh's greatness led ultimately to the development of a genuinely monotheistic faith. But it is also the prophets who repeatedly proclaimed Yahweh's faithfulness to Israel in spite of the people's faithlessness, a proclamation that was fundamental to the hope for restoration and return that became the basis for a restored community after the exile. Because Israel survived not as a political and territorial state but as an ethnic and a religious community, the ultimate judgment passed on its historical leaders was necessarily based on religious rather than political standards. The one true king of Israel was Yahweh, and his servants who led his people on earth—whether as kings, governors, judges, or prophets—were judged successful only to the extent that they ensured the people's obedience to the covenant and, through it, their faithfulness to Yahweh as their god.

CHAPTER FOURTEEN

Syria–Palestine: Suffering and Death

Ideas about the Fate of the Dead

The religious cultures of Syria–Palestine endorsed the common view that death was the inevitable fate of all human beings. After death, the departed would be buried and descend into the Underworld, a dark realm far removed from the concern of the gods in heaven. There the dead continued to exist in a semiconscious state, below the surface of earth but above the waters of the abyss. Since the dead were cut off from the gods that controlled daily life they were also deprived of the blessings those gods offered, including light, happiness, and the vigor of life.

There was a deity ruling the Underworld as his or her royal domain, but usually the god was subject to the same dreary conditions there as the dead themselves. In Syria–Palestine, the god of the dead was Mot ("Death") who, as his name indicates, was essentially a personification of death itself, a voracious devourer of human beings. In the surviving mythology Mot represents not only death but all the forces that oppose life. As a result, he is cast as an enemy of the other gods, who in turn represent dynamic life in all its aspects. This idea lies behind Baal and Anat's combat with Mot, for example. Although Baal and Anat overcome Mot he continues to exist, but only as a tamed constituent of an ordered cosmos rather than as an anticreative force of chaos. In this respect, Mot is much like Tiamat after her defeat by Marduk in Babylonian mythology.

In Israel there are traces in the surviving literature of the pervasive ancient belief that those who went down into the Underworld (called "Sheol" in Hebrew) were largely cut off from the divine realm. As a result, the dead were no longer able to praise Yahweh and were beyond the scope of his concern (cf. Psalms 6:5; 30:9; cp. Isaiah 38:13). The situation of the dead could at its best be compared to sleep, as when someone died a blessed death: "Then David slept with his ancestors" (1 Kings 2:10a). This turn of phrase seems to reflect a belief that the dead are insensible and inactive, not consciously involved in any continued existence in the Underworld or in the world of the living.

At the same time, throughout Syria–Palestine we find evidence of the belief the dead had continuing connections with the present world that might result in benefits for the living. In Israel, for example, the people's common identity as the people of Israel implied community and continuity between dead and living. Just as previous generations had enjoyed the covenantal blessing in the past, so their descendants enjoyed them in the present, at whatever point in history that "present" might be (cf. 2 Samuel 7:22–24; 1 Kings 3:50–54; Nehemiah 9).

But more often in Syria–Palestine the dead were believed to be a more immediate source of supernatural benefits for the living. There is some evidence of offerings made to the dead in Ugaritic texts, notably to dead kings or to ancestors, but the references are few and open to interpretation. The same is true for the limited evidence that might suggest the existence of a (largely suppressed) cult of the dead in Israel (cf. Isaiah 29:4). Better attested by the surviving evidence is the practice of necromancy, consultation of oracular spirits among the dead in order to gain insights into the present or future. It is uncertain how this practice was introduced to Syria–Palestine. Deuteronomy 18:9–14 forbids necromancy and other forms of divination as a violation of exclusive covenantal devotion to Yahweh and identifies necromancy as a practice of the other peoples of Syria–Palestine that Israel must shun. In Samuel, a work powerfully influenced by Deuteronomy's ideal of Israel, after Saul becomes king he banishes mediums and wizards from Israel. But Saul later consults a medium in Endor to raise the dead spirit of Samuel, who accurately foretells Saul's death and the scattering of his army by the Philistines (1 Samuel 28). In Kings the villainous Manasseh of Judah consults mediums and wizards (2 Kings 21:6) while the exemplary Josiah banishes both (2 Kings 23:24). Isaiah refers to mediums consulting the spirits of the dead, apparently in Judah (Isaiah 8:19–22), and among the Egyptians (Isaiah 19:3). In both cases the people who do this are condemned to distress and hardship with no help from their gods. It is worth noting that necromancy is condemned in the Hebrew Bible for reasons that have nothing to do with the reliability of the information gained by the practice, and in fact the story in 2

Samuel 28 instead apparently affirms that necromancy can provide reliable insight into the future.

Burial practices in Syria–Palestine also reveal something about prevailing beliefs about the fate of the dead and their relationship to those left behind. Remains of burials in Ugarit dating from the Late Bronze Age include group burials in underground chambers under houses and the king's palace. This practice appears to reflect a belief that the dead continue to share membership in the family and the community. Phoenician burials from the Iron Age, on the other hand, were located away from the houses of the living, indicating a degree of separation between the living and the dead. The abode of the dead was set apart from the hustle and bustle of the world of the living, and tomb inscriptions warn the reader not to disturb the deceased's rest.

In Israel and Judah during the time of the kingdoms, bodies were initially placed on stone benches in cave-like tombs. After the bodies decomposed, the bones would be gathered and reinterred in niches under the bench. Later ossuaries—covered stone boxes to hold bones—were used for secondary burials. Funerary items were sometimes included in Israelite burials during this time, including bowls and jars, lamps and small figurines whose purpose is unknown. These archaeological remains, along with traces of mourning practices in the surviving literature, suggest that in Israel the deceased were believed to continue as part of the community. The dead therefore remained a proper object of community concern, quite apart from any specific ideas of an afterlife or situations in which the dead might consciously interact with the living.

Although in Syria–Palestine the gods could and did sometimes die, they were not bound by mortality in the same way that human beings were, invariably fated to die. In the surviving stories in which a god such as Baal dies, those gods are associated with fertility. As we have seen, other gods (Osiris) and goddesses (Inanna) associated with fertility also die. But when fertility gods die, it is also a necessary part of the story that they return to life in some way, and by so doing establish the cycle of fertility.

There also seem to have been some human beings who were believed to be exempt from the universal human fate of death. Because of the close association between the gods and the king, deceased kings were sometimes awarded divine status in Syria–Palestine. Deified kings enjoyed immortality in the divine realm where they would continue to watch out for the interests of their people. In the Hebrew Bible, there are references to people who did not die but were "taken up," presumably into the heavens. One is the ancient patriarch Enoch, who "walked with [Elohim]; then he was no more, because [Elohim] took him" (Genesis 5:24). Another is the prophet Elijah, who was taken up in a fiery chariot as his disciple Elisha watched (2 Kings 2:11–12). Both Enoch and Elijah were venerated in later Jewish tradition, especially in the context of expectations about the progression of events that would lead to the end of the world.

Apart from these unusual cases, however, in the religious cultures of Syria–Palestine death was believed to be the common fate of all human beings. It was usually felt necessary to explain this fact in mythic explanations of human origins, as part of "the way things came to be." The Israelite story of Adam and Eve, like most explanations for the origins of humanity's subjection to death, places the blame on early human beings who fail to obey a divine command. At the same time, there is often also a sense in such stories that the god to some extent shares culpability, as in the Mesopotamian story of Adapa. There are traces of this idea in the Israelite story of Adam and Eve—why plant the forbidden tree in the center of the Garden of Eden?—but the notion that Yahweh Elohim might share any guilt is considerably muted.

Death, Suffering, and the Meaning of Life

As elsewhere in the ancient Near East, in Syria–Palestine the inevitability of death raised the problem of the ultimate purpose and worth of human life. What seems to have been the earliest and most common view accepted the inevitability of death as a given, and understood the realm of human action and divine reward to be the present life. This meant the good would be rewarded and the wicked punished during their lifetimes, with the assumption that a person's final situation would be an accurate reflection of the sort of life he or she had lived. As we have seen, this is a common view among ancient Near Eastern religious cultures in general, and the principle of retributive justice was a guiding assumption. The entire concept of doing what the gods require and rendering them due honor is based on the expectation that doing so will bring a person into the realm of divine blessing, as the gods reward those who obey and honor them. Those who ignore the gods or do things that displease them, on the other hand, will be punished.

The principle of retributive justice is fundamental to much of ancient Near Eastern wisdom literature in particular. Wisdom teaching is based on the idea that the person who follows the counsel of the wise can thereby exert control over his or her life and ensure long life and prosperity as the fitting reward for proper action. On the other hand, actual experience of life in the world—then as now—often seemed to deny that very idea. Instead it seems in life that the good often suffer and the wicked often prosper, as if there were no governing principle of justice in operation at all. This was the subject of some discussion in the surviving wisdom literature of Israelite religious culture.

The wisdom book included in the Hebrew Bible that comes closest to entirely surrendering the principle of retributive justice in the face of life experience is Ecclesiastes (also known as Qoholeth, "the Teacher"). The book dates from around 300 BCE, during a time when Judah was under the authority of the Macedonian king Ptolemy I Soter of Egypt (305–285 BCE), after the conquest under Alexander the Great. Ecclesiastes expresses skepticism about the entire concept of wisdom, its practicality and desirability, questioning its value in the light of the unpredictability of human life and its ultimate ending in death. The author bases this skepticism on his own observations of the world and the course of human life. "I, the Teacher . . . applied my mind to seek and to search out by wisdom all that is done under heaven: it is an unhappy business that [Elohim] has given to human beings to be busy with" (Ecclesiastes 1:13). The refrain of the work is "Vanity of vanities . . . vanity of vanities! All is vanity!" (Ecclesiastes 1:2; cp. 12:8) and the vanity of human endeavor is its primary theme. "Vanity" translates the Hebrew *hebel*, which means "vapor" or "mist," and commonly refers to an exhalation of breath—it signifies something that is less than nothing. The word also carries the image of ephemerality, the idea of something that dissipates almost as soon as it comes into being, like vapor in the air.

But the Teacher's assessment of the vanity of human endeavor is not based only on the inevitability of death. It is a necessary concomitant of the partial and temporal nature of human effort. The Teacher dismisses pleasure—representing gratification of the body—as an unworthy human pursuit because of its inherent limitations. But he also dismisses wisdom—representing the highest function of the human mind—as ultimately futile because true wisdom is unattainable (Ecclesiastes 7:23–24). Both the wise man and the fool must die (Ecclesiastes 2:13–15; 9:1–6), so what the wise man learns does him little good, and in fact is not what it claims to be at all. Even the pursuit of justice—representing the common good of the community—is vain because it is inevitable that wickedness will sometimes flourish while the good suffer (Ecclesiastes 3:16). The Teacher goes so far as to question the value of doing good, both because of the inherent dangers involved (Ecclesiastes 7:15–16) and the uncertainty that the good person will receive any sort of reward after death (Ecclesiastes 3:17–21).

The Teacher emphasizes the heedlessness of creation to human ambition and needs. The cycles of nature move on continuously and eternally, which means that "there is nothing new under the sun" and one's own existence is only a very small part of the cycle (Ecclesiastes 1:4–11). There is a time and season for everything, so an action may be appropriate at one time and at another time may be completely inappropriate. If what is right depends on times and seasons, how can one be wise (Ecclesiastes 3:1–8)? A number of the "wise sayings" the Teacher includes are either examples of irony (cf. Ecclesiastes 10:8–9) or ironically refute common opinion (cf. Ecclesiastes 7:1–5), reflecting the distinction between what human beings believe and what Elohim alone knows to be true. Elohim is ultimately in charge, but it is impossible for even the wisest person to know his thoughts (Ecclesiastes 5:1–2, 18–20; 6:1–2, 10–12; 8:16–17; 9:11–12; 11:5). This is the crux of the argument: It is impossible for human beings to know the mind of Elohim.

Ecclesiastes concludes with an apparent editorial addition (Ecclesiastes 12:9–14) that attempts to put the words of the Teacher into a more traditionally optimistic light. But despite touches of traditional piety in the work, it is generally deeply pessimistic. Not surprisingly, the final judgment of the Teacher recalls words found in the Harpers' Songs in Egypt and in the mouth of Siduri the alewife in *Gilgamesh*: "There is nothing better for mortals than to eat and drink, and find enjoyment in their toil" (Ecclesiastes 2:24; cp. 5:18; 8:15; 9:7–10).

Despite repeated assertions that one must obey the god who is in control of human destiny, the general attitude expressed in Ecclesiastes represents something of a theological dead end. Its pessimism and fatalism undercut the association between how the community stands in the eyes of its god and how the community fares on earth. In other words, the author more or less completely rejects the idea of retributive justice and severs any connection between the people's behavior and the course their lives may take. But this connection—the idea that how human beings relate to the divine has real consequences for their life in the world—lies behind virtually all religious belief and action. For this reason, some version of retributive justice is maintained throughout the religious cultures of the ancient Near East, even by those that acknowledge the limits death places on human happiness. Even the advice offered in Ecclesiastes and elsewhere to enjoy the pleasures life has to offer while it lasts is a counsel of wisdom, based on a particular idea of what actions are most likely to give human life meaning. In fact, the primary problem encountered in maintaining or defending belief in the principle of retributive justice is not death but human suffering. Death can be seen as essentially just, since all human beings must die. But the problem of human suffering—and more especially suffering that is perceived to be unjust—is a problem that only becomes more acute as in the context of a henotheistic or monotheistic religious culture.

Human Suffering and Divine Justice

The existence of natural and human evil that results in suffering is the primary theological problem for any religious culture that posits a powerful and morally upright chief deity. As we have seen, religious belief and practice at the most basic level are ways of maintaining balance and harmony between the human and the divine worlds. Balance and harmony are maintained in part through the exchange of benefits. If the religious community lives in relationship to a powerful and morally upright chief deity, its members reasonably expect that the benefits they provide for the god will invariably be balanced by benefits granted to them by the god in return. If they suffer from some sort of evil instead, the god appears to be unjust.

The problem of undeserved suffering is relatively easy to explain in the context of a polytheistic religious system, where the benevolent intentions of one god toward a devotee may be thwarted by the ill-will of another god. In polytheistic systems, the gods have competing interests just as human beings do. Conflicts between gods may produce unfortunate results for human beings, even if (and sometimes because) a person is particularly devoted to one of the gods involved. In a polytheistic system there is a general imperative to worship and honor all the gods, since this is what the gods deserve and expect. There is also a general belief that failure to do what the gods require—or even what a single god among the multitude requires—will result in punishment for human beings. But there is no corresponding reassurance that proper behavior among human beings will ensure divine blessings, and certainly not that individuals who do the right thing will be rewarded. In polytheistic religious cultures human beings live more or less at the mercy of divine whims. The gods are not required to act justly, and in any event ultimate power lies not with the gods, but with some impersonal force that controls both the gods and humanity. This force may be fate or destiny or simply a result of the fundamental nature of created existence, "the way things are."

In a henotheistic or monotheistic religious culture, the problem of evil becomes more difficult. The community and its patron god are understood to have a relationship based on mutual recognition and obligation. The community is responsible for obeying and worshipping the patron god and the patron god is obliged to provide for the well-being of the community. The god's moral character is understood in terms of his or her commitment and obligation to protect and bless the community.

A monotheistic religious culture must confront and explain the problem of evil in terms of the central conviction of a single god who is both all-powerful and entirely righteous. Since there is no other power comparable to the power of the single god, there is nothing outside of the god that can act against the god's will. While the god may be limited in action in some way as a result of the god's own character or the conditions the god has imposed on creation—for example, the nature of the created order may prevent the god from making something both uniformly green and uniformly red at the same time—the god cannot be opposed by any force or will external to the god's own.

The god is also understood as the absolute arbiter of right and wrong, the perfect moral judge, and so also morally perfect. The god is always both willing and able to interact with creation and his or her people in accord with the god's perfect moral character. But the existence of both natural and human evil seems to contradict the perfect moral character of the creator and the suffering that evil inflicts on innocent human beings seems to contradict divine justice. In short, the problem presented by evil in a monotheistic religious culture is, in the words of the playwright Archibald MacLeish, "If God is God he is not good; if God is good he is not God." Either the god's power or the god's righteousness comes into question.

For this reason, in monotheistic religious cultures it becomes necessary to explain the apparent contradiction between the god's omnipotent power and absolute righteousness on the one hand, and the existence of natural and human evil and suffering on the other. Any explanation for the problem of evil is called "theodicy" (Greek, "God is in the right"). Theodicy attempts to "justify the ways of God to men," as Milton put it in *Paradise Lost* (I, 26). Its intention is to demonstrate that God is in the right under any and all circumstances, despite any appearances to the contrary.

As the religious culture of Judah gradually developed from henotheism to an overt monotheism as a result of prophetic preaching during and after the Babylonian exile, the need to make sense of Yahweh's actions toward his people became more and more pressing. The traditional explanation for suffering, either for the community or for an individual, was human sinfulness. Most often specific instances of misfortune or suffering were identified as divine retribution for specific, identifiable sins the person suffering had committed against Yahweh.

This is true for the general situation of human suffering as well as specific instances of misfortune in Israel's past. As we've seen, the explanation for the introduction of death and hardship into human life was traced in Genesis 2–3 to human sinfulness, specifically Adam and Eve's offense when they ate the fruit of the tree of the knowledge of good and evil when explicitly commanded by Yahweh not to do so. In the story of Israel's wilderness wandering, there is often swift and direct punishment for offenses committed by all or some of the people, leaving the connection between human wickedness and divine punishment in no doubt (cf. Exodus 32:35; Leviticus 10:1–3; Numbers 11:31–34; 12:1–5, 10–15; 14:26–35; 16:1–35). We find the same idea in operation in the books of Samuel and Kings. The author pronounces moral judgment on all the kings of Israel and Judah, and attributes the downfall of both kingdoms to disobedience to Yahweh's covenantal commands (2 Kings 17:7–23; 21:10–15).

Second Isaiah similarly explained the fall of Jerusalem and the exile as Yahweh's own work as a form of punishment for Judah's rejection of the covenant (Isaiah 42:24–25; 43:22–24). But after the exiles returned to Judah from Babylon, the fortunes of the renewed covenantal community did not significantly improve, despite the rebuilding of the Jerusalem temple under Haggai and Zerubbabel, despite social and religious reforms under Nehemiah and Ezra. Hopes among the Jews for divine deliverance and independence from foreign dominion were continually frustrated. This historical experience, and the simple day-to-day observation that the good were not always rewarded in this life nor the evil always punished, provoked theological wrestling with the problem of evil and the human suffering that results from it. One result, as we've seen, is the fatalism of Ecclesiastes. But this wrestling with the problem of evil reaches its fullest expression in the book of Job, a prolonged meditation on human suffering.

The book of Job is usually dated to the period of the Babylonian exile during the sixth century BCE, although dates have been suggested ranging from the seventh to the fourth centuries BCE. The story of Job appears to have been well-known even before it became the basis for the book of Job as we now have it. Ezekiel, for example, in his preaching before the fall of Jerusalem refers to Job as a proverbially blameless man comparable to Noah and Daniel, two other stellar examples of human righteousness (Ezekiel 14:14, 20).

In the book of Job, the relatively simple story of Job's persistent trust in Yahweh under affliction (Job 1:1–2:13) and his eventual reward at Yahweh's hands (Job 42:7–17) provides the context for an extended reflection on human suffering. The bulk of the book of Job as it now exists is dedicated to a debate between Job and three of his friends over the question of whether it is just that Yahweh allows Job to suffer as he does. The sudden appearance of a fourth friend, the young man Elihu, is clearly a later interpolation. His extended speech (Job 32:1–37:24) disconnects Job's final self-confident words from Yahweh's reply to Job, and in fact anticipates some of Yahweh's later words to Job.

The book of Job approaches its subject from an unorthodox angle. Usually in the ancient world the problem of evil was posed in terms of the unjust prosperity and well-being of the wicked rather than the unjust suffering of the innocent. The more usual approach may reflect a reluctance to postulate that a person could be totally innocent, so blameless that any suffering he or she might experience puts divine justice to the test. Or it may just reflect habitual human resentment directed against the prosperous and the related suspicion that those who become wealthy do so only through dishonesty. Prosperity in the ancient world indicated a lack of equilibrium within a community, a situation best remedied by acts of charity and generous hospitality.

In Job, however, the main character is a man who is both rich and entirely righteous. He is subjected to a series of grievous misfortunes: the death of his children in a natural disaster, the loss of all his property to thieves and enemy soldiers, and finally debilitating illness. Although Job is well-known for his righteousness before these calamities befall him, his blameless behavior in the face of misfortune is presented as even more remarkable. "In all this Job did not sin or charge [Elohim] with wrong-doing" (Job 1:22), even when his wife goads him to do so (Job 2:9–10). Job is joined by his three friends, who listen to him as he expresses his grief and questions the meaning of his existence. But they then begin to debate with Job. They all affirm the traditional view that Yahweh rewards the innocent and punishes the guilty. They argue that Job's sufferings are proof that he must be guilty of sin. In reply Job asserts that he is innocent of any offense. Yahweh is punishing him unjustly, and Job demands to know why he is suffering.

The usual modern emphasis on "the problem of Job"—why do the innocent suffer?—overlooks the fact that the audience knows from the outset of the story precisely why Job is subjected to a series of evils. Yahweh allows terrible things to happen to Job because Yahweh has made a wager about Job's response. The prologue to Job provides a heavenly view of Job's situation that grants the audience access to Yahweh's council chamber. This is where the heavenly beings (literally, "sons of Elohim") appear before Yahweh and the place where Yahweh makes his decisions in governing the cosmos and its creatures. Among the heavenly beings is the Adversary or Accuser (in Hebrew, *satan*) in Yahweh's court. The Adversary is responsible for arguing the case against the human beings that appear before Yahweh for judgment (cp. Zechariah 3:1–2). He is the prosecutor in the divine court and as such he fills a necessary and important function in the formulation of the judicial rulings made by a righteous god. He is true to his nature in this story. He raises doubts about Job's righteousness by arguing that Job is obedient only because he expects to be rewarded in return.

The Adversary's question, "Does Job fear Elohim for nothing?" raises a basic religious problem. Are human beings righteous if they obey and worship the gods or a god only in hope of receiving some benefit in return, or are they righteous only if they worship the gods because the reverence due to them compels them to without any thought of reward? The Adversary's question effectively forces Yahweh to accept the wager. If Yahweh were to refuse, it would appear the Adversary was right and Yahweh was afraid to admit it. But when Yahweh accepts the wager, he at least appears to act against his own nature, because the wager means he must allow the Adversary to heap misfortune on a righteous man who has done nothing to deserve it. The Adversary's later role as the tempter Satan is already in view here.

The prologue frames the story in a way that determines how the audience will understand what follows. By virtue of their glimpse into the heavenly court, the audience from the outset knows exactly why Job has suffered the various calamities that have befallen him. Before the debate between Job and his friends begins the audience already knows that Job is in fact innocent of any wrongdoing and that his suffering is a test from Yahweh. The audience from the beginning possesses knowledge utterly unavailable to Job and his friends as characters in the story. The audience hears the entire story and follows the entire debate fully aware that there is no way the human actors in the story can guess the true nature of Job's situation. In this way the story emphasizes—and forces the audience to acknowledge—that human beings are inevitably ignorant of the full range of factors behind the divine will, the knowledge of just what motivates Yahweh's actions.

The bulk of the book is devoted to Job's protestations of innocence alternating with his wish to confront Yahweh, and his friends' arguments that he must be guilty of sin. Job argues that he is innocent of any sin and so it is unjust that he should suffer as he does, since suffering is only justified when it is a punishment for sinfulness. Job's friends argue in reply that Job's suffering in itself is proof that he must be guilty of some hidden sin, since only grievous sin would justify the suffering he is experiencing at Yahweh's hands. Both Job and his friends subscribe to the principle of retributive justice as the way to understand why Yahweh bestows blessings on some and sufferings on others. But beyond that, both Job and his friends further believe that the motivations for all Yahweh's actions must be transparent to human observers. In other words, not only must Yahweh's actions be righteous, but they must be readily *seen* to be righteous by human beings. This attitude toward Yahweh—that somehow he is accountable to his human creation for his actions—is also reflected in several of Job's speeches in the book. In addition to his complaints, Job repeatedly expresses his desire to confront Yahweh with the injustice of what he has done, to call Yahweh into court to accuse him of violating his own nature by not treating Job according to his deserts.

Yahweh's reply to Job out of the whirlwind at the climax of the story essentially grants Job's wish. Job is at least theoretically provided with the opportunity to make his case against Yahweh. But in fact Yahweh's reply puts Job in his place, making him aware that as a human being, as a creature, he is in no position to understand or judge his god's actions. Instead of answering Job directly, Yahweh points to all the marvels of creation, all of them under his dominion and all with a purpose only he fully understands. Yahweh assaults Job with a series of rhetorical questions, each beginning either with *Who* or *Do you know*. Yahweh's questions all focus on the details of creation, either in terms of its mysteries (cf. Job 38:16–24; 39:1–4) or the power needed to tend to its operations (cf. Job 38:25–27, 31–35) or to control its greatest creatures, such as Leviathan (cf. Job 41:1–34). In each case, the only (unspoken) answer Job might be able to make truthfully to these rhetorical questions would only reinforce Yahweh's argument that Job is in no position to judge him. The only reply Job could offer to "Who?" is "Yahweh," to "Do you know?" is "No, I don't," and to "Can you?" is "No, I can't." The questions themselves enforce these answers, and Job need not offer a reply for Yahweh's point to be made. The unanswered questions Yahweh puts to Job are meant to demonstrate the difference in knowledge and power between Yahweh as creator of the cosmos and Job as only one of an infinite number of Yahweh's creatures. In response to Yahweh's recitation of the marvels of his creation, Job can only keep silence and "repent," not for sin, but for presuming that he has the standing and the capacity to judge his creator.

The epilogue of the book of Job leaves theological discussion behind and returns to the storytelling motifs and language of the prologue, once again framing the theological debate with a fairly straightforward narrative. Yahweh commends Job and rebukes his friends. Job is presumably commended for his steadfast righteousness and his repentance for his presumption in wanting to judge his god. His friends are rebuked because they did not speak justly of Yahweh as Job did (Job 42:7). Apparently Yahweh finds Job's searching questions preferable to his friends' smug assurance. Yahweh fully restores Job's health and fortunes—"[Yahweh] gave Job twice as much as he had before" (Job 42:10b)—thereby "making good" his former suffering. This conclusion leaves aside the question of whether all losses can be made good—new children to replace dead children, for example—but it satisfies the ancient world's idea that one's "last state" in life determined one's happiness. Job is rewarded for his faithfulness and becomes even more prosperous than he was before. The framing story is apparently intended to have it both ways: Yahweh manages to demonstrate to the Adversary that Job is righteous without any expectation of reward, but also upholds the principle of retributive justice by lavishly rewarding Job for his righteousness as the end of the story.

The happy ending that restores Job's fortunes might easily be taken as a denial of the basic premise of Yahweh's reply to Job at the climax of the book. There Yahweh argues that neither he nor his actions are accountable to his human creation and that he need not do what human beings expect. Yet at the end of the story Yahweh restores Job's fortunes. But in fact the conclusion does not violate the point of the book. Yahweh does not explicitly compensate Job for the suffering he has endured, and the restoration of his fortunes is not said to be a reward for his righteousness or his steadfastness in the midst of his troubles. Yahweh's reasons for compensating Job are essentially as mysterious to his human subjects as the reasons for first allowing him to suffer. Ultimately the book of Job leaves the answer to the problem of evil in the hands of Yahweh whose will is his own and utterly unfathomable to human reason.

Expectations about the End

The evolving monotheism in the exilic and post-exilic community of the people of Israel prompted reconsideration of issues surrounding the difficulties of human life—not only the problem of innocent suffering, but even the finality of death itself. As the power of Yahweh came to be perceived as absolute—that is, restricted by nothing outside himself—his eternal faithfulness to the covenant was emphasized. Both before and during the exile, the message of the prophets focused on Yahweh's continuing faithfulness to the covenant with Israel, in spite of the people's continual failure to be faithful. This is a major theme of the prophet Hosea, for example, who preached in Israel toward the end of the reign of Jeroboam II and during the decline of the kingdom that followed (cf. Hosea 2:14–23; 5:15–6:6; 11:1–11; 14:1–9). During the exile, Yahweh's faithfulness to his covenantal promises became the basis for the hope of return and restoration among the Judahites in Babylon. This is the major topic of Ezekiel's later prophecies, and virtually the sole topic of the exilic prophet we know as Second Isaiah (cf. Isaiah 41:8–16; 44:21–28; 54:1–10). After the return, the prophets Haggai and Zechariah reiterated Yahweh's care for his people, again basing their proclamation on Yahweh's covenantal promises (cf. Haggai 1:15b–2:9; Zechariah 1:1–6, 7–17).

Yahweh's eternal faithfulness to his people Israel is also sometimes expressed in terms of his faithfulness to individuals, particularly those who trust in his mercy (cf. Psalms 3, 16, 59). Many of the psalms express the psalmist's trust in Yahweh in spite of hardships or the speaker's previous offenses, a trust based in Yahweh's faithfulness (cf. Psalms 51, 86, 102, 130). This is not an uncommon religious motif, and we find many examples in prayers and invocations from other Near Eastern religious cultures. But in a few of the psalms Yahweh's mercy extends to rescuing the suppliant from death (cf. Psalms 16:9–10; 49:15; 73:23–26). Psalm 73:26 makes the point well: "My flesh and my heart may fail, but [Elohim] is the strength of my heart and my portion forever." The psalmist trusts in Yahweh because his faithfulness is eternal. Still, these verses in some psalms are only hints. Yahweh's covenantal faithfulness to Israel was eternal, and so was his covenantal promise to David and his descendants; but in texts originating after the exile we begin to find evidence of a belief that Yahweh's covenantal fidelity to individual people might not be limited to the span of a person's life.

Both the problem of innocent suffering and Yahweh's covenantal fidelity to his people as a community and as individuals are addressed in apocalypticism. Apocalypticism is a form of religious thought based on anticipation of the imminent end of the world as it now exists through direct divine agency. Among the Jews after the Babylonian exile, apocalypticism was expressed through the expectation that Yahweh would at some point directly intervene into human history to save and vindicate his people Israel. Although apocalypticism may have roots in other ancient Near Eastern religious cultures, it is in many ways a natural outcome of Israel's religious ideas. The people of Israel understood their history as a people specifically as a history lived out in covenantal relationship to Yahweh as their god and sovereign protector. The prophets and the writers whose work is preserved in the Hebrew Bible tended to depict historical events in mythic terms, understanding history as only the visible manifestations of the invisible work of Yahweh on his people's behalf.

This idea also affected how the kingdoms of Israel and Judah understood their own historical situation. A tradition about "the Day of Yahweh" visualized a day when Yahweh would act decisively in history to deliver and vindicate his faithful people by defeating their enemies (cf. Isaiah 13:6–22). This tradition was a mythic expression of an historical aspiration, the hope that one day Israel and Judah would be freed from fear of their enemies and enjoy peace and prosperity. History did not bear out this expectation. As a result, the hope for military victory and vindication against the nation's enemies came to be expressed less as an historical event to be carried out by human agencies on Yahweh's behalf, and more in mythic terms as an earthshaking interruption of the normal course of human history carried out by the explicit agency of Yahweh himself.

The prophecies of Zechariah provide a good example of this transition from prophetic hope for divine vindication to apocalyptic expectation. Zechariah's early chapters employ a number of symbolic figures and actions that refer to anticipated historical events, notably the restoration of the community of Judah after exile under the leadership of Zerubbabel and Joshua the high priest (cf. Zechariah 3–4). Zechariah's visions include heavenly figures who explain to the prophet the meaning of the things he sees. Both obscure symbolism and the use of heavenly figures as interpreters of the visions later became typical of apocalyptic literature, notably the New Testament book of Revelation. Both Zechariah 8 (taken by scholars to be the last part of the book that may be credited to Zechariah) and Zechariah 14 (attributed by scholars to a later writer) are visions of Yahweh's vindication of his people and its aftermath. Zechariah 14 includes details of Yahweh's final battle against the nations (Zechariah 14:1–7). But both chapters depict the peoples of all the nations coming to Jerusalem to worship Yahweh, with his faithful people the Jews serving as mediators (cf. Zechariah 8:23; 14:20–21). "The Day of Yahweh" has now come to be understood as the "day" Yahweh's direct supernatural intervention would make Israel the center of a renewed world.

"The Day of Yahweh" as a mythic day of reward and vindication carries with it an implicit condemnation of the world's present state. Apocalypticism addresses the problem of evil and suffering in part by presenting a present world dominated by forces hostile to Yahweh and in open rebellion against him. The cosmos Yahweh created has turned against him as a result of human sinfulness. The first human offense led to a downward spiral of further sinfulness, as sin piles upon sin after the Flood just as it did in the generations before Noah (Genesis 6:5–7). The human world in its sinfulness has exalted all that rejects Yahweh and the faithful descendants of Noah, the people of Israel. The earthly forces that oppress Israel—notably the foreign empires that reject Yahweh's sovereignty over the world and wield unjust dominion over his people—are identified with the spiritual forces that oppose Yahweh. In short, apocalyptic expectations among the Jews cast the nations that oppress Yahweh's people as agents of cosmic evil. Although creation was made good, it is now so corrupted by human sin that it utterly rejects Yahweh and his people and embraces everything that stands in opposition to his sovereign will.

The consequences of this view are not unexpected. Apocalypticism turns the usual understanding of retributive justice on its head. It is no longer the case that Yahweh rewards those who obey him with material blessings and peace in the present life. In its present state, the only people who can be at ease in the world are the wicked who align themselves with the evil spiritual powers that govern it. Instead, those who obey Yahweh and are pleasing to him *suffer* in the present age, specifically at the hands of those who oppose Yahweh. Earthly prosperity is a sign of evil, since in an evil world prosperity can only be the result of collusion with the wickedness the world encourages.

But in apocalyptic belief the idea of divine reward for the faithful remains operative. The principle of retributive justice is still in effect, but the context of its operation has changed. Now the blessings that are the just reward for the good and the punishments that are the just deserts of the wicked are postponed until after Yahweh's intervention at the end of the current age. After the Day of Yahweh the faithful will finally be vindicated and receive their reward in the form of blessings bestowed upon them in the new age. Those who opposed Yahweh will either be destroyed in the battles he fights to establish his sovereignty over the earth or will repent and gather to worship Yahweh with his faithful people in Jerusalem. It is worth noting that in Zechariah 8 and 14 what is excluded from the new age is not people—the foreign nations, those who rebel against God—but behaviors, wickedness, and disobedience. Those who repent, no matter who they are, are welcome to gather in Jerusalem with the Jews to worship Yahweh.

Apocalypticism is most typically expressed through apocalyptic literature, a mythic representation of historical events as a series of steps in the progress toward the end of the age. Apocalyptic literature typically presents a vision experienced by a revered figure of the past, who sees the events of history "properly," that is, from the heavenly perspective. Because they are seen from the heavenly perspective, the events of history are narrated in mythic, symbolic terms. But the review of history is also presented in the apocalyptic context as a vision of the future. From the perspective of the visionary, a person of the past, intervening events of the more recent past and the present are part of his "future." After the visionary experiences the vision, he is often instructed to write it down and then hide it until the time has come for the vision to be fulfilled (cf. Daniel 12:4, 9). The very fact that an audience hears the words of the text "proves" that their own time is the time of the end. They hear about recent historical events in the guise of the visionary's prophecies of the future that were delivered in the past. Most apocalyptic literature can in fact be dated by finding the point in history when the "vision" becomes inaccurate because it is no longer a recounting of the author's past but reflects his or her genuine attempt to look into the future.

One of the few consistently recurring themes of apocalyptic literature is the suffering of Yahweh's faithful people in the events leading up to the apocalyptic crisis, when Yahweh will finally act to vindicate them and destroy their enemies. The suffering of Yahweh's people is symptomatic of the current fallen nature of the cosmos, now prey to forces that oppose Yahweh. But the suffering of Yahweh's people is also a guarantee of their righteousness. In apocalyptic thought the suffering of the righteous is not a problem, but rather the inevitable consequence of their faithfulness to Yahweh. Their suffering is also a sign of the progress of the apocalyptic course of events, an indication that Yahweh will soon act to bring an end to their struggles.

Apocalyptic literature is notably less concerned with the new situation of the righteous after their vindication than with the events leading up to the destruction of their enemies and the victory of Yahweh's people. But one constant in the depiction of the redemption of Yahweh's people is what scholars call an "apocalyptic reversal." This is the reversal of fortunes that is the result of Yahweh imposing his sovereignty over a rebellious creation and imposing retributive justice. After Yahweh's victory, the wicked who formerly prospered during the previous evil age will be punished, and the righteous who suffered at the hands of the wicked will be rewarded for their faithfulness. Yahweh will apportion praise and blame justly, but only after the end of the current evil age.

One important result of the apocalyptic way of thinking, but appearing late in the history of the people of Israel, is the possibility of some sort of life after death. The idea of life after death is a form of theodicy related to apocalypticism that apparently first appeared during the Hellenistic era, in the third century BCE. This idea arose in response to the severe persecution of the Jews by the Syrian king Antiochus IV Epiphanes, who outlawed obedience to the covenantal law and killed those Jews who continued to obey it. These calamitous events raised a theological problem. How could those Jews who had remained faithful to the covenant to the point of death receive their just reward from Yahweh? On the one hand, these martyrs had demonstrated the highest degree of obedience to the covenant and Yahweh as their god by remaining faithful until death. On the other hand, their death meant they could not receive any reward for their obedience during the life they had been forced to forfeit. The end of their life, what would normally be assumed as the "final state" that determined its worth, was persecution and death. But it was inconceivable that such fidelity and such suffering could go uncompensated in some way by Yahweh, their god who rewards the faithful.

This apparent conundrum led to the reluctant acknowledgment among at least some groups of Jews that divine recompense could come after death, even if it was restricted to the very good and the very evil. We find this idea at the end of Daniel—a book written in part in reaction to the persecution under Antiochus—where Daniel is told he will be included among those who will rise "at the end of the days" (Daniel 12:1–3; cp. Ezekiel 14:14, 20). An angel assures Daniel, "Many of those who sleep in the dust of the earth shall awake, some to everlasting life, and some to shame and everlasting contempt" (Daniel 12:2). It is worth noting that posthumous retribution also includes the very evil, an apparent acknowledgment that not all the wicked will receive their just punishment either in the present age or in the inauguration of the new age.

Belief in divine recompense after death also necessitated a belief in resurrection, the return of the body to life. The Jews, like the other peoples of Syria–Palestine as well as the Mesopotamians and the Egyptians, believed the self could not exist in any real sense apart from the body—this was why those in Sheol were mere shadows. "Life" in any real sense necessarily meant the life enjoyed as an embodied person. In the resurrection, the shades of those chosen to "awake . . . to everlasting life" would be reunited with their dead bodies, bodies given life once again by the divine breath/spirit.

But belief in bodily resurrection and a future life after death remained contested beliefs in the subsequent history of Judaism, with the older, more pessimistic view of death often prevailing in the popular mind and among the leaders of the community. Belief in resurrection of the body apparently had little to no effect on Jewish burial practices before the turn of the age, certainly nothing comparable to the elaborate preparation of the body for burial among the Egyptians. But this may in part reflect the contested nature of the belief; not enough Jews believed in resurrection to lead to a wholesale revision of burial customs and traditions. There might be another explanation as well. The Jews believed Yahweh alone was responsible for the work of raising the dead to new life. Yahweh was responsible for creating the world and giving life to its creatures—including human beings—in the beginning, and it was his justice and fidelity to the covenant that would lead him to give new life to the dead. There was no need for human beings to prepare the bodies of the dead for the resurrection, should it come. Yahweh's creative power would again give life where there was none. It was the Jews' belief in Yahweh's faithfulness, his justice, and power that was the basis of their hope for divine vindication during their lifetimes, and for some his faithfulness, justice, and power became the basis of their hope for divine vindication after death.

CHAPTER FIFTEEN

Syria–Palestine: The Human World

Ritual Worship in Syria–Palestine

As was the case elsewhere in the ancient Near East, the primary means of worship and interaction with the gods in Syria–Palestine was through rituals conducted in temples and at shrines. Rituals of worship and sacrifice were carried out in major temples by a host of functionaries acting under the king's authority and on his behalf. But elsewhere the number of cultic personnel involved in worship might be relatively small, and in some cases, such as the Israelite celebration of the Passover, no cultic personnel were required at all.

In Syria–Palestine both daily maintenance of ritual worship and supervision of various other temple functions were the responsibility of the chief priest. There were different sorts of priesthoods among and within the various states of Syria–Palestine, with different levels of sacral authority. Many of these priesthoods were hereditary. The chief priest of a god's cult was also the administrator of the god's temple and supervisor of the cultic personnel, who were arranged in a hierarchy according to the kind of work they did in the temple.

Both men and women might serve as cultic personnel. In addition to the priests who performed ritual sacrifices, there were other personnel who were responsible for consecrating the worship space and its paraphernalia. There were diviners who used various methods to discern the will of the gods. Other people who served in the temple itself included bearers, singers, and sacred prostitutes, both male and female. Lower functionaries did work in the temple precinct that was both practical and necessary. They included butchers, bakers, guards, water carriers, maintenance men, and so on. Cultic personnel also routinely included official temple prophets who were empowered to receive and proclaim divine oracles. Such revelations might either be responses to specific questions posed through the prophet or given spontaneously by the god.

The temple precincts in Syria–Palestine seem to have been smaller than those in Egypt and Mesopotamia, and were generally restricted to the immediate area of the temple building itself. Temples in Syria–Palestine usually incorporated an extended porch or courtyard outside of the temple building proper. The main feature of the temple building was a large central room with an altar where sacrifices were offered, along with other sacred furniture such as a large basin to hold the water needed in sacrificial rituals. A temple would sometimes be built with towers or a second story, and might include shrines for other gods in addition to the primary god worshipped in the temple.

The book of Kings in the Hebrew Bible gives an extended description of the temple in Jerusalem built during the reign of Solomon, during the second third of the tenth century BCE. The temple was apparently built on a Phoenician design, if it is true that Phoenician builders were sent to Solomon in Jerusalem by Hiram, king of Tyre and became major contributors to its construction (1 Kings 5). The temple was rectangular, with internal measurement of about 32 meters long, 10.7 meters wide and about 16 meters high. The interior was divided into the sanctuary or Holy Place, measuring about 21.3 meters long and 10.7 meters wide, and the smaller inner sanctuary or Holy of Holies, a cubic space measuring about 10.7 meters in height, length, and width. The Holy of Holies was where the Ark of the Covenant was kept, along with other sacred objects. Storerooms surrounded the outside walls of the sanctuary on three sides. At the short end of the temple opposite the Holy of Holies was the entrance, leading out to a porch flanked by two bronze pillars. Ten stairs led down from the porch to the temple courtyard. To the left and right in front of the temple in the courtyard were the altar of sacrifice and the Sea of Bronze, a large basin of water for ceremonial uses. The entire temple courtyard was surrounded by a wall marking off the sacred precinct from the surrounding area. As large and impressive as the Jerusalem temple was, it formed only a portion of Solomon's extensive palace complex. If the book of Kings is accurate, it took some seven years to build the temple, but thirteen to finish the entire palace complex (1 Kings 6:37–7:1).

The people of Syria–Palestine worshipped not only at temples but also at open-air altars and other sacred sites, most of them also served by the official priests. The people of both Israel and Judah, for example, had a number of altars and shrines apart from their primary places of worship, the temples of

View of modern Jerusalem showing the Wailing Wall and the Dome of the Rock, the site of Solomon's temple ©. 2008 Jupiterimages Corporation

Yahweh in Jerusalem and Samaria. Some of them had close associations with Israel's ancestors, notably the shrines at Bethel and Dan. All of these altars were officially sanctioned and were served by Levitical (i.e., officially authorized) priests (cf. 2 Kings 23:8–9), at least until the reforms instituted by Hezekiah of Judah and later again instituted by Josiah (2 Kings 18:4, 22; 23:8, 15–20).

Apart from Israel and Judah, we do not have much information about the rituals of worship in Syria–Palestine. What information we have is mostly about the goods offered as sacrifices for the gods, for example the lists of sacrifices in the archives at Ebla, dating to around 2350 BCE. In Syria–Palestine offerings seem to have encompassed almost anything of value in human life. All sorts of animals were offered with no apparent restrictions on the type or condition of the animal. In some cases certain parts of the animal, such as the head or the entrails, were specified as appropriate, either for specific rituals or as the portion set aside for the cultic personnel. Other sorts of foods, including grains and vegetables, might also be offered to the gods, reflecting the fact that sacrificial rituals were thought of primarily as sacred banquets provided for the gods by their worshippers. Libations of oil, wine, and beer were offered as well, poured out on an altar in honor of the god. These libations were notably offerings of goods produced through the efforts of human beings, since it required human labor to squeeze the oil, prepare the wine, and brew the beer from the ingredients nature provided. Similarly, offerings of cloth and bread represented the results of human efforts that turned the products of nature into a new, useful form.

We do not know what role representations of the gods played in these rituals, whether cult statues received the same elaborate care they did in Egypt and Mesopotamia, or whether the presence of a cult statue was even necessary for sacrifice. It appears certain that there was no representation of Yahweh, the god of Israel, in his temple in Jerusalem in Judah nor in Samaria in Israel. The traditional means of indicating the presence of Yahweh appears to have been the creation of a royal "footstool" over which his presence or glory was believed to abide. This was the apparent intention of the Ark of the Covenant (cf. 1 Samuel 4:4; 2 Kings 19:15; Psalm 99:1) and may have been the intention of the golden bull calves created by Jeroboam of Israel for the shrines of Bethel and Dan (1 Kings 12:28–30) as well. But the divine presence of other gods was represented in Israel and elsewhere by such objects as the stylized trees honoring Asherah (cf. Exodus 34:13; Judges 6:25; 1 Kings 14:15), sacred stones (*masseboth*; cf. Deuteronomy 7:5; 2 Kings 17:10; Micah 5:13), and cultic statues. The inventory of items removed from the Jerusalem temple at the order of Josiah as part of his religious reforms, whether historically accurate or not, suggests the wide variety of cultic para-phernalia found in temples in Syria–Palestine in the late seventh century BCE (2 Kings 23:4–7).

Ritual practice in Israel and later in the two kingdoms had points of con-tinuity with what we know of sacrifice elsewhere in Syria–Palestine, but there were also differences. The covenantal law required every adult male to make offerings to Yahweh at regional cultic sites during festivals three times a year. In early spring offerings were made during the Passover, a commemo-ration of the Exodus combined with an agricultural festival of unleavened bread. In late spring offerings were made during the festival of Weeks, asso-ciated with the harvest. In fall offerings were part of the festival of Booths or Tabernacles, a commemoration of establishment of the covenant at Sinai that became associated with an agricultural festival of ingathering.

There were rules in Israel governing the animals to be offered for sacrifice. Only certain animals of specific ages, with no disabilities or disfigurements, could be offered to Yahweh. There were also specific regulations about which animals were appropriate for specific cultic occasions, with some allowances made for people of limited means (cf. Leviticus 5:7–8, 11–12). Regulations also determined how animals were to be prepared for sacrifice and how the sacrifice itself was to be offered, indicating which parts of the animal were to be burned and which parts distributed to the priests to be eaten (cf. Leviti-cus 7:1–10). There was particular concern with draining the blood from the animal before it was offered or consumed, arising from the belief that blood carried the force of life, and was therefore sacred to Yahweh and to be "re-turned" to him. As part of the sacrifice for sin, for example, the blood of the sacrificial animal was sprinkled on the altar and the remainder poured out at its foot (Leviticus 4:5–7, 16–18, 25, 30). As this practice indicates, in Israel and Judah offerings were not carried out in the presence of a cultic statue but on an altar in the open air outside the place the divine presence was believed to "abide." Similarly, at least in the surviving documents, offerings are thought of not as nourishment for Yahweh, but rather as a "sweet savor in his nostrils," suggesting a less corporeal idea of the deity. Sacrifices were offered to atone for sin, for purification, as thanksgiving, and to mark specific occa-sions during the year or in the course of human life. Different occasions called for other sorts of offerings, including wine libations and offerings of grain, the offering of first-fruits and first-born animals.

Regulations concerning worship in Israel and Judah show definite signs of development in the surviving texts. The most notable development was prob-ably the restriction of ritual worship in Judah to the temple in Jerusalem. This was a change in both practice and attitude that was apparently first instituted under Hezekiah (715–687 BCE) and again under Josiah (640–609 BCE). The restriction of ritual worship to the Jerusalem temple became the dominant model for the restored community of the Jews after the Babylonian exile. But as the religious reaction under Hezekiah's son Manasseh (687–642 BCE) and among Josiah's successors suggests, the restriction of a state's ritual worship to a single location was at odds with the consensus of religious belief and practice throughout the ancient Near East.

Family-Based Religious Practice in Syria–Palestine

Popular religious beliefs and practices in Syria–Palestine seem to have focused on ritual actions directed toward personal gods on the one hand and ancestors on the other. The evidence for popular or family religious practice outside of Israel is sparse and represents different eras, and its applicability to the average family in Syria–Palestine at any specific point in history is open to question. In Ugarit during the thirteenth century BCE, for example, among the duties that apparently fell to the male head of the family was the responsibility to participate in ritual worship in the temples of El and Baal and "to [erect] the stele of his divine ancestor" (Johnston, 427). In this case, participating in ritual worship meant taking part in a sacred meal in the temple. The "divine ancestor" was apparently a deified progenitor; the word *ilib* combines *il*, "god," and *ab*, "father," and so seems to mean an ancestor who has been elevated to divine status after his death. The idea that a family's ancestors were capable of acting for the benefit of their living descendants stood in tension with more commonly attested ideas about the finality of death and the passivity of the dead in the Underworld.

Household worship centered on the family altar or shrine. Archaeological excavations have uncovered many family altars from different eras in Syria–Palestine. The altar was used to make offerings to the household god in times of trouble, such as sickness or injury, or during a woman's pregnancy or the delivery of her child. The altar might include statues of the household god, a figure of the patron god of the family, or figurines related to particular situations, such as representations of women in childbirth. Possession of the statues of the household gods apparently represented legitimate authority as leader of the household. This is why the theft of his household gods prompted Laban's anger against Jacob in a story recounted in Genesis 31:19, 31–37. Later in the accounts of the history of Israel we find household gods as possessions of Saul's family when he was king of Israel (1 Samuel 19:13–17). These stories appear to indicate that worship of patron gods within the family could coexist in Israel with the acknowledgment of Yahweh as the god of Israel. Devotion to patron gods is also represented by the names given to children, specifically names that included a theophoric ("god-bearing") element, such as Elijah ("Yahweh is my god").

We have already considered the practice of referring to "personal gods" who serve as a person or a family's advocate and defender in the heavenly council. In Syria–Palestine, the family god might be referred to as "the god of the house" (the family in its largest sense) or "the god of my father" (Johnston, 429). We find clear instances of this practice in Israelite religious culture as it is depicted in the texts of the Hebrew Bible. Foreigners in Israel or Judah will often refer to Yahweh as the god of the person they are addressing. The queen of Sheba, for example, says to Solomon, "Blessed be Yahweh your god who has delighted in you and set you on the throne of Israel" (1 Kings 10:9). There is also the frequent explicit identification of Yahweh as "the god of Abraham, of Isaac and of Jacob" (cf. Exodus 3:15a, 16a). In this case, the ancestral god of the family of Abraham is also the god of his extended "family," the people of Israel.

In keeping with the origins of the community, many religious practices in Israel reflected the situation of the nomadic family, since they were performed by family members and required neither priest nor temple. Circumcision, for example, is enjoined on male Israelite children eight days after birth (Genesis 17:12; Leviticus 12:3) as a sign of their inclusion in the covenantal promises. There are some indications that adolescent and adult males were also sometimes circumcised (cf. Genesis 17:25; 34:14–24). Circumcision was presumably performed by the father of the child or the senior father of the household (cf. Genesis 17:11, 23), although the ritual is most often described in the passive voice (cf. Genesis 17:12–14, 24–27). Circumcision was not restricted to Israel in the ancient Near East, and its origins may lie in a puberty ritual or an attempt to ward off evil spirits (cf. Exodus 4:24–26).

The Passover as it is described in Exodus 12:1–13:6 appears to be a composite of several traditions, but it clearly represents a family-based ritual. The Passover was probably originally a shepherd's festival marking the transition from winter to summer pasturage, with the intention of eliciting divine protection for the flocks. Later this pastoral festival was reconciled with the feast of Unleavened Bread, an agricultural festival apparently celebrated in Palestine before the Israelite settlement in Canaan. The pastoral and familial nature of the Passover may explain why it was not celebrated by the people of Israel after their settlement in the land until the time of Josiah of Judah, assuming the account of Josiah's reform in 2 Kings 23:21–23 is reliable.

The primary religious observance in Israel and Judah was the Sabbath (from Hebrew *shabbat*, "to cease, desist"), a mandated day of rest from all work for the entire household. The Sabbath did not originally demand any sort of religious activity, although later various practices became associated with the day. The essential idea of the Sabbath is rest. It is justified in the first creation story found in Genesis 1:1–2:3 as a commemoration of Yahweh's rest after his six days of creative work. But the justification for the Sabbath runs deeper in the Israelite tradition than that. It is a reflection of the idea of rest and renewal within the very fabric of creation. The Sabbath was intended to allow all members of the household, including the animals, to rest (cf. Exodus 23:12; Deuteronomy 5:12–15). The same principle is at work in the idea of the Sabbath year for the land (Leviticus 25:1–7) and the Jubilee year that occurs every fiftieth year as a "Sabbath of Sabbaths" (Leviticus 25:8–17; 8–55). Yahweh was believed to be a good steward of everything he had made. He allowed human beings, animals, and even the land to enjoy periodic rest from the work necessary for the good of his creation, thereby showing his mercy and love to his creatures. The observance of the Sabbath in Israel stands in contrast to the prevailing notion among the religious cultures of the ancient Near East that human beings exist only to serve the gods. It enshrines in a weekly observance the idea that human beings exist also so they may enjoy the pleasures of life granted to them by a benevolent creator.

Diviners, Seers, and Prophets

As we have seen, there were various methods for gaining insight into the divine world in the ancient Near East, including necromancy, extispicy, and various other forms of divination, but in Israel and Judah at least prophecy eventually became the dominant method. Various kinds of seers familiar from elsewhere in the ancient Near East appear in the texts of the Hebrew Bible. In those texts seers and their practices are often rejected as illegitimate, but there are also indications that some of those practices were at one time considered an acceptable part of Israelite religious culture.

In the story of Joseph in Genesis 37, 39–50, for example, after Joseph is sold into slavery in Egypt by his brothers, he gains favor with the Egyptians in part through his ability to divine the future. He does this both by interpreting dreams and by reading the dregs of the wine in a cup (Genesis 40–41; 44:5, 15). Both of these skills are treated as legitimate in the story, and are in fact signs of Yahweh's favor toward Joseph. We find instances of oracles derived from the sound and movement of trees in stories about Israel's early history in Canaan. Judges 9:37 refers to a location called Diviners' Oak (*Elonmeonenim*), and in the book of Samuel Yahweh tells David in response to an inquiry to listen for the sounds of marching in the tops of the balsam trees as a sign to attack, "for then [Yahweh] has gone out before you to strike down the army of the Philistines" (2 Samuel 5:24).

Necromancy, consultation of dead spirits, was theoretically forbidden in Israel (cf. Leviticus 20:27; Deuteronomy 18:11; cp. 1 Samuel 28:3). But the story about Saul consulting the medium of Endor in 1 Samuel 28 suggests this may have been a not entirely successful attempt to squelch a popular practice. As we have seen, the story acknowledges that necromancy is an effective way of divining the future at the same time that it rejects the practice as forbidden. Necromancy apparently continued to be a popular method for gaining insight into the future in Judah at least until the time of Isaiah of Jerusalem (Isaiah 8:19–20).

It appears that other sorts of divination were not only popular in the kingdoms of Israel and Judah, but often enjoyed royal patronage. Jeremiah rejects the false reassurances of the diviners, dreamers, soothsayers, and sorcerers who are part of the court of the king of Judah (Jeremiah 27:9; 29:8). Similarly, Zechariah 10:2 rejects the oracles of divining instruments and the dreams and visions of seers in favor of Yahweh's word revealed through the prophet. It appears that the prophets in particular were concerned with delegitimizing alternative, competing forms of discerning Yahweh's will in Israel and Judah.

Just as Samuel in the Hebrew Bible represents the transition from the regional rule of the judges to the military rule of kings, he also represents the transition from the spiritual authority of the seer to the preeminent spiritual authority of the inspired prophet. Samuel appears in the role of a seer in 1 Samuel 9, when Saul consults him to find his donkeys. The story appears to be independent of the stories about Samuel that precede it, and reintroduces Samuel as "a man of [Elohim] . . . a man held in honor. Whatever he says always comes true" (1 Samuel 9:6). Samuel's standing as a judge in Israel is not a part of this story. In this story he is primarily a seer, someone who will—for a fee—use supernormal insight to help people find something lost or to foretell the future. In the context of the story this is a legitimate occupation, and Samuel is repeatedly referred to as "the man of Elohim" (*ish ha-elohim*), a title later also used for other prophets, including Elisha (cf. 2 Kings 5:8; 6:6).

To harmonize Samuel's roles as both seer and prophet, the author adds the explanatory note, "Formerly in Israel, anyone who went to inquire of [Elohim] would say, 'Come, let us go to the seer'; for the one who is now called a prophet was formerly called a seer" (1 Samuel 9:11). Here the author is doing two things to make the details of his history conform to the standards of his own time. First, he presents consultation with a seer even for fairly mundane purposes such as finding a lost donkey as "inquiring of Elohim." The seer is not consulted and paid to use his or her own inherent gifts, but to act as a mediator between the client and Yahweh, who is the source of the information the seer conveys. In short, the seer functions in much the same way as a prophet. Second, the author is careful explicitly to conflate the role of the "seer"—a role no longer legitimate in the religious culture of Judah at the time he wrote—with the more religiously respectable role of "prophet." In the stories concerning him, Samuel performs functions that are typically also fulfilled by prophets in the later history of Israel and Judah, but many of these functions also recall Moses, who is regarded as the first prophet in the Israelite tradition. The writer portrays Samuel in such a way that Samuel represents the sort of inspired prophecy that was dominant after his time, rather than the historical reality of the other, later discredited forms of gaining insight into Yahweh's will.

Although prophecy is to some extent continuous with these other methods of discerning the divine will, it also stands apart as a distinctive religious phenomenon in several respects. For one thing, the prophetic vocation is less a gift than a calling. The diviner is someone skilled in various techniques for discovering divine intentions, often by virtue of a divinely bestowed gift of insight. But the prophet is someone who is believed to be set apart by the gods. The prophet submits to them, proclaiming their message on the basis of some form of religious experience. The prophet usually feels that he or she is under constraint to speak the message given by the gods, whether he or she wishes to or not. The Greek *prophetes* means "*forth*-teller—not "*fore*-teller"— because the prophet proclaims the message given to him or her by the god. The prophet always indicates that the god, not the prophet, is the source of the message he or she proclaims.

The prophet's ministry usually begins with an inaugural experience when the prophet receives his or her call to prophesy. The prophetic call takes the form of a vision or an audition, that is, something seen or something heard that is understood to be a message from the god. Both visions and auditions are ecstatic phenomena. Ecstatic phenomena are unusual states of mind when a person seems to "stand outside" him- or herself. In states of ecstasy people are caught up in some sort of interior experience while their normal participation in everyday reality is temporarily diminished or interrupted. There are varying degrees of ecstasy. They may range from preoccupation to daydreaming to intense concentration to total immersion in another (mental or spiritual) reality. Generally speaking, the intensity of an ecstatic experience is determined by the extent that the person affected remains aware of the normal stream of activity that surrounds him or her.

Experiencing a vision usually presupposes a fairly intense ecstatic experience as the effected person sees something that is in fact not there. But sometimes a vision may involve insight into the true nature or significance of something that is in fact present. For example, Jeremiah has an ecstatic experience involving an almond branch in Jeremiah 1:11–12. It is immaterial to the message whether the almond branch he sees is actually there or not. The point of the experience—based both on the budding of branches in spring and a play on words in the Hebrew—is that Yahweh proclaims a message beforehand that something will happen in the future and then "watches over" his word to bring it to pass. Here Jeremiah is able to "look past" the everyday reality of the almond branch to discern the message Yahweh conveys through it.

An audition—a religious experience in which something is heard rather than seen—does not presuppose as intense an ecstatic experience as a vision, since one may often hear a message clearly while still remaining aware that other things are happening at the same time. Visions most often seem to include an auditory element, a voice that explains the meaning of the vision to the prophet. What is true in all forms of prophetic experience, however, is the prophet's conviction that the god has conveyed a specific message through the experience, and that the prophet in turn is required to proclaim that message on the god's behalf.

The prophet's proclamation of the message he or she receives from the god is not restricted to words spoken in a public forum, but includes other forms of communication and other possible audiences. The prophetic message might be addressed to the king. Prophets employed by the court or the temple had a primary duty to address the king on the gods' behalf, to reveal the gods' intention for both the king and his people. We have already seen examples of this sort of prophecy in both Egypt and Mesopotamia. The prophet might address other individuals or a group, such as the court or the ruling elite. Or a prophet might proclaim the divine message publicly, to the people in general. What person or people were to be addressed with the proclamation was a part of the divine message the prophet received.

Sometimes the prophet undertakes a particular set of actions as part of the message he or she wishes to convey. These "prophetic actions" may be either individual deeds or habitual behaviors and may take a wide range of forms. An example of an individual action would be Jeremiah's purchase of property in Anathoth to indicate that after the Babylonian conquest of Judah, Yahweh would ultimately bring the exiles back home and their property would once again have value (Jeremiah 32:6–15). Jeremiah also provides an example of a habitual behavior that served as a prophetic action, when he wore a yoke on his neck as a symbol of the "yoke" of submission that would be placed on Judah by the Babylonians (Jeremiah 27:1–13). Jeremiah's yoke was later seized and broken by another prophet, Hananiah, in a prophetic action he said symbolized Yahweh's intention to break Babylon's yoke of oppression within two years (Jeremiah 28:10–11). As we will see, the conflict between the messages of the prophets Jeremiah and Hananiah opens up the entire problem of true and false prophecy.

Major events in the prophet's own life might also serve to symbolize his message in a prophetic action. The prophet Hosea, for example, married a prostitute to symbolize Yahweh's "marriage" through the covenant to an unfaithful Israel. Hosea's prophecies equate infidelity to Israel's covenantal relationship to Yahweh with marital infidelity, and the practice of worshipping cult statues with adultery, an equation we find elsewhere among the prophets (cf. Jeremiah 3:1–18; cp. Hosea 4:12–19). At Yahweh's direction Hosea first marries a prostitute, Gomer, and then has three children with her (Hosea 1). Hosea then repudiates Gomer and her children but later reconciles with her and the children after she repents (Hosea 3). The children are given names symbolic of Hosea's prophetic message for Israel. The first son is named Jezreel, recalling Jehu's violent elimination of the Omride dynasty. A daughter is named Lo-ruhamah, "not pitied" (1:6) and Hosea's second son is Lo-ammi, "not my people." The daughter's name means Yahweh will not pity Israel, and the second son's name is not only an accusation of illegitimacy—not my child—but also a repudiation of the covenantal relationship. Both names represent Yahweh's rejection of his people for their unfaithfulness. But again at Yahweh's instruction, the children's names are later changed—or rather, reversed—to Ruhamah, "pitied," and Ammi, "my people," (Hosea 2:23). The names now symbolize the renewal of the covenantal relationship—also symbolized by the renewal of the marital relationship between Hosea and Gomer—when Yahweh will forgive Israel, have pity on them, and once again say, "You shall be my people, and I shall be your god" (Hosea 2:14–23). So Hosea's entire family history is a prophetic action illustrating the message he proclaims, that Israel has been unfaithful to Yahweh and will be punished, but Yahweh will ultimately forgive Israel and renew the covenant with his people.

Not only was the prophet's message often acted out through symbolic actions, but more significantly, it was also often written down. Part of a prophet's mission might be to have his prophecies recorded in writing, to serve as a witness of the words that the god had spoken to the prophet. A written record was particularly significant in cases where a prophecy foresaw specific events in the future. In such cases, the written record would prove the prophecy had been spoken before it was fulfilled. Written prophecies stand as a witness that Yahweh is the one who controls events, who first speaks the word through his prophets and then fulfills it.

Writing down prophecies also ensures their preservation for later generations. In some cases it appears that the prophets themselves ensured that their prophecies were recorded. In the book of Jeremiah, the prophet dictated his prophecies to his secretary Baruch at Yahweh's command. Baruch later read the prophecies to the people of Judah, the members of the court, and finally to King Jehoiakim himself. After the king burned the scroll of prophecies, Yahweh ordered Jeremiah to produce another scroll like it (Jeremiah 36). More often it appears that followers of a prophet first memorized his prophecies and passed them on to others orally before they were ultimately written down. In the process they apparently sometimes added other prophecies, proclaimed by themselves or by others, speaking the word of Yahweh in the prophet's name and continuing his prophetic tradition. Scholars see this phenomenon of preservation and addition in the distinct parts of the books of Isaiah (Isaiah 1–39, 40–55, 56–66) and Zechariah (Zechariah 1–8, 9–14).

The Hebrew Bible includes both large and small collections of written prophecies. The tradition of transcribing prophecies became so well-established that by the time of the Babylonian conquest, Ezekiel could have a vision of Yahweh's words being given to him in the form of a scroll. In the vision he eats the scroll and then he speaks the word of Yahweh that is now "inside" him to the people of Israel (Ezekiel 2:9–3:11). There is an interesting interplay between the word of Yahweh spoken by the prophet and the preservation of the word through writing. The word is written down so it may "come alive" again when it is read aloud, allowing the prophet—and through the prophet Yahweh—to speak Yahweh's word anew. Writing prophecies also allows them to be reinterpreted and applied to new situations even centuries later, as new audiences find the prophecies "fulfilled" in ways that might have little to do with their original meaning or historical context.

Prophecy in Israel and Judah

Biblical scholars have identified three primary sorts of prophet in ancient Israel and Judah: guild prophets, official prophets, and independent prophets. These divisions among prophets are not mutually exclusive, and there was some overlap among the categories. In fact, the most prominent prophets usually represented two of these categories, while Samuel represented all three. But delineating the distinctions among the three divisions still has some value in helping us understand the different historical and social contexts in which prophets proclaimed their message.

Guild prophets were prophets who lived and prophesied in groups, usually under a leader. Prophets of this sort were known as "the sons of the prophets" (cf. 2 Kings 2:3, 5, 7). Guild prophets were under the authority of a head prophet, with the rest of the group sharing equal status as "sons." In stories concerning them, both Samuel and Elisha are associated with groups of prophets as their leaders, although both are also portrayed acting independently of the group. Bands of prophets might either remain in a single location or move from place to place. Guild prophets were found not only in Israel and Judah but throughout Syria–Palestine, notably in Canaan and Phoenicia. The prophets of Baal who opposed Elijah in the story of the contest on Mt. Carmel were probably guild prophets, since they exhibit the forms of prophetic ecstasy that were typical of such prophets (1 Kings 18:26, 28–29).

Guild prophets typically experienced extreme forms of prophetic ecstasy that are often described as "frenzies" (cf. 1 Samuel 10:5, 10). Their ecstasies might be expressed through dancing, whirling, going into catatonic trances, or stripping naked (cf. 1 Samuel 19:23–24). The prophetic ecstasy the guild prophets experienced was contagious. In 1 Samuel 10:9–13, for example, Saul falls into a prophetic frenzy among a band of prophets, something the author explains as part of the demonstration that Yahweh has given him "another heart" (10:9; cp. 10:5–6). 1 Samuel 19:18–24 tells how some of Saul's soldiers and later Saul himself go into ecstasies among a band of prophets in Naioth in Ramah.

Guild prophets appear to have set themselves apart by their appearance as well as their behavior. They were apparently easily recognized. They probably wore distinctive clothing and may have had some characteristic mark that indicated their status as prophets. In 1 Kings 20:38–41, for example, a guild prophet is able to disguise himself with a bandage over his eyes. Ahab of Israel recognizes him as a prophet only when the bandage is removed, apparently because some sort of mark on the forehead indicated the man's prophetic status. Or what Ahab saw may have been a distinctive haircut, like a monk's tonsure. In 2 Kings 2:23–25 the prophet Elisha, who was a leader of a band of prophets, curses a group of boys in Bethel because they jeered him with cries of "Go away, baldhead!" The curse—and the subsequent mauling of the boys by two bears—makes some sense if the boys were mocking Elisha's distinctive prophetic tonsure, but even so the story remains problematic.

As this story demonstrates, guild prophets seem to have been regarded with both awe and ridicule. In one story, Elisha orders one of them to anoint the army commander Jehu as king over Israel (2 Kings 9:1–10). After the young man anoints Jehu outside of a tent where he is meeting with his officers, the officers ask, "Why did that madman come to you?" Jehu replies, "You know the sort and how they babble" (2 Kings 9:11). When the priest Amaziah calls the prophet Amos a "seer," Amos replies, "I am no prophet, nor a prophet's son" (Amos 7:12–14). Amos rejects the title "seer" but also the title "prophet" and the role of the sons of the prophets. Although itinerant bands of prophets probably continued to carry out their work in Syria–Palestine after the fall of the independent kingdoms, the surviving texts do not refer to them after that time.

A second sort of prophet in ancient Syria–Palestine was the official prophet. Official prophets were employed as prophets within the context of the royal court or a cultic site to divine or declare the gods' intentions for individuals and the state. Court prophets served as advisors to kings in formulating domestic and foreign policy, and in time of war advised the king on strategy and tactics. In each case, the role of the court prophet was to discern and declare the will of the gods in regard to a particular situation. Kings who depended on the oracles of court prophets of course ran the danger of being told only what the prophets thought the king wanted to hear. In a story about Ahab of Israel and Jehoshaphat of Judah preparing to go into battle against Ramoth-gilead, Jehoshaphat asks Ahab to seek an oracle from Yahweh. Four hundred of Ahab's prophets prophesy victory, but Jehoshaphat holds out for an oracle from another prophet. That prophet, Micaiah son of Imlah, correctly prophesies disaster, as Ahab knew he would (1 Kings 22:1–18).

Cultic prophets were associated with the temples and shrines dedicated to the country's gods. It was their responsibility to bring inquiries to the god or to discern the god's will either for individual petitioners or for the proper maintenance of cultic worship. Cultic prophets were part of the personnel associated with a temple or shrine, with duties similar to those of diviners, although their methods of interacting with the gods were different. Cultic prophets were part of the religious establishment of a state, and tended to conform to the prevailing orthodoxy of their time as dictated by the king and the chief priests. They were an essentially conservative religious force, since they served at the king's pleasure. Like the court prophets, the cultic prophets too tended to deliver oracles that were favorable to the king and denounced only his enemies. As a result, official prophets are sometimes regarded with suspicion by the authors of the biblical texts, especially when they come into conflict with an independent prophet, as the court prophet Hananiah did with Jeremiah (Jeremiah 28). At the same time, several of the major independent prophets were apparently cultic prophets as well, including Isaiah of Jerusalem, Ezekiel, and Haggai.

The third sort of prophet was the independent prophet. The independent prophet spoke on Yahweh's behalf without the legitimating authority conferred by the royal court or a cultic site. In fact the independent prophets whose oracles have come down to us most often spoke out in opposition to both king and cult. They provided an alternative version of the traditions and history that undergirded the religious cultures of Israel and Judah and with it a dissenting view of the obligations of the people and leaders to their god under the stipulations of the Sinai covenant.

Independent prophets seem to have been called from a variety of professions to proclaim oracles at Yahweh's instigation. Some, like Samuel and Elisha, were associated with the wandering guild prophets as leaders over them (cf. 1 Samuel 19:20; 2 Kings 2:15). Amos, the earliest prophet whose oracles have been collected into a surviving book, was one "among the shepherds of Tekoa" in Judah (Amos 1:1). He described himself as "a herdsman and a dresser of sycamore trees" (Amos 7:14). Jeremiah belonged to the family of priests descended from Abiathar, David's priest who was banished to Anathoth after supporting Adonijah's bid to succeed his father (Jeremiah 1:1; 1 Kings 2:26). Ezekiel was a Zadokite priest who was among the first wave of exiles sent to Babylon with Jehoiachin of Judah in 598 BCE. Isaiah of Jerusalem and some of the other independent prophets appear to have served as cultic prophets as well, but their authority derived from their proclamation of divine oracles independent of the duties of their office. Some of the prophets—notably Ezekiel—filled several authoritative roles in the religious establishment, while others were defined solely by their role as independent prophets. What set them apart from their peers was the authority granted to them by the force of the divine oracles they proclaimed, the conviction among those who heard them that they truly spoke the word of Yahweh.

The prophets Elijah and Jeremiah may be taken as primary examples of independent prophets in Israel and Judah. Elijah's words and deeds have survived in the book of Kings. In the stories about him, Elijah speaks out repeatedly against the political and religious policies of Ahab and Jezebel of Israel in both word and action, and he is hounded by royal officials as a result, effectively forcing him underground (cf. 1 Kings 19:1–18). Jeremiah provoked strong opposition with his prophetic message in Judah and he, too, suffered persecution as a result (cf. Jeremiah 38:1–13). But even when Jeremiah attempted to keep silent, the force provoking him to speak overwhelmed him, and he could not hold in the message he felt compelled to deliver (cf. Jeremiah 20:7–12).

The phenomenon of independent prophecy—a phenomenon predicated on the idea that the gods may choose through whom to speak to their people—

raises the difficult problem of distinguishing true from false prophecy. Although the inaugural visions of the prophet are a subjective experience that assures them they are receiving divine messages, there is no objective test by which the proclamation of a genuine word of a god might be distinguished from some other sort of proclamation. The source of false prophecy is open to question in the surviving texts. In 1 Kings 13, one prophet simply lies to another and gives a false oracle (1 Kings 13:18). The independent prophet Micaiah in his conflict with the prophets serving Ahab in 1 Kings 22:1–40 claims that false prophecy is the result of Yahweh sending lying spirits to mislead and destroy those who disobey him (1 Kings 22:19–23). Since we are not aware of how official prophets were chosen for their offices, it may be that there were different varieties of prophetic inspiration.

But the question remained, how was an audience to distinguish true prophecy from false prophecy? Jeremiah in his conflict with the official prophet Hananiah offers two tests. First, he says, a true prophet proclaims a message consistent with the message of the earlier prophets, a message of war, famine, and pestilence rather than peace. Second, if a prophet does prophesy peace, the truth of his word will only be proven when Yahweh fulfills the prophecy (Jeremiah 28). We find this idea of prophecy and fulfillment used as a major motif in the history of Israel and Judah as it is depicted in the books of Samuel and Kings (cf. 1 Kings 13:1–6; 2 Kings 23:15–18). But we have also seen that not all the words of "true" prophets find fulfillment. A notable example is the prophetic words of Second Isaiah (Isaiah 40–55), which promised a glorious return from exile to a renewed land of Judah, a promise whose failure later apparently inspired in part the prophecies of Haggai. The real test of a prophet's authority seems to have been the words and deeds of the prophet himself, to the extent that those words and deeds were perceived by their audiences to be self-authenticating, indicating by their very force and compelling content that they were in fact a true proclamation of the word of Yahweh.

Literary Expressions of Personal Religion in Israel and Judah

Apart from the theological presentation of Israel's history in the biblical texts, there are other literary texts that reflect the nature of personal religion among the people of Israel. The psalms, for example, are devotional poems. Although they were apparently written to be used in communal worship, they also often reflect the lamentations or thanksgiving of an individual worshipper.

The book of Psalms is a collection of 150 poems that is comprised of five smaller collections (Psalms 1–41, 42–72, 73–89, 90–106, and 107–150). The divisions are marked by doxologies, formulas of praise to God that appear at the end of each collection (Psalms 41:13; 72:18–19; 89:52; 106:48; 150). The language of praise found in the psalms is comparable to similar language found in the same context throughout the ancient Near East, including elsewhere in Syria–Palestine. Most of the language and imagery employed in praising Yahweh the God of Israel is based on common human ideas of majesty, power, glory, and beneficence. Similarly, there is nothing unique in the human concerns the psalms address. The psalmists beseech Yahweh to protect them against their enemies, to vindicate their faithfulness, to save them in times of trouble, to grant wisdom and power to the king, and to bless the people. But in spite of the common language and concerns, the psalms also provide some insight into Israel's ritual worship, its religious festivals, and the religious sentiments of its people.

Several types of psalms can be distinguished according to their content, and content often suggests a particular setting for their use. Hymns of praise, for example, were probably used within the context of worship at the Jerusalem temple and presented either individually or chorally to praise Yahweh's greatness and mercy as exhibited in his works of power. Laments may reflect either an individual or communal situation. They follow a standard pattern including an invocation, a complaint, a confession of trust, a petition for help, and a concluding vow that thanksgiving will be offered when the petition is answered. Songs of thanksgiving combine elements of the hymn of praise and the lament to look back on difficulties the speaker has experienced in the past and to give thanks that those difficulties have been overcome through Yahweh's help. There are also songs of Zion, hymns celebrating the enthronement of Yahweh as god over Israel or the enthronement of the king as Yahweh's viceroy on earth. Finally, there are royal songs in praise of the king, since the blessings associated with his rule come from Yahweh.

Of these different sorts of psalm, the hymns of praise, laments, and songs of thanksgiving often represent the voice of a single individual either praising Yahweh or invoking his aid. As worship in Israel and Judah came to focus more and more on Yahweh alone to the exclusion of other gods, invocation of Yahweh in any and all circumstances replaced earlier resort to gods with specialized realms of power. To the extent that individual forms of worship and praise mimicked those of official religious culture, the language and sentiments of temple worship also became the language of private religious devotion.

There are also psalms which reflect piety of a more individual sort, a form of piety usually associated with the period after the Babylonian exile. Some psalms, for example, are meditations on the covenant and the blessings granted to Israel through observance of the covenantal stipulations (cf. Psalms 1:1–6; 19:7–14; 119). These psalms reflect the conviction that both group and individual adherence to the covenant not only ensures Yahweh's blessings but also leads to a worthwhile life guided by its principles.

This same idea is, perhaps not surprisingly, also found in Israelite wisdom literature. There the focus on the covenantal law represents a substantial deviation within the ancient Near Eastern wisdom tradition. Wisdom literature in Israel and Judah is comparable in many ways to the wisdom literature we have discussed in connection with Egypt and Mesopotamia. The surviving writings reflect the same general concern with pragmatic wisdom, the knowledge of how to get along in the world, and apparently developed in the same context, the scribal school, where it formed a basic part of the curriculum. The Israelite tradition shares with other wisdom traditions the contrast between the wise man and the fool, between the student who learns wisdom and lives a life according to its precepts, and the one who learns wisdom but disregards it and suffers as a result. Wisdom literature in Israel and Judah also shares the primary form of expression (the proverb) with other forms of wisdom literature found in Egypt and Mesopotamia. In fact in some cases we find extensive parallels to writings from other wisdom traditions, notably the portions of Proverbs 22:17–23:11 (subtitled "Sayings of the Sages") that have very close parallels to parts of the Egyptian wisdom text *The Wisdom of Amenemope*.

Wisdom literature from Israel and Judah also shares with the other traditions the distinction between what we may call "optimistic" and "pessimistic" wisdom, as we have seen in our discussion of "pessimistic" wisdom in Ecclesiastes and Job. The optimistic tradition is best represented by the book of Proverbs, where a discernible pattern and predictability in life allows the wise person to take steps to determine his or her fate, confident in the principle of retributive justice. But the optimistic wisdom tradition is also exemplified by later books such as the Wisdom of ben-Sirach (also known as Ecclesiasticus, c. 180 BCE) and the book of Wisdom (first century BCE), although with some modifications in keeping with exposure to Hellenistic culture and the intervening experience of the Jews.

But the Israelite wisdom tradition, despite its parallels to other ancient wisdom traditions in the ancient Near East, also reflects a trust not just in the predictability of life and the principle of retributive justice, but in Yahweh as the god who establishes order in human life. The key principle appears repeatedly: "The fear of [Yahweh] is the beginning of wisdom; they have sound sense who practice it" (Psalm 111:10; cp. Proverbs 1:7; 9:10; 15:33; Job 28:28). Whether this is an early or a late principle in the Israelite wisdom tradition, it represents a new development of the tradition in light of henotheistic belief, consistent with some of what we find in Job.

One of the more remarkable instances of this idea appears in Proverbs 8, where a personified wisdom calls out to those who seek instruction. Here Wisdom appears as a woman who offers her goods to anyone who wishes to have them. She says, "I love those who love me, and those who seek me diligently find me. Riches and honor are with me, enduring wealth and prosperity" (Proverbs 8:17–18). Wisdom is also the essence of virtue: "All the words of my mouth are righteous; there is nothing twisted or crooked in them" (8:8). This is because wisdom is based on fear of Yahweh, which ensures the wise will shun wickedness: "The fear of [Yahweh] is hatred of evil" (8:13a).

But this personified wisdom also identifies herself very closely with Yahweh's work in creation, as the divine attribute that served Yahweh in all his creative work. Here again the speaking of a word in the act of creation "breathes/inspires" wisdom already present in the god's mind: "[Yahweh] created me at the beginning of his work, the first of his acts of long ago" (8:22). But the creative word of wisdom is again personified, now as a partner in Yahweh's creative work. "When he marked out the foundations of the earth, then I was beside him, like a master worker, and I was daily his delight" (8:29c–30). Israelite wisdom literature ultimately finds wisdom—which is divine wisdom, based in the fear of Yahweh—in the very fabric of creation itself, because it is also inherent in the nature of Yahweh himself. Like other Israelite religious traditions preserved in the Hebrew Bible, the wisdom tradition recasts all of human existence in terms of the unique lordship of Yahweh.

Conclusion: Change and Continuity in the Hellenistic Age

Alexander's Conquest and Its Consequences

The shape of Hellenistic culture, which prevailed throughout the eastern Mediterranean basin from the fourth century BCE through the early centuries of the Roman Empire, was largely determined by the efforts of one man: Alexander the Great. Alexander inherited control of the armies of Greece, but through brilliant military strategy and tactics became the master of most of the Mediterranean world. His father, Philip of Macedon, united the warring cities of Greece through skillful warfare and canny statesmanship, and became leader of a Panhellenic alliance in 338 BCE. With Greece united behind him, Philip planned a campaign against Persia in retaliation for its fifth-century invasion of Greece, but his plans were cut short by his assassination in 336 BCE.

Philip was succeeded by his twenty-year-old son, Alexander III, who carried out his plan to invade Persia, and in the process conquered most of the Near East. As Alexander's armies moved east, pieces of the Persian Empire fell into his hands: Asia Minor, Egypt, Syria–Palestine, Mesopotamia, and finally Persia itself. Alexander's conquest of the Persian Empire with a relatively small army was a tribute to his military genius, but also to the reforms his father had brought to the Greek way of fighting a war. Alexander eventually crossed the Indus River and campaigned in India, but his troops finally rebelled and refused to fight any longer. Alexander died of fever in Babylon in 323 BCE, at thirty-three. His young son soon died also, and three of Alexander's generals divided his empire among themselves.

Alexander was an imperialist in the classic sense, someone who wished not only to conquer territories but also to create a cosmopolitan culture that would unify his vast domains. Although he was Macedonian and not a Greek, Alexander was a fervent Hellenist who intended to bring the blessings of Greek classical culture to the former subjects of the Persian kings. For the vast majority of his subjects, of course, the change in imperial leadership meant little. They were still governed by regional officials who were now subject in turn to Greek-speaking Macedonians instead of Aramaic-speaking Persians. In time, however, Alexander's conquests did result in the development of a single cosmopolitan culture throughout his domains, at least at its upper levels, through a gradual process of assimilation. The resulting culture was Hellenistic (i.e., "Greek-like"), a culture that was primarily Greek but included elements of many of the native cultures of territories conquered under Alexander. The Macedonian kings of Egypt and Syria (including Mesopotamia) legitimized their rule by adopting the traditional royal trappings and customs of the peoples under their control. But they also established within their domains the dominant institutions of Hellenic culture, in part to assimilate the native aristocracies and make them their supporters.

Central to Hellenistic culture was a simplified version of the classical Greek language called *koiné* ("common") Greek. Greek became the language of government administration and in time, the *lingua franca* of the Hellenistic world. The Greek educational system indoctrinated sons of the native aristocracies. Along with these changes came the spread of the Greek reverence for athletics, Greek ideals of beauty and order, and the influence of Greek philosophy, including natural science and mathematics.

New cities were established throughout Alexander's domains. The most notable of these was probably Alexandria in Egypt, built on the Mediterranean coast in the Nile Delta. These new cities were based on the model of a Greek city-state (*polis*), with written constitutions, limited citizenship, and public facilities including temples built in the Greek style, gymnasia for athletics, marketplaces, libraries, and so on. Greek-style city constitutions also reestablished existing cities as Greek *poleis*, with the public facilities and policies befitting their new status.

Probably the most influential change arising from the Macedonian conquest was in religious culture, since the new cosmopolitanism led to widely spread syncretism. Syncretism is the synthesis of elements—gods, rituals, and mythologies—taken from distinct religious cultures into new forms and combinations. This process often included reinterpretation of existing rituals and mythology to give them a more universal significance. Syncretism was often actively encouraged by Hellenistic rulers to legitimate their power and to unite their subjects in a common religious culture. Alexander himself, for example, consulted an Egyptian oracle that he claimed named him the son of Amun, thereby establishing a divine patrimony similar to that attributed to the kings of Egypt.

Religious syncretism also resulted in the creation of new gods who combined the attributes of several others, as well as the reinvention of traditional gods as savior figures. Gods from the conquered nations tended to become "Hellenized" by being presented and worshipped according to Greek models. In their new form their "foreignness" became primarily an indication of their ancient origins or their universal appeal rather than a challenge to Greek hegemony. The Hellenistic era also saw widespread worship of some traditional Greek gods, notably Demeter and Dionysus, who were now worshipped as universal gods who controlled the powers of life, death, and rebirth.

The Hellenistic era saw a return to the worship of ancient earth-based (chthonic) deities, as the fertility rituals surrounding them were reinterpreted as salvation rituals. The power of these deities, usually goddesses, was based on their association with the cycle of fertility, an association that often broadened, as we have seen, into control over the cycles of life, cosmic rhythms, and all aspects of dynamic life. These deities were worshipped in "mystery religions," so-called because the devotee went through a secret initiation ritual that represented a death to the old life and rebirth as a devotee of the deity. Some of the mysteries, notably those devoted to the Egyptian goddess Isis, featured multiple secret initiations. The appeal of the mystery religions was that they offered devotees personal access to the deity as a patron or patroness. This relationship between a divine patron and individual human worshippers stood in contrast to much of the traditional religious culture of the ancient Mediterranean world.

One became a follower of a mystery religion by choice and submitted to the rituals of initiation in order to be admitted into the select group of the god's devotees. The mysteries emphasized the bond between the deity and the initiate in terms of the initiate's devotion toward the god, and the god's benevolent protection in response. The "salvation" offered by the mystery religions was not salvation from death, but salvation from the blind power of fate. The ritual of initiation brought the devotee under the patronage of a powerful deity who could provide protection against the buffets of fate, and in some cases, blessedness in the afterlife. The hope was that, just as the goddess herself in the cultic mythology overcame adversity to eventually regain her loved one from the power of death and to return home with him in peace, so she would also protect her devotee during life's wanderings and bring him or her safely "home."

Religious Change in the Near East in the Hellenistic Age

The nations whose religious cultures we have considered—Egypt, Mesopotamia, and the states of Syria–Palestine—suffered different fates as a result of Alexander's conquests. Egypt came under the control of Alexander's general Ptolemy and his descendants, who continued to rule Egypt until the Roman period. But the Ptolemies, like Alexander, legitimized their rule over Egypt by adhering to Egypt's royal traditions. The Ptolemies founded and renovated traditional Egyptian temples dedicated to the traditional Egyptian gods, and presented themselves—and were represented in religious art—in terms of traditional royal symbolism. The Ptolemies generally respected the two major groups among their subjects, Greeks and Macedonians on the one hand and native Egyptians on the other. Egyptian law remained in force even as it was supplemented by Greek law. Although *koiné* Greek was the language of commerce and government, Egyptian continued in use both as a spoken and as a written language, even in literature. With support from the Ptolemies, Egyptian religious culture continued for the most part undisturbed in all its particulars, although Greek iconography and ideas were gradually introduced into traditional religious art and beliefs.

Mesopotamia's situation was more unsettled, both as a part of the Hellenistic kingdom of Syria under the Seleucids, and later under the dominion of the Parthians. After Alexander defeated the Persians at Gaugamela in October 331 BCE, Persian troops in Babylon surrendered the city to him. Following his practice of legitimating his rule through recognition of a territory's traditional gods, Alexander offered a thanksgiving sacrifice to Marduk and ordered the rebuilding of destroyed temples in Babylon. The Babylonians welcomed Alexander and his plans for the city, but the conqueror soon departed. He led his armies to the east for continued campaigning and only returned to Babylon in 323 BCE, when he died there of a fever.

Dominion over Mesopotamia changed hands among Alexander's generals several times before the territory finally fell to Seleucus as part of the kingdom of Syria in 301 BCE. Seleucus built his royal capital Antioch on the Orontes, near the Mediterranean coast. The relocation of the center of political power left Mesopotamia in relative peace but also outside the mainstream of culture and commerce. Hellenistic cities in Mesopotamia were built along the major trade routes to Central Asia, often on the ruins of older cities. Babylon and other old cities were not rebuilt, although they often gained Greek-style civic buildings and temples. Some of the old cities of Mesopotamia prospered under the new regime under the Seleucids but others, like Babylon, were largely depopulated and filled with ruins. Although traditional Mesopotamian religious culture was fostered first by Alexander and later by the Seleucids through benefactions to temples, the continuation of traditional forms of worship was apparently largely restricted to those temples and the few people who continued to venerate the old gods.

The Parthians entered Iran from the northeast around 250 BCE, after having established dominion over the former heart of the Persian Empire a century earlier. They moved into Mesopotamia as far as the Tigris and claimed the territory in its entirety. After a brief reassertion of Seleucid power, the Parthian king Artabanus II regained control of Mesopotamia. Mesopotamia remained under Parthian control with only two brief interruptions until it fell to the Sassanian Persians in 227 CE. During this time the Parthians controlled the trade routes between east and west. They built new settlements and enlarged existing cities, filling them with new settlers. This newest mixed-ethnic incursion severely diluted Mesopotamian identity even as the territory's ancient cultural legacy, including its religious culture, slowly faded away.

The Seleucids finally wrested control over Syria–Palestine from the Ptolemies in 198 BCE and retained control until the Roman conquest under Pompey in 63 BCE. Throughout the Hellenistic period there were supporters of both dynasties, the Ptolemies and the Seleucids, in Syria–Palestine. This led to endless intrigues meant to promote the interests of one dynasty over the other, or to curry favor with one side or the other, among the local political authorities.

The Seleucid king Antiochus IV Epiphanes came to power in Syria in 175 BCE, and his desire to establish Hellenization among his subjects quickly made him a legendary opponent to Judaism. Antiochus was a fervent Hellenist and initially found support among the pro-Syrian faction in Jerusalem, made up almost exclusively of aristocrats. Antiochus deposed Jason, the leader of the faction, as high priest in Jerusalem and replaced him with Menelaus, an even more fervent supporter of the Seleucid dynasty and its policies. The king's blatant manipulation of the high priesthood led to a conservative reaction among the Jews that culminated in an insurrection against Antiochus in Jerusalem. Antiochus put down the rebellion and attempted to enforce Hellenization by forbidding the practice of Judaism and forcing Jews to eat unclean foods. The final affront came in 167 BCE with the rededication of the Jerusalem temple to the worship of Zeus, with whom Antiochus identified himself.

Soon a guerilla action began in the Judaean hill country, led by a priest named Mattathias and his five sons. The third son, Judas, nicknamed "Maccabee" ("the Hammer"), became the leader of the rebellion against the Syrian king. Judas had a number of notable victories, culminating in the capture of Jerusalem and the rededication of the temple to the worship of Yahweh in 164 BCE, an event commemorated in the celebration of Chanukah. As a result of the rebellion, the Jews gained territorial autonomy in 142 BCE. Members of Judas's family, the Hasmoneans, ruled Palestine as high priests until 63 BCE, although the territory remained under the nominal authority of the Seleucids.

Near Eastern Religious Cultures at the Beginning of the First Century BCE

What can we say about the religious cultures of Egypt, Mesopotamia, and Syria–Palestine at the beginning of the first century BCE, before the Roman conquest? Despite the continuation of traditional Egyptian religious culture under the Ptolemies, the vigorous dynamism of Hellenistic culture introduced new religious ideas and iconography, a development that would eventually lead to Egypt's full integration into the mainstream of Mediterranean religious culture during the first century of the Roman Empire. Mesopotamian religious culture, on the other hand, effectively disappeared under Parthian rule. Even its chief cities and religious monuments disappeared without a trace, although many of its religious ideas and practices—most notably extispicy and astrology—continued to exert an influence on Western thought.

Much of the religious culture of Syria–Palestine was assimilated into prevailing Greco-Roman religious culture, although the assimilation was never complete. Judaism, centered in Jerusalem and the surrounding territory controlled by the Hasmoneans, was sustained by ritual worship in the Jerusalem temple and communal worship in congregations both in Palestine and throughout much of the Hellenistic world, primarily in major cities. Local congregations fostered a vision of the Jews as Israel, Yahweh's chosen people, characterized by obedience to the covenantal law of Sinai. Although Judaism shared with the religions of the surrounding peoples the practice of ritual sacrifice, it attracted outsiders as a monotheistic religious culture with a clear ethical character, defining a way of life that set the Jews apart from other religious groups.

But what can we say about the religious *influence* of Egypt, Mesopotamia, and Syria–Palestine at the beginning of the first century BCE, before the Roman conquest? Perhaps most important, the goddess Isis became the central deity of a mystery religion more widespread than any other in the ancient Mediterranean world. The relevant aspects of Isis's divine character for her mystery rituals were first her role in Osiris's death and resurrection and second her protection of Horus, both as a child and in his contests with Seth. Together these mythic roles represented Isis's power over life and death and maternal love for those who made themselves her devotees. Osiris was known both under his own name and as Serapis, which was essentially his Hellenized identity as a universal god. Sanctuaries of Serapis and Isis were established throughout the Mediterranean basin in major ports and cities, where their worshippers tended to be well-educated and socially prominent. The public rituals associated with Isis worship were daily rituals of prayer and meditation at her sanctuaries, with major festivals recalling parts of Isis's story. Some of these rituals, as well as the religious emotions that characterized Isis worship, are reflected in the later chapters of *The Golden Ass*, a novel written by Apuleius of Madaurus in the second half of the second century CE.

The most influential remnant of Mesopotamian culture in the Hellenistic and later Roman world was the Neo-Babylonian (Chaldean) science of astrology. Astrology appealed to the desire to gain insight into the gods' will for the present and the future through a superficially "scientific" observation and calculation of the movement of the stars. Astrologers were popular among the Romans, who included them among the other practitioners who claimed to be able to divine the gods' intentions, including the interpreters of omens, augers, and seers who practiced extispicy, another popular divination technique among the Mesopotamians.

The Hellenistic era also saw the spread of a mystery religion devoted to a deity known as "the Syrian goddess." Atargatis was apparently related to the goddess Astarte of Syria–Palestine, and was herself related in turn to the Mesopotamian goddess Ishtar. The mystery religion was apparently first spread by Syrians who were slaves in other Mediterranean nations, beginning in the third century BCE. The satirist Lucian of Samosata (born c. 120 CE) in his treatise, "The Syrian Goddess," is a primary source for information about the Syrian goddess, as is Apuleius's *The Golden Ass*. In her temple at Hieropolis in Syria, a statue of the goddess was apparently displayed with others of El (whom Lucian identified as Zeus) and Baal or Hadad (whom Lucian identified as a bearded image of Apollo). On the basis of the appearance of the image found in her temple, Lucian writes that Atargatis "is certainly Hera, but she also has something of Athena, Aphrodite, Selene, Rhea, Artemis, Nemesis and the Fates" (*The Syrian Goddess*, 32).

The events of the persecution under Antiochus IV Epiphanes were arguably the origin of several trends in Judaism that were to have substantial impact in the Roman world after the turn of the age. Apocalyptic expectations arose in reaction to the persecution, which seemed to be the ultimate expression of the hostility of the powers controlling the present age against Yahweh and his people. The persecution under Antiochus IV appears to have inspired the apocalyptic scenario found in Daniel 10–12, for example. As we have seen, belief in the resurrection from the dead of both the very good and the very wicked seems to have arisen in response to the martyrdom of faithful Jews under Antiochus. At the same time, the revived ideal of military action to defend Yahweh's people against their enemies, exemplified by the struggle of the Maccabeans, continued to attract adherents, notably those who later led the Jewish revolt against Rome in 66 CE. The Hasmonean era in Palestine also saw the rise of parties and sectarian groups within Judaism, notably the Sadducees, Pharisees, and the sectarians whose beliefs and ways of life are reflected in the writings known as the Dead Sea Scrolls.

The ancient Near Eastern religious cultures that would prove the most influential in the Roman era were Egyptian Isis worship and Judaism. Each offered an alternative to the religious cultures of Greece and Rome in the form of the worship of a single powerful deity. Each demanded that its followers devote themselves to the god and adopt a distinctive way of life that would set them apart from mainstream society. Each offered divine protection for the believer in the present life and freedom from the blind power of fate, with some hope for a blessed rest in the world to come. In short, both Isis worship and Judaism at the turn of the age offered their devotees the fulfillment of the perennial religious yearnings of the peoples of the ancient Near East.

Bibliography for Further Reading

General

Glenn Holland. *Divine Irony*. Selinsgrove, PA: Susquehanna University Press, 2000.

Sarah Iles Johnston, ed. *Religions of the Ancient World*. Harvard University Press Reference Library. Cambridge, MA: Belknap/Harvard University Press, 2004.

James B. Pritchard, ed. *The Ancient Near East*. Volume 1: *An Anthology of Texts and Pictures*. Volume 2: *A New Anthology of Texts and Pictures*. Princeton: Princeton University Press, 1958, 1975.

Marc Van de Mieroop. *A History of the Ancient Near East ca. 3000-323 BC*. 2nd edition. Blackwell. History of the Ancient World. Malden, MA: Blackwell, 2007.

Robin W. Winks and Susan P. Mattern-Parkes. *The Ancient Mediterranean World: From the Stone Age to A.D. 600*. New York: Oxford University Press, 2004.

Egypt

Jan Assmann. *The Search for God in Ancient Egypt*. Translated by David Lorton. Ithaca, NY: Cornell University Press, 2001.

Jan Assmann. *Death and Salvation in Ancient Egypt*. Translated by David Lorton. Ithaca, NY: Cornell University Press, 2005.

John Baines, Leonard H. Lesko, and David P. Silverman. *Religion in Ancient Egypt: Gods, Myths, and Personal Practice*. Edited by Byron E. Shafer. Ithaca, NY: Cornell University Press, 1991.

Kathryn A. Bard. *An Introduction to the Archaeology of Ancient Egypt*. Malden, MA: Blackwell, 2008.

Raymond Faulkner, trans. *The Egyptian Book of the Dead: The Book of Going Forth by Day*. 2nd rev. ed. San Francisco: Chronicle Books, 1998.

John L. Foster, ed. and trans. *Ancient Egyptian Literature: An Anthology*. Austin: University of Texas Press, 2001.

Lucia Gahlin. *Egypt: Gods, Myths and Religion*. New York: Barnes and Noble, 2002.

George Hart. *Egyptian Myths*. The Legendary Past. Austin: University of Texas Press, 1990.

Erik Hornung. *Idea Into Image: Essays on Ancient Egyptian Thought*. Translated by John Baines. Ithaca, NY: Cornell University Press, 1982.

Erik Hornung. *Conceptions of God in Ancient Egypt: The One and the Many*. Translated by Elizabeth Bredeck. Princeton: Timken, 1992.

Erik Hornung. *History of Ancient Egypt: An Introduction*. Translated by David Lorton. Ithaca, NY: Cornell University Press, 1999.

Salima Ikram and Aidan Dodson. *The Mummy in Ancient Egypt: Preparing the Dead for Eternity*. London: Thames & Hudson, 1998.

Miriam Lichtheim. *Ancient Egyptian Literature: A Book of Readings. Volume I: The Old and Middle Kingdoms. Volume II: The New Kingdom*. Berkeley and Los Angeles: University of California Press, 2006.

Bojana Mojsov. *Osiris: Death and Afterlife of a God*. Malden, MA: Blackwell, 2005.

Dominic Montserrat. *Akhenaten: History, Fantasy and Ancient Egypt*. New York: Routledge, 2000.

Stephen Quirke. *The Cult of Ra: Sun-Worship in Ancient Egypt*. London: Thames & Hudson, 2001.

John Ray. *Reflections of Osiris: Lives from Ancient Egypt*. New York: Oxford University Press, 2002.

Donald B. Redford, ed. *The Ancient Gods Speak: A Guide to Egyptian Religion*. New York: Oxford University Press, 2002.

Ian Shaw, ed. *The Oxford History of Ancient Egypt*. New York: Oxford University Press, 2000.

William Kelly Simpson. *The Literature of Ancient Egypt: An Anthology of Stories, Instructions, Stelae, Autobiographies, and Poetry*. 3rd edition. New Haven, CT: Yale University Press, 2003.

A. J. (Alan Jeffrey) Spencer. *Death in Ancient Egypt*. New York: Penguin, 1982.

Claude Traunecker. *The Gods of Egypt*. Translated by David Lorton. Ithaca, NY: Cornell University Press, 2001.

Richard H. Wilkinson. *Symbol and Magic in Egyptian Art*. London: Thames & Hudson, 1994.

Mesopotamia

Jeremy Black and Anthony Green. *Gods, Demons and Symbols of Ancient Mesopotamia: An Illustrated Dictionary*. Austin: University of Texas Press, 2003.

Jean Bottéro. *Everyday Life in Ancient Mesopotamia*. Translated by Antonia Nevill. Baltimore: Johns Hopkins University Press, 2001.

Jean Bottéro. *Religion in Ancient Mesopotamia.* Translated by Teresa Lavender Fagan. Chicago: University of Chicago Press, 2001.

Nicole Brisch, ed. *Religion and Power: Divine Kingship in the Ancient World and Beyond.* Oriental Institute Seminars 4. Chicago: Oriental Institute of the University of Chicago, 2008.

Stephanie Dalley, ed. and trans. *Myths from Mesopotamia: Creation, the Flood, Gilgamesh, and Others.* Oxford World's Classics. Revised edition. New York: Oxford University Press, 1989.

Thorkild Jacobsen. *The Treasures of Darkness: A History of Mesopotamian Religion.* New Haven, CT: Yale University Press, 1976.

Samuel Noah Kramer. *The Sumerians: Their History, Culture, and Character.* Chicago: University of Chicago Press, 1963.

Samuel Noah Kramer. *Sumerian Mythology: A Study of Spiritual and Literary Achievement in the Third Millennium B.C..* Revised edition. Philadelphia: University of Pennsylvania Press, 1972.

Samuel Noah Kramer. *History Begins at Sumer: Thirty-Nine Firsts in Recorded History.* 3rd edition. Philadelphia: University of Pennsylvania Press, 1981.

Stephen Mitchell. *Gilgamesh: A New English Version.* New York: Free Press, 2004.

Karen Rhea Nemet-Nejat. *Daily Life in Ancient Mesopotamia.* Peabody, MA: Hendrickson, 2002.

Joan Oates. *Babylon.* Revised edition. New York: Thames & Hudson, 1986.

Susan Pollock. *Ancient Mesopotamia: The Eden that Never Was.* New York: Cambridge University Press, 1999.

George Roux. *Ancient Iraq.* 3rd edition. New York: Penguin, 1992.

N. K. Sandars, ed. and trans. *Poems of Heaven and Hell from Ancient Mesopotamia.* Penguin Classics. London: Penguin, 1971.

N. K. Sandars, ed. and trans. *The Epic of Gilgamesh.* Penguin Classics. Revised edition. London: Penguin, 1972.

Marc Van de Mieroop. *The Ancient Mesopotamian City.* Oxford: Clarendon Press, 1997.

Diane Wolkstein and Samuel Noah Kramer. *Inanna, Queen of Heaven and Earth: Her Stories and Hymns from Sumer.* New York: Harper & Row, 1983.

Syria–Palestine

Yohanan Aharoni. *The Land of the Bible: A Historical Geography.* Translated by Anson F. Rainey. Revised edition. Philadelphia: Westminster, 1979.

Joseph Blenkinsopp. *A History of Prophecy in Israel: From the Settlement in the Land to the Hellenistic Period.* Revised edition. Philadelphia: Westminster John Knox, 1996.

Richard J. Clifford, ed. *Wisdom Literature in Mesopotamia and Israel.* Symposium 36. Atlanta: Society of Biblical Literature, 2007.

John J. Collins. *Introduction to the Hebrew Bible.* Minneapolis: Fortress, 2004.

Michael D. Coogan, ed. *The Oxford History of the Biblical World*. New York: Oxford University Press, 1998.

Frank Moore Cross. *Canaanite Myth and Hebrew Epic: Essays in the History of the Religion of Israel*. Cambridge, MA: Harvard University Press, 1973.

John Day. *Molech: A God of Human Sacrifice in the Old Testament*. New York: Cambridge University Press, 1989.

John Day. *Yahweh and the Gods and Goddesses of Canaan*. New York: Sheffield Academic Press, 2002.

Israel Finkelstein and Neil Asher Silberman. *The Bible Unearthed: Archaeology's New Vision of Ancient Israel and the Origin of Its Sacred Texts*. New York: Touchstone, 2001.

Israel Finkelstein and Neil Asher Silberman. *David and Solomon: In Search of the Bible's Sacred Kings and the Roots of the Western Tradition*. New York: Free Press, 2006.

Henry Jackson Flanders, Jr., Robert Wilson Crapps, and David Anthony Smith. *People of the Covenant: An Introduction to the Hebrew Bible*. 4th edition. New York: Oxford University Press, 1996.

John H. Hayes and J. Maxwell Miller. *A History of Ancient Israel and Judah*. 2nd edition. Louisville, KY: Westminster John Knox, 2006.

Siegfried Hermann. *A History of Israel in Old Testament Times*. 2nd edition. Philadelphia: Fortress, 1981.

Klaus Koch. *The Prophets: Volume 1: The Assyrian Period. Volume 2: The Babylonian and Persian Periods*. Philadelphia: Fortress, 1983, 1984.

Jon Levenson. *Sinai and Zion: An Entry into the Jewish Bible*. New York: Harper & Row, 1987.

Johannes Lindblom. *Prophecy in Ancient Israel*. Philadelphia: Fortress, 1967.

Steven L. McKenzie. *King David: A Biography*. New York: Oxford University Press, 2000.

Dennis Pardee. *Ritual and Cult at Ugarit*. Writings from the Ancient World 10. Atlanta: Society of Biblical Literature, 2002.

Mark Smith. *The Early History of God: Yahweh and the Other Deities in Ancient Israel*. 2nd edition. Grand Rapids, MI: Wm. B. Eerdmans, 2002.

Glossary

Akkadian—a Semitic language dominant in Mesopotamia from the nineteenth century to the twelfth century BCE.

Ammit—(Egyptian) "the Gobbler"; the composite beast in Duat that devours the souls of those whose evil deeds during their earthly lives have made their hearts heavy.

Amorites—a Semitic people from the region of Syria who established states north of Sumer c. 2900 BCE and later settled in various parts of Syria–Palestine.

Amurru—a state in Syria in the fourteenth and thirteenth centuries BCE.

ankh—Egyptian symbol of eternal life, a vertical cross with an oval loop forming the top arm just above the crossbar.

anthropomorphic—from Greek; in human form.

Anunnaki—(Akkadian) initially identified as the gods of heaven, but later they appear as the gods of earth and the Underworld.

apocalyptic reversal—the vindication of the poor and the outcast over the rich and powerful at the end of the age.

apocalypticism—the expectation that God will directly intervene in human history at some future point to save and vindicate his people.

Aramaeans—a Semitic people who settled in northwestern Mesopotamia and Syria–Palestine between 1500 and 1000 BCE, and established city-states in Syria.

Aramaic—alphabetic Semitic language, dominant in Mesopotamia from the twelfth century BCE.

Archaic era—era in Egyptian history, comprising Dynasties 1 and 2, c. 3000–2686 BCE.

asheroth—(Hebrew) stylized trees sacred to the goddess Asherah.

audition—an ecstatic experience that is primarily aural.

ba—(Egyptian) a person's activity or spiritual presence perceivable to others in what he or she does; the persona of an individual; self-consciousness.

bamoth—(Hebrew) "altars," often called "high places"; national shrines in Israel and Judah.

bark—a boat-shaped shrine carried by the god's priests.

BCE—before the Common Era; the Common Era theoretically began with the birth of Jesus of Nazareth.

Bel Matati—(Akkadian) "Lord of the World"; a title of Marduk.

Benben—(Egyptian) the primeval hill that emerged from Nun, the sea of chaos; shaped like a pyramid, it provided the creator god with a place to stand while doing the work of creation.

The Book of Going Forth by Day—Egyptian collection of texts of instruction for the deceased, including versions of the Pyramid Texts and the Coffin Texts; often called *The Egyptian Book of the Dead*.

canopic jars—containers for a mummy's internal organs.

CE—Common Era, the current era, theoretically beginning with the birth of Jesus of Nazareth.

cenotaph—a memorial stone dedicated to a deceased person, comparable to a tomb but not located at his or her burial place.

Chaldeans—a Semitic people who established the Neo-Babylonian Empire in the seventh century BCE.

charismatic—derived from a spiritual gift or grace (Greek, *charisma*).

chthonic deities—earth-based gods and goddesses.

Coffin Texts—instructions for the dead painted inside coffins in Egypt during the Middle Kingdom.

cosmogony—from Greek, an account of the origin of the cosmos.

cult—the collection of rituals and associated activities involved in the worship of a particular god.

Day of Yahweh, in Israelite religious culture, the day when Yahweh will act decisively to deliver and vindicate his faithful people.

deities—self-conscious controllers of sacred power; gods.

Deshret—(Egyptian) "the Red Land," the Egyptian desert; also the name of the upswept red crown of Lower Egypt.

dingir—(Sumerian) "one of heaven," "god".

djet—(Egyptian) time as the transcendent reality of the changeless, associated with Osiris.

droît du seigneur—(French) "right of the lord"; a lord's prerogative to have sexual intercourse with virgin brides before they marry.

Duat—the Egyptian Underworld, the realm of Osiris.

ecstatic phenomena—from Greek, "to stand outside"; what is experienced in a state of mind when one "stands outside" one's self and one's normal perception of reality is temporarily interrupted.

effective cursing—using access to the spiritual world to call wrath down upon one's enemies.

Ennead—the nine chief gods of the Egyptian pantheon, in some accounts the first products of divine creation.

epic poem—verse story about a hero who undertakes a series of adventures lived out in conscious relationship to the divine world.

execration texts—names of enemies written on clay vessels that are then smashed, effectively "breaking" the enemy's power.

First Intermediate Period—era in Egyptian history, comprising Dynasties 9–11, c. 2160–2055 BCE.

guild prophets—prophets who lived and prophesied in groups, usually under a leader.

hedjet—(Egyptian) the white crown of Upper Egypt, shaped like a fat bowling pin.

heka—(Egyptian) magic or divine energy; one of the three godly powers necessary for the work of creation.

Hellenic—from Greek, *Hellas* ("Greece"); Greek in nature.

Hellenistic—from Greek, *hellenistikos*, "Greek-like"; resembling or related to the Greeks.

henotheism—a religious culture devoted to worshipping one god out of the many gods that exist.

hieros gamos—(Greek) "sacred marriage"; sexual intercourse between a male devotee and a female temple functionary, intended to promote the fertility of crops through the imitation of the sexual intercourse between a fertility deity and his or her consort.

history—a realm of discourse concerning what can reasonably be surmised to have happened in the past on the basis of verifiable and acceptable data and systematic analysis.

Hittites—an Indo-European people that established a civilization and a kingdom in Asia Minor, dominant from the eighteenth century to the beginning of the twelfth century BCE.

hu—(Egyptian) divine utterance, one of the three godly powers necessary for the work of creation.

Hurrians—a people led by an Indo-European ruling class that entered the Near East in the third millennium BCE and established the kingdom of Mitanni in northern Syria in the fifteenth and fourteenth centuries BCE.

HWY—(Hebrew) "to be".

Hyksos—a Semitic people who founded Dynasty 15 and claimed authority over Upper and Lower Egypt and parts of Syria–Palestine during the Second Intermediate Period (c. 1650–1550 BCE).

ideogram—a symbol used in a writing system to picture the thing to which it refers, rather than to represent a sound.

Igigi—(Akkadian) initially identified as the gods of earth and the Underworld, but later they appear as the gods of heaven.

ilu—(Akkadian) "god," "one of heaven".

immanent—permeating and operating through the realm of creation as its driving force.

inaugural experience—an ecstatic experience usually taking the form of a vision and/or an audition (i.e., something seen and/or something heard) that first calls a prophet to prophesy.

independent prophets—individual prophets who speak on a god's behalf apart from the authority granted by the king of a state or the priests of a religious community.

isfet—(Egyptian) disorder; identified with Seth.

ka—(Egyptian) the interaction between mind and body that allows a person to live and act; the individual identity of a person, his or her character, and the way character determines the shape and ultimate nature of a person's life.

Kassites—an Iranian people led by an Indo-European warrior elite that ruled Mesopotamia for over four centuries during the second millennium BCE.

Kemet—(Egyptian) "the Black Land"; the Nile Valley.

koiné—(Greek) "common"; the Greek of the Hellenistic culture of the eastern Mediterranean from the fourth century BCE.

libation—a liquid poured out as an offering to a god.

lingua franca—(Italian) "Frankish tongue"; the common (usually second) language of diverse people united in a common cosmopolitan culture.

maat—(Egyptian), divine harmony or balance; also deified as a goddess.

masseboth—(Hebrew) "sacred stones," "sacred pillars".

material culture—the physical remains of a human culture, discovered through archaeology.

me—(Sumerian) "authority," "supernatural power".

Mesolithic era—the Middle Stone Age, the period c. 17,000–c. 8300 BCE.

Mesopotamia—from Greek, "Between the Rivers"; the territory defined by the Tigris and Euphrates.

Middle and Late Bronze Ages—the period c. 2200–1200 BCE.

Middle Kingdom—era in Egyptian history comprising part of Dynasty 11 as well as Dynasties 12 and 13, 2055–1650 BCE.

Mishnah—a collection of rabbinic commentaries on the teachings of Torah; compiled c. 200 CE.

Mitanni—a Hurrian kingdom located in northern Syria, dominant over Assyria in the fifteenth and fourteenth centuries BCE.

monotheism—a religious culture reflecting devotion to the one god, the only god believed to exist.

mystery religion—a religious group devoted to a "savior god," usually a goddess with fertility associations, with voluntary membership based on participation in secret initiation rituals.

myth—a realm of discourse involving any idea of what motivates or drives history, or what lies behind or above history, including the influence of forces usually identified as "supernatural".

mythology—legendary accounts of the activities and interactions of gods and heroes.

name—an expression of the deepest sense of the self, the essential reality of a human being or a god.

natron—a solution used in Egyptian mummification, comprising various mixtures of sodium bicarbonate, sodium carbonate, sodium sulfate, and sodium chloride.

"natural" religious communities—religious communities coextensive with a social community.

necromancy—the summoning up of oracular spirits from the dead to gain insight into the present or to foresee the future.

neheh—(Egyptian) the perpetual passage of heavenly and earthly events that accumulate as history, associated with Ra.

Neolithic era—the New Stone Age, c. 8300–c. 4000 BCE.

New Kingdom—era in Egyptian history, comprising Dynasties 18–20, c. 1550–1069 BCE.

nisu-bity—(Egyptian) usually translated "King of Upper and Lower Egypt," a royal title in Egypt from the third millennium.

nome—regional territory in Egypt under control of a leader called a nomarch.

numinous—associated with or indicative of the sacred.

Nun—(Egyptian) the dark waters of the limitless depths.

official prophets—professional prophets who worked within the context of the royal court or the ritual cult.

Ogdoad—(Greek) "group of eight"; four pairs of primeval Egyptian gods and goddesses instrumental in creation in the Hermopolis account.

Old Kingdom—era in Egyptian history, comprising Dynasties 3–6, c. 2686–2125 BCE.

"Opening of the Mouth"—in Egypt, a ritual believed to make it possible for something to live, or in the case of the dead body, to live again.

Opet—an annual festival in Egypt when the king traveled to the temple of Luxor at Thebes to have his royal power renewed by Amun-Ra.

Paleolithic era—the Old Stone Age, began about two million years ago, ended c. 17,000 BCE.

Pharaoh—from the Egyptian *Per Ao*, "great house"; a title for the Egyptian king during the New Kingdom and after.

polis—(Greek) a regional city-state based on a constitution and ruled by a council of citizens.

polytheism—a religious culture that recognizes and offers worship to many different gods.

prophetes—(Greek) "forth-teller," "proclaimer"; a prophet.

prophetic action—a particular behavior enacted by a prophet as part of the prophetic message.

Pyramid Texts—Egyptian religious inscriptions in the chambers of Old Kingdom pyramids, offering instructions for the dead.

regicide—murder of a ruling king.

sacred, the—that which permeates, influences, and relates to material reality and yet is recognized as part of another reality not subject to the limitations of the material.

šā mūti—(Akkadian) "bread of death".

šāmūti—(Akkadian) "bread of heaven".

sanctuary—sacred space devoted to worship, including temple, altar, and associated buildings and space.

Second Intermediate Period—era in Egyptian history, comprising Dynasties 13–17, c. 1759–1539 BCE.

sed-festival—a celebration and renewal of the pharaoh's divine authority to rule, observed after about thirty years of the king's rule.

serdab—(Egyptian) an enclosed chamber adjacent to the funerary chapel in royal tombs, in which one or more statues of the deceased and his or her family were placed.

shabtis—(Egyptian) "answerers"; tomb models of male and female slaves believed to serve the needs of the deceased in the afterlife, sometimes called *ushebtis*.

shadow—in Egyptian religious culture, the physical presence of a person distinct from the body, both during life and after death.

Sheol—(Hebrew) the Underworld, the dwelling-place of the dead.

sia—(Egyptian) divine knowledge, one of the three godly powers necessary for the work of creation.

sistrum—a type of musical rattle, comprising a handle surmounted by a metal loop with loose metal pieces attached to produce noise when shaken.

Sokar festival—in Egypt, a somber commemoration of the death of Osiris.

stele (pl. stelae)—a column or standing stone, usually inscribed as a commemoration.

suzerainty treaty—a treaty in which a subject people accepts a king as its sovereign, with stipulations placed on both sides.

syncretism—the synthesis of different elements taken from distinct religious cultures into new forms and combinations.

theodicy—from Greek, "god is in the right"; a demonstration that a god's actions are in keeping with the god's righteous character, despite appearances to the contrary.

theogony—from Greek, an account of the origins of the gods.

theophoric element—from Greek, "god-bearing"; the part of a personal name that incorporates the name of a god.

Third Intermediate Period—era in Egyptian history, comprising Dynasties 21–25, c. 1069–664 BCE.

Ubaid—Neolithic culture in southeastern Mesopotamia during the fifth millennium BCE.

Upper Paleolithic era—30,000–17,000 years ago.

uraeus—the sacred cobra portrayed on Egyptian crowns, representing supreme power.

Urim and Thummin—in Israelite religion, a divining apparatus used to discover Yahweh's will, part of the high priest's apparel.

vision—an ecstatic experience that is primarily visual in nature.

voluntary religious communities—communities one chooses to join as a result of a conversion experience.

wedjat—Egyptian, "sound one"; an amulet representing a left eye lined with kohl and an eyebrow with the markings of a falcon; also called "Eye of Horus".

Yahweh—reconstructed pronunciation of the Hebrew YHWH, the name of the god of Israel.

YHWH—(Hebrew) the name of the god of Israel.

ziggurat—massive pyramidal brick building, intended in ancient Mesopotamia to represent the sacred mountain

Index

Aaron, 223
Abiathar, 272
Abraham, 209–10, 234, 263
Absalom, 207, 221
Abydos, 4, 8, 43
abyss, 34, 36, 123–24, 147, 149, 185, 215–16, 239. *See also* depths
Adad, 117, 180
Adam, 214–15, 242, 246
Adapa, 115, 126–28, 157, 165; story of, 126, 128
administration, 4, 38, 50, 78, 100–101, 102, 104, 106, 133, 139, 199, 257; royal, 9–10, 38, 102, 106, 113
administrators, 82, 197, 225
Adonai, 208
Adonijah, 221, 272
afterlife, 5, 21, 23, 25, 57–61, 64–67, 70, 74–75, 81, 86, 90, 149, 151–52, 163, 241, 279
agriculture, 9, 60, 99–100, 115, 117, 119
Ahab, 212, 227–28, 270–73
Ahaz, 197, 227
Ahmose, 10, 28

Akhenaten, 11, 28–30, 50, 79, 84, 194, 202. *See also* Amenhotep IV
Akhetaten, 11, 30, 84
Akkad, 99, 104
Akkadian (language), 101, 104–5, 111, 118, 123, 128, 131–32, 137, 140–41, 155–58, 164, 179, 182–83, 185
Akkadian (people), 100–2, 116, 123, 131, 141, 154, 169, 193
alewife, 146–47, 154, 244
Alexander III of Macedon, 14, 198, 243, 277–81
altars, 206, 212, 222–23, 258, 260–62
Amarna, 11, 194
Amenemhat I, 8, 52–54, 92–93
Amenhotep I, 10–11
Amenhotep IV, 11, 28, 79. *See also* Akhenaten
Ammit, 71, 75, 150
Amorites, 102–3, 123, 224
Amos, 271–72
amulets, 62, 86, 169, 178–79
Amun, 8, 11–12, 20–21, 28–30, 34–36, 50–51, 81–84, 199, 279; priests of, 28–29

Amun-Ra, 28, 37, 40, 79, 81
Amurru, 11, 194
Anat, 47, 200, 203–4, 206–7, 213, 239
animals: sacred, 77, 82, 85; sacrificial,
    78, 180, 261
ankh, 18
Anshar, 118, 124–25
Antiochus IV Epiphanes, 255, 281,
    283–84
Anu, 114, 124–25, 127, 132, 138–39,
    144, 160–61, 164, 184, 186–87
Anubis, 21, 23, 25, 70–72
Anunnaki, 113, 156
apocalypticism, 252–55
apocalyptic reversal, 255
Apophis, 44, 47, 68, 216
Apsu, 112–13, 123–25, 148
Arabian Desert, 105, 191, 195–96
Aramaeans, 196
Aramaic, 105, 131, 182, 191, 278
Aram-Damascus, 196–97, 227
Archaic Period (Egyptian history), 4–5,
    16, 20, 35, 39
architecture, 4, 8, 10, 16, 54–55, 84,
    138
archives, 103, 137, 194, 202, 260
Ark of the Covenant, 222, 230, 258,
    260
Aruru, 139, 141
Asherah, 203–4, 206, 213, 260
Asshur, 103, 114, 118, 126, 134
Assur-bannipal, 13, 107–8, 135, 185
Assyria, 13, 99, 103, 105–8, 118, 126,
    134, 137, 155, 196–97, 212, 227,
    237
Assyrians, 13, 105, 118, 131, 197, 228
Astarte, 45, 47, 200, 203, 206–7, 228
astrology, 181, 282–83
Aten, 11, 28–30, 79, 202
Athena, 121, 283
Atrahasis, 127, 165, 184, 186–88
Atum, 18, 20, 27–28, 32–36, 68, 213
Avaris, 9, 193

ba, 58–59, 61–63, 79, 82, 90
Baal, 118, 202–4, 206–9, 211–13, 221,
    224, 228, 239, 241, 262, 270, 283
Baalat, 200
Babylon, 13, 103–9, 114–15, 118, 123,
    126, 128, 134–35, 173–76, 197–98,
    228, 230, 247, 251, 272, 277, 280
Babylonia, 99, 101, 103, 109, 118,
    197–98
Babylonian conquest of Judah, 228, 267,
    269
Babylonian creation story, 112, 118, 123.
    See also Enuma Elish
Babylonian exile, 191, 229, 246–47, 252,
    262, 274
Babylonians, 13, 103–5, 107–8, 131, 197,
    228–31, 237, 267, 280
"The Babylonian Theodicty," 183
beetle, sacred, 27, 86. *See also* scarab
Belshazzar, 109, 135
Benben, 32, 34
Bes, 23, 84
Bethel, 222, 224, 260, 270
blood, 25, 92, 121, 126, 128, 164, 186,
    195, 212, 261
boat, 46, 67–68, 80, 147, 173, 185–87
Bronze Age, 105, 192–93; Late, 193–94,
    196, 241; Middle, 193
Bubastid dynasty in Egypt, 12
Bull El, 203, 213, 223
Bull of Heaven, 144–45, 148, 155, 164
burial, 4, 21, 58–60, 63, 65, 67, 73, 95,
    150–52, 192, 241, 256
Byblos, 5, 8, 193–94, 200

calendar, 81, 115, 125
Canaan, 9, 192–93, 195–96, 208,
    210–11, 223, 233, 235, 264, 270
Canaanites, 208, 235
Chaldeans, 108, 118, 131, 134, 181, 283
chaos, 34, 109, 122–25, 127–28, 139,
    145, 155, 164, 167, 174, 185, 188,
    213, 215–16, 239

chapels, 63, 83–84
Chemosh, 207
childbirth, 25, 84, 117, 178–79, 215, 262
city-states, 100–101, 103, 192, 199
cobra, 18, 21, 33, 68
Code of Hammurabi, 103–4, 133
coffins, 60, 62, 66, 95
Coffin Texts, 33, 66–67
"Contendings of Horus and Seth," 17, 25–26, 42, 86, 207
cosmogonies, 30–32, 122
"Counsels of Wisdom," 182
"The Courtship of Inanna and Dumuzi," 119–20
covenant, 196, 209–11, 218, 222, 228–30, 233–37, 247, 251, 255–56, 258, 260–61, 268, 274–75
covenantal relationship, 210, 228, 230–34, 236–37, 252, 268
creation, work of, 5, 27, 32, 125–26, 128, 213–18
creation of humanity, 34, 114, 117, 126, 168, 186, 216
creation stories, 30–32, 34, 37, 42, 118, 122–24, 126, 129, 134, 162, 174, 186, 212–15, 217–18, 234, 264; Egyptian, 20, 30–32, 34, 36
creator, 5, 18, 27, 31–33, 35–36, 118, 128, 201–2, 208, 212–13, 217, 246, 250, 264
cult, 27, 125, 206, 211, 219, 226–27, 240, 257, 272. See also ritual worship
cultic personnel, 78, 134, 171–72, 220, 257–58, 260
cultic sites, 32, 222, 237, 261, 271–72
cultic statues, 40, 79–80, 82, 172–73, 175, 229–30, 260–61
cults, national, 83, 169, 223
culture: Egyptian, 15–16, 57, 131; Mesopotamian, 131, 152, 177, 283
cuneiform, 101, 111, 185
curses, 144–45, 270

Cutting the Grain (Egyptian festival), 173
Cyrus of Persia, 13, 109, 197

Dagon, 208
Damkina, 115, 124, 178
Dan, 222, 260
dance, 25–26, 78
Daniel, 247, 254–56, 284
Darius I, 13
David, 196, 207, 221–22, 227–28, 230, 235–36, 240, 252, 264, 272
Davidic dynasty, 196, 221–22, 228–29, 232, 236
Day of Atonement, 174
Day of Yahweh, 253–54
Dead Sea Scrolls, 284
death, fear of, 145–47, 153
debate, 90–91, 182–84, 247–50
deities, 21, 26–28, 33, 61, 84, 117, 160, 169, 183, 200, 216, 261, 279, 282–84
demons, 47, 153, 158, 169, 178–79, 183
depths, 31–32, 34, 36, 115, 123–24, 147–48, 155. See also abyss
Descent of Ishtar, 154, 173. See also Inanna's descent
Deuteronomy, 206, 223, 240, 260, 264–65
devotees, 11, 19, 30, 48–49, 83–84, 96, 201, 245, 279, 283–84
devotion, 28, 135, 201, 240, 263, 274, 279
dingir, 111, 128
disorder, 17, 39, 44, 47, 49–50, 80, 85, 127
"Dispute between the Tamarisk and the Date Palm," 182
divine authority, 20, 112–13, 125, 158, 226
divine couples, 20, 33–34, 36
divine energy, 32, 35, 124, 126–28
divine essence, 27, 35
divine hierarchy, 94, 114, 186, 217–18

divine honors, 39, 118, 136, 172
divine justice, 104, 187, 245–46, 248
diviners, 168, 171, 180–81, 183, 257,
    264–66, 271
divine warrior, 203–4, 213
djet, 19, 39, 74
Djoser, 5, 23, 84
dreams, 85, 135, 141–42, 145, 171,
    180–81, 183, 204, 264–65
Duat, 62–63, 66, 68–69, 71, 74, 90–91.
    See also Osiris, kingdom of
Dumuzi, 115, 119–20, 155, 158–59,
    163, 172–73, 179

Ea, 112–13, 115–16, 124–27, 157,
    160–61, 178, 184–86
Ebla, 202, 260
Ecclesiastes, 92, 243–44, 247, 275
Ecclesiasticus, 275
ecstasy, 181, 266–67, 270
Eden, 214, 229, 242
Edom, 195, 235
Egypt: history, 4–5, 15, 25, 38, 57, 79;
    Lower, 3–5, 8, 12, 20–21, 49, 51,
    105; Middle, 34; Upper, 3–5, 12–13,
    21, 44, 49, 70; Upper and Lower,
    3–4, 8–9, 20, 38, 40, 44, 52, 71
Egyptian, 17–18, 20, 23, 27, 47, 163,
    279–80
Egyptian Book of the Dead, 7, 66
Egyptian mythology, 23, 65, 122
Egyptian pantheon, 19, 23, 37, 69, 94
Egyptian religious culture, 15–18, 25,
    30, 35, 37, 58, 95–96, 149–50, 200,
    280, 282
El, 202–4, 206, 208, 212–13, 221, 234,
    262, 283
Elam, 102, 105–8
El-Elyon, 221
elemental gods, 20, 31, 33, 36, 123
Elijah, 211–12, 227–28, 241–42, 263,
    272
Elisha, 242, 265, 270, 272

Elohim, 213, 215–17, 234, 241, 243–44,
    248, 252, 265
El Shaddai, 203, 208
Enki, 112, 114–15, 117, 121, 156–57,
    159, 186–87
Enkidu, 139–46, 148, 150, 153
Enlil, 114–15, 117–18, 123, 132,
    142–43, 156, 161, 184, 186–87
Ennead, 20, 35–36, 45
Ennugi, 117, 184
Enoch, 242
Enuma elish, 123, 126–28, 134, 168,
    186–87, 215, 217
Epic of Gilgamesh, 120, 136–39, 145,
    154–55, 164–65, 182, 184–85,
    187–88
Ereshkigal, 117–18, 132, 153, 155–64,
    179
Eridu, 115, 126
erotic love, 21, 25–26, 43, 119–20, 144,
    173
Esagil, temple of Marduk, 175, 183
Esarhaddon, 13, 106–7, 135
Esau, 234
eternal life, 17–18, 67, 145–46, 148,
    153–54
Euphrates, 99–100, 103, 117, 184
Evil-Merodach, 109
execration texts, 73
Exodus, 208–10, 213, 223, 233, 235,
    247, 260–61, 263–64
exorcism, 179
extispicy, 180–81, 264, 282–83
Ezekiel, 210, 229, 247, 251, 256, 269,
    271–72
Ezra, 232, 247

falcon, 5, 18, 20, 51, 86
farmers, 38, 117, 119, 204, 211
fate, 23, 65, 71, 89, 91, 138, 148–50,
    152–54, 156, 163–65, 215, 236, 239,
    241–42, 245, 275, 279, 284
Fertile Crescent, 106, 191

fertility, cycle of, 43, 121, 163, 216, 241, 279
fertility deities, 115, 119, 121, 144, 159, 203–4, 206, 241
Festival of Drunkenness, 26
firmament, 21, 125, 186, 216
First Intermediate Period, 7, 28, 51–52, 86, 92
flood, great, 3, 33, 112, 136, 147, 167, 184, 187–88
food offerings, 40, 63, 73, 84, 172
friendship, 141, 144, 148
funerary temples, 40, 42, 65

Garden of Eden, 214, 229, 242
Gaza, 106, 195
Geb, 20, 33, 35–36, 42, 114
Genesis, 105, 209–10, 213–18, 233–35, 241, 246, 253, 262–64
Geshtinanna, 158, 163
ghosts, 53, 74, 150
Gideon, 224–25
gifts, spiritual, 225
Gilgal, 224
Gilgamesh, 112, 120, 137–48, 150, 153–54, 163, 183, 224, 244
Gilgamesh and Enkidu, 141–42, 145–46, 148, 155, 164
the Gobbler, 71–72, 75, 150. See also Ammit
gods: chief, 27, 35, 113–14, 118; Egyptian, 17–18, 20, 23, 27, 47, 163, 279–80; high, 155, 160, 184, 186; household, 262; lesser, 23, 113–14, 124–25, 162, 169, 186, 200; Mesopotamian, 113–14, 117–18, 121, 152; national, 84, 95, 168–69; patron, 38, 118, 135, 177, 220–21, 262–63; personal, 169, 209, 262–63; regional, 21, 203; sun, 20, 27, 29; traditional, 279–80; universal, 21, 23, 279
goods, funeral, 60, 63, 150–51

graves, 59–60, 150–51
Greece, 137, 198, 277, 284
Gugal-ana, 117

Habakkuk, 228
Hadad, 203, 283
Haggai, 231, 247, 251, 271, 273
Hall of Truth, 70, 75, 86
Hammurabi, 103–4, 133
Hananiah, 268, 271
harmony, 17, 39, 44, 53–54, 77, 127, 162, 168, 210, 233, 245
Har-pa-khered, 44, 49. See also Horus the child
Harpers' Songs, 75, 91–92, 147, 154, 244
harp players, 91–92
Harran, 109, 160
Hathor, 21, 23–27, 46, 200
Hatshepsut, 10, 24, 41
heart, 33, 35, 54, 61, 71–72, 75, 86, 91, 135, 252, 270, 281
Hebrew, 191, 196, 207–8, 227, 240, 248, 267
Heka, 32, 35
Heliopolis, 27, 32, 34–35
Hellenistic Age, 192, 255, 277–84
Hellenistic culture, 275, 277–78, 282
Helopolis creation story, 35
henotheism, 200–202, 226–27, 235, 244–46
Hermopolis, 21, 34
hero, 111–12, 123–24, 128, 131–39, 141–43, 145–48, 153, 165, 167, 233
Herodotus, 61, 173
Hezekiah, 13, 106, 197, 212, 237, 260, 262
hieroglyph, 4, 44, 71
hieros gamos, 119, 172, 203. See also sacred marriage
Hittites, 11, 104, 194–95, 236
Horeb, 222
horns, 18, 23, 26, 44, 200

horses, 120, 144
Horus, 5, 18, 20–21, 23, 25–26, 28, 36–37, 39–40, 42–52, 54, 69, 84, 86, 135, 200, 207, 283; eye of, 46, 86; sons of, 23, 61
Horus the child, 44, 48, 83
Hosea, 251, 268
hospitality, 127, 157, 161, 248
household devotions, 84–85, 169
Hu, 32, 35
human condition, 126–27, 146, 164–65, 169, 184, 186, 188
Humbaba, 141–46, 148, 153
Hurrians, 102, 104, 193
Huwawa;, 141, 143. See also Humbaba
Hyksos, 9–10, 28
hymns, 80, 84, 119, 177, 274
"Hymn to Osiris," 42

Igigi, 113
illness, 23, 30, 44, 57, 82, 85, 146, 187, 248
ilu, 111, 128, 202
Imhotep, 23, 84
immortality, 112, 127, 153, 187, 215, 241
Inanna, 112, 114–15, 117–22, 155–59, 163–64, 172–73, 179, 241
Inanna's descent, 117, 155, 162, 179, 204. See also Descent of Ishtar
incense, 7, 79, 84, 172
Indo-Europeans, 105
inscriptions, 4, 11, 17, 42, 62, 66, 73, 101, 191, 194
The Instruction of Any, 90–91
"The Instruction for Merykara," 51, 52
Iran, 109, 136, 281
Iranian people, 104, 108
Iron Age, 195, 241
irony, 143, 164, 244
irrigation, 99, 115, 119, 133, 184
Isaac, 209, 234, 263

Isaiah, Second, 229–31, 247, 251, 273
Isaiah of Jerusalem, 227, 229, 240, 265, 269, 271–72
Ishbaal, 196, 221
Ishmael, 234
Ishtar, 115–16, 135, 138, 144, 148, 154–58, 161–64, 172–73, 175, 186, 188, 200. See also Inanna
Ishtar Gate, 175–76
Ishtar of wisdom, 154
Isis, 20–21, 23, 25–26, 33, 35–36, 42–49, 69–71, 83–85, 113, 122, 282–83
Isis and the seven Scorpions, 83
Isis worship during the Hellenistic era, 283–84
Israel, history, 213, 232–33, 246, 273
Israelite kingdoms, 192, 196, 213, 224
Israelite religion, 209, 217, 221
Israelite tradition, 209, 218, 264, 266, 275
"I Will Praise the Lord of Wisdom," 183

Jacob, 209, 234–35, 262–63
Jebusites, 196, 207, 221–22
Jedidiah, 221. See also Solomon
Jehoiachin, 108, 272
Jehoshaphat, 208, 271
Jehu, 196, 268, 270–71
Jeremiah, 206, 210, 229, 265, 267–69, 271–73
Jeroboam, 196, 251, 260
Jerusalem, 106–8, 197, 207–8, 212, 221–23, 227–29, 231–32, 237, 247, 253–54, 258–61, 265, 271–72, 281–82
Jews, 231–32, 247, 252–56, 262, 275, 281–82, 284
Jezebel, 212, 227, 272
Job, 183–84, 213, 247–51, 275–76
Jonathan, 208, 221
Jordan River, 192

Jordan valley, 195
Joseph, 235, 264
Joshua, 223–24, 253
Josiah, 197, 208, 212, 237, 260, 262–63
Judah, religious culture of, 206–7, 246, 261, 266
Judahites, 197, 222, 231, 251
Judaism, 256, 281–84
Judas Maccabee, 281–82
judges, 23, 71, 153, 156, 208, 221, 224–25, 235, 237, 246, 250, 260, 264–65
Judgment Hall of Osiris, 72
justice, 39, 47, 70, 79, 104, 113, 115, 128, 133, 139, 186, 243, 256

ka, 35, 40, 58–59, 61–63, 79, 82
ka-priests, 59, 63
Karnak, 10, 21, 28, 40, 82–83
Kassites, 104, 131
ka-world, 63–64
Kheprer, 27, 68–69
Kheti, 89–90
Khety, 51–52
Khnum, 21, 34, 36, 59
Khonsu, 21
Khufu, 6–7
kings: divine, 5, 7, 40, 49, 51, 57, 67, 74, 81; ideal, 53, 136; legendary, 4, 136
kingship, 28, 40, 42–43, 47, 49–50, 54, 69, 121, 132–35, 138–39, 148, 154, 174, 219; Egyptian, 37, 42, 131; Egyptian myth of, 26, 42–44, 47, 54, 69, 163
Kushites, 13

labor, manual, 5, 9, 74, 82, 89–90, 100, 114, 125, 128, 186, 196, 215, 260
Late Period (Egyptian history), 13, 192
law code, 102–4
laws, covenantal, 232, 255, 261, 275, 282

leadership: charismatic, 195, 221, 224–25; political, 15, 38, 225–26, 228, 232
Lebanon, 5, 8, 142, 192, 194
Lehem, 221
Leviathan, 206, 213, 250
Levites, 222, 226, 260
Leviticus, 174, 247, 261, 263–65
libations, 84–85, 260
Libya, 5, 11–14, 131
life: earthly, 57, 63, 67, 74, 85, 150, 216; everlasting, 146, 165, 256; power of, 65, 159, 162, 279; source of, 26–27, 39, 71, 150, 164
literature: apocalyptic, 253–55; Egyptian, 91, 163; Mesopotamian, 184
Lothan, 206, 213, 216
Lower Egypt, 3–5, 8, 12, 20–21, 49, 51, 105
Luxor, 28, 81

maat, 17, 30, 36, 39, 47, 50, 53–54, 71, 77, 79, 89, 94, 174
Maccabeans, 281, 284
Macedonia, 198, 277
Macedonians, 14, 109, 232, 243, 278, 280
magic, 19, 26, 32, 43–46, 48–49, 62–63, 66–67, 70, 83–86, 112–13, 115, 125, 178
magical practices, 85, 113, 177–80
Mami, 186
Manasseh, 197, 207, 240, 262
Marduk, 109, 112, 115, 118, 123–28, 132, 134–35, 168, 174–75, 183, 199, 213, 217, 239, 280
Mari, 103
marriage, 26, 118, 120, 160, 220, 232, 235, 268
masseboth, 260
mastabas, 63

Maxims of Ptahhotep, 87
Medes, 108–9, 197
Media, 105–6, 109
mediators, 29, 219, 223, 233, 235, 253, 266
Mediterranean Sea, 3–4, 104–5, 167, 191, 194, 198, 206, 277–78, 280, 282–83
mediums, 240, 265
Megiddo, 193
Melqart, 207
Memphis, 4, 8, 11, 33, 35, 82, 107, 215
Memphis creation story, 35
Menes, 4
Merneptah, 11–12
Mesopotamia: history, 104–5, 135–36; lower, 99–101, 104, 143, 160, 192; northern, 99, 104, 160, 191
Micah, 260
Middle Kingdom (Egyptian history), 8–9, 34, 38, 40, 42, 51–53, 61, 64, 66, 78, 82, 85, 87, 89, 92–93, 193
migration, 104–5, 191–92
Milky Way, 67, 70
Minoan Crete, 194–95
Mitanni, 104–5, 193–94
Moab, 195, 207
Molech, 207
monotheism, 28–29, 159, 200–202, 226–27, 229, 237, 244–46, 251, 282
monsters, 44, 47, 68, 71, 112, 117, 122, 125, 141–43, 145–46, 206, 216
Montu, 28
moon, 20–21, 46, 109, 115, 134–35, 149, 216
Moses, 208, 210, 223–24, 227, 235
Mot, 204, 206, 213, 239
Mount Carmel, 211–12, 270
mourning, 26, 43, 70, 75, 127, 157–58, 204, 241
mummies, 7, 58, 61–63, 65, 86
mummification, 59–62, 81
Mummu, 123–25

Muwatalli, 11, 194
Mycenaean Greece, 11, 105, 194–95
Myth of Kingship (Egypt), 42–43
mythology: Egyptian, 23, 65, 122; Mesopotamian, 112, 122, 126, 144, 168
myths, 16, 20, 30, 35, 43, 48, 101, 131, 163, 173, 199–200, 206, 217, 278

Nabonidus, 109, 134–35
Nabopolassar, 108
Nabu, 134
names, secret, 35, 43, 48–49
Namtar, 158, 160–62, 164
Nanna, 102, 114–15, 156
Nanna-Suen, 115
Naram-Sin, 102, 136
Narmer, 4
Nebuchadnezzar, 13, 108–9, 176, 197
necromancy, 240–41, 264–65
necropolis, 15, 65, 74
Nefertiti, 30
neheh, 19, 39, 74
Nehemiah, 231–32, 240, 247
Neith, 45, 78, 207
Neo-Babylonians, 108, 118, 134, 174, 181, 283
Neolithic era, 3, 38, 58–60, 192
Nephthys, 20, 23, 33, 35–36, 43, 70–71
Nergal, 114–15, 117, 132, 153, 160–64, 203, 207
New Kingdom (Egyptian history), 10, 28, 35, 38, 40, 42, 45, 50, 61, 64–67, 78–81, 83–84, 207
New Year, 26, 81, 123, 134, 173–75, 179
Nile, heavenly, 67, 70
Nile delta, 4, 9, 70, 107, 193, 278
Nile River, 3, 26, 34, 39, 43, 53, 82, 99
Nile Valley, 3, 15, 57, 60, 70
Nineveh, 108, 155
Ninshubar, 155–56
Ninsun, 138

Nintu, 186–88
Ninurta, 114, 117, 184, 186
Nippur, 102, 143, 155
Noah, 147, 217, 247, 253
nomadic herders, 103, 115, 119, 209–11, 222, 234, 263
nomes, 4, 23, 71
nonexistence, 32, 71, 150, 152
Nubia, 8–11, 13–14, 38, 53, 131
Nun, 27, 32–34, 68, 122
Nut, 20, 27, 33, 35–36, 42, 67, 114, 163

offenses, 70, 84, 127, 179, 228–29, 237, 246, 248, 252–53
Ogdoad, 28, 34–35
Old Babylonian (language), 137, 141, 154, 183
Old Kingdom (Egyptian history), 5, 7, 16, 23, 27, 32–33, 38–40, 42, 61, 66–67, 78, 82, 86–87, 193, 200
omens, 134, 180, 283
Omri, 196, 223, 228, 268
Opening of the Mouth ceremony, 64–65, 70
Opet (festival), 81
oracles, 80, 82, 85, 92, 135, 169, 182, 264–65, 271–73
Osiris, 7–8, 18–21, 23, 26, 33, 35–36, 42–49, 54, 66–73, 82, 89, 156, 163, 241, 283 kingdom of, 58, 62, 67, 69–71, 74, 86, 149–50, 152, 163. *See also* Duat
ossuaries, 59, 241

palace coup, 8, 12, 53–54, 93
Palestine, 11, 13, 192–95, 198, 207, 223–24, 263, 282
Papyrus of Ani, 66, 72
Parthians, 280–82
Passover, 209, 257, 261, 263
patron deities, 25, 45, 49, 83, 94, 134, 145, 279

Pazuzu, 179
Pentateuch, 210, 213, 223
Persia, 13–14, 109, 197–98, 230, 232, 277, 280
Persian empire, 14, 169, 197–98, 230–31, 277–78, 280–81
Persian Gulf, 99–100, 106
"Pessimistic Dialogue between Master and Servant, A" 182
pestilence, 160, 162, 203, 273
petitions, 19, 84, 177, 184, 271, 274
pharaoh, 9–12, 14, 27, 38, 92, 95
Pharisees, 284
Philip of Macedon, 198, 277
Philistines, 11–12, 195–96, 208, 224, 235–36, 240, 265
Phoenicia, 193–96, 200, 206–7, 241, 258, 270
piety, 5, 30, 83–85, 92, 244, 274
polytheism, 23, 31, 159, 168, 199–203, 209, 211, 229, 245
power: creative, 27, 125, 217, 256; god's, 18, 79, 201, 212, 246; magical, 43, 69, 122; sovereign, 18, 21, 50, 113; spiritual, 225, 254
prayers, 19, 50, 73, 78, 83, 86, 94–95, 153, 168, 174, 183, 212, 230, 233, 252, 283
priestesses, 28, 119, 171–73, 175, 203
priesthoods, 12, 78–79, 222–23, 226, 257, 281
promises, 49, 143–44, 161, 183, 188, 209, 227, 231, 273; covenantal, 229, 234, 251–52, 263
prophecies, 92, 169, 181–82, 228–29, 231, 251, 253–54, 264, 266–69, 272–73; false, 268, 273
"The Prophecy of Neferty," 92–93, 181
prophetic action, 228, 267–68
prophets, 92, 181–82, 212, 219, 221, 223–33, 235, 237, 251–53, 258, 264–73; court, 271; cultic, 271–72; guild, 269–70, 272; independent,

227, 269, 271–72; official, 227, 258, 269, 271, 273
prostitutes, 120, 140, 145, 257, 268
prostitution, sacred, 173, 203
Proverbs, book of, 87, 89, 275–76
psalms, 213, 222, 231, 240, 251–52, 260, 273–75
Ptah, 18, 23, 27, 33, 35, 51, 73, 83–84, 213, 215
Ptolemies, 14, 84, 198, 280–82
Punt, 7–8
purification, 65, 79, 174, 261
pyramids, 5, 7, 13, 32, 66–67, 84
Pyramid Texts, 7, 33, 42, 66–67

Qadesh, 11, 51, 193–94
Qingu, 125–26, 128, 168
Qoholeth, 243. See also Ecclesiastes
queen, 7, 9, 12, 21, 26, 28, 47, 70, 73, 121–22, 133, 156, 159, 162, 263
Queen of Heaven and Earth, 121–22, 159

Ra, 7, 18–19, 21, 25–28, 32–33, 35, 39, 44–49, 65, 67–69, 81, 115, 122, 163, 200, 207; journey in the Underworld, 68–69; names of, 27–28, 43, 48–49
Ra of Foreign Lands, 200
Rahab, 213
Ra-Horakhty, 28
Rameses II, 11–12, 40, 50–51, 83–84, 194
Rameses III, 12, 83, 195
Rehoboam, 196
reign of, 195
religion: mystery, 279, 282–83; official, 15, 80, 95; popular, 80, 83, 177, 223
religious authority, 100, 221, 223, 225–26
religious communities, 199, 231, 237, 245
religious practices, 15, 30, 83–85, 95, 168–69, 192, 211, 223–24, 262–64

religious rituals, 77, 101, 119, 134, 158, 169, 172, 177–78, 203, 211, 228
religious sentiment, 80, 83, 85–86, 91, 177, 274
repentance, 229, 235, 250, 254, 268
resurrection, 67, 256, 283–84
retributive justice, 242–44, 249, 251, 253–55, 275
Revelation, book of, 253
revelations, 169, 180, 208, 253, 258
revenge, 42, 46, 89, 121, 125, 144, 164
reverence, 7, 66, 175, 177, 217, 249
righteousness, 246–48, 250–51, 255
ritual cult, 220, 227
ritual practices, 70, 155, 174, 180, 207, 261–62
rituals: family-based, 263; funerary, 95, 153; magical, 178; mystery, 283; sacrificial, 258, 260
ritual sacrifice, 226–28, 236, 282
ritual worship, 40, 77–78, 84–85, 171, 223, 226, 231–32, 257, 261–62, 282
Roman Empire, 49, 137, 198, 277, 281–84
Romans, 109, 232, 283
Royal Cemetery of Ur, 151

Sabbath, 209, 217, 263–64
sacred marriage, 119, 171–73, 175. See also hieros gamos
sacrifices, 65, 148, 171, 174, 186–87, 204, 212, 219, 231, 233–34, 257–58, 260–61
Sadducees, 284
sages, 89, 111–12, 126, 128, 136, 147, 165, 167, 183–84
Salim, 207, 221
salvation, 230, 279
Samaria, 197, 212, 223, 228, 260
Samson, 224
Samuel, 208, 220–22, 224–25, 232, 235–36, 240–41, 247, 260, 262, 265–66, 269–70, 272–73

sanctuaries, 171, 175, 258, 283
Sargon II, 102, 107, 197
Sargon of Agade, 101–3, 136
Sarpanitum, 174, 183
"The Satire of the Trades," 89–90
Saul, 196, 221, 225–26, 235–36, 240, 262, 265, 270
"Sayings of the Sages," 275
scarab, 27, 69
scorpion, 4, 83–84
Scorpion, King, 44
scribes, 4, 23, 38, 66, 71, 82, 84, 87–90, 101, 134, 193
sea, primeval, 33–34, 36, 68
Sea Peoples, 11–12, 105, 194–95
Second Intermediate Period, 9
sed-festival (Egypt), 40, 81
seer, 264–66, 271, 283
Sekhmet, 25
Seleucids, 198, 280–82
Semitic language, 105
Semitic peoples, 9, 101, 103–4, 108, 123
Sennacherib, 106, 212
Senusret, 8–9, 53–54, 93–94
Serapis, 283
servants, 64, 78, 133, 141, 151–53, 168, 171, 175, 182, 218, 237
Seth, 5, 18, 20–21, 23, 25–26, 33, 35–36, 42–50, 54, 69, 86, 156, 200, 207, 283
Seth-animal, 18, 42
Sety, 11–12, 68
sexual intercourse, 31, 33, 114–15, 119–20, 122, 140, 157, 161–62, 172, 175, 177, 186, 203
sexuality, 119–21, 157, 159
shabtis, 64, 70, 151
shadow, 58–59, 62–63, 256
Shalmaneser, 106
Shamash, 104, 115–16, 142, 144–46, 154, 180, 183
Shamhat, 140–41, 145

Shechem, 9, 224
Sheol, 239, 256
Sherida, 115
Sheshonq, 12
Shiloh, 222
shrines, 9, 28, 43, 78–80, 85, 95, 102, 155, 173, 207, 212, 222, 226, 257–58, 260, 262, 271
Shu, 20, 33, 35
Shuruppak, 182, 184
Sia, 32, 35
Sidon, 194
Siduri, 146–48, 154, 183, 244
sin, 109, 115, 134–35, 174, 179, 183, 214–15, 246, 248–50, 253, 261
Sinai, 210, 222, 233, 235, 261, 282
Sinai covenant, 210, 272
Sinai Peninsula, 8, 10, 191
sinfulness, 246, 249, 253
singers, 25, 78, 257
Sinuhe, 54, 93–95
slaves, 9, 64, 70, 104, 153, 168, 171, 177, 204, 235, 283
snakes, 34, 49, 147
Sneferu, 5, 92
Sokar festival (Egypt), 81
solar disk, 18, 23, 26, 28, 33, 200
Solomon, 12, 196, 207, 221–23, 227, 236, 258–59, 263
songs, 54, 91–92, 274
souls, 23, 35, 58, 67, 150
space, sacred, 77–78, 80
spell, 33, 84–85, 112–13, 124
spirit, 32, 35, 58–59, 73, 75, 84, 96, 142, 215, 240
stars, 21, 58, 63, 67, 74, 120–21, 181, 216, 283
statues, 19, 26, 40, 63, 71, 79, 172, 212, 230, 262, 283; cult, 19, 80, 84, 155, 175, 230, 260; funerary, 64
"statues of evil," 174–75
stelae, 11, 63, 84, 104, 194–95, 262
storytellers, 47, 137, 142, 184

storytelling, 155, 233, 250
suffering, 144, 157, 159, 183–84, 242, 244–46, 248–51, 253–55
Sumer, 99, 114, 117–18
Sumeria, 101–2, 103, 114, 136, 151, 192
Sumerian literature, 101, 117, 137, 141, 150, 155–58, 164, 179, 182–83
Sumerians, 100–102, 103, 111, 117, 121, 128, 131–32, 152, 179
sun disk, 11, 18, 20, 29
syncretism, 199–200, 278–79
Syria, 10–11, 70, 93, 99, 103–6, 108, 192–94, 196, 198, 202–3, 280–81, 283
Syrians, 12, 93, 281, 283
Syro-Ephraimite War, 227

tabernacle, 222, 261
Tablet of Destinies, 112, 114, 125
The Tale of Sinuhe, 53, 93–95, 191
Ta-tenen, 27, 32, 35
Tefnut, 20, 26, 33, 35–36
temple complexes, 78, 80, 82, 100, 173, 257–58
temple personnel, 78, 171–72
temple rituals, 79–80, 169, 219, 226, 257, 274
"The Testament of Amenemhat," 52
thanksgiving, 183, 219, 261, 273–74, 280
Thebes, 8–12, 21, 28, 34–35, 67, 81–82, 84, 108
theodicy, 246, 255
Third Dynasty of Ur, 102–3, 118, 170
Third Intermediate Period, 12, 90
Thoth, 21, 23, 30, 34, 47, 71–72, 81, 86
throne name, 5, 7, 11
Thutmose, 10, 68, 193
Tiamat, 112, 123–25, 134, 187, 213, 216, 239
Tiglath-Pileser III, 105–6, 196

Tigris, 99–100, 117, 281
tombs, royal, 40, 42, 63, 151–52
trade, 5, 7–9, 82, 89–90, 100–101, 109, 172, 191–95, 200, 280–81
trees, 74, 107, 115, 143, 206, 214, 242, 246, 264, 272
Tutankhamun, 11, 51
Tyre, 194, 207, 212, 228, 258

Ubaid period, 100, 151
Ugarit, 193, 203–4, 206–8, 240–41, 262
Underworld, Egyptian, 23, 62, 69. See also Duat, Osiris, kingdom of
Ur, 101, 102–3, 137, 152, 170, 173
uraeus, 18, 22, 33
Urartu, 106
Ur-Nammu, 102, 170
Uruk, 101, 136–41, 144–45, 147–48, 154–55, 160
Uruk period in Mesopotamia, 100
Ut-napishtim, 146–48, 153, 184–87
story of, 184, 188
Utu, 114–15

Valley Feast (Egypt), 82
votive offerings, 82, 95
vows, 188, 274

Wadjit, 51
Wag festival (Egypt), 81
wedjat, 46, 86. See also Horus, eye of
wilderness, 139–41, 144–46, 174, 196, 209–10, 221
wisdom: literature, 82, 86–87, 89–92, 182–83, 242–43, 275; Egyptian, 87, 275; Israelite, 275–76; Mesopotamian, 182–84
The Wisdom of Amenemope, 89, 275
Wisdom of ben-Sirach, 275
wisdom teaching, 87, 89, 91, 242
wisdom traditions, 51, 86, 90, 101, 275–76

"The Words of Ahiqar," 182
worship, popular, 20, 84, 262
worship rituals, 25–26, 77, 171, 208,
    226, 257, 260, 271
worship spaces, 171, 206, 257

Yahweh, 206–13, 218, 220–37, 240,
    246–56, 260–61, 263–76, 282, 284;
the Day of, 252; worship of, 208,
    211–12, 220–23, 226–28, 236, 282
Yahweh Elohim, 213–15, 242
Yamm, 204, 206, 213

Zadok, 221
Zechariah, 248, 251, 253–54, 265, 269
Zerubbabel, 247, 253